D0566218

Cooking Light®
COOKBOOK 1995

Cooking Light
COOKBOOK 1995

Oxmoor House

Book Division of Southern Progress Corporation
P.O. Box 2463, Birmingham, Alabama 35201

Library of Congress Catalog Number: 87-61020
ISBN: 0-8487-1408-3
ISSN: 1043-7061

Manufactured in the United States of America
Second Printing 1995

Editor-in-Chief: Nancy J. Fitzpatrick
Senior Foods Editor: Katherine M. Eakin
Senior Editor, Editorial Services: Olivia Kindig Wells
Art Director: James Boone

Cooking Light® Cookbook 1995

Editor: Caroline A. Grant, M.S., R.D.
Foods Editors: Deborah Garrison Lowery, Cathy A. Wesler, R.D.
Copy Editors: Holly Ensor, Cecilia C. Robinson
Editorial Assistant: Lisa C. Bailey
Director, Test Kitchens: Kathleen Royal
Assistant Director, Test Kitchens: Gayle Hays Sadler
Test Kitchen Home Economists: Susan H. Bellows, Christina A. Crawford, Iris Crawley, Sarah Davidson, Michele Brown Fuller, Elizabeth Luckett, Angie Neskaug Sinclair, Jan A. Smith
Senior Photographer: Jim Bathie
Photographer: Ralph Anderson
Senior Photo Stylist: Kay E. Clarke
Photo Stylist: Virginia R. Cravens
Designer: Faith Nance
Director of Production and Distribution: Phillip Lee
Production Manager: Gail Morris
Associate Production Manager: Theresa L. Beste
Production Assistant: Marianne Jordan
Recipe and Menu Developers: Tanya Barnes, Patricia Coker, Noreen Eberly, Trish Leverett, Karen Mangum, Debby Maugans, Susan Reeves, Jane Ingrassia Reinsel, Patricia Schmidt, Elizabeth J. Taliaferro
Text Consultants: Maureen Callahan, M.S., R.D.; Office of the Vice President of Health Affairs, University of Alabama at Birmingham: Julius Linn, M.D., Executive Director, and Lisa Latham, Associate Editor

Cover: *Fresh Tomato and Cheese Pizza (page 143)*
Back cover: *Black Forest Trifle (page 232)*
Frontispiece: *Barbecued Turkey Burger with Sweet Onions (page 54), Vegetable Coleslaw (page 55), Grilled Potato Wedges (page 55), and Pineapple-Citrus Spritzer (page 54)*

Contents

The Food & Fitness Connection

Welcome to *Cooking Light Cookbook 1995*

For more than a decade, *Cooking Light* annual cookbooks have brought you great-tasting, healthy recipes and up-to-date information on nutrition and fitness. And this year is no exception. As the registered dietitian responsible for this edition, I've made sure each recipe fits our standards for fat, calories, cholesterol, and more. And along with our taste panel of test kitchen home economists, registered dietitians, and food editors, I evaluated each recipe for flavor. (Yes, we literally ate our way through this book!) If a recipe didn't please our palates, you won't find it on these pages. An important part of our evaluation was checking for realistic serving sizes. You won't find any skimpy portions.

To help you visualize how attractive light food can be, we've included plenty of full-color photographs to show you easy yet attractive garnish ideas. But there's much, much more! Other features you'll find in this edition of *Cooking Light* include the following:

- **Up-to-date news from the nutrition front:** We explain the latest news and how it relates to you on pages 9–11.
- **Sneaky ways to exercise:** Find easy ways to add exercise to your daily routine on pages 14 and 15.
- **Ways to turn your home into a gym:** You can get as good a workout at home as at the gym—for a lot less money. See how on pages 16 and 17.
- **Ways to make it light:** Don't miss the how-tos for making your all-time favorite lasagna recipe lower in calories, fat, and sodium on page 19.
- **Information on biotechnology:** Is it best? You decide. Consider all the issues on pages 20 and 21.
- **Twenty eye-catching, mouth-watering menus:** Each has less than 30 percent calories from fat.
- **More than 350 recipes:** All have our seal of approval for flavor and nutrition.
- **Tips for convenience cooking:** You'll find helpful hints for easier, faster cooking.
- **A seven-day meal plan:** Choose the 1,200- or 1,600-calorie set of menus for a delicious way to lose weight.

We hope you'll enjoy *Cooking Light* as a resource, a guidebook, and a cookbook for many years to come. So join me, and the staff of *Cooking Light Cookbook 1995*, for a lifetime of eating and living well.

Caroline Grant

Caroline A. Grant, M.S., R.D.

Update

The exciting news on the food and nutrition front is that finally, finally, most of it is good news. Here in a nutshell are the headline highlights from 1994 and what they mean for you.

Butter vs. Margarine

Stick with margarine for now, but watch for new, more conclusive findings in the battle for bringing back butter.

Give me that old-time flavor—butter may not be so bad after all, say some researchers. In fact, some scientists say butter may even be better for you than margarine.

But before you go back to the real thing, know that the American Heart Association (AHA) doesn't agree. Margarine, says the AHA, is made with vegetable fat and provides no dietary cholesterol. So it's still wise to spread your bread with margarine instead of butter.

The firmer margarine appears, the more saturated fat it contains.

So who started all the hoopla about butter being better? The debate centers on margarine's trans fatty acids (TFAs) and a study that appeared in the *American Journal of Public Health* in an article by Dr. Walter C. Willet and Dr. Alberto Ascherio of the Harvard School of Public Health. They argued that TFAs (the fats found in margarine and other processed foods) could be responsible for as many as 30,000 heart disease-related deaths in this country each year.

TFAs form when unsaturated oils are partially hydrogenated. The hydrogenation process converts oils into solids, making them last longer before spoiling. Concerns arose about the effects of TFAs when Dutch researchers fed one group of people diets rich in saturated fat and another group diets rich in TFAs. The TFAs boosted the "bad" low-density lipoprotein (LDL) cholesterol levels almost as much as did saturated fats. And unlike the saturated fat, TFAs actually lowered the blood level of "good" high-density lipoprotein (HDL) cholesterol.

Despite the results of this one study, the message here is one of moderation. In other words, you can eat margarine, or butter for that matter, in moderation without worrying.

Meanwhile, researchers continue to battle it out. And if they come to a definitive conclusion in the next few months, we'll let you know about it in *Cooking Light Cookbook 1996*. So stay tuned. . . .

New Ways to Lower Cholesterol

Keep up the diet, and have your HDL level screened regularly. Then, if needed, lose weight and increase your activity to boost HDL levels, recommends the National Cholesterol Education Program.

If you've had a blood cholesterol reading on the high side, chances are you've memorized one of the charts that indicates the milligrams of cholesterol in a list of foods. But you can do more, says the National Cholesterol Education Program in its newly released guidelines for lowering cholesterol. The revised guidelines emphasize that increased physical activity and weight loss in addition to a low-fat diet help lower total blood cholesterol levels and increase levels of HDL, the "good" cholesterol.

What's Your Risk?

Your chance of having a heart attack is greater if your HDL cholesterol count is 35 milligrams per deciliter or less than if it's 60 milligrams per deciliter or more. So ask for a separate reading of HDL at your regular checkups, beginning as early as age 20.

So along with your total blood cholesterol screening, request readings of your HDL and LDL levels. The best news you can get is that your HDL is high and your LDL is low—that means your risk of heart disease is low. If the readings are the opposite, take steps to lower your cholesterol, because you are at greater risk of heart disease.

Here are more suggestions for keeping cholesterol levels in check:

Eat less saturated fat—it raises levels of "bad" LDL cholesterol. Also, keep dietary cholesterol amounts you consume to an average of 300 milligrams a day.

Load up on carbohydrates such as whole grains, peas, beans, fruits, and vegetables. These foods are low in fat and provide dietary fiber, which can help lower blood cholesterol levels.

If you drink alcohol, do so in moderation. (No more than two drinks daily for men, and one for women.) In moderation, alcohol may decrease the risk of heart disease up to 40 percent. But before having a drink a day, consider that alcohol also has been shown to increase the risk of breast cancer.

Eat more citrus fruits, dark green leafy vegetables, and dark yellow and orange vegetables. These foods are rich in the antioxidants beta carotene and vitamins C and E, which soak up destructive particles in the arteries. Damage from these particles allows cholesterol to adhere more easily to artery walls.

Season with fresh garlic. Yes, garlic. Studies show that eating garlic may decrease cholesterol by 15 to 20 percent. So skip the garlic pills, but if you like garlic, add it liberally to your meals.

Lose weight if you're overweight. For every extra two pounds, your total blood cholesterol rises by 1 milligram per deciliter.

Get moving. Exercise raises "good" HDL cholesterol and lowers "bad" LDL cholesterol.

Stub out the cigarettes. Smoking damages artery walls, constricts blood vessels, and lowers levels of protective HDL.

Eat More B *(Vitamins, That Is)*

Foods such as beans and dark green, leafy vegetables that are rich in the B vitamins—B_6, B_{12}, and folic acid—may help prevent heart attacks. People who don't get enough of these B vitamins tend to have high levels of homocysteine, an amino acid linked to a 40 percent increased risk of heart attack.

Foods to Help Fight Disease

We now know that all those foods Mom insisted you eat really are good for you—in more ways than even she knew. They're nature's way of warding off two of the most common diseases.

Eat more antioxidants. . . . Eat five fruits and vegetables a day. . . . Don't forget to eat your cruciferous veggies. . . . These phrases are repeated in magazines, newspapers, and every other place you get health and nutrition information. And for good reason. Researchers agree that the foods moms push on their children have protective qualities.

In the foods-to-fight-cancer message, antioxidants are the most well-known of the phytochemicals (a group of hundreds of naturally occurring substances in plants that help the body stay healthy). Other phytochemicals have such textbook-sounding names as isoflavones, phytosterols, flavonoids, and indoles. (See chart on page 11 for more on phytochemicals.)

But if you're not chemistry-minded, all you need to remember is to eat foods rich in beta carotene and vitamins C and E. (See "Pass the Antioxidants, Please!" in the next column.)

The positive research to date doesn't mean that more is better. So before you stock up on antioxidant vitamin supplements, know that results of some studies suggest caution. For example, a study of smokers by the National Cancer Institute showed that vitamin E and beta carotene seemed to give no protection against lung cancer. Beta carotene even seemed to increase the risk.

What that means is that nothing can undo the results of a lifestyle that includes smoking, a high-fat diet, and lack of exercise. So if you're adjusting your diet to include disease-fighting foods, make sure the rest of your lifestyle takes a healthy turn, too.

Pass the Antioxidants, *Please!*

They're in greatest amounts in the following foods:

- apricots
- broccoli
- brussels sprouts
- cabbage
- cantaloupes
- carrots
- citrus fruits
- green beans
- lettuce
- mangoes
- peaches
- peas
- plums
- pumpkins
- red peppers
- spinach
- strawberries
- sweet potatoes
- tomatoes
- winter squash

Why Not High-Fat?

Along with causing weight gain and clogged arteries, a high-fat diet may be a significant link to several kinds of cancer. If these types run in your family, take note and watch your diet.

Fat from some foods has been connected to the development or progression of prostate, lung, breast, colon, uterine, and pancreatic cancers. Recent studies on the diet-and-cancer connection include research in the following four areas:

Red meat and prostate cancer: Men who ate more beef, pork, lamb, processed meat, bacon, and hot dogs had the highest risk of advanced prostate cancer, according to a Harvard study. Results also showed that the speed at which the prostate cancer advanced was directly related to the amount of animal fat in the diet.

Saturated fat and lung cancer: Women in a National Cancer Institute study were six times more likely to develop lung cancer when they ate a diet heavy in saturated fat (15 percent or more of total daily calories) than were women who got 10 percent or less of their total daily calories from saturated fat. At highest risk were women whose diets included more than 40 percent of calories from total fat.

Fat and breast cancer: A diet high in fat may cause existing breast tumors to grow at a faster rate than tumors in women who eat a leaner diet. Scientists theorize that this is because the fat increases the production of the female hormone estrogen.

Fat and colon cancer: A high-fat, low-fiber diet increased the risk of developing precancerous colon polyps by four times in a Harvard study. People who ate diets high in saturated fats and red meat were more likely to develop colon cancer than was a similar group of people who ate more seafood and chicken, according to another study.

Why You Should Eat Your Veggies

Phytochemicals, including antioxidants, are the naturally occurring substances found in plants that help prevent some diseases. This chart shows what you can eat to help you stay healthy.

Beneficial Phytochemical	Helps Prevent	Where to Get It
Allylic Sulfide	cancer, heart disease	onions, garlic
Beta Carotene	cancer, heart disease	deep yellow or orange fruits and vegetables
Capsaicin	cancer, heart disease	hot peppers
Flavonoids	cancer, formation of blood clots	onions, apples
Indoles	breast and uterine cancers	broccoli, cabbage, brussels sprouts
Isoflavones and Phytosterols	breast and prostate cancers, heart disease	soy beans, soy products
Lycopene	cancer, heart disease	red fruits, tomatoes, red peppers, carrots
Sulforaphane	cancerous tumors	broccoli, cauliflower, brussels sprouts, turnips
Vitamin C	mouth, stomach, and esophageal cancers	citrus fruits; strawberries; red peppers; dark green, leafy vegetables
Vitamin E	breast, cervical, gastrointestinal, lung, prostate, and stomach cancers	soy products, avocados, nuts, vegetable oils

Bone Up on Calcium

Adults may need to consume more calcium than called for in the previous Recommended Daily Allowance (RDA), says a national health committee. But there's more you can do to prevent osteoporosis, a bone-thinning disease.

If you're aged 25 years or older, you need to increase your calcium intake from 800mg to 1,200mg a day, or to 1,500mg if you are a post-menopausal woman not taking estrogen for hormone replacement. This suggestion to raise the RDA for calcium comes from a National Institutes of Health committee in an effort to reduce the incidence of osteoporosis. Similar recommendations come from the National Osteoporosis Foundation.

The best way to get calcium is to eat low-fat dairy products and green, leafy vegetables. Other ways to increase bone density include participating regularly in weight-bearing exercise such as walking or jogging. Also, lifting weights builds bone and strengthens muscles so that bones and joints are better protected if you fall. And you're less likely to fall if you lift weights regularly because the training increases balance and mobility.

Nutrition Basics for *Cooking Light*

Your calls and letters tell us that most of you are interested in losing weight or maintaining a low-fat diet. The information on these pages is provided to help you do just that. By following these guidelines and tips, you can safely meet your goals for a healthy lifestyle.

PLANNING A DIET OF 30 PERCENT FAT OR LESS

If your diet is ideal, 30 percent or less of the calories you consume each day come from fat, at least 50 percent are from carbohydrates, and about 20 percent come from protein. That's a good guideline to follow, according to the American Heart Association (AHA) and the American Dietetic Association. But it's a bit complicated to calculate exactly.

What's simplest to remember is this: Eat less protein, eat less fat, and eat more carbohydrates. What the AHA means by recommending the 30 percent fat limit is that, over the course of a day or even a period of days, your diet should average no more than 30 percent of calories from fat. You'll notice that not every *Cooking Light* recipe has less than 30 percent fat, and that's okay. Just remember to pair these recipes with lower-fat recipes to create balanced meals.

Therefore, it's more important to look at the number of fat grams you're eating per serving than to calculate just what percent of calories are coming from where.

Dial a Dietitian

If you want an expert to figure the ideal percentage and grams of fat, protein, and carbohydrates you should eat, contact a registered dietitian. To locate a dietitian near you, call a local hospital and ask to speak with someone in the dietary department. Most hospitals have dietitians on staff who can help you or will recommend a dietitian who can.

The American Dietetic Association also provides local referrals through its nutrition hotline. Call 1-800-366-1655 and ask for a listing of dietitians near you.

Figure the Fat

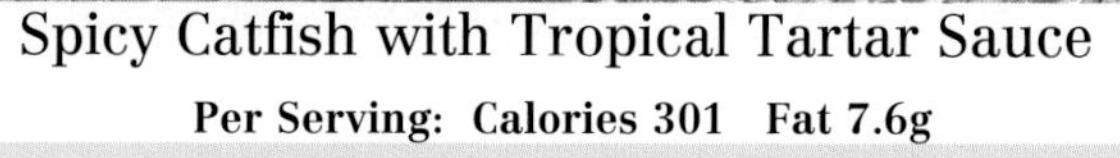

Spicy Catfish with Tropical Tartar Sauce

Per Serving: Calories 301 Fat 7.6g

If you want to determine the percentage of calories from fat for a particular food or recipe, use the following formula. We used Spicy Catfish with Tropical Tartar Sauce as an example.

7.6g Number of fat grams per serving
x 9 Multiplied by the number of calories per fat gram
68.4 Equals total calories from fat
÷301 Divided by the total number of calories per serving
.227 Equals percent fat from calories. Round three numbers off to two. For this example, .227 rounds to .23 or 23 percent fat.

HOW TO MAKE OUR RECIPES WORK FOR YOU

Using the nutrient listing at the end of each recipe is an easy way to find recipes that fit into your healthy-eating plan. If you're eating low-fat, specific figures for total fat, saturated fat, and cholesterol will help you stick to your goal. If you're trying to shed a few pounds, the calorie and fat numbers will be of most interest to you. And if you want to maintain good health, notice the calcium, iron, and fiber information included in each analysis; these nutrients do play an important role in health and well-being.

How the Recipes Are Analyzed

We derived the nutrient information for each recipe from a computer analysis based primarily on U.S. Department of Agriculture figures. The analysis is as accurate as possible based on these guidelines:

- When a range is given for an ingredient (for example, 3 to 3½ cups flour), the lesser amount is used in the calculation.
- Some alcohol calories evaporate during heating; we reflect that.
- Only the amount of marinade absorbed by the food is used.
- Garnishes and optional ingredients are not used in the calculation.

YOUR DAILY NUTRITION GUIDE

	Women Ages 25 to 50	*Women Over 50*	*Men Over 24*
Calories	2,000	2,000 or less	2,700
Protein	50g*	50g or less	63g
Fat	67g or less	67g or less	90g or less
Saturated Fat	22g or less	22g or less	30g or less
Carbohydrates	299g	299g	405g
Fiber	25g to 35g	25g to 35g	25g to 35g
Cholesterol	300mg** or less	300mg or less	300mg or less
Iron	15mg	10mg	10mg
Sodium	3,300mg or less	3,300mg or less	3,300mg or less
Calcium	800mg	800mg	800mg

* (grams is abbreviated throughout the book as g)
** (milligrams is abbreviated throughout the book as mg)

Keep in mind that these numbers are estimates; calorie requirements vary according to your size, weight, and level of activity. These numbers are to be used as a general guide; additional nutrients are needed during different stages of life. For example, children's calorie and protein needs are based on height and vary greatly as they grow. Teenagers require less protein but more calcium and iron than adults. Pregnant or breast-feeding women need more protein, calories, and calcium. The need for iron increases during pregnancy but returns to normal afterward.

HOW TO LOSE WEIGHT

It's easier said than done. Here are tips for the healthiest ways to take off the pounds:

- For a rough estimate of how many calories you can eat without gaining or losing weight, multiply your current weight by 15. For another quick estimate, check the calorie listing in the appropriate column for your age in the nutrition guide above. Once you've determined your maintenance calorie level, subtract 500 calories from that number, and use the total as a guide for the number of calories to eat each day. With this change you should lose about a pound per week.
- Don't try to lose weight quickly. Losing more than two pounds each week isn't a good idea; you'll be more likely to put back on whatever you've lost (and more) eventually. With each subsequent diet, losing weight can become even more difficult.
- Avoid diets that suggest eating fewer than 1,200 calories a day, unless it's recommended by your doctor. Severely limiting your food intake can prevent you from getting the essential nutrients you need to stay healthy.
- Use the *"Cooking Light* 1995 Menu Plans," pages 246 through 249, for great-tasting, healthy meal plans that are ideal for a weight-control diet.

Exercise—The Perfect Partner

If you garden, walk the dog, wash the car, or sweep the sidewalk, you're lowering your risk of developing heart disease, diabetes, high blood pressure, osteoporosis, stroke, and cancer.

Vigorous activity still is considered to be a good way to improve cardiovascular endurance, gain strength, and lose weight. But the latest research shows that the hard-and-fast rules that have applied to exercise for years—continuous, vigorous aerobic activity for at least 30 minutes, three to five days a week—aren't the only rules in the fitness game. Promoting the advantages of *moderate* exercise are the Centers for Disease Control and Prevention, the American College of Sports Medicine, the President's Council on Physical Fitness and Sports, the National Cancer Institute, and other scientific groups.

Moderate exercise is part of many daily activities, and a bonus is that your activities can be broken into chunks throughout the day. Short sessions have a cumulative effect, making them roughly equal to a sustained workout.

You can attack household chores with greater enthusiasm now that you know they're actually good for you. But if you love that power-packed workout—don't quit. Your extra efforts will pay off in better health, too.

MAKE A CLASSIC MOVE

If movin' to the groovin' is how you enjoy exercise, pick Brahms instead of the Rolling Stones. Researchers at the University of Tennessee found that people exercised longer and harder when listening to soft, slow, easy-listening music (100 beats per minute) than when rocking out to loud, fast, upbeat music (140 beats per minute) or listening to no music at all.

The best news: The soothing melodies fooled people into thinking they weren't working out nearly as hard as they were. Surprisingly, exercisers felt they worked just as hard when no music was played as when they listened to the upbeat music.

SNEAK IN SOME EXERCISE

Squeezing fitness into your already busy schedule isn't as hard as you may think. Just seize any opportunity to move around. Here's how:

- Make the most of your lunch hour. Take a walk (10 to 15 minutes) around the office building—inside or outside—before eating lunch.
- Take the stairs instead of the elevator at work and even at the mall.
- Do some things inefficiently. Make several trips up the stairs with the clean clothes instead of one trip. When you shop at the mall, don't go from one store to the next; walk past a few stores you want to go in, and then backtrack.
- Do stretching exercises, sit-ups, push-ups, or use an exercise machine at home while you watch the evening news.
- Take your children to the park and play along with them.
- Vacuum, dust, and rock 'n' roll. Pop in your favorite tape, put on your headphones, and turn housework into a workout.
- When you travel, make reservations at a hotel that has a pool or an exercise room, or pack a jump rope and do some jumping before your day begins. On vacation trips, sign up for walking tours of local attractions and scenic highlights.

HOW TO STICK WITH IT

Sometimes it just isn't enough to know that the sooner you begin a regular exercise program, the better your health and quality of life will be. Studies show that the best motivation for sticking to a diet or an exercise program is to do it with someone else. So convince a friend or a family member to be your exercise partner. You'll both feel better, look better, and reduce your health risks. And remember, it's never too late to begin.

WHAT MODERATE EXERCISE CAN DO FOR YOU

- Reduce risk of heart attack
- Lower blood pressure
- Reduce body fat
- Decrease risk of developing diabetes
- Lessen symptoms of menopause
- Reduce stress
- Decrease risk of cancer
- Increase bone strength
- Strengthen heart and lungs
- Strengthen muscles
- Improve sleep
- Increase energy

Set Yourself Up for Success with a Home Gym

If you're committed to exercise but your schedule isn't, check out the following advantages of a home gym.

1. It's convenient. Night owls can pedal while watching the late movie; early birds can stair-climb through the morning news.
2. It's private. You can wear baggy shorts and a T-shirt and avoid comparing yourself with those half your age and size.
3. It can be done anytime. You can pop in an exercise video and sweat to the oldies while dinner's cooking.
4. It saves time. In the time you spend driving to and from the gym, you can be finished with your exercise routine.
5. It saves money. No matter how much your equipment costs, you'll end up saving money over a club membership.

SMART TIPS FOR BUYING LARGE EQUIPMENT

Resist impulse buying. If you don't need it, or haven't made a commitment to use it, don't buy it.

Try it out first. Visit an exercise equipment store, a health club, or your local gym to be sure the machine is the right size for your body and is comfortable and easy to use.

Perform a safety check. Be sure all movable or motorized parts have protective coverings. If the equipment runs on cables, inspect the lines carefully to be sure the cables aren't frayed and that all bolts are tightened down securely.

Stick with reputable stores with knowledgeable sales staffs. Ask about the machine's warranty and service contract, which should cover parts and labor for at least a year.

Resist "real steals." You usually get what you pay for. A $99 cross-country ski machine ordered from a television advertisement is unlikely to withstand regular use. Plus, the noisier, bumpier, and more uncomfortable it is, the less likely you are to use it.

Stay away from equipment advertised as being able to reduce specific areas of the body. This type of equipment comes from the myth that you can spot-reduce. Truth is, you can't dictate where your body puts on fat or where you take it off. That's why overall body conditioning is so important.

BUYING HOME GYM EQUIPMENT: A GUIDE TO THE BASICS

For $250 or less, you can buy the first seven pieces of equipment listed below and create a home gym that provides a complete body workout. When you're ready to go beyond the basics, consider adding one or more of the large pieces of equipment.

EQUIPMENT	PRICE RANGE	PURPOSE	BUYING TIPS
Floor mat	$30 to $100	provides protection and comfort on hard floor surface	Look for a firm foam rubber mat or any type of firm carpet.
Dumbbells	60¢ to 70¢ a pound	tones and strengthens arms, legs, and other muscles	To work out every major muscle group, fitness trainers recommend that women buy a series of dumbbells ranging from 3 to 20 pounds; men, 10 to 35 or 50 pounds.
Weight bench	$15 to $50	provides comfort and support when working with weights	Look for a sturdy, heavy bench that won't tip over easily.
Leg weights	$8 to $15	strengthens and tones legs and buttocks	Avoid leg weights covered with plastic, which can crack and irritate your skin.
Chin-up bar	$15 to $25	strengthens and tones arms and shoulders	Look for a bar that bolts into the wall.
Jump rope	$8 to $11	provides aerobic conditioning	To work your upper body while you jump, look for a weighted rope or one that has weighted handles.
Step bench with aerobics video	$60 to $80	provides aerobic conditioning	Look for a bench that has add-on platforms for a more challenging workout as you master the basics.
LARGE EQUIPMENT			
Multistation weight machine	$300 to $1,500	strengthens all major muscle groups	Make sure the machine is comfortable and that you understand how to operate it.
Stationary bicycle	$250 to $350, basic models; $500 to $3,000, computerized models	provides aerobic conditioning; strengthens and tones legs	To work out your upper body as well, look for a bike with pumping handle bars.
Treadmill	$300 to $600, nonmotorized; $1,000 to $5,000, electronically powered	provides aerobic conditioning; strengthens and tones legs	Be sure you have room to accommodate the machine. It requires a lot of space.
Rowing machine	$700 to $1,600	provides aerobic conditioning; strengthens and tones most major muscle groups	Be sure you have room to accommodate the machine. It requires a lot of space.
Stair climber	$250 to $500, basic models; $1,000 to $3,000, computerized models	provides aerobic conditioning; strengthens and tones legs, hips, and buttocks	Look for a machine with independent stepping action.
Cross-country ski machine	$250 to $700	provides aerobic conditioning; strengthens most major muscle groups	If you have balancing problems, don't buy this machine.

The *Cooking Light* Kitchen

Mama mia! It's Italian, and it's fattening—right? Not any more! If you make lasagna only when you feel you can splurge on fat and calories, take a look at our Vegetable Lasagna. We used a typical "fat-filled" version as the blueprint for our new light lasagna recipe that appears on page 140.

Try our techniques with your family's favorite lasagna recipe. If you substitute low-fat or nonfat ingredients, keep in mind that some of these products are higher in sodium than the regular versions.

Here are some of the secrets we used to lighten high-fat lasagna and make it healthier for you:

- Replaced 1 pound of ground beef with 7½ cups of flavorful vegetables.
- Reduced the amount of cottage cheese as well as substituted 1% low-fat cottage cheese for the higher-fat cream-style cottage cheese, cutting out 26 grams of fat.
- Used ½ cup egg substitute instead of 2 whole eggs, which further reduced fat and cholesterol.
- Cut the total amount of mozzarella cheese from 4 cups to 1 cup, used part-skim mozzarella instead of regular, and omitted the Parmesan cheese, reducing the fat another 92 grams. These changes also helped reduce the sodium.
- Replaced regular canned tomatoes and tomato paste with no-salt-added tomato sauce.

Before

CLASSIC LASAGNA

1 pound ground beef
1 (16-ounce) can whole tomatoes, undrained
2 (6-ounce) cans tomato paste
1 teaspoon dried parsley flakes
1 teaspoon dried basil
½ teaspoon garlic powder
½ teaspoon pepper
2 (12-ounce) cartons cream-style cottage cheese
2 eggs, beaten
8 lasagna noodles (cooked with salt and fat)
4 cups (16 ounces) shredded mozzarella cheese
½ cup grated Parmesan cheese

Calories: 544
Percentage of Calories from Fat: 48%
Cholesterol: 153mg
Sodium: 1157mg

After

VEGETABLE LASAGNA

1 cup thinly sliced zucchini
1 cup thinly sliced yellow squash
1 cup thinly sliced carrot
2 cups broccoli flowerets
Vegetable cooking spray
1½ cups thinly sliced fresh mushrooms
1 cup chopped onion
3 cups no-salt-added tomato sauce
1 teaspoon garlic powder
1 teaspoon Italian seasoning
1 teaspoon dried basil
¾ to 1 teaspoon pepper
½ teaspoon salt
1 (16-ounce) carton 1% low-fat cottage cheese
½ cup frozen egg substitute, thawed
8 lasagna noodles (cooked without salt or fat)
1 cup (4 ounces) shredded part-skim mozzarella cheese

Calories: 234
Percentage of Calories from Fat: 14%
Cholesterol: 10mg
Sodium: 500mg

Look for the complete recipe for Vegetable Lasagna on page 140.

What's New in the Marketplace?

Enjoy juicy summer tomatoes year-round. . . . Will biotechnology feed the hungry? . . . Plan your diet and meals on a computer.

Fine-Tuning Nature's Handiwork

If you think of mutant corn and killer tomatoes when you hear the terms *biotechnology* or *genetic engineering*, relax. Humans have practiced basic forms of genetic engineering for a thousand years by selectively breeding plants and animals that have certain attributes. It's just a way to enhance the health benefits and nutritional value of certain foods.

But the nineties method of genetic engineering—isolating specific genes to breed into plant foods—brings controversy. Consider the issues of both sides . . .

PRAISING THE POSITIVES

Year-round availability. Longer shelf life. A longer period of peak flavor for fresh foods. These are just a few benefits consumers will recognize right away. (See the tomato story below.) But proponents of biotech engineering say that these benefits will make a major impact on the world at large by the year 2000 by helping . . .

. . . Improve the Nutritional Quality of Food

- It's possible to alter food to better meet dietary needs—for instance, a modified potato that has more starch and less water. A higher-starch potato would absorb less oil, meaning lighter, healthier chips and French fries.
- Foods that are already nutritious, such as soy beans, can be made more flavorful.
- Nutrients that already exist in a particular food can be enhanced to provide additional health benefits. For example, garlic could be produced with more allicin, an active ingredient that reportedly lowers cholesterol.

. . . Preserve the Environment

- Development of pest- and disease-resistant crops would help reduce the need for fungicides, herbicides, insecticides, and pesticides.
- Instead of planting five acres to guarantee one acre of harvest, growers could plant only the yield needed.

. . . Feed the Hungry

- Crops could be produced to be heat- and drought-resistant and to grow on barren soil, which would help increase the food supply in areas where starvation is rampant.
- Fruits and vegetables could be enriched with more vitamins and protein, which would also aid starving populations that receive these foods.

NOW YOU CAN HAVE GARDEN-FRESH TOMATOES YEAR-ROUND

The Flavr Savr™ tomato, the first genetically engineered food to enter the marketplace, promises homegrown taste in store-bought tomatoes. By isolating the gene that causes tomatoes to soften, and then copying and inserting it backwards into tomato plants, Calgene Fresh, the California-based producer of Flavr Savr, claims to have created a tomato that offers consumers what they can't get in the average supermarket tomato—taste.

Ordinarily, farmers pick tomatoes when they're hard and green so they won't spoil before reaching your local grocer. But thanks to the marvels of genetic engineering, Flavr Savr tomatoes can ripen on the vine days longer and still be shipped long distances and stored for several weeks while maintaining a delicious homegrown taste.

WRESTLING WITH THE RISKS

Although supporters of genetic engineering are confident that engineered foods are actually safer than those developed through traditional breeding methods, some scientists and activist groups have voiced ethical, religious, and safety concerns. Their unresolved questions include the following:

What about the environment? Environmentalist groups question whether plants bred to resist pests will pollinate with a related weed, making the weed harder to kill. Biotechnologists say that engineered plants are no more dangerous to the environment than are traditional-bred plants.

What about people who abstain from certain foods? Vegetarians and others who avoid some foods for religious or ethical reasons worry about genes from their "taboo" foods being introduced into foods they do eat. Pro-biotech scientists say it's not a problem because plants, animals, and bacteria already share a number of similar genes.

"Biotechnology is going to give us cheaper, better foods."

David Wheat, Ph.D.
President of The Bowditch Group
and leading biotechnology expert

What about allergens? Another concern is the possibility of introducing allergens into foods. For example, a gene from a food that commonly triggers allergic reactions, such as peanuts, might be introduced into another food. But current Food and Drug Administration (FDA) policy requires any genetically engineered food that contains an allergen to be clearly labeled. Any food developed through biotechnology also is subject to the same stringent FDA regulatory requirements.

Opponents of genetically engineered foods feel the FDA's May 1992 policy pertaining to plant-based, genetically modified foods falls short because the tests are based on the characteristics of the food instead of the processes used to produce them. Opponents prefer to see these new foods tested as food additives before receiving approval. The FDA argues that genetically engineered foods don't contain substances significantly different from those already in the diet, so they don't need approval as food additives.

Despite the controversy, you'll be hearing more about genetic engineering and agricultural biotechnology. We'll keep you posted on the progress in *Cooking Light Cookbook 1996*.

Disk Drive to Healthier Eating

Computer technology has pulled up a chair to your kitchen table. According to manufacturers of such diet and nutrition computer programs as Perfect Diet and Nutripak, with a few keyboard commands you can do the following:

- calculate a food plan based on your weight-loss goals and fitness regimen;
- compute percentage of daily calories from fat, carbohydrates, and protein;
- track your daily intake of nutrients and compare nutrient values of foods;
- tally the number of calories you consume in a day, subtracting calories expended during physical activity;
- search a database of up to 5,000 foods and organize and index hundreds of recipes; and
- print out a shopping list based on the recipes you select.

And that's only the beginning. With the advent of CD-ROMs (compact disk read-only memory), you'll be able to watch the recipe being prepared—complete with step-by-step oral instructions.

The basic programs sell for about $19, but bells and whistles raise the price. Before buying, make sure (1) the program comes in a version that runs on your computer (DOS, Windows, or Macintosh); (2) your computer has enough memory and hard-disk space to operate the program; (3) your monitor is capable of displaying the graphics; and (4) the program is compatible with your printer. Also, CD-ROM programs require a CD-ROM player, which costs about $300 to $600.

Although no program can lose the weight or buy healthy foods for you, one may be the catalyst to help you achieve your 1995 healthy-eating goals.

Healthy American Meals

Choose from These Twenty Great Menus

Fret no more about planning flavorful, low-fat menus. Each menu in this chapter meets the guidelines for healthy eating. The total calories for each menu come from these sources:

- at least 50 percent from carbohydrates
- about 20 percent from protein
- less than 30 percent from fat, with 10 percent or less from saturated fat

If you've kept up with the latest nutrition recommendations, you know that these percentages are in line with the preferred goals for healthy eating. Just choose the right menu to fit the occasion, including the following choices:

Breakfast and Brunch menus begin on page 26 . . .
- Breakfast in the Great Outdoors (page 26) is a fun way to cook and eat outside.
- Romantic French Breakfast (page 31) is perfect for pampering your true love.
- Bridesmaids Brunch (page 35) honors the bride-to-be and her attendants.

Quick and Easy menus begin on page 38 . . .
- Picnic at the Park (page 38) lets you whip up a fun, carry-along feast.
- Tune In for Dinner (page 45) is one way to warm up a winter evening with a good movie, great food, and special friends.

That's Entertaining menus begin on page 50 . . .
- Supper on the Patio (page 53) creates a relaxing atmosphere for the party.
- An Evening in Japan (page 56) takes you and your friends on a culinary trip to the Orient.
- Mexican Fiesta (page 63) awakens the taste buds with bold-flavored recipes.

Holiday Celebrations menus begin on page 66 . . .
- Valentine Dinner for Dad (page 66) helps your children serve up a delicious surprise.
- Labor Day Barbecue (page 72) ushers in fall with a robust feast from the grill.
- The Sweetest Christmas (page 79) treats guests to a tempting dessert buffet.

Overleaf: *Use the natural beauty of the outdoors to enhance an elegant meal of Poached Salmon with Cucumber-Dill Sauce, Golden Honey Crescent Rolls, and Sugar Snap Pea and Hearts of Palm Salad. (Menu begins on page 50.)*

Right: *Relish a breakfast of garden-fresh flavors with Cheddar-Potato Frittata, Garden Greens with Red Pepper Dressing, Melon with Sweet Onion Dressing, and Zucchini-Orange Bread. (Menu begins on page 33.)*

Breakfast & Brunch

Breakfast in the Great Outdoors

Raisin Bread French Toast with Apple Syrup

Spicy Pork Sausage

Grilled Oranges and Grapefruit

Cranberry-Raspberry Tea

SERVES 4
TOTAL CALORIES PER SERVING: 368
(Calories from Fat: 15%)

Outdoors is a splendid setting for a leisurely breakfast. To get maximum time in the fresh air, try this breakfast that cooks on the grill. Just follow each recipe's easy grilling instructions. The fruit may be served with the meal or as a prelude to the French toast and sausage (two links per serving).

The combination of delicious food and relaxed morning atmosphere is sure to keep everyone lingering at the table longer than usual.

Wake up with Raisin Bread French Toast with Apple Syrup, Grilled Oranges and Grapefruit, Spicy Pork Sausage, and Cranberry-Raspberry Tea.

RAISIN BREAD FRENCH TOAST WITH APPLE SYRUP

¼ cup unsweetened apple cider
2 tablespoons low-sugar apple jelly
1 tablespoon brown sugar
½ teaspoon cornstarch
Vegetable cooking spray
½ cup plus 2 tablespoons frozen egg substitute, thawed
¼ cup skim milk
½ teaspoon vanilla extract
4 (1-ounce) slices cinnamon-raisin bread

Combine first 4 ingredients in a saucepan. Place grill rack on grill over medium-hot coals (350° to 400°). Place saucepan on rack; cook, stirring constantly, until jelly melts and mixture is slightly thickened. Remove from heat; set aside, and keep warm.

Coat a 10-inch cast-iron skillet with cooking spray; place on rack until hot. Combine egg substitute, milk, and vanilla in a bowl. Dip 2 bread slices in egg mixture. Place in skillet; cook, covered, 5 to 7 minutes on each side or until browned. Repeat with remaining bread and egg mixture. Serve warm with cider mixture. Yield: 4 servings (134 calories per serving).

Per Serving:

Protein 6.2g	Fat 1.0g	(Saturated Fat 0.2g)
Carbohydrate 24.7g	Fiber 1.1g	Cholesterol 1mg
Iron 1.1mg	Sodium 177mg	Calcium 55mg

SPICY PORK SAUSAGE

If prepackaged lean ground pork is not available at your grocery store, ask the butcher to grind some lean pork loin for you.

⅓ pound lean ground pork
1½ tablespoons fine, dry breadcrumbs
1 tablespoon finely chopped onion
1 egg white, lightly beaten
½ teaspoon ground sage
¼ teaspoon fennel seeds, crushed
¼ teaspoon ground thyme
¼ teaspoon hot sauce
⅛ teaspoon salt
⅛ teaspoon garlic powder
⅛ teaspoon ground red pepper
⅛ teaspoon pepper
Vegetable cooking spray

Combine first 12 ingredients in a medium bowl, stirring well. Shape mixture into 8 links.

Place grill rack on grill over medium-hot coals (350° to 400°). Coat a large cast-iron skillet with cooking spray, and place on rack until hot. Place sausage links in skillet, and cook 9 to 10 minutes or until browned, turning frequently. Drain links on paper towels. Serve warm. Yield: 8 links (36 calories each).

Per Link:

Protein 4.5g	Fat 1.5g	(Saturated Fat 0.5g)
Carbohydrate 1.0g	Fiber 0.1g	Cholesterol 11mg
Iron 0.3mg	Sodium 63mg	Calcium 6mg

GRILLED ORANGES AND GRAPEFRUIT

1 cup fresh grapefruit sections
1 cup fresh orange sections
1 tablespoon water
2½ teaspoons brown sugar
2 teaspoons reduced-calorie margarine, melted
2 teaspoons chopped pecans, toasted

Arrange grapefruit and orange sections evenly on one half of a large piece of heavy-duty foil.

Combine water, brown sugar, and margarine; brush fruit evenly with brown sugar mixture. Sprinkle with pecans. Fold foil over fruit; crimp edges to seal.

Place grill rack on grill over medium-hot coals (350° to 400°). Place foil packet on rack; grill, covered, 1 to 2 minutes or until thoroughly heated.

To serve, remove fruit mixture from foil packet, and transfer to individual serving plates. Serve warm. Yield: 4 servings (67 calories per ½-cup serving).

Per Serving:

Protein 0.9g	Fat 2.2g	(Saturated Fat 0.2g)
Carbohydrate 12.5g	Fiber 2.6g	Cholesterol 0mg
Iron 0.2mg	Sodium 19mg	Calcium 29mg

CRANBERRY-RASPBERRY TEA

This tea is delightful when served warm, but it's also a refreshing thirst-quencher when served chilled over ice.

2½ cups water
6 regular-size tea bags
1½ cups cranberry-raspberry-strawberry juice blend
2 tablespoons honey

Bring water to a boil in a saucepan. Add tea bags; remove from heat. Cover and steep 5 minutes. Remove and discard tea bags. Add juice blend and honey; stir well.

Serve tea warm or chilled. Yield: 4 cups (95 calories per 1-cup serving).

Per Serving:

Protein 0.1g	Fat 0.0g	(Saturated Fat 0g)
Carbohydrate 24.9g	Fiber 0g	Cholesterol 0mg
Iron 0.1mg	Sodium 7mg	Calcium 7mg

Add sparkle to the night with Crabmeat Omelet Crêpes, Spicy Peach Sweet Rolls (page 30), Champagne-Marinated Grapes (page 30), and Cinnamon-Chocolate Coffee (page 30).

Midnight Breakfast

Crabmeat Omelet Crêpes
Spicy Peach Sweet Rolls
Champagne-Marinated Grapes
Cinnamon-Chocolate Coffee

SERVES 8
TOTAL CALORIES PER SERVING: 407
(Calories from Fat: 12%)

A late-night party is especially elegant and dramatic. Whether it's after the theater, a concert, or even the midnight movie, late hours seem magical. Nocturnal parties need to be planned around food that's easy to serve and requires as little fuss as possible at the last minute.

Spicy Peach Sweet Rolls (one per person) and Champagne-Marinated Grapes can be made the morning of the party. Even the "egg crêpes" can be prepared and filled ahead of time, and then warmed and ready to serve in just a few minutes after you return home.

CRABMEAT OMELET CRÊPES

Butter-flavored vegetable cooking spray
1 cup sliced fresh mushrooms
1 cup chopped green onions
2 teaspoons minced garlic
1 tablespoon all-purpose flour
2 tablespoons no-salt-added tomato paste
1½ teaspoons curry powder
1 teaspoon hot sauce
¼ teaspoon salt
⅛ teaspoon ground white pepper
1¼ cups plus 2 tablespoons skim milk, divided
1 pound fresh lump crabmeat, drained
⅓ cup minced fresh parsley
1¼ cups plus 2 tablespoons frozen egg substitute, thawed
¼ teaspoon salt
¼ teaspoon ground white pepper
Green onion tops (optional)

Coat a large nonstick skillet with cooking spray. Place over medium-high heat until hot. Add mushrooms, green onions, and garlic; sauté 2 to 3 minutes or until vegetables are tender.

Reduce heat to low. Stir in flour and next 5 ingredients. Cook, stirring constantly, 1 minute. Gradually stir in 1 cup milk. Cook over medium heat, stirring constantly, until thickened and bubbly. Stir in crabmeat and parsley; cook until thoroughly heated. Set aside, and keep warm.

Combine egg substitute, remaining milk, ¼ teaspoon salt, and ¼ teaspoon pepper.

Coat a 7- or 8-inch crêpe pan or nonstick skillet with cooking spray; place over medium heat until hot. Pour 2 tablespoons egg substitute mixture into pan, and quickly tilt pan in all directions so mixture covers pan in a thin film. Cook 2 minutes or until crêpe can be shaken loose from pan. Flip crêpe; cook about 30 seconds. Place crêpe on a towel to cool. Stack between layers of wax paper to prevent sticking. Repeat procedure until all egg mixture is used.

Spoon 3 rounded tablespoons crabmeat mixture down center of each crêpe. Roll up crêpes, and place 2 crêpes, seam side up, on each individual plate. Garnish with green onion tops, if desired. Yield: 8 servings (108 calories per 2 crêpes).

Make-ahead directions: Prepare filling and crêpes; assemble as directed. Cover and refrigerate up to 8 hours. Bake at 350° for 20 minutes or until heated.

Per Serving:

Protein 16.7g	Fat 1.7g	(Saturated Fat 0.2g)
Carbohydrate 6.0g	Fiber 0.8g	Cholesterol 52mg
Iron 1.8mg	Sodium 383mg	Calcium 135mg

SPICY PEACH SWEET ROLLS

2¼ cups all-purpose flour, divided
¼ teaspoon baking soda
3 tablespoons sugar
¼ teaspoon salt
¼ teaspoon ground cinnamon
¼ teaspoon ground nutmeg
1 package active dry yeast
½ cup skim milk
2 tablespoons margarine
1 egg
1 teaspoon vanilla extract
⅓ cup diced dried peaches
1 teaspoon all-purpose flour
Vegetable cooking spray
⅓ cup sifted powdered sugar
1½ teaspoons lemon juice

Combine ½ cup flour, baking soda, and next 5 ingredients in a large mixing bowl, stirring well. Combine milk and margarine in a saucepan; cook over medium heat until margarine melts, stirring occasionally. Cool to 120° to 130°.

Gradually add milk mixture to flour mixture, beating well at low speed of an electric mixer. Beat an additional 2 minutes at medium speed. Add egg and vanilla; beat well. Add peaches; stir well. Gradually stir in enough of the remaining 1¾ cups flour to make a soft dough.

Sprinkle 1 teaspoon flour over work surface. Turn dough out onto floured surface, and knead until smooth and elastic (about 10 minutes). Place dough in a large bowl coated with cooking spray, turning to coat top. Cover and let rise in a warm place (85°), free from drafts, 45 minutes or until dough is doubled in bulk.

Punch dough down, and divide into 12 equal portions. Roll each portion into a 12-inch rope. Shape each rope into a coil on a large baking sheet; coat top of each coil with cooking spray. Cover and let rise in a warm place, free from drafts, 30 minutes or until doubled in bulk.

Bake at 350° for 10 to 12 minutes or until lightly browned. Combine powdered sugar and lemon juice, stirring well. Drizzle over warm rolls. Yield: 1 dozen (156 calories each).

Make-ahead directions: Prepare the dough as directed, and shape into coils on a large baking sheet. Cover and refrigerate up to 8 hours. Before baking, remove from refrigerator, and let stand 30 minutes or until doubled in bulk. Bake as directed.

Per Roll:

Protein 3.8g	Fat 3.0g	(Saturated Fat 0.6g)
Carbohydrate 28.4g	Fiber 1.2g	Cholesterol 19mg
Iron 1.5mg	Sodium 109mg	Calcium 22mg

CHAMPAGNE-MARINATED GRAPES

4 cups seedless green grapes
¾ cup unsweetened pineapple juice
⅔ cup champagne
2 tablespoons sugar
1 teaspoon grated lemon rind
Lemon curls (optional)
Fresh mint sprigs (optional)

Place grapes in a shallow dish. Combine pineapple juice and next 3 ingredients; pour over grapes. Cover and marinate in refrigerator at least 8 hours, stirring occasionally.

Spoon grapes and liquid into 8 individual compotes. If desired, garnish with lemon curls and mint. Yield: 8 servings (105 calories per ½-cup serving).

Per Serving:

Protein 0.7g	Fat 0.5g	(Saturated Fat 0.2g)
Carbohydrate 22.8g	Fiber 1.5g	Cholesterol 0mg
Iron 0.4mg	Sodium 3mg	Calcium 15mg

CINNAMON-CHOCOLATE COFFEE

5⅔ cups strong brewed coffee
⅓ cup chocolate syrup
1 teaspoon vanilla extract
½ teaspoon ground cinnamon

Combine all ingredients in a medium saucepan. Cook over medium heat until thoroughly heated, stirring occasionally. Yield: 1½ quarts (38 calories per ¾-cup serving).

Per Serving:

Protein 0.6g	Fat 0.2g	(Saturated Fat 0g)
Carbohydrate 8.2g	Fiber 0g	Cholesterol 0mg
Iron 1.0mg	Sodium 11mg	Calcium 7mg

A romantic combination includes Breakfast in a Bread Basket, Fresh Strawberries with Creamy Yogurt Topping, and Hazelnut Café au Lait (recipes on page 32).

Romantic French Breakfast

Breakfast in a Bread Basket
Fresh Strawberries with Creamy Yogurt Topping
Hazelnut Café au Lait

SERVES 2
TOTAL CALORIES PER SERVING: 453
(Calories from Fat: 16%)

With recipes designed just for two, this meal sets the mood for the rest of the day. An occasion such as this, inspired by the romantic reputation of the French, calls for the use of your favorite china and silver.

Breakfast in a Bread Basket is a hearty entrée that's similar to a quiche. While it bakes, slice the strawberries and prepare the coffee. You can prepare the topping for the fruit the night before and refrigerate.

BREAKFAST IN A BREAD BASKET

Vegetable cooking spray
½ cup plus 2 tablespoons low-fat baking mix
2 tablespoons skim milk
3 tablespoons chopped sweet red pepper
3 tablespoons chopped green onions
2 eggs, lightly beaten
1 egg white, lightly beaten
2 tablespoons skim milk
¼ teaspoon garlic powder
¼ teaspoon pepper
Fresh basil sprigs (optional)

Coat 2 (10-ounce) custard cups with cooking spray; set aside. Combine baking mix and 2 tablespoons milk in a small bowl, stirring well. Divide dough into 3 equal portions; shape 2 portions into balls. (Keep remaining portion covered.)

Gently press 1 ball of dough into a 2-inch circle between 2 sheets of heavy-duty plastic wrap. Roll dough, still covered, into a 5-inch circle. Remove top sheet of plastic wrap. Invert and press dough into bottom and 2 inches up sides of prepared custard cup. Remove remaining plastic wrap. Repeat procedure with remaining ball of dough. Divide remaining portion of dough into 4 equal pieces. Roll each piece into a 15-inch rope. Twist 2 ropes together. Repeat procedure with remaining 2 ropes.

Moisten top edge of dough in custard cups with water. Gently press a twisted rope around dough in each cup, joining ends of ropes together. Set aside.

Coat a small nonstick skillet with cooking spray; place over medium-high heat until hot. Add red pepper and green onions; sauté until tender.

Combine sautéed vegetables, 2 eggs, and next 4 ingredients, stirring well. Pour mixture into pastry shells. Bake at 350° for 35 to 40 minutes or until set. Remove from oven; let stand 5 minutes.

Remove from cups, and garnish with fresh basil sprigs, if desired. Yield: 2 servings (269 calories per serving).

Per Serving:		
Protein 13.2g	Fat 6.1g	(Saturated Fat 1.7g)
Carbohydrate 39.3g	Fiber 1.1g	Cholesterol 222mg
Iron 5.9mg	Sodium 709mg	Calcium 234mg

FRESH STRAWBERRIES WITH CREAMY YOGURT TOPPING

1 (8-ounce) carton vanilla low-fat yogurt
1 tablespoon powdered sugar
¼ teaspoon almond extract
1 cup fresh strawberry halves
1 teaspoon brown sugar

Spoon yogurt onto several layers of paper towels; spread to ½-inch thickness. Cover with additional paper towels; let stand 5 minutes. Scrape yogurt into a bowl, using a rubber spatula. Stir in powdered sugar and almond extract. Cover and chill.

Spoon strawberries evenly onto individual plates. Top with yogurt mixture; sprinkle with brown sugar. Yield: 2 servings (139 calories per serving).

Per Serving:		
Protein 6.0g	Fat 1.7g	(Saturated Fat 0.9g)
Carbohydrate 25.8g	Fiber 1.8g	Cholesterol 6mg
Iron 0.4mg	Sodium 76mg	Calcium 205mg

HAZELNUT CAFÉ AU LAIT

1 cup skim milk
1 teaspoon instant hazelnut-flavored coffee granules
1 cup boiling water

Place milk in a small saucepan, and cook over medium heat until thoroughly heated. (Do not boil.) Combine coffee granules and water. Pour ½ cup coffee and ½ cup milk into each mug; stir. Serve warm. Yield: 2 servings (45 calories per 1-cup serving).

Per Serving:		
Protein 4.3g	Fat 0.2g	(Saturated Fat 0.1g)
Carbohydrate 6.4g	Fiber 0g	Cholesterol 2mg
Iron 0.5mg	Sodium 66mg	Calcium 153mg

Bumper Crop Brunch

Cheddar-Potato Frittata

Garden Greens with Red Pepper Dressing

Zucchini-Orange Bread

Melon with Sweet Onion Dressing

Coffee

SERVES 6
TOTAL CALORIES PER SERVING: 362
(Calories from Fat: 20%)

Invite your favorite gardening buddies over to celebrate the results of your hard work. This menu of quick and easy recipes brings summer's abundant harvest to your table.

Uncomplicated preparation promotes the garden-fresh flavors of tomatoes, zucchini, lettuce, and sweet red peppers. Except for Cheddar-Potato Frittata, this menu may be prepared in advance, leaving plenty of time for sharing gardening tips over a freshly brewed cup of coffee.

Enjoy a bountiful harvest of fresh vegetables in Cheddar-Potato Frittata.

CHEDDAR-POTATO FRITTATA

1½ cups coarsely chopped round red potato
Vegetable cooking spray
1 cup chopped tomato
¼ cup chopped green onions
½ teaspoon pepper
¼ teaspoon salt
1½ cups frozen egg substitute, thawed
½ cup (2 ounces) shredded reduced-fat sharp Cheddar cheese
Green onions (optional)

Cook chopped potato in a saucepan in boiling water to cover 10 to 12 minutes or until tender. Drain well.

Coat a large nonstick skillet with cooking spray; place over medium-high heat until hot. Add potato, tomato, and next 3 ingredients; sauté until onion is tender. Pour egg substitute over vegetable mixture. Cover; cook over medium-low heat 15 minutes or until set. Sprinkle with cheese. Cover; cook 2 minutes or until cheese melts. Cut into 6 wedges, and serve immediately. Garnish with green onions, if desired. Yield: 6 servings (100 calories per serving).

Per Serving:

Protein 10.1g	Fat 2.1g	(Saturated Fat 1.1g)
Carbohydrate 10.5g	Fiber 1.4g	Cholesterol 6mg
Iron 1.9mg	Sodium 263mg	Calcium 115mg

GARDEN GREENS WITH RED PEPPER DRESSING

1 large sweet red pepper
3 tablespoons white wine vinegar
2 tablespoons water
2 teaspoons olive oil
¼ teaspoon salt
⅛ teaspoon ground red pepper
1 tablespoon minced fresh basil
2 cups torn red leaf lettuce
2 cups torn green leaf lettuce
2 cups torn romaine lettuce
1 cup chopped tomato
1 cup chopped cucumber

Cut pepper in half lengthwise; remove and discard seeds and membrane. Place pepper, skin side up, on a foil-lined baking sheet. Bake at 425° for 20 to 25 minutes or until skin is browned. Cover with aluminum foil; let cool. Peel and discard skin.

Place roasted pepper, vinegar, and next 4 ingredients in container of an electric blender. Cover and process until mixture is smooth; transfer to a small bowl. Stir in basil. Cover and chill at least 1 hour.

Combine lettuces, tomato, and cucumber in a large bowl; toss gently. Arrange lettuce mixture evenly on individual plates. Spoon red pepper mixture over salads. Yield: 6 servings (38 calories per 1-cup serving).

Per Serving:		
Protein 1.2g	Fat 1.9g	(Saturated Fat 0.3g)
Carbohydrate 5.0g	Fiber 1.8g	Cholesterol 0mg
Iron 1.0mg	Sodium 106mg	Calcium 26mg

ZUCCHINI-ORANGE BREAD

1 cup finely shredded zucchini
1¾ cups all-purpose flour
2½ teaspoons baking powder
¼ teaspoon salt
½ cup sugar
1 teaspoon grated orange rind
½ cup unsweetened orange juice
⅓ cup frozen egg substitute, thawed
2 tablespoons vegetable oil
½ teaspoon orange extract
Vegetable cooking spray

Press zucchini between paper towels to remove excess moisture. Combine zucchini, flour, and next 4 ingredients in a large bowl. Combine orange juice, egg substitute, oil, and orange extract, stirring well. Add to dry ingredients, stirring just until dry ingredients are moistened.

Spoon batter into an 8½- x 4½- x 3-inch loafpan coated with cooking spray. Bake at 375° for 40 to 45 minutes or until a wooden pick inserted in center comes out clean. Let cool in pan 10 minutes; remove from pan, and let cool completely on a wire rack. Yield: 16 servings (98 calories per ½-inch slice).

Per Serving:		
Protein 2.1g	Fat 1.9g	(Saturated Fat 0.3g)
Carbohydrate 18.1g	Fiber 0.4g	Cholesterol 0mg
Iron 0.9mg	Sodium 45mg	Calcium 48mg

MELON WITH SWEET ONION DRESSING

2 cups cantaloupe balls
2 cups honeydew melon balls
2 cups watermelon balls
¼ cup sugar
¼ cup unsweetened orange juice
1 tablespoon minced onion
2 teaspoons vegetable oil
¾ teaspoon poppy seeds
¼ teaspoon salt
¼ teaspoon dry mustard

Place melon balls in a large bowl; set aside.

Combine sugar and remaining ingredients in a small jar; cover tightly, and shake vigorously. Pour orange juice mixture over melon balls, and toss gently. Cover and chill. Toss gently before serving. Serve with a slotted spoon. Yield: 6 servings (121 calories per 1-cup serving).

Per Serving:		
Protein 1.5g	Fat 2.3g	(Saturated Fat 0.6g)
Carbohydrate 25.8g	Fiber 1.8g	Cholesterol 0mg
Iron 0.4mg	Sodium 112mg	Calcium 27mg

Bridesmaids Brunch

Ham-and-Cheese Strata
Steamed Asparagus
Apple-Currant Biscuits
Amaretto Fruit Medley
Cranberry Fizz

SERVES 10
TOTAL CALORIES PER SERVING: 605
(Calories from Fat: 14%)

Honor the bride-to-be and her bridesmaids with this elegant brunch that's easy on the cook. The entrée is made the night before and refrigerated. Pop it in the oven about an hour before guests arrive.

Prepare the fruit salad as well as the beverage base in the morning. Prepare the biscuits before guests arrive, but wait to bake them just before you are ready to serve (two biscuits per serving). Steam the asparagus (2½ pounds) while the biscuits bake.

Amaretto Fruit Medley (page 36) provides a refreshing boost of energy for the bride and her attendants.

HAM-AND-CHEESE STRATA

Vegetable cooking spray
4 cups sliced fresh mushrooms
¾ cup chopped green onions
½ cup chopped sweet red pepper
1 (16-ounce) loaf French bread, torn into bite-size pieces
⅔ cup Chablis or other dry white wine
1¼ cups chopped reduced-fat, low-salt ham
1 cup (4 ounces) shredded reduced-fat Swiss cheese
1½ cups frozen egg substitute, thawed
1½ cups skim milk
½ teaspoon dried thyme
½ teaspoon dry mustard
¼ teaspoon pepper
⅛ teaspoon salt

Coat a large nonstick skillet with cooking spray; place over medium-high heat until hot. Add mushrooms, onions, and red pepper; sauté until tender.

Coat a 13- x 9- x 2-inch baking dish with cooking spray. Place bread pieces in dish. Spoon mushroom mixture over bread. Pour wine over mushroom mixture. Sprinkle with ham and cheese.

Combine egg substitute and remaining ingredients; stir with a wire whisk. Pour over layers in dish. Cover; chill 8 hours. Let stand at room temperature 20 minutes before baking. Cover; bake at 325° for 1 hour. Yield: 10 servings (237 calories per serving).

Per Serving:

Protein 17.4g	Fat 4.3g	(Saturated Fat 2.0g)
Carbohydrate 31.1g	Fiber 1.8g	Cholesterol 19mg
Iron 2.5mg	Sodium 543mg	Calcium 221mg

APPLE-CURRANT BISCUITS

You can use apple juice in place of the apple bourbon if you prefer.

⅓ cup currants
¼ cup apple bourbon
1¾ cups all-purpose flour
2 teaspoons baking powder
⅛ teaspoon salt
2 tablespoons sugar
1¼ teaspoons ground cinnamon
½ cup nonfat buttermilk
3 tablespoons margarine, melted
1 tablespoon all-purpose flour
Vegetable cooking spray
½ cup sifted powdered sugar
2 tablespoons unsweetened apple juice

Combine currants and bourbon in a small bowl; let stand 10 minutes. Drain, reserving liquid and currants. Set liquid and currants aside.

Combine 1¾ cups flour and next 4 ingredients in a medium bowl; make a well in center of mixture. Combine reserved liquid, buttermilk, and margarine; add to dry ingredients, stirring just until dry ingredients are moistened. Stir in currants.

Sprinkle 1 tablespoon flour evenly over work surface. Turn dough out onto floured surface, and knead lightly 4 or 5 times. Roll dough to ½-inch thickness; cut into rounds with a 1½-inch biscuit cutter. Place rounds on a baking sheet coated with cooking spray. Bake at 400° for 10 to 12 minutes or until biscuits are golden.

Combine powdered sugar and apple juice. Drizzle over warm biscuits. Serve warm. Yield: 26 biscuits (65 calories each).

Per Biscuit:		
Protein 1.2g	Fat 1.5g	(Saturated Fat 0.3g)
Carbohydrate 11.9g	Fiber 0.3g	Cholesterol 0mg
Iron 0.5mg	Sodium 33mg	Calcium 32mg

AMARETTO FRUIT MEDLEY

For a nonalcoholic version of this fruit dessert, stir in orange juice in place of the amaretto.

⅓ cup sliced almonds
3 tablespoons sugar
6 fresh nectarines, pitted and sliced
2 medium-size oranges, peeled and sectioned
2 fresh plums, pitted and sliced
¼ cup amaretto

Combine almonds and sugar in a small nonstick skillet; cook over low heat, stirring constantly, 20 minutes or until sugar melts and coats almonds. Let cool. Break almond mixture into small chunks.

Place fruit in a large bowl; pour amaretto over fruit mixture, and toss gently. Cover and chill thoroughly. Spoon fruit mixture evenly into 10 compotes. Top evenly with almond mixture. Yield: 10 servings (117 calories per serving).

Per Serving:		
Protein 1.6g	Fat 1.6g	(Saturated Fat 0.2g)
Carbohydrate 23.3g	Fiber 4.1g	Cholesterol 0mg
Iron 0.3mg	Sodium 0mg	Calcium 24mg

CRANBERRY FIZZ

4½ cups cranberry juice cocktail
3 cups unsweetened orange juice
2½ cups club soda, chilled

Combine cranberry juice and orange juice in a large pitcher, stirring well. Cover and chill.

Stir in club soda just before serving. Serve over ice. Yield: 2½ quarts (101 calories per 1-cup serving).

Per Serving:		
Protein 0.5g	Fat 0.1g	(Saturated Fat 0g)
Carbohydrate 25.4g	Fiber 0.1g	Cholesterol 0mg
Iron 0.2mg	Sodium 18mg	Calcium 13mg

Herb and Cheese Tomatoes, Savory Polenta with Sautéed Mushrooms, and Lamb Chops Dijon are perfectly portioned for a cozy dinner. *(Menu begins on page 47.)*

Quick & Easy

Picnic at the Park

Mexican Turkey Sandwiches
Vegetable-Pasta Salad
Fresh Orange Wedges
Mocha Chip Cookies
Sparkling Fruit Soda

SERVES 6
TOTAL CALORIES PER SERVING: 576
(Calories from Fat: 18%)

When the next sunny weekend comes along, head to the park for fun and games. You'll be set for the day when you carry along this portable meal.

Prepare the sandwiches and salad in the morning. Keep them, along with one small orange per person, over ice until serving time. The cookies (one per person) can be made up to two days in advance.

Combine the juices for the beverage before you go, but wait until serving time to add the sparkling water. All that's left to do is collect your "toys"—kite, balls and bats, toy sailboats, or whatever you fancy.

Lunch is a picnic when you prepare Mexican Turkey Sandwiches, Mocha Chip Cookies, Sparkling Fruit Soda, and Vegetable-Pasta Salad.

MEXICAN TURKEY SANDWICHES

2/3 cup light process cream cheese product, softened
1/4 cup chopped onion
1/4 cup commercial no-salt-added salsa
2 tablespoons chopped ripe olives
6 (6-inch) flour tortillas
10 ounces thinly sliced smoked turkey breast
1/4 cup plus 2 tablespoons commercial no-salt-added salsa
1/2 cup (2 ounces) shredded fat-free Cheddar cheese
1 cup tightly packed shredded leaf lettuce

Beat cream cheese at medium speed of an electric mixer until smooth. Add onion, 1/4 cup salsa, and olives; stir well.

Spread cream cheese mixture evenly over tortillas; arrange turkey evenly over cream cheese mixture. Spoon 1 tablespoon salsa over each tortilla; top with cheese and lettuce. Roll up tortillas jellyroll fashion. Cover with plastic wrap; chill thoroughly. Yield: 6 servings (213 calories per serving).

Per Serving:

Protein 19.0g	Fat 7.6g	(Saturated Fat 3.2g)
Carbohydrate 17.6g	Fiber 1.5g	Cholesterol 43mg
Iron 1.4mg	Sodium 738mg	Calcium 162mg

VEGETABLE-PASTA SALAD

8 ounces farfalle pasta, uncooked
1 cup quartered cherry tomatoes
¾ cup frozen English peas, thawed
2 small sweet yellow peppers, seeded and cut into strips
3½ tablespoons commercial reduced-calorie Italian dressing
2 tablespoons grated Parmesan cheese

Cook pasta according to package directions, omitting salt and fat. Drain; rinse pasta under cold water, and drain again. Place in a bowl; add tomatoes, peas, and pepper, tossing gently.

Combine Italian dressing and Parmesan cheese in a jar; cover tightly, and shake vigorously to blend. Pour dressing mixture over pasta mixture, and toss well. Cover and chill thoroughly. Yield: 6 servings (182 calories per 1-cup serving).

Per Serving:

Protein 7.1g	Fat 1.7g	(Saturated Fat 0.5g)
Carbohydrate 34.6g	Fiber 2.7g	Cholesterol 1mg
Iron 2.3mg	Sodium 183mg	Calcium 38mg

MOCHA CHIP COOKIES

The flavor of these dark, rich-tasting cookies gives no hint that they're low in fat.

¼ cup reduced-calorie margarine, softened
⅓ cup sugar
¼ cup firmly packed brown sugar
¼ cup frozen egg substitute, thawed
1 cup all-purpose flour
½ teaspoon baking soda
¼ teaspoon salt
¼ cup unsweetened cocoa
1 tablespoon instant coffee granules
⅓ cup semisweet chocolate mini-morsels
Vegetable cooking spray

Beat margarine at medium speed of an electric mixer until creamy; gradually add sugars, beating well. Add egg substitute; beat well. Combine flour, baking soda, salt, cocoa, and coffee granules. Add to margarine mixture; beat just until blended. Stir in chocolate morsels.

Drop dough by level tablespoonfuls, 2 inches apart, onto cookie sheets coated with cooking spray. Bake at 375° for 5 to 6 minutes.

Remove from cookie sheets, and let cool completely on a wire rack. Yield: 22 cookies (71 calories each).

Per Cookie:

Protein 1.3g	Fat 2.3g	(Saturated Fat 0.7g)
Carbohydrate 11.6g	Fiber 0.2g	Cholesterol 0mg
Iron 0.6mg	Sodium 81mg	Calcium 7mg

SPARKLING FRUIT SODA

2 cups unsweetened peach juice blend
2 cups unsweetened apple juice
2 cups lemon-lime-flavored sparkling water, chilled

Combine peach juice and apple juice. Cover and chill thoroughly.

Just before serving, stir in sparkling water. Serve over ice. Yield: 6 servings (83 calories per 1-cup serving).

Per Serving:

Protein 0.5g	Fat 0.1g	(Saturated Fat 0g)
Carbohydrate 20.3g	Fiber 0.2g	Cholesterol 0mg
Iron 0.3mg	Sodium 8mg	Calcium 17mg

After enjoying Mock Muffuletta, Cheese-and-Olive Stuffed Celery, Peanut Butter Snack Squares, and Flash Fruit Quencher, you'll feel like getting off the sidelines and into the game.

Sideline Soccer Social

Mock Muffuletta
Cheese-and-Olive Stuffed Celery
Peanut Butter Snack Squares
Flash Fruit Quencher

SERVES 4
TOTAL CALORIES PER SERVING: 585
(Calories from Fat: 24%)

Have you noticed that soccer is exploding in popularity among children and adults? One reason is that it requires no specific physical attributes—only practiced skills and athletic endurance. Another reason is that it's just plain fun!

Whether you are a "presock" Mom or a uniformed player, this portable supper will fuel your team spirit. The Mock Muffuletta is a hand-held meal of roast beef, cheese, and salad. The flavors blend when it's wrapped airtight and chilled over crushed ice in a cooler. Cheese-and-Olive Stuffed Celery (three per serving) makes a crisp sandwich accompaniment. Peanut Butter Snack Squares are a satisfying postmeal treat (one per person).

MOCK MUFFULETTA

The flavors intensify as this sandwich chills; prepare it at least two hours before serving.

3 cups finely shredded romaine lettuce
½ small purple onion, thinly sliced and separated into rings
¼ cup crumbled blue cheese
3 tablespoons commercial oil-free Italian dressing
1 tablespoon red wine vinegar
1 tablespoon water
4 (2-ounce) submarine rolls, split
2 plum tomatoes, thinly sliced
½ teaspoon coarsely ground pepper
6 ounces thinly sliced cooked roast beef

Combine first 6 ingredients in a bowl; toss well. Spoon lettuce mixture onto bottom halves of rolls. Top with tomato slices; sprinkle with pepper. Arrange roast beef over tomato. Top with remaining roll halves. Wrap in aluminum foil; chill at least 2 hours. Yield: 4 servings (294 calories per serving).

Per Serving:

Protein 16.4g	Fat 8.9g	(Saturated Fat 3.0g)
Carbohydrate 37.4g	Fiber 1.7g	Cholesterol 41mg
Iron 4.1mg	Sodium 781mg	Calcium 64mg

CHEESE-AND-OLIVE STUFFED CELERY

¼ cup nonfat cream cheese product, softened
1 tablespoon finely chopped green onions
1 teaspoon sesame seeds, toasted
4 pimiento-stuffed olives, finely chopped
24 (2-inch-long) celery sticks

Combine first 4 ingredients in a small bowl, stirring well. Spoon cream cheese mixture evenly into 12 celery sticks. Top with remaining 12 celery sticks, pressing edges together. Cover and chill. Yield: 1 dozen (9 calories each).

Per Stuffed Celery Snack:

Protein 0.9g	Fat 0.2g	(Saturated Fat 0g)
Carbohydrate 0.9g	Fiber 0.3g	Cholesterol 1mg
Iron 0.1mg	Sodium 113mg	Calcium 21mg

PEANUT BUTTER SNACK SQUARES

⅓ cup reduced-calorie margarine, softened
¼ cup reduced-fat peanut butter
⅔ cup sugar
½ cup frozen egg substitute, thawed
¾ cup all-purpose flour
½ teaspoon baking powder
⅛ teaspoon salt
½ cup finely chopped, unsalted dry-roasted peanuts
½ teaspoon vanilla extract
Vegetable cooking spray

Beat margarine and peanut butter at medium speed of an electric mixer until creamy; gradually add sugar, beating well. Add egg substitute, and beat until well blended.

Combine flour, baking powder, and salt. Add to margarine mixture, beating well. Stir in peanuts and vanilla.

Spread mixture into an 8-inch square pan coated with cooking spray. Bake at 350° for 25 minutes or until lightly browned. Yield: 16 servings (126 calories each).

Per Square:

Protein 3.5g	Fat 6.2g	(Saturated Fat 0.9g)
Carbohydrate 15.6g	Fiber 0.7g	Cholesterol 0mg
Iron 0.6mg	Sodium 84mg	Calcium 16mg

FLASH FRUIT QUENCHER

2 cups cranberry juice cocktail, chilled
1 cup unsweetened pineapple juice, chilled
1 cup unsweetened orange juice, chilled

Combine all ingredients in a large pitcher, stirring well.

Serve over crushed ice. Yield: 4 cups (138 calories per 1-cup serving).

Per Serving:

Protein 0.6g	Fat 0.2g	(Saturated Fat 0g)
Carbohydrate 34.6g	Fiber 0.2g	Cholesterol 0mg
Iron 0.4mg	Sodium 6mg	Calcium 20mg

Send your taste buds back to "the good old days" with Simple Baked Chicken and Basil Mashed Potatoes topped with Home-Style Gravy and accompanied with Stewed Tomatoes and Onions (page 44).

Dine Down Memory Lane

Simple Baked Chicken
Basil Mashed Potatoes
Home-Style Gravy
Stewed Tomatoes and Onions
S'More Brownies
Skim Milk

SERVES 6
TOTAL CALORIES PER SERVING: 546
(Calories from Fat: 20%)

Meals are getting back to basics these days, but with a twist. Old favorites are being enjoyed for their flavor as well as for their place in a healthy lifestyle. Although no longer heavy and fat-laden, these updated home-style recipes will still take your thoughts down memory lane.

The baked chicken gets its spark from lemonade concentrate and lots of freshly ground pepper, and mashed potatoes are the perfect side dish. Use yogurt to add zip, and add basil to bring this comfort food into the nineties.

What could be more appropriate to accompany these favorites than Home-Style Gravy? Ladle 2 tablespoons of warm gravy over each serving of chicken and 2 tablespoons over the potatoes.

Use red, ripe, juicy tomatoes for the best flavor in Stewed Tomatoes and Onions, a nostalgic dish that's making a comeback. Keep diners reminiscing with S'More Brownies, flavored with graham crackers, marshmallows, and chocolate. Enjoy these gooey treats with glasses of cold skim milk. (Serve one brownie and 1 cup milk per person.)

SIMPLE BAKED CHICKEN

1 (3-pound) broiler-fryer, cut up and skinned
Vegetable cooking spray
½ cup frozen lemonade concentrate, thawed and undiluted
2 tablespoons canned low-sodium chicken broth, undiluted
½ teaspoon garlic powder
1 teaspoon dried rosemary, crushed
1 teaspoon freshly ground pepper

Place chicken on a rack in a roasting pan coated with cooking spray.

Combine lemonade concentrate, chicken broth, and garlic powder, stirring well. Sprinkle chicken with rosemary and pepper; brush with some of lemonade mixture.

Bake at 400° for 45 to 50 minutes or until chicken is done, turning and basting occasionally with remaining lemonade mixture. Yield: 6 servings (235 calories per serving).

Per Serving:		
Protein 28.6g	Fat 7.5g	(Saturated Fat 2.0g)
Carbohydrate 12.1g	Fiber 0.2g	Cholesterol 87mg
Iron 1.6mg	Sodium 87mg	Calcium 21mg

BASIL MASHED POTATOES

2½ cups peeled, sliced baking potato
3 tablespoons skim milk
2 tablespoons plain nonfat yogurt
¼ teaspoon salt
⅛ teaspoon ground white pepper
1½ tablespoons minced fresh basil
Fresh basil sprigs (optional)

Place potato in a medium saucepan; add water to cover. Bring to a boil; cook 15 minutes or until tender. Drain potato, and place in a large bowl. Beat at medium speed of an electric mixer 1 minute or until smooth.

Combine milk and next 3 ingredients; gradually add milk mixture to potato, beating at medium speed until smooth. Stir in minced basil. Garnish with fresh basil sprigs, if desired. Yield: 6 servings (68 calories per ½-cup serving).

Per Serving:		
Protein 2.2g	Fat 0.1g	(Saturated Fat 0g)
Carbohydrate 15.0g	Fiber 1.3g	Cholesterol 0mg
Iron 0.6mg	Sodium 110mg	Calcium 27mg

HOME-STYLE GRAVY

This virtually fat-free gravy is the perfect accompaniment to baked chicken, roasted pork, or mashed potatoes.

Vegetable cooking spray
½ cup chopped onion
1 teaspoon dried thyme
1½ tablespoons cornstarch
¼ cup water
1¼ cups canned low-sodium chicken broth, undiluted
¼ teaspoon salt
¼ teaspoon pepper
¼ teaspoon poultry seasoning

Coat a medium saucepan with cooking spray, and place over medium-high heat until hot. Add onion and dried thyme; sauté 3 minutes or until onion is tender.

Combine cornstarch and water, stirring until smooth; stir in broth. Add cornstarch mixture, salt, pepper, and poultry seasoning to onion mixture. Bring to a boil over medium heat, stirring constantly. Cook, stirring constantly, until thickened and bubbly. Yield: 1½ cups (5 calories per tablespoon).

Per Tablespoon:		
Protein 0.2g	Fat 0.1g	(Saturated Fat 0g)
Carbohydrate 0.9g	Fiber 0.1g	Cholesterol 0mg
Iron 0.2mg	Sodium 29mg	Calcium 2mg

STEWED TOMATOES AND ONIONS

Vegetable cooking spray
½ cup chopped green pepper
¼ cup thinly sliced celery
1 small onion, thinly sliced and separated into rings
1 clove garlic, minced
3 cups peeled, coarsely chopped tomato
1 tablespoon red wine vinegar
2 teaspoons sugar
⅛ teaspoon pepper

Coat a large nonstick skillet with cooking spray; place over medium-high heat until hot. Add green pepper, celery, onion, and garlic; sauté 5 minutes or until vegetables are tender. Add tomato and remaining ingredients; bring to a boil. Cover, reduce heat, and simmer 15 minutes, stirring occasionally. Yield: 6 servings (37 calories per ½-cup serving).

Per Serving:		
Protein 1.2	Fat 0.5g	(Saturated Fat 0.1g)
Carbohydrate 8.3g	Fiber 1.8g	Cholesterol 0mg
Iron 0.7mg	Sodium 14mg	Calcium 11mg

S'MORE BROWNIES

½ cup sugar
⅓ cup water
2½ tablespoons vegetable oil
½ teaspoon vanilla extract
2 egg whites, lightly beaten
½ cup all-purpose flour
¾ teaspoon baking powder
⅛ teaspoon salt
⅓ cup graham cracker crumbs (about 5 squares)
¼ cup unsweetened cocoa
Vegetable cooking spray
2 cups miniature marshmallows
1 (1-ounce) square semisweet chocolate, grated

Combine first 4 ingredients in a medium bowl. Add egg whites, stirring well. Combine flour and next 4 ingredients. Add to sugar mixture; stir well.

Pour batter into an 8-inch square pan coated with cooking spray. Bake at 350° for 22 minutes or until a wooden pick inserted in center comes out clean. Sprinkle with marshmallows; bake an additional minute or until marshmallows melt. Sprinkle with grated chocolate. Let cool completely. Cut into bars. Yield: 16 brownies (100 calories each).

Per Brownie:		
Protein 1.6g	Fat 3.1g	(Saturated Fat 0.9g)
Carbohydrate 17.2g	Fiber 0.2g	Cholesterol 0mg
Iron 0.6mg	Sodium 53mg	Calcium 14mg

A RAINBOW A DAY?

Eat carrots because they're orange? Tomatoes because they're red? Yes! Research continues to show that carotenoids (the pigments that give fruits and vegetables their brilliant colors) have positive health benefits.

The best known carotenoid is orange-yellow beta carotene, which abounds in carrots, sweet potatoes, apricots, and deep green leafy vegetables. This antioxidant (so named because it helps prevent damage to body cells by oxygen free radicals) also appears to play a role in preventing some cancers as well as heart disease.

Lycopene, a deep red carotenoid found in tomatoes, red peppers, and ruby-red grapefruit, seems to be a potent antioxidant as well as a protectant against cancer. One study found that women who ate a lycopene-rich diet had only one-fifth the risk of developing a precancerous condition of the cervix than did those whose diets were low in lycopene.

Results from a study of mice suggest that canthaxanthin, a carotenoid found in some mushrooms and used as a coloring agent by the food industry, may help prevent breast cancer. But studies in humans are needed before any conclusions can be made.

Tune In for Dinner

Turkey-Black Bean Chili
Wilted Bacon Salad
Buttermilk Corn Muffins
Cranberry-Apple Cobbler

SERVES 5
TOTAL CALORIES PER SERVING: 561
(Calories from Fat: 11%)

Pair this speedy, casual winter supper with a favorite video—choose a classic, a comedy, or even an animated story. Whatever the mood, one whiff of this meal will tell family or friends that they're in for a treat.

The entire supper takes less than an hour to assemble. All the ingredients for the chili are full-flavored, so there's no need for a lengthy simmering time. Serve cornbread muffins (one per serving) to eat with or even crumble into the chili.

Toss the salad just before serving to make sure the dressing will still be warm. Remember to pause the movie long enough to serve dessert.

Settle in with your remote control in hand for Turkey-Black Bean Chili, Buttermilk Corn Muffins (page 46), and Wilted Bacon Salad (page 46).

TURKEY-BLACK BEAN CHILI

Vegetable cooking spray
1 cup coarsely chopped onion
½ cup sliced celery
2 (16-ounce) cans no-salt-added black beans
1 (10-ounce) can whole tomatoes and green chiles, undrained and chopped
6 ounces diced, cooked turkey breast
1 tablespoon chili seasoning mix
¼ cup plus 1 tablespoon nonfat sour cream alternative
Sweet red pepper strips (optional)

Coat a small Dutch oven with cooking spray. Place over medium-high heat until hot. Add onion and celery; sauté until tender. Let cool slightly. Transfer mixture to container of an electric blender.

Drain beans; reserve liquid. Add half of beans and all of liquid to blender. Cover; process until smooth. Stop once to scrape down sides. Return to Dutch oven.

Add remaining beans, tomato and chiles, turkey, and chili seasoning to Dutch oven. Cook over medium heat until heated. Ladle into bowls; top evenly with sour cream. Garnish with pepper strips, if desired. Yield: 5 cups (259 calories per 1-cup serving).

Per Serving:

Protein 22.7g	Fat 2.0g	(Saturated Fat 0.4g)
Carbohydrate 36.1g	Fiber 6.7g	Cholesterol 23mg
Iron 4.6mg	Sodium 442mg	Calcium 71mg

WILTED BACON SALAD

Using turkey bacon instead of regular bacon cut the fat in this recipe by 2.2 grams per serving.

⅓ cup chopped onion
3 tablespoons brown sugar
3 tablespoons cider vinegar
4 slices turkey bacon, cooked and crumbled
7 cups mixed baby salad greens

Combine first 4 ingredients in a small saucepan; bring to a boil. Reduce heat; simmer, uncovered, 5 minutes, stirring until sugar dissolves.

Place salad greens in a large bowl; pour vinegar mixture over greens, tossing gently. Serve warm. Yield: 5 servings (50 calories per 1¼-cup serving).

Per Serving:		
Protein 1.3g	Fat 0.8g	(Saturated Fat 0.2g)
Carbohydrate 9.8g	Fiber 0.4g	Cholesterol 3mg
Iron 0.3mg	Sodium 75mg	Calcium 9mg

BUTTERMILK CORN MUFFINS

¾ cup yellow cornmeal
¾ cup all-purpose flour
1½ teaspoons baking powder
¼ teaspoon baking soda
¼ teaspoon salt
2 teaspoons sugar
1 cup nonfat buttermilk
¼ cup frozen egg substitute, thawed
1 tablespoon vegetable oil
½ cup canned no-salt-added whole-kernel corn, drained
Vegetable cooking spray

Combine first 6 ingredients in a medium bowl, stirring well. Make a well in center of mixture. Combine buttermilk, egg substitute, and oil. Add to dry ingredients, stirring just until dry ingredients are moistened. Fold in corn.

Spoon batter into muffin pans coated with cooking spray, filling two-thirds full. Bake at 425° for 18 to 20 minutes or until muffins are golden. Remove muffins from pans immediately. Yield: 10 muffins (106 calories each).

Per Muffin:		
Protein 3.5g	Fat 1.8g	(Saturated Fat 0.4g)
Carbohydrate 18.7g	Fiber 0.8g	Cholesterol 1mg
Iron 1.1mg	Sodium 127mg	Calcium 75mg

CRANBERRY-APPLE COBBLER

Commercial whole-berry cranberry sauce adds a tangy twist to this cobbler without adding fat.

3 cups peeled, coarsely chopped Rome apple (about 2 medium)
Butter-flavored vegetable cooking spray
1 (16-ounce) can jellied whole-berry cranberry sauce
¼ cup unsweetened orange juice
⅓ cup quick-cooking oats, uncooked
¼ cup all-purpose flour
2½ tablespoons brown sugar
2 tablespoons reduced-calorie margarine, softened

Place chopped apple in an 8-inch square pan coated with cooking spray. Combine cranberry sauce and orange juice, stirring well. Spoon cranberry sauce mixture evenly over apple.

Combine oats, flour, and brown sugar; cut in margarine with a pastry blender until mixture resembles coarse meal. Sprinkle oat mixture evenly over cranberry mixture. Coat oat mixture with cooking spray. Bake at 375° for 35 minutes or until apple is tender. Let stand 10 minutes before serving. Yield: 10 servings (146 calories per serving).

Per Serving:		
Protein 1.4g	Fat 2.1g	(Saturated Fat 0.3g)
Carbohydrate 32.0g	Fiber 1.8g	Cholesterol 0mg
Iron 0.6mg	Sodium 37mg	Calcium 9mg

Dinner Just for Two

Lamb Chops Dijon
Savory Polenta with Sautéed Mushrooms
Herb and Cheese Tomatoes
Orange Amaretti
Sparkling Apple Juice
Coffee

SERVES 2
TOTAL CALORIES PER SERVING: 631
(Calories from Fat: 28%)

When an opportunity arises, serve this simple dinner designed for couples only. Sip on sparkling apple juice (combine ¾ cup apple juice and ¼ cup sparkling water per serving) while you assemble dinner.

Begin by preparing the polenta. Next, broil the lamb chops, adding the polenta to the oven part way through the lamb cooking time. Make the mushroom topping while the lamb and polenta cook.

As you arrange the lamb and polenta on the dinner plates, bake the tomatoes. Let the sherbet soften while you enjoy dinner; assemble the dessert just before serving.

For a luscious yet low-fat alternative to plain ice cream that's just as cool and creamy, serve Orange Amaretti (page 48).

LAMB CHOPS DIJON

2 (5-ounce) lean lamb loin chops (1 inch thick)
Vegetable cooking spray
2 teaspoons Dijon mustard
1 teaspoon lemon juice
¼ teaspoon minced garlic
Dash of pepper
Dash of dried thyme

Trim fat from chops; place chops on rack of a broiler pan coated with cooking spray. Combine mustard and remaining ingredients in a small bowl, stirring well. Brush half of mustard mixture evenly over 1 side of chops.

Broil 5½ inches from heat (with electric oven door partially opened) 5 to 6 minutes; turn chops, and brush with remaining mustard mixture. Broil 5 to 6 minutes or to desired degree of doneness. Yield: 2 servings (194 calories per serving).

Per Serving:

Protein 25.6g	Fat 8.9g	(Saturated Fat 3.0g)
Carbohydrate 0.7g	Fiber 0g	Cholesterol 81mg
Iron 1.8mg	Sodium 220mg	Calcium 18mg

SAVORY POLENTA WITH SAUTÉED MUSHROOMS

Polenta is a cooked cereal that is eaten warm like mush or is chilled, shaped, and reheated (as in this recipe). For added flavor, we stirred in grated Parmesan cheese.

2½ cups water
¼ teaspoon salt
⅔ cup instant polenta
3 tablespoons grated Parmesan cheese
Olive oil-flavored vegetable cooking spray
1¼ cups sliced mushrooms
½ teaspoon dried Italian seasoning
½ cup Marsala
¼ teaspoon coarsely ground pepper

Combine 2½ cups water and salt in a medium saucepan; bring to a boil. Add polenta in a slow, steady stream, stirring constantly. Reduce heat to medium, and cook, stirring constantly, 20 minutes or until mixture pulls away from sides of pan. Add cheese, stirring until cheese melts. Spoon into an 8½- x 4½- x 3-inch loafpan coated with cooking spray. Set aside, and let cool completely.

Coat a large nonstick skillet with cooking spray. Place over medium-high heat until hot. Add mushrooms and Italian seasoning; sauté until mushrooms are tender. Add Marsala; cook over medium-high heat, stirring constantly, until most of the liquid evaporates. Set aside, and keep warm.

Turn polenta out onto a cutting board; cut polenta in half crosswise. Cut half of polenta into 4 (½-inch-thick) slices; reserve remaining polenta for another use. Place polenta slices on a baking sheet coated with cooking spray. Coat polenta lightly with cooking spray, and sprinkle with pepper. Broil 5½ inches from heat (with electric oven door partially opened) 5 minutes on each side or until crusty and golden. Place 2 polenta slices on each individual serving plate. Top evenly with mushroom mixture. Serve warm. Yield: 2 servings (113 calories per serving).

Per Serving:

Protein 4.6g	Fat 2.5g	(Saturated Fat 0.9g)
Carbohydrate 19.6g	Fiber 3.1g	Cholesterol 3mg
Iron 2.2mg	Sodium 231mg	Calcium 73mg

HERB AND CHEESE TOMATOES

4 plum tomatoes, halved lengthwise
Olive oil-flavored vegetable cooking spray
1 tablespoon goat cheese
1 teaspoon chopped ripe olives
½ teaspoon dried basil
¼ teaspoon pepper
Fresh oregano sprigs (optional)
Fresh thyme sprigs (optional)

Cut a thin slice from rounded side of 4 tomato halves; place prepared halves, rounded side down, in a 9-inch pieplate coated with cooking spray.

Combine cheese and next 3 ingredients; spread mixture over tomato halves in pieplate. Top with remaining tomato halves, cut side down; coat with cooking spray. Bake at 425° for 8 minutes or just until thoroughly heated. Serve immediately. Garnish with oregano and thyme sprigs, if desired. Yield: 2 servings (64 calories per 2 tomatoes).

Per Serving:

Protein 2.6g	Fat 2.9g	(Saturated Fat 1.2g)
Carbohydrate 8.8g	Fiber 2.5g	Cholesterol 6mg
Iron 1.2mg	Sodium 136mg	Calcium 54mg

ORANGE AMARETTI

¼ cup reduced-calorie frozen whipped topping, thawed
1 amaretti cookie, crushed
¾ cup orange sherbet, softened
2 amaretti cookies

Fold whipped topping and crushed cookie into sherbet. Pipe or spoon into dessert dishes. Serve each with 1 cookie. Serve immediately. Yield: 2 servings (168 calories per serving).

Per Serving:

Protein 1.6g	Fat 5.3g	(Saturated Fat 2.4g)
Carbohydrate 30.5g	Fiber 0.3g	Cholesterol 4mg
Iron 0.4mg	Sodium 92mg	Calcium 47mg

Treat guests to a festive meal of Mexican-Spiced Pork Tenderloins, Orange-Jicama Salsa, and Fiesta Rice. *(Menu begins on page 63.)*

That's Entertaining

Gather in the Garden

Summer Squash Soup

Poached Salmon with Cucumber-Dill Sauce

Sugar Snap Pea and Hearts of Palm Salad

Golden Honey Crescent Rolls

Raspberry Swirl Angel Food Cake

SERVES 6
TOTAL CALORIES PER SERVING: 642
(Calories from Fat: 22%)

Use the natural beauty of your surroundings this spring and summer by entertaining in your own backyard.

Serve the creamy squash soup first. Follow it with tender salmon fillets, a crisp vegetable salad, and fresh-baked crescent rolls. Then offer each guest a slice of Raspberry Swirl Angel Food Cake. (Menu calories reflect one roll and one slice of cake per serving.)

Raspberry Swirl Angel Food Cake (page 52) is a light dessert that blends with the pastel beauty of spring flowers.

SUMMER SQUASH SOUP

Vegetable cooking spray
1 tablespoon reduced-calorie margarine
½ cup minced onion
1 clove garlic, minced
7 cups thinly sliced yellow squash (about 8 small)
1 small potato (about 4 ounces), peeled and cubed
2 cups canned no-salt-added chicken broth, undiluted
¾ cup 1% low-fat milk
2 teaspoons minced fresh thyme
¼ teaspoon salt
⅛ teaspoon ground white pepper
Fresh thyme sprigs (optional)

Coat a large nonstick skillet with cooking spray; add margarine. Place over medium-high heat until margarine melts. Add minced onion and garlic; sauté until tender. Add squash slices, potato cubes, and chicken broth. Bring mixture to a boil; cover, reduce heat, and simmer 15 minutes or until vegetables are tender.

Transfer mixture to an electric blender; cover and process until smooth. Pour mixture into a large bowl. Stir in milk, minced thyme, salt, and pepper. Cover and chill thoroughly.

To serve, ladle soup into individual bowls. Garnish with thyme sprigs, if desired. Yield: 1½ quarts (78 calories per 1-cup serving).

Per Serving:

Protein 3.3g	Fat 2.0g	(Saturated Fat 0.4g)
Carbohydrate 12.5g	Fiber 2.8g	Cholesterol 1mg
Iron 0.8mg	Sodium 137mg	Calcium 69mg

POACHED SALMON WITH CUCUMBER-DILL SAUCE

The salmon is refreshing when served chilled, but it is just as delicious when served warm with the chilled sauce.

2 cups Chablis or other dry white wine
2 cups water
½ teaspoon chicken-flavored bouillon granules
6 peppercorns
4 sprigs fresh dillweed
2 bay leaves
1 stalk celery, chopped
1 small lemon, sliced
6 (4-ounce) salmon fillets (½ inch thick)
Cucumber-Dill Sauce
Fresh dillweed sprigs (optional)

Combine first 8 ingredients in a skillet. Bring to a boil; cover, reduce heat, and simmer 10 minutes.

Add fillets to mixture in skillet, and cook 10 minutes or until fish flakes easily when tested with a fork. Transfer fillets to a platter, using a slotted spoon; cover and chill thoroughly. Discard liquid mixture remaining in skillet.

To serve, place fillets on individual serving plates; spoon Cucumber-Dill Sauce evenly over fillets. Garnish with fresh dillweed sprigs, if desired. Yield: 6 servings (217 calories per serving).

Cucumber-Dill Sauce

⅓ cup peeled, seeded, and finely chopped cucumber
⅓ cup nonfat sour cream alternative
⅓ cup plain nonfat yogurt
2 teaspoons chopped fresh dillweed
1 teaspoon Dijon mustard

Combine all ingredients in a small bowl, stirring well. Cover and chill thoroughly. Yield: 1 cup.

Per Serving:

Protein 25.9g	Fat 9.8g	(Saturated Fat 1.7g)
Carbohydrate 2.5g	Fiber 0.1g	Cholesterol 77mg
Iron 0.7mg	Sodium 121mg	Calcium 47mg

SUGAR SNAP PEA AND HEARTS OF PALM SALAD

1 cup fresh Sugar Snap peas
2 cups torn Boston lettuce
2 cups torn romaine lettuce
1 cup sliced canned hearts of palm, drained
¼ cup sliced green onions
Honey-Orange Vinaigrette

Arrange peas in a vegetable steamer over boiling water. Cover and steam 1 minute or until peas are crisp-tender. Set aside, and let cool.

Combine peas and next 4 ingredients in a large bowl; toss well. Pour Honey-Orange Vinaigrette over lettuce mixture; toss gently. Yield: 6 servings (59 calories per 1-cup serving).

Honey-Orange Vinaigrette

2 tablespoons cider vinegar
2 tablespoons unsweetened orange juice
1 tablespoon honey
2 teaspoons vegetable oil
⅛ teaspoon onion powder
⅛ teaspoon ground red pepper

Combine all ingredients in a small bowl, stirring well with a wire whisk. Yield: ¼ cup.

Per Serving:

Protein 1.3g	Fat 1.6g	(Saturated Fat 0.3g)
Carbohydrate 11.3g	Fiber 0.9g	Cholesterol 0mg
Iron 0.8mg	Sodium 5mg	Calcium 15mg

GOLDEN HONEY CRESCENT ROLLS

These rolls will keep in an airtight container for up to three days. To warm them, bake at 350° for 10 minutes or until thoroughly heated.

1½ cups all-purpose flour
¼ teaspoon salt
1 package active dry yeast
⅓ cup skim milk
¼ cup honey
2 tablespoons margarine
1 tablespoon water
¼ cup frozen egg substitute, thawed
1 cup whole wheat flour
1 tablespoon all-purpose flour
Vegetable cooking spray

Combine first 3 ingredients in a large mixing bowl, stirring well. Combine milk and next 3 ingredients in a saucepan; heat until margarine melts, stirring occasionally. Cool to 120° to 130°.

Gradually add liquid mixture to flour mixture, beating at low speed of an electric mixer until blended. Add egg substitute, and beat an additional 2 minutes at medium speed. Gradually stir in enough whole wheat flour to make a soft dough.

Sprinkle 1 tablespoon all-purpose flour evenly over work surface. Turn dough out onto floured surface, and knead until smooth and elastic (about 10 minutes). Place dough in a large bowl coated with cooking spray, turning to coat top. Cover and let rise in a warm place (85°), free from drafts, 1 hour or until doubled in bulk.

Punch dough down; turn out onto work surface, and knead lightly 4 or 5 times. Roll dough into a 16-inch circle. Cut into 12 wedges. Roll up each wedge, beginning at wide end. Place, point side down, on a baking sheet coated with cooking spray; curve into crescent shapes. Cover and let rise in a warm place, free from drafts, 30 to 40 minutes or until doubled in bulk. Bake at 375° for 8 to 10 minutes or until golden. Yield: 1 dozen (139 calories each).

Per Roll:

Protein 4.0g	Fat 2.3g	(Saturated Fat 0.4g)
Carbohydrate 26.1g	Fiber 1.9g	Cholesterol 0mg
Iron 1.4mg	Sodium 83mg	Calcium 18mg

RASPBERRY SWIRL ANGEL FOOD CAKE

½ (10½-ounce) package frozen unsweetened raspberries, thawed
1 cup plus 1 tablespoon water, divided
1 (16-ounce) package angel food cake mix
Fresh raspberries (optional)
Fresh mint sprigs (optional)

Position knife blade in food processor bowl; add thawed raspberries, and process until smooth. Place raspberry puree in a wire-mesh strainer over a bowl; press with back of spoon against the sides of the strainer to squeeze out juice. Discard pulp and seeds remaining in strainer. Place ¼ cup raspberry puree in a small bowl. Reserve remaining puree for another use. Add ¼ cup plus 2½ tablespoons water to ¼ cup raspberry puree; stir well.

Place half of egg white powder packet from cake mix in a large bowl; add raspberry-water mixture. Beat at low speed of an electric mixer until combined; beat at high speed until stiff peaks form. Sprinkle half of flour packet from cake mix over raspberry-egg white mixture; fold into raspberry-egg white mixture. Set aside.

Place remaining egg white powder in a large bowl; add remaining ½ cup plus 2½ tablespoons water. Beat at low speed until blended; beat at high speed until stiff peaks form. Sprinkle remaining half of flour packet over beaten egg white mixture; fold into egg white mixture.

Spoon half of raspberry cake mixture into an ungreased 10-inch tube pan; top with half of plain cake mixture. Repeat layers, using remaining raspberry cake and plain cake mixtures. Gently swirl batters with a knife. Bake at 375° for 40 minutes or until cake springs back when lightly touched. Remove cake from oven; invert pan, and cool completely. Loosen cake from sides of pan, using a narrow metal spatula; remove from pan. If desired, garnish with fresh raspberries and mint sprigs. Yield: 12 servings (149 calories per serving).

Per Serving:

Protein 3.2g	Fat 0.1g	(Saturated Fat 0g)
Carbohydrate 34.2g	Fiber 0.9g	Cholesterol 0mg
Iron 0.2mg	Sodium 72mg	Calcium 42mg

Cool and creamy Frozen Rum Custard (page 55) caps off an evening of casual outdoor dining.

Supper on the Patio

Pineapple-Citrus Spritzers
Barbecued Turkey Burgers with Sweet Onions
Grilled Potato Wedges
Vegetable Coleslaw
Frozen Rum Custard

SERVES 8
TOTAL CALORIES PER SERVING: 792
(Calories from Fat: 13%)

For a relaxed midsummer meal, serve a casual menu on the patio. With a little advance preparation, you'll be able to unwind with friends instead of being left in the kitchen slaving over the meal. Prepare the coleslaw the morning of the party so the flavors can blend. Next, assemble the turkey burgers, onions, and potatoes up to the point of grilling. Then combine the custard ingredients, and chill.

When the guests arrive, fire up the grill, and then freeze the custard (½ cup per serving). As the meal cooks on the grill and the ice cream maker whirrs, sit back and relax with lively conversation and cool Pineapple-Citrus Spritzers.

PINEAPPLE-CITRUS SPRITZERS

2½ cups unsweetened grapefruit juice
2 cups unsweetened pineapple juice
½ cup frozen limeade concentrate, thawed and undiluted
¼ cup sugar
1¾ cups lemon-flavored sparkling mineral water, chilled
1 cup Chablis or other dry white wine, chilled

Combine first 4 ingredients in a large pitcher, stirring well. Cover and chill thoroughly.

Just before serving, stir in sparkling water and wine. Yield: 2 quarts (142 calories per 1-cup serving).

Per Serving:		
Protein 0.7g	Fat 0.1g	(Saturated Fat 0g)
Carbohydrate 31.0g	Fiber 0.1g	Cholesterol 0mg
Iron 1.9mg	Sodium 14mg	Calcium 20mg

BARBECUED TURKEY BURGERS WITH SWEET ONIONS

Vegetable cooking spray
2 sweet onions, thinly sliced
2 teaspoons margarine, melted
2 teaspoons honey
1 teaspoon water
¼ teaspoon paprika
⅛ teaspoon salt
2 pounds freshly ground raw turkey breast
¾ cup fine, dry breadcrumbs
Tangy Barbecue Sauce
8 green leaf lettuce leaves
8 tomato slices
8 reduced-calorie whole wheat hamburger buns

Coat a 12-inch square of heavy-duty aluminum foil with cooking spray. Place onion slices on one half of coated side of foil. Combine margarine and next 4 ingredients, stirring well. Brush margarine mixture over onion. Fold foil over onion; crimp edges to seal.

Coat grill rack with cooking spray; place on grill over medium-hot coals (350° to 400°). Place foil packet on rack; grill, covered, 20 minutes or until onion is tender. Set aside, and keep warm.

Combine turkey, breadcrumbs, and ⅔ cup Tangy Barbecue Sauce; shape mixture into 8 patties. Place patties on rack; grill, covered, 5 minutes on each side or until turkey is done, basting frequently with remaining Tangy Barbecue Sauce.

Place a lettuce leaf and a tomato slice on bottom half of each bun; top with turkey patties. Spoon onion slices evenly over patties. Top with remaining bun halves. Yield: 8 servings (322 calories per serving).

Tangy Barbecue Sauce

Vegetable cooking spray
⅔ cup finely chopped onion
1 clove garlic, minced
1 (8-ounce) can no-salt-added tomato sauce
⅓ cup reduced-calorie catsup
3 tablespoons brown sugar
1½ tablespoons red wine vinegar
1½ tablespoons lemon juice
1 teaspoon chili powder
2 teaspoons low-sodium Worcestershire sauce
½ teaspoon pepper
¼ teaspoon salt

Coat a large nonstick skillet with cooking spray; place over medium-high heat until hot. Add onion and garlic; sauté 5 minutes or until tender. Stir in tomato sauce and remaining ingredients; bring to a boil. Cover, reduce heat, and simmer 15 minutes. Yield: 1¼ cups.

Per Serving:		
Protein 31.3g	Fat 4.5g	(Saturated Fat 1.2g)
Carbohydrate 37.0g	Fiber 3.7g	Cholesterol 69mg
Iron 3.0mg	Sodium 513mg	Calcium 52mg

GRILLED POTATO WEDGES

4 medium-size baking potatoes (about 2 pounds)
Butter-flavored vegetable cooking spray
½ teaspoon dried thyme
¼ teaspoon garlic powder
¼ teaspoon salt
¼ teaspoon pepper
¼ teaspoon paprika
⅛ teaspoon sugar
⅛ teaspoon ground red pepper

Scrub potatoes. Cut each lengthwise into 12 wedges; lightly coat with cooking spray. Set aside.

Combine thyme and remaining ingredients in a large heavy-duty, zip-top plastic bag; add potato wedges. Seal bag, and shake until potato wedges are well coated.

Place grill rack on grill over medium-hot coals (350° to 400°). Cover rack with heavy-duty aluminum foil coated with cooking spray. Place potato wedges on foil; grill, covered, 20 to 30 minutes or until tender, turning every 10 minutes. Serve warm. Yield: 8 servings (87 calories per serving).

Per Serving:		
Protein 2.5g	Fat 0.4g	(Saturated Fat 0g)
Carbohydrate 19.1g	Fiber 1.9g	Cholesterol 0mg
Iron 1.5mg	Sodium 81mg	Calcium 17mg

VEGETABLE COLESLAW

1½ cups shredded red cabbage
1 cup shredded carrot
¾ cup shredded yellow squash
¾ cup shredded zucchini
½ cup chopped green pepper
⅓ cup finely chopped onion
¼ cup unsweetened pineapple juice
1½ tablespoons sugar
3 tablespoons cider vinegar
2 tablespoons water
½ teaspoon chicken-flavored bouillon granules
¼ teaspoon paprika
¼ teaspoon celery seeds
⅛ teaspoon garlic powder
Dash of ground red pepper

Combine first 6 ingredients in a large bowl.

Combine pineapple juice and remaining ingredients in a bowl, stirring well. Pour over vegetable mixture; toss gently. Cover and chill at least 4 hours. Yield: 8 servings (38 calories per ½-cup serving).

Per Serving:		
Protein 1.0g	Fat 0.3g	(Saturated Fat 0.1g)
Carbohydrate 8.8g	Fiber 1.5g	Cholesterol 0mg
Iron 0.5mg	Sodium 59mg	Calcium 24mg

FROZEN RUM CUSTARD

Egg yolk gives this custard its creamy texture and rich taste, but it contributes less than 1 gram of fat to each serving.

½ cup sugar
¼ cup instant nonfat dry milk powder
2 tablespoons cornstarch
2 cups 1% low-fat milk, divided
1 (12-ounce) can evaporated skimmed milk
2 tablespoons light rum
1 egg yolk, beaten
2 teaspoons vanilla extract
½ cup semisweet chocolate mini-morsels

Combine first 3 ingredients in a large saucepan. Stir in 1 cup low-fat milk, evaporated milk, and rum. Bring to a boil over medium heat, stirring constantly. Cook, stirring constantly, 1 minute or until mixture thickens slightly. Gradually stir about one-fourth of hot mixture into egg yolk; add to remaining hot mixture, stirring constantly. Remove from heat; stir in remaining low-fat milk and vanilla. Cover; chill.

Stir in chocolate morsels. Pour mixture into freezer can of a 2-quart hand-turned or electric freezer. Freeze according to manufacturer's instructions. Pack freezer with additional ice and rock salt; let stand 1 hour before serving. To serve, scoop ½ cup frozen custard into each individual dessert bowl. Serve immediately. Yield: 4 cups (203 calories per ½-cup serving).

Per Serving:		
Protein 7.4g	Fat 5.8g	(Saturated Fat 3.1g)
Carbohydrate 31.5g	Fiber 0.1g	Cholesterol 32mg
Iron 0.6mg	Sodium 101mg	Calcium 253mg

An Evening in Japan

Shrimp Mirin
Warmed Sake
Soba Noodles in Broth
Beef Teriyaki
Steamed Rice
Sesame Vegetable Medley
Sweet Oranges with Strawberries
Green Tea

SERVES 10
TOTAL CALORIES PER SERVING: 758
(Calories from Fat: 13%)

Invite some friends on a culinary trip to Japan. Start with Shrimp Mirin, and serve each person 4 ounces of warmed sake (a sweet Japanese wine). Next, offer a bowl of Soba Noodles in Broth, followed by Beef Teriyaki, steamed rice (½ cup per serving), and Sesame Vegetable Medley. End with a cup of steaming green tea and Sweet Oranges with Strawberries.

Visit the Orient with Beef Teriyaki and Sesame Vegetable Medley (page 58).

SHRIMP MIRIN

½ cup mirin (rice wine)
1 tablespoon sugar
1 tablespoon peeled, chopped gingerroot
3 tablespoons low-sodium soy sauce
1 teaspoon lemon juice
⅛ teaspoon salt
20 large fresh shrimp, peeled and deveined
2 tablespoons rice wine vinegar
1 tablespoon mirin
⅛ teaspoon salt
1½ cups shredded daikon (oriental radish)
Vegetable cooking spray
10 lemon slices
10 cucumber slices

Combine ½ cup mirin and next 5 ingredients. Reserve half of mirin mixture. Pour remaining half of mirin mixture into a large heavy-duty, zip-top plastic bag; add shrimp. Seal bag, and shake until shrimp are well coated. Marinate in refrigerator up to 4 hours, turning bag occasionally.

Combine vinegar, 1 tablespoon mirin, and ⅛ teaspoon salt in a bowl. Add daikon; toss gently.

Remove shrimp from marinade; discard marinade. Place shrimp on rack of a broiler pan coated with cooking spray. Broil shrimp 5½ inches from heat (with electric oven door partially opened) 3 to 4 minutes on each side or until shrimp turn pink.

Place 1 lemon slice and 1 cucumber slice on each plate. Top each with daikon mixture and 1 shrimp.

Bring reserved half of mirin mixture to a boil in a saucepan. Pour into small bowls. Serve warm with shrimp. Yield: 10 servings (44 calories per serving).

Note: If mirin isn't available, substitute sherry. Add ¼ teaspoon sugar for every tablespoon sherry used.

Per Serving:		
Protein 6.6g	Fat 0.4g	(Saturated Fat 0.1g)
Carbohydrate 2.3g	Fiber 0.2g	Cholesterol 60mg
Iron 1.1mg	Sodium 195mg	Calcium 20mg

SOBA NOODLES IN BROTH

Look for soba noodles at oriental markets. If unavailable, substitute spaghetti noodles.

3½ cups canned low-sodium chicken broth
¼ pound skinned, boned chicken breast halves
2 stalks celery, cut into 2-inch pieces
1 small onion, quartered
1 carrot, cut into 2-inch pieces
3 quarts water
6 ounces soba (buckwheat) noodles, uncooked
2 tablespoons sugar
2½ tablespoons low-sodium soy sauce
1 tablespoon tahini
½ teaspoon pepper
¼ teaspoon salt
¼ pound fresh spinach, trimmed and chopped
2 tablespoons sliced green onions

Combine first 5 ingredients in a saucepan; bring to a boil. Cover, reduce heat, and simmer 20 minutes. Remove chicken; set aside. Discard celery, onion, and carrot. Skim fat from broth; set broth aside.

Bring 3 quarts water to a boil in a Dutch oven; add noodles. Reduce heat; simmer, uncovered, 5 to 7 minutes or until tender. Drain; set aside.

Shred chicken; return to broth. Add noodles, sugar, and next 5 ingredients; cook over medium heat 2 minutes, stirring frequently. Ladle into soup bowls; sprinkle with green onions. Yield: 10 servings (107 calories per ½-cup serving).

Per Serving:		
Protein 6.9g	Fat 1.9g	(Saturated Fat 0.2g)
Carbohydrate 16.8g	Fiber 0.9g	Cholesterol 8mg
Iron 1.4mg	Sodium 221mg	Calcium 24mg

BEEF TERIYAKI

¾ cup dry sherry
¾ cup low-soduim soy sauce
1 tablespoon vegetable oil
½ teaspoon dry mustard
⅛ teaspoon onion powder
3 cloves garlic, minced
2 pounds boneless top sirloin steak (1 inch thick)
1½ tablespoons dark corn syrup
1 tablespoon water
2 teaspoons cornstarch
Vegetable cooking spray
1 tablespoon plus 2 teaspoons dry mustard
1 tablespoon water
Green onion fans (optional)

Combine first 6 ingredients, stirring well. Reserve ½ cup sherry mixture. Pour remaining sherry mixture into a large heavy-duty, zip-top plastic bag. Add steak; seal bag, and shake until steak is well coated. Marinate in refrigerator up to 4 hours, turning bag occasionally.

Combine reserved sherry mixture, corn syrup, 1 tablespoon water, and cornstarch in a small saucepan, stirring well. Bring to a boil over medium-low heat, and cook, stirring constantly, 1 minute. Remove from heat. Set aside, and keep warm.

Remove steak from marinade, discarding marinade. Place steak on rack of a broiler pan coated with cooking spray. Broil 5½ inches from heat (with electric oven door partially opened) 6 to 7 minutes on each side or to desired degree of doneness. Slice steak diagonally across grain into ¼-inch-thick slices. Arrange steak strips on individual serving plates. Brush cooked sherry mixture evenly over steak strips.

Combine 1 tablespoon plus 2 teaspoons mustard and 1 tablespoon water in a small bowl, stirring well with a wire whisk. Spoon mustard mixture evenly alongside steak strips. Garnish with green onion fans, if desired. Yield: 10 servings (167 calories per serving).

Per Serving:		
Protein 22.5g	Fat 6.1g	(Saturated Fat 2.1g)
Carbohydrate 3.5g	Fiber 0g	Cholesterol 65mg
Iron 2.6mg	Sodium 267mg	Calcium 12mg

SESAME VEGETABLE MEDLEY

1 cup small fresh shiitake mushrooms
Vegetable cooking spray
2 teaspoons sesame oil
1 pound fresh snow pea pods, trimmed
1 cup diagonally sliced carrot
½ cup canned bamboo shoots, drained
1 clove garlic, minced
2 tablespoons water
1 tablespoon low-sodium soy sauce
2 teaspoons sugar
¼ teaspoon cornstarch
¼ teaspoon chicken-flavored bouillon granules
¼ teaspoon Dijon mustard
1 tablespoon sesame seeds, toasted

Remove and discard mushroom stems.

Coat a large nonstick skillet with cooking spray; add sesame oil. Place over medium-high heat until hot. Add mushroom caps, snow peas, and next 3 ingredients; sauté 2 to 3 minutes or until vegetables are crisp-tender.

Combine water and next 5 ingredients, and add to vegetable mixture. Cook, stirring constantly, until sauce is slightly thickened. Arrange evenly on individual serving plates, and sprinkle with sesame seeds. Yield: 10 servings (64 calories per ½-cup serving).

Per Serving:		
Protein 2.2g	Fat 1.6g	(Saturated Fat 0.2g)
Carbohydrate 10.0g	Fiber 2.2g	Cholesterol 0mg
Iron 1.1mg	Sodium 70mg	Calcium 25mg

SWEET ORANGES WITH STRAWBERRIES

Honor your guests with this sweet creation. Oranges are considered a prized dessert in the Orient.

6 small oranges
¾ cup water
¾ cup rosé wine
½ cup sugar
2 whole cloves
2 (1-inch) slices peeled gingerroot
1 (2-inch) stick cinnamon
½ vanilla bean, split lengthwise
2 cups halved fresh strawberries

Peel oranges, removing white layer of skin just under the orange peel. Cut oranges crosswise into ⅛-inch-thick slices. Remove and discard seeds. Set aside orange slices.

Combine water and next 6 ingredients in a medium saucepan; bring to a boil. Cover, reduce heat, and simmer 15 minutes. Pour mixture through a wire-mesh strainer into a bowl, discarding solids remaining in strainer. Add orange slices to hot syrup. Cover and chill.

Just before serving, stir in strawberries. Spoon fruit and liquid evenly into individual dessert dishes. Yield: 10 servings (68 calories per ½-cup serving).

Per Serving:		
Protein 0.6g	Fat 0.2g	(Saturated Fat 0g)
Carbohydrate 17.2g	Fiber 2.6g	Cholesterol 0mg
Iron 0.2mg	Sodium 2mg	Calcium 22mg

DIET AND EXERCISE—THE WINNING COMBINATION

It now seems likely that less stringent dieting coupled with more exercise may be the answer to better weight control. Boston researchers divided a group of older dieters—one group exercised (twice-a-day workouts on an exercise cycle to burn 360 calories) but did not diet, the other group dieted (360 fewer calories per day) but did not exercise.

After 12 weeks, the exercisers had lost the most weight. Not only did they peel off an average of 16 pounds, but these active folks also gained 3 pounds of muscle mass. If you translate this into terms of actual fat lost (the most important health issue in the study), the exercisers lost almost 19 pounds of body fat. The dieters, on the other hand, lost 11 pounds. However, 6 of those pounds were lean muscle, making net fat loss a meager 4½ pounds. The conclusion: *Increased activity* combined with healthy eating habits helps you lose weight or control your weight.

Seafood Lasagna (page 60), Mixed Greens with Walnut Vinaigrette (page 61), and Lemon Squash (page 60) make an elegant meal. Add a lovely centerpiece made by stacking decorative bowls of flowers set in oasis.

Engagement Party Buffet

Seafood Lasagna
Lemon Squash
Mixed Greens with Walnut Vinaigrette
Commercial French Rolls
Orange Marmalade Tea Cakes
Mocha Cappuccino
Sparkling Fruit Champagne

SERVES 8
TOTAL CALORIES PER SERVING: 807
(Calories from Fat: 23%)

Celebrate the upcoming union of a loving couple with this easy yet elegant buffet. The day before the party, assemble and refrigerate the lasagna. Tear the lettuces, and slice the red pepper and the squash; store in zip-top bags in the refrigerator. Just before guests arrive, pop the lasagna in the oven, and toss the salad (without the dressing).

A few minutes before you're ready to serve, warm the rolls (one per person), prepare the squash, and toss the salad with the vinaigrette. Brew the coffee during dinner; serve it with cookies (one per serving). End the event with fruit champagne (½ cup juice and ½ cup champagne per serving) and a toast to the happy couple.

SEAFOOD LASAGNA

2 (10-ounce) packages frozen chopped spinach, thawed
1¼ pounds unpeeled small fresh shrimp
6 cups water
Vegetable cooking spray
½ cup chopped onion
½ cup chopped green pepper
2 cloves garlic, minced
1 (8-ounce) package Neufchâtel cheese
1 (16-ounce) container 1% low-fat cottage cheese
¾ cup (3 ounces) shredded reduced-fat Swiss cheese, divided
¼ cup frozen egg substitute, thawed
2 tablespoons skim milk
1½ tablespoons chopped fresh basil
¼ teaspoon salt
¼ teaspoon pepper
⅓ cup all-purpose flour
1¾ cups skim milk
⅓ cup Chablis or other dry white wine
½ pound fresh lump crabmeat, drained
6 lasagna noodles (cooked without salt or fat)
¼ cup freshly grated Parmesan cheese
½ teaspoon paprika
Cooked shrimp with tails (optional)

Drain spinach, and press dry between layers of paper towels; set aside.

Peel and devein 1¼ pounds shrimp. Bring 6 cups water to a boil; add shrimp, and cook 3 to 5 minutes or until shrimp turn pink. Drain, and set aside.

Coat a medium saucepan with cooking spray; place over medium-high heat until hot. Add onion, green pepper, and garlic; sauté until tender. Transfer to a bowl. Wipe saucepan dry with a paper towel.

Add Neufchâtel cheese to saucepan, and cook over medium heat, stirring constantly, until cheese melts. Add melted Neufchâtel cheese, cottage cheese, ½ cup Swiss cheese, and next 5 ingredients to onion mixture; stir well. Set aside.

Place flour in a medium saucepan. Stir in 1¾ cups milk. Cook over medium heat, stirring constantly, 5 to 7 minutes or until thickened. Remove from heat; stir in 1¼ pounds cooked shrimp, wine, and crabmeat.

Coat a 13- x 9- x 2-inch baking dish with cooking spray. Place 3 lasagna noodles in bottom of dish. Top with half of cottage cheese mixture, half of spinach, and half of seafood mixture. Repeat layers with remaining noodles, cottage cheese mixture, spinach, and seafood mixture.

Combine remaining ¼ cup Swiss cheese, Parmesan cheese, and paprika; sprinkle over lasagna. Cover and bake at 350° for 40 minutes. Uncover and bake an additional 10 minutes. Let lasagna stand 10 minutes before serving. Garnish with shrimp, if desired. Yield: 8 servings (355 calories per serving).

Per Serving:

Protein 36.1g	Fat 11.7g	(Saturated Fat 6.5g)
Carbohydrate 26.2g	Fiber 3.2g	Cholesterol 138mg
Iron 4.4mg	Sodium 750mg	Calcium 428mg

LEMON SQUASH

This recipe can be made from start to finish in about 15 minutes.

2¼ cups diagonally sliced yellow squash
2¼ cups diagonally sliced zucchini
¼ cup canned no-salt-added chicken broth, undiluted
1 tablespoon lemon juice
1 teaspoon cornstarch
2 teaspoons reduced-calorie margarine
¼ teaspoon dried oregano
¼ teaspoon salt
¼ teaspoon pepper
Fresh oregano sprigs (optional)

Arrange squash and zucchini in a vegetable steamer over boiling water. Cover and steam 6 minutes or until crisp-tender; place in a serving bowl.

Combine chicken broth and next 6 ingredients in a small saucepan, stirring until smooth. Cook over medium heat, stirring constantly, until slightly thickened. Pour mixture over vegetables; toss gently. Garnish with oregano sprigs, if desired. Yield: 8 servings (18 calories per ½-cup serving).

Per Serving:

Protein 0.7g	Fat 0.7g	(Saturated Fat 0.1g)
Carbohydrate 2.9g	Fiber 0.7g	Cholesterol 0mg
Iron 0.3mg	Sodium 84mg	Calcium 13mg

MIXED GREENS WITH WALNUT VINAIGRETTE

2 cups torn curly endive
2 cups loosely packed watercress leaves
2 cups torn fresh spinach
2 cups torn red leaf lettuce
½ cup sliced water chestnuts
½ cup julienne-sliced sweet red pepper
⅓ cup rice wine vinegar
1 tablespoon chopped fresh chives
1 tablespoon water
2 teaspoons walnut oil
1 teaspoon white wine Worcestershire sauce
½ teaspoon sugar
⅛ teaspoon salt
⅛ teaspoon pepper
2½ tablespoons finely chopped walnuts, toasted

Combine first 6 ingredients in a large bowl; toss well, and set aside.

Combine vinegar and next 7 ingredients in a small bowl, stirring well with a wire whisk. Stir in walnuts; pour over lettuce mixture, and toss gently. Yield: 8 servings (41 calories per 1-cup serving).

Per Serving:		
Protein 1.4g	Fat 2.8g	(Saturated Fat 0.2g)
Carbohydrate 3.1g	Fiber 1.1g	Cholesterol 0mg
Iron 0.7mg	Sodium 55mg	Calcium 29mg

ORANGE MARMALADE TEA CAKES

To store these cookies, stack between sheets of wax paper, and place in an airtight container.

¼ cup margarine, softened
1½ ounces Neufchâtel cheese, softened
2 tablespoons frozen egg substitute, thawed
1 teaspoon vanilla extract
⅔ cup all-purpose flour
½ teaspoon baking powder
3 tablespoons sugar
¼ cup low-sugar orange marmalade
Vegetable cooking spray
½ cup sifted powdered sugar
2 teaspoons unsweetened orange juice

Combine margarine and Neufchâtel cheese in a bowl; beat at medium speed of an electric mixer until creamy. Add egg substitute and vanilla; beat well.

Combine flour, baking powder, and 3 tablespoons sugar; add to margarine mixture, beating well. Stir in marmalade.

Drop dough by level tablespoonfuls, 2 inches apart, onto cookie sheets coated with cooking spray. Bake at 350° for 10 to 12 minutes or until edges are golden. Remove from cookie sheets, and let cool completely on wire racks.

Combine powdered sugar and orange juice, stirring until smooth. Spread over cooled cookies. Yield: 1½ dozen (70 calories each).

Per Cookie:		
Protein 0.9g	Fat 3.2g	(Saturated Fat 0.9g)
Carbohydrate 9.4g	Fiber 0.1g	Cholesterol 2mg
Iron 0.3mg	Sodium 42mg	Calcium 13mg

MOCHA CAPPUCCINO

For a nonalcoholic beverage, omit the Frangelico, and increase the chocolate syrup to ½ cup.

5½ cups warm brewed coffee
¼ cup plus 2 tablespoons chocolate syrup
2 tablespoons Frangelico or other hazelnut-flavored liqueur
½ cup reduced-calorie frozen whipped topping, thawed
1 tablespoon plus 1 teaspoon grated semisweet chocolate

Combine first 3 ingredients, stirring well. Pour evenly into serving mugs. Top each serving with 1 tablespoon whipped topping and ½ teaspoon grated chocolate. Serve immediately. Yield: 1½ quarts (69 calories per ¾-cup serving).

Per Serving:		
Protein 0.8g	Fat 1.3g	(Saturated Fat 0.7g)
Carbohydrate 12.1g	Fiber 0g	Cholesterol 0mg
Iron 1.0mg	Sodium 16mg	Calcium 9mg

Frozen Margarita Pie (page 64) won't waste away once guests take a bite of this lime-flavored creation with a pretzel crust. Keep it cool by setting the pieplate in a larger one filled with ice.

Mexican Fiesta

Avocado Dip
Mexican-Spiced Pork Tenderloins
Fiesta Rice
Orange-Jicama Salsa
Frozen Margarita Pie

SERVES 6
TOTAL CALORIES PER SERVING: 588
(Calories from Fat: 19%)

Create a casual party around this south-of-the-border menu. You can make the chips for Avocado Dip a couple of days in advance; then whip up the dip right before guests arrive. The salsa for the tenderloins can be kept two days in the refrigerator (1/4 cup per serving).

The pie can be made up to a week ahead and kept tightly covered in the freezer. For extra flavor, rub the tenderloins with the spice mixture, and refrigerate a couple of hours before baking. Prepare the rice while the pork cooks. Decorate with sombreros, colorful blankets, and maracas.

AVOCADO DIP

6 (6-inch) corn tortillas
1/2 cup nonfat cottage cheese
1/3 cup mashed ripe avocado
1/4 cup canned chopped green chiles
1/4 cup nonfat sour cream alternative
1 teaspoon lemon juice
1/4 teaspoon salt
1/8 teaspoon pepper
1/8 teaspoon garlic powder
Dash of hot sauce
3/4 cup seeded, chopped tomato
1 tablespoon chopped ripe olives

Cut each tortilla into 6 wedges, and place on an ungreased baking sheet. Bake at 350° for 8 to 10 minutes or until crisp. Set aside.

Position knife blade in food processor bowl. Add cottage cheese and next 8 ingredients. Process until smooth. Transfer to a serving bowl; top with tomato and olives. Serve with baked chips. Yield: 6 servings (95 calories per 3 tablespoons dip and 6 chips).

Per Serving:

Protein 5.2g	Fat 2.5g	(Saturated Fat 0.4g)
Carbohydrate 13.9g	Fiber 1.8g	Cholesterol 1mg
Iron 0.7mg	Sodium 276mg	Calcium 60mg

MEXICAN-SPICED PORK TENDERLOINS

2 (3/4-pound) pork tenderloins
1 teaspoon ground cumin
1 teaspoon chili powder
1/2 teaspoon dried oregano
1/4 teaspoon garlic powder
1/4 teaspoon salt
1/4 teaspoon black pepper
1/8 teaspoon ground red pepper
Vegetable cooking spray

Trim fat from tenderloins. Combine cumin and next 6 ingredients. Rub spice mixture evenly over tenderloins. Place tenderloins on a rack in a roasting pan coated with cooking spray. Insert meat thermometer into thickest part of tenderloin, if desired. Bake at 375° for 45 minutes or until meat thermometer registers 160°.

Transfer tenderloins to a serving platter. Let stand 10 minutes; slice diagonally across grain into thin slices. Yield: 6 servings (153 calories per serving).

Per Serving:

Protein 25.9g	Fat 4.6g	(Saturated Fat 1.5g)
Carbohydrate 0.6g	Fiber 0.2g	Cholesterol 83mg
Iron 1.7mg	Sodium 163mg	Calcium 15mg

FIESTA RICE

Vegetable cooking spray
1 teaspoon vegetable oil
½ cup chopped sweet red pepper
¼ cup chopped onion
1 clove garlic, minced
1¼ cups no-salt-added chicken broth, undiluted
½ cup long-grain rice, uncooked
½ cup frozen whole-kernel corn, thawed
½ cup commercial no-salt-added salsa
½ cup drained canned black beans
1 tablespoon chopped fresh cilantro
¼ teaspoon salt
Orange slices (optional)
Fresh cilantro sprigs (optional)

Coat a large saucepan with cooking spray; add oil. Place over medium-high heat until hot. Add red pepper, onion, and garlic; sauté until crisp-tender. Add broth and next 3 ingredients. Bring to a boil; cover, reduce heat, and simmer 20 minutes. Remove from heat; let stand 5 minutes or until liquid is absorbed. Stir in beans, chopped cilantro, and salt. If desired, garnish with orange slices and cilantro sprigs. Yield: 3 cups (118 calories per ½-cup serving).

Per Serving:		
Protein 3.8g	Fat 1.3g	(Saturated Fat 0.2g)
Carbohydrate 22.8g	Fiber 1.6g	Cholesterol 0mg
Iron 1.5mg	Sodium 201mg	Calcium 28mg

ORANGE-JICAMA SALSA

After removing the husk from the tomatillo, wash the fruit to remove the sticky residue.

¾ cup chopped fresh orange
¼ cup peeled, chopped jicama
¼ cup husked, chopped tomatillo
¼ cup chopped purple onion
3 tablespoons chopped fresh cilantro
1 small jalapeño pepper, seeded and minced
2 tablespoons unsweetened orange juice
1 tablespoon lime juice
½ teaspoon sugar
⅛ teaspoon salt

Combine first 6 ingredients in a small bowl, and toss well. Combine orange juice and remaining ingredients, stirring well. Pour over orange mixture; toss gently. Cover and chill at least 2 hours. Yield: 1½ cups (6 calories per tablespoon).

Per Tablespoon:		
Protein 0.1g	Fat 0.0g	(Saturated Fat 0g)
Carbohydrate 1.6g	Fiber 0.4g	Cholesterol 0mg
Iron 0.1mg	Sodium 13mg	Calcium 5mg

FROZEN MARGARITA PIE

2½ cups small pretzels, finely crushed
¼ cup reduced-calorie margarine, melted
1 tablespoon sugar
6 cups vanilla nonfat frozen yogurt, softened
¼ cup tequila
3 tablespoons frozen limeade concentrate, thawed and undiluted
1 teaspoon grated fresh lime rind
1 tablespoon fresh lime juice
Lime slices (optional)
Edible flowers (optional)
Lime rind curls (optional)

Combine first 3 ingredients in a small bowl, stirring well. Press mixture evenly into bottom and up sides of a 9-inch pieplate. Freeze crust 1 hour.

Combine yogurt and next 4 ingredients in a bowl, stirring well. Spoon yogurt mixture into prepared crust. Cover and freeze until firm. Let stand at room temperature 5 minutes before slicing. If desired, garnish with lime slices, edible flowers, and lime rind curls. Yield: 10 servings (198 calories per serving).

Per Serving:		
Protein 5.1g	Fat 3.8g	(Saturated Fat 0.6g)
Carbohydrate 34.5g	Fiber 0g	Cholesterol 0mg
Iron 0.6mg	Sodium 263mg	Calcium 163mg

For a new angle on a romantic holiday, let the kids surprise Dad with Lemonade Chicken, Heartfelt Pasta Salad, and Green Beans with Tomato-Bacon Topping. (Menu begins on page 66.)

Holiday Celebrations

Dad will adore the chocolaty-good taste of From-the-Heart Brownie Sundaes (page 68).

Valentine Dinner for Dad

Lemonade Chicken
Green Beans with Tomato-Bacon Topping
Heartfelt Pasta Salad
From-the-Heart Brownie Sundaes

SERVES 5
TOTAL CALORIES PER SERVING: 677
(Calories from Fat: 26%)

Let the children present a grand dinner to their favorite fella. You'll treasure their proud looks as they serve Dad these recipes that are designed to include their help in the kitchen.

Older children can cut and chop vegetables, while younger ones can measure ingredients. When they aren't busy with cooking tasks, encourage them to decorate and set the table for the special meal.

Homemade valentines can serve as place cards; scraps of ribbons and lace wrapped around candles can create a simple centerpiece.

LEMONADE CHICKEN

½ (6-ounce) can frozen lemonade concentrate, thawed
2 tablespoons white wine Worcestershire sauce
2 tablespoons water
1 tablespoon raspberry vinegar
½ teaspoon minced fresh rosemary
1 clove garlic, crushed
5 (8-ounce) chicken leg quarters, skinned
Vegetable cooking spray
Lemon slices (optional)
Fresh rosemary sprigs (optional)

Combine first 6 ingredients in a large heavy-duty, zip-top plastic bag. Add chicken; seal bag, and shake until chicken is well coated. Marinate in refrigerator 1 hour, turning bag occasionally.

Remove chicken from marinade; reserve marinade. Place chicken on a rack in a roasting pan coated with cooking spray. Bake at 350° for 55 minutes or until done, basting frequently with reserved marinade. Place chicken on a serving platter. If desired, garnish with lemon slices and rosemary sprigs. Yield: 5 servings (226 calories per serving).

Per Serving:		
Protein 25.2g	Fat 9.0g	(Saturated Fat 2.4g)
Carbohydrate 9.8g	Fiber 0.1g	Cholesterol 85mg
Iron 1.4mg	Sodium 145mg	Calcium 23mg

GREEN BEANS WITH TOMATO-BACON TOPPING

Substituting turkey bacon for regular bacon cut the fat by 1.6 grams per serving in this recipe.

1 (10½-ounce) can low-sodium chicken broth, divided
1 pound fresh green beans
Vegetable cooking spray
1 cup chopped plum tomatoes
¼ cup chopped onion
1 clove garlic, minced
4 slices turkey bacon, cooked and crumbled
¼ teaspoon dried basil
⅛ teaspoon salt

Set aside ¼ cup chicken broth. Pour remaining broth into a large saucepan.

Wash beans; trim ends, and remove strings. Bring broth to a boil, and add beans. Cover, reduce heat, and simmer 10 minutes or until tender. Drain beans; set aside, and keep warm.

Coat a saucepan with cooking spray. Place over medium-high heat until hot. Add tomato, onion, and garlic; sauté until onion is crisp-tender. Add reserved ¼ cup broth, and cook until onion is tender and liquid has almost evaporated, stirring frequently. Stir in bacon, basil, and salt. To serve, spoon beans evenly onto individual serving plates. Spoon tomato mixture evenly over beans. Serve warm. Yield: 5 servings (66 calories per serving).

Per Serving:		
Protein 3.8g	Fat 2.0g	(Saturated Fat 0.5g)
Carbohydrate 9.4g	Fiber 2.5g	Cholesterol 7mg
Iron 1.3mg	Sodium 220mg	Calcium 39g

HEARTFELT PASTA SALAD

If heart-shaped pasta is not available, substitute an equal amount of elbow macaroni. (See page 272 for information about ordering heart-shaped pasta.)

6 ounces heart-shaped pasta, uncooked
1¼ cups small fresh broccoli flowerets
¾ cup diced sweet red pepper
½ cup sliced carrot
⅓ cup commercial reduced-calorie Caesar dressing

Cook pasta according to package directions, omitting salt and fat. Drain and rinse with cold water; drain again.

Combine pasta and remaining ingredients in a medium bowl, tossing gently. Cover and chill thoroughly. Yield: 5 servings (156 calories per 1-cup serving).

Per Serving:		
Protein 5.4g	Fat 1.3g	(Saturated Fat 0.1g)
Carbohydrate 29.4g	Fiber 2.3g	Cholesterol 0mg
Iron 1.9mg	Sodium 122mg	Calcium 23mg

FROM-THE-HEART BROWNIE SUNDAES

Vegetable cooking spray
½ cup unsweetened cocoa
⅓ cup all-purpose flour
½ teaspoon baking powder
¼ cup plus 2 tablespoons sugar
¼ cup firmly packed brown sugar
½ cup frozen egg substitute, thawed
¼ cup vegetable oil
1 teaspoon vanilla extract
Unsweetened cocoa powder
1 cup fresh or frozen raspberries, thawed
½ cup apricot nectar
1½ teaspoons sugar
1½ teaspoons cornstarch
1¼ cups vanilla nonfat frozen yogurt

Line an 8-inch square pan with a large sheet of aluminum foil, allowing foil to extend 1 inch over sides of pan. Coat foil with cooking spray; set aside.

Combine ½ cup cocoa, flour, and baking powder in a medium bowl; make a well in center of mixture.

Combine ¼ cup plus 2 tablespoons sugar and next 4 ingredients; add to dry ingredients, stirring just until dry ingredients are moistened. Spoon batter into prepared pan. Bake at 350° for 22 minutes or until a wooden pick inserted in center comes out clean. Cool completely on a wire rack.

Carefully lift foil out of pan. Dip a 3-inch heart-shaped cutter in cocoa powder, and cut brownie into 5 hearts. Reserve remaining brownie for another use. Set brownie hearts aside.

Combine raspberries and nectar in container of an electric blender; cover and process until smooth. Place raspberry mixture in a wire-mesh strainer over a bowl; press with back of spoon against the sides of the strainer to squeeze out juice. Discard pulp and seeds remaining in strainer. Transfer raspberry mixture to a small saucepan. Add 1½ teaspoons sugar and cornstarch; stir until smooth. Cook over medium heat, stirring constantly, until thickened. Cool slightly.

To serve, place a brownie heart on each individual dessert dish; spoon 1½ tablespoons raspberry sauce around each. Spoon ¼ cup raspberry sauce in small circles around edges of dishes. Drag the tip of a wooden pick through one side of each circle, creating a paisley design. Place ¼ cup yogurt on each brownie heart. Drizzle remaining sauce evenly over each scoop of yogurt. Yield: 5 servings (229 calories per serving).

Per Serving:		
Protein 5.2g	Fat 6.9g	(Saturated Fat 1.5g)
Carbohydrate 37.9g	Fiber 2.2g	Cholesterol 0mg
Iron 1.7mg	Sodium 55mg	Calcium 103mg

Dark Chocolate Brownies: To make traditional pan brownies, prepare and bake brownies as directed. Cool in pan on a wire rack. Cut into 16 bars. Yield: 16 brownies (88 calories each).

Per Brownie:		
Protein 1.8g	Fat 3.8g	(Saturated Fat 0.8g)
Carbohydrate 11.6g	Fiber 0.1g	Cholesterol 0mg
Iron 0.8mg	Sodium 14mg	Calcium 18mg

HOW TO GARNISH BROWNIE HEARTS

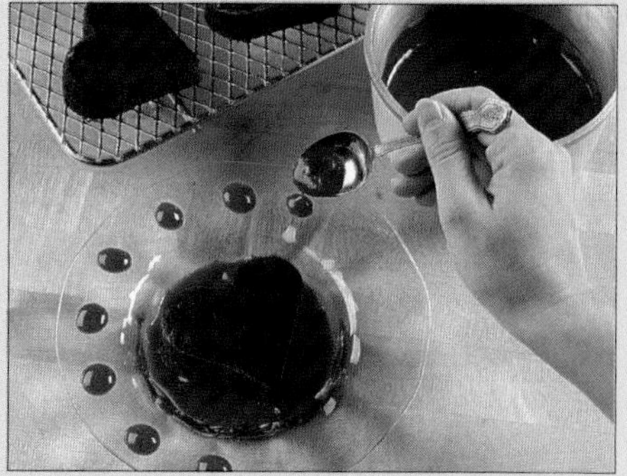

Spoon 1½ tablespoons raspberry sauce around brownie heart on each dish. Spoon ¼ cup sauce in small circles around edges of dishes.

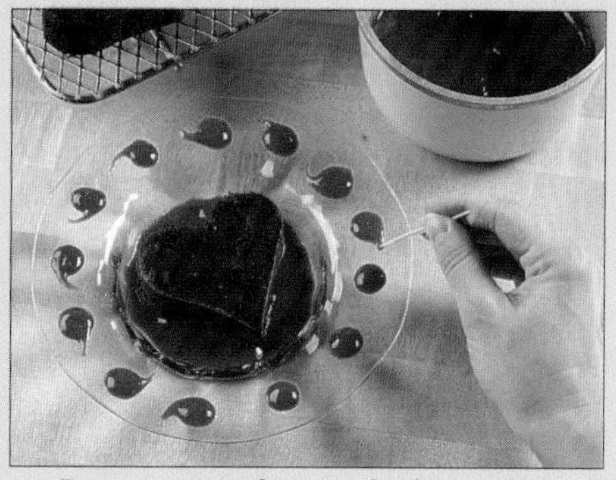

Drag a wooden pick through one side of each circle, creating a paisley design.

Any meal is special when you prepare Oriental Sherry Chicken and Orange-Almond Rice (page 70).

Easter Sunday Dinner

Oriental Sherry Chicken
Orange-Almond Rice
Roasted Asparagus with Onions
Miniature Carrot Cake Muffins
Frozen Lemon Angel Cake

SERVES 6
TOTAL CALORIES PER SERVING: 696
(Calories from Fat: 18%)

Easter morning is a whirlwind: surprises from the Easter bunny, egg hunts, and making sure dresses and shirts are pressed and faces are chocolate-free. Easter meal preparations often have to wait until the morning tide has calmed.

To ease your schedule, make the dessert (to be covered with whipped topping right before serving) and the muffins (two per serving) the day before. If you have enough room in the oven, bake the chicken and add the asparagus and onions about 15 minutes before the chicken is done. The vegetables are also delicious served at room temperature and may be baked earlier, if needed. Also, cook the rice while the chicken bakes. All that's left is to gather the family and enjoy a memorable meal on this special occasion.

ORIENTAL SHERRY CHICKEN

1 (3-pound) broiler-fryer, skinned
2 cups dry sherry
½ cup white wine vinegar
½ cup low-sodium teriyaki sauce
⅓ cup firmly packed brown sugar
5 cloves garlic, minced
Vegetable cooking spray
Orange slices (optional)
Fresh parsley sprigs (optional)

Trim fat from chicken. Remove giblets and neck from chicken; reserve for another use. Rinse chicken under cold water; pat dry with paper towels. Combine sherry and next 4 ingredients; cover and refrigerate ½ cup sherry mixture. Place remaining mixture in a large heavy-duty, zip-top plastic bag; add chicken. Seal bag; shake until chicken is coated. Marinate in refrigerator 8 hours, turning bag occasionally.

Remove chicken from marinade; discard marinade. Place chicken, breast side up, on a rack in a roasting pan coated with cooking spray. Insert meat thermometer into meaty part of thigh, making sure it does not touch bone. Cover and bake at 400° for 40 minutes; uncover and bake an additional 30 minutes or until meat thermometer registers 180°, basting occasionally with ½ cup sherry mixture. If desired, garnish with orange slices and parsley sprigs. Yield: 6 servings (167 calories per serving).

Per Serving:		
Protein 23.8g	Fat 6.2g	(Saturated Fat 1.7g)
Carbohydrate 2.5g	Fiber 0g	Cholesterol 73mg
Iron 1.0mg	Sodium 118mg	Calcium 14mg

ORANGE-ALMOND RICE

Cooking the rice in broth and juice adds flavor but no fat to this side dish.

2½ cups canned no-salt-added chicken broth, undiluted
1½ cups unsweetened orange juice
¼ teaspoon salt
¾ cup wild rice, uncooked
¼ cup chopped onion
1 cup long-grain rice, uncooked
⅓ cup canned mandarin oranges in light syrup, drained
¼ cup sliced almonds, toasted
2 tablespoons chopped fresh parsley
¼ teaspoon pepper

Combine chicken broth, unsweetened orange juice, and salt in a medium saucepan; bring mixture to a boil.

Add wild rice and chopped onion to mixture in saucepan; cover, reduce heat, and simmer 20 minutes. Add long-grain rice; cover and simmer an additional 30 minutes or until rice is tender and liquid is absorbed.

Add oranges and remaining ingredients to rice mixture in saucepan; stir well. Yield: 6 servings (264 calories per 1-cup serving).

Per Serving:		
Protein 6.8g	Fat 2.9g	(Saturated Fat 0.3g)
Carbohydrate 51.7g	Fiber 2.2g	Cholesterol 0mg
Iron 2.2mg	Sodium 105mg	Calcium 35mg

ROASTING VEGETABLES INTENSIFIES THEIR FLAVOR

To add more flavor to vegetables, roast them in your oven. Roasting vegetables—asparagus, carrots, garlic, onions, peppers, potatoes, tomatoes, or zucchini, for example—concentrates their flavors and brings out their natural sweetness. Roasted root vegetables make a great topping for couscous or rice and, when pureed, become a wonderful sauce for meats.

Cut vegetables into uniform pieces before roasting. Root vegetables such as carrots, potatoes, and turnips can be parboiled before roasting to reduce roasting time. To parboil, immerse the vegetables in boiling water for two minutes; then drain and let cool.

Most vegetables take 10 to 15 minutes to roast. For roasting, they should first be spread in a single layer on a baking sheet, and then coated with cooking spray. Root vegetables, onions, and garlic should be prepared the same way, but they need 15 to 20 minutes to roast while being stirred occasionally.

ROASTED ASPARAGUS WITH ONIONS

1 pound fresh asparagus spears
1 large purple onion, thinly sliced
Vegetable cooking spray
2 tablespoons balsamic vinegar
1½ teaspoons grated orange rind
2 tablespoons fresh orange juice
1 teaspoon dark sesame oil
½ teaspoon freshly ground pepper
¼ teaspoon salt
¼ teaspoon sugar

Snap off tough ends of asparagus. Remove scales from stalks with a knife or vegetable peeler, if desired. Arrange asparagus and onion separately on 2 baking sheets coated with cooking spray. Bake asparagus at 400° for 12 to 15 minutes or until crisp-tender. Bake onion at 400° for 15 to 18 minutes or until lightly browned, stirring twice.

Combine vinegar and remaining ingredients in a small jar; cover and shake vigorously. Arrange asparagus and onion on a serving platter. Drizzle vinegar mixture over vegetables. Serve warm or at room temperature. Yield: 6 servings (37 calories per serving).

Per Serving:		
Protein 1.6g	Fat 1.1g	(Saturated Fat 0.1g)
Carbohydrate 6.4g	Fiber 1.7g	Cholesterol 0mg
Iron 0.6mg	Sodium 100mg	Calcium 21mg

MINIATURE CARROT CAKE MUFFINS

1¼ cups sifted cake flour
1 teaspoon baking powder
¾ teaspoon baking soda
¼ teaspoon salt
⅔ cup sugar
½ teaspoon ground cinnamon
¼ cup apple butter
1 tablespoon vegetable oil
3 egg whites, lightly beaten
¾ cup grated carrot
⅓ cup canned crushed pineapple in juice, drained
Vegetable cooking spray

Combine first 6 ingredients in a medium bowl; make a well in center of mixture. Combine apple butter, oil, and egg whites; add to dry ingredients, stirring just until dry ingredients are moistened. Gently fold in carrot and pineapple.

Spoon batter into miniature (1¾-inch) muffin pans coated with cooking spray, filling three-fourths full. Bake at 375° for 13 minutes or until golden. Remove from pans immediately. Yield: 2½ dozen (47 calories each).

Per Muffin:		
Protein 0.7g	Fat 0.6g	(Saturated Fat 0.1g)
Carbohydrate 9.7g	Fiber 0.3g	Cholesterol 0mg
Iron 0.4mg	Sodium 57mg	Calcium 11mg

FROZEN LEMON ANGEL CAKE

For this dessert, you can replace the lemon ice milk with your favorite flavor of low-fat ice cream, frozen yogurt, or sherbet.

1 (10½-ounce) loaf commercial angel food cake
1½ cups lemon ice milk, softened
1 (10-ounce) package frozen sliced strawberries in light syrup, thawed and drained
1¼ cups reduced-calorie frozen whipped topping, thawed
Fresh strawberries (optional)
Lemon slices (optional)
Fresh mint sprigs (optional)

Cut a ½-inch slice off top of cake; set aside. Hollow out center of cake, leaving a ½-inch-thick shell. Reserve inside of cake for another use. Combine ice milk and sliced strawberries, stirring well. Spoon ice milk mixture into cake shell; top with reserved cake slice. Cover and freeze 4 hours or until firm.

Place cake on a serving platter; spread whipped topping evenly over top and sides of cake. If desired, garnish with fresh strawberries, lemon slices, and mint sprigs. Serve immediately. Yield: 10 servings (134 calories per serving).

Per Serving:		
Protein 2.8g	Fat 2.4g	(Saturated Fat 1.5g)
Carbohydrate 26.3g	Fiber 0.1g	Cholesterol 4mg
Iron 0.2mg	Sodium 67mg	Calcium 70mg

Labor Day Barbecue

Grilled Lamb Patties
Italian Vegetable Medley
Grilled Polenta
Roasted Pepper Catsup
Papaya Sorbet

SERVES 6
TOTAL CALORIES PER SERVING: 485
(Calories from Fat: 22%)

This menu has been designed for the grill. First, grill the vegetables. Next, grill the lamb and the polenta together, if there's room. There are no last-minute kitchen tasks. Both Roasted Pepper Catsup (3 tablespoons per serving) and Papaya Sorbet can be prepared up to two days ahead.

GRILLED LAMB PATTIES

1 pound lean ground lamb
½ pound freshly ground raw turkey
¼ cup soft breadcrumbs
2 teaspoons fennel seeds, crushed
½ teaspoon ground cumin
½ teaspoon freshly ground pepper
¼ teaspoon salt
2 cloves garlic, crushed
Vegetable cooking spray

Position knife blade in food processor bowl; add lamb, turkey, breadcrumbs, fennel seeds, cumin, pepper, salt, and garlic. Process until mixture is finely ground. Remove mixture from processor bowl, and shape into 6 patties.

Coat grill rack with cooking spray; place on grill over medium-hot coals (350° to 400°). Place patties on rack; grill, covered, 4 to 5 minutes on each side or until done. Yield: 6 servings (162 calories per serving).

Per Serving:

Protein 24.3g	Fat 5.9g	(Saturated Fat 2.0g)
Carbohydrate 1.5g	Fiber 0.2g	Cholesterol 74mg
Iron 2.3mg	Sodium 183mg	Calcium 28mg

ITALIAN VEGETABLE MEDLEY

12 medium-size fresh shiitake mushroom caps
1 medium-size yellow squash, sliced
1 medium zucchini, sliced
1 medium-size sweet red pepper, cut into strips
1 medium-size sweet yellow pepper, cut into strips
2 small purple onions, cut into wedges
1 tablespoon olive oil
Vegetable cooking spray
8 sun-dried tomatoes, cut into thin strips
2 tablespoons minced fresh oregano
1 tablespoon capers
2 tablespoons balsamic vinegar
1 clove garlic, crushed

Combine first 6 ingredients; add olive oil, and toss. Place vegetables in a grilling basket.

Coat grill rack with cooking spray; place on grill over medium-hot coals (350° to 400°). Place basket on rack; grill, covered, 18 minutes or until vegetables are tender, turning occasionally. Transfer vegetables to a bowl. Stir in tomato, oregano, and capers. Combine vinegar and garlic. Pour over vegetable mixture; toss. Yield: 6 servings (81 calories per ¾-cup serving).

Per Serving:

Protein 2.3g	Fat 3.4g	(Saturated Fat 0.5g)
Carbohydrate 12.7g	Fiber 2.9g	Cholesterol 0mg
Iron 1.6mg	Sodium 244mg	Calcium 40mg

A sizzling menu includes Grilled Lamb Patties, Grilled Polenta (page 74), and Italian Vegetable Medley.

GRILLED POLENTA

4 cups water
½ teaspoon salt
1 cup instant polenta
¼ cup freshly grated Parmesan cheese
2 tablespoons minced fresh dillweed
Olive oil-flavored vegetable cooking spray
Fresh dillweed (optional)

Combine water and salt in a large saucepan; bring to a boil. Add polenta in a slow, steady stream, stirring constantly. Reduce heat to medium; cook, stirring constantly, 20 minutes or until mixture pulls away from sides of pan. Remove from heat, and stir in Parmesan cheese and minced dillweed.

Spoon polenta mixture into a 13- x 9- x 2-inch pan coated with cooking spray, pressing to smooth top. Let cool completely.

Turn polenta out onto a cutting board; cut into 12 squares. Coat both sides of each polenta square with cooking spray. Coat grill rack with cooking spray; place on grill over medium-hot coals (350° to 400°). Place polenta on rack; grill, covered, 5 minutes on each side or until browned. To serve, cut each polenta square in half diagonally. Place 4 triangles on each serving plate. Garnish with dillweed, if desired. Yield: 6 servings (94 calories per serving).

Per Serving:		
Protein 3.4g	Fat 2.1g	(Saturated Fat 0.9g)
Carbohydrate 16.0g	Fiber 2.3g	Cholesterol 3mg
Iron 0.9mg	Sodium 279mg	Calcium 65mg

ROASTED PEPPER CATSUP

3 large sweet red peppers
⅓ cup reduced-calorie catsup
1 teaspoon Hungarian sweet paprika
1 teaspoon brown sugar
2 teaspoons balsamic vinegar
1 clove garlic

Cut peppers in half lengthwise; remove and discard seeds and membrane. Place peppers, skin side up, on a baking sheet, and flatten with palm of hand. Broil 5½ inches from heat (with electric oven door partially opened) 15 to 20 minutes or until charred. Place in ice water until cool; peel and discard skins.

Coarsely chop peppers, and place in container of an electric blender. Add catsup and remaining ingredients; cover and process until smooth, stopping once to scrape down sides. Yield: 1½ cups plus 3 tablespoons (7 calories per tablespoon).

Per Tablespoon:		
Protein 0.2g	Fat 0.1g	(Saturated Fat 0g)
Carbohydrate 1.4g	Fiber 0.3g	Cholesterol 0mg
Iron 0.3mg	Sodium 1mg	Calcium 2mg

PAPAYA SORBET

¾ cup sugar
¾ cup water
1¾ cups peeled, seeded, and pureed papaya (about 2 large)
¼ cup lime juice

Combine sugar and water in a small saucepan; bring to a boil over medium heat, stirring until sugar dissolves. Remove from heat, and let cool completely. Stir in pureed papaya and lime juice. Cover and chill thoroughly.

Pour mixture into freezer can of a 2-quart hand-turned or electric freezer. Freeze according to manufacturer's instructions. Pack freezer with additional ice and rock salt, and let stand 1 hour before serving. Scoop sorbet into individual bowls. Serve immediately. Yield: 3 cups (127 calories per ½-cup serving).

Per Serving:		
Protein 0.5g	Fat 0.1g	(Saturated Fat 0g)
Carbohydrate 32.9g	Fiber 1.3g	Cholesterol 0mg
Iron 0.1mg	Sodium 3mg	Calcium 18mg

Guests will be thankful when you present Hickory-Smoked Turkey Breast (page 76), Shredded Brussels Sprouts Gratin (page 77), Pureed Root Vegetables with Caraway (page 76), and Cranberry-Pear Relish (page 77).

Come Over for Thanksgiving Dinner

Hickory-Smoked Turkey Breast
Pureed Root Vegetables with Caraway
Shredded Brussels Sprouts Gratin
Cranberry-Pear Relish
Pumpkin Spice Cake

SERVES 8
TOTAL CALORIES PER SERVING: 600
(Calories from Fat: 21%)

Are you waiting for December to bring relatives to fill the seats at your dinner table? Fill those seats now with friends in the same situation.

Instead of traditional turkey and dressing, serve this menu that boasts a fragrant smoked turkey breast. Hearty side dishes are made with brussels sprouts and root vegetables. And we've included a delicious sweet-and-tangy version of cranberry relish (¼ cup per serving). End the meal with moist Pumpkin Spice Cake (one slice per serving).

You can easily set up the meal on a buffet dressed up in your best china and silver. Or serve it "bistro-style" by baking and serving the side dishes in rustic casseroles and colorful pottery.

HICKORY-SMOKED TURKEY BREAST

Hickory chips
1 (3-pound) skinned, boned turkey breast
1 tablespoon olive oil
2 teaspoons lemon juice
1 teaspoon dried basil
½ teaspoon dried oregano
½ teaspoon dried thyme
¼ teaspoon salt
¼ teaspoon garlic powder
¼ teaspoon paprika
Vegetable cooking spray
Fresh thyme sprigs (optional)

Soak hickory chips in water at least 30 minutes.

Rinse turkey breast with cold water; pat dry. Tuck loose ends under thickest part of breast. Secure turkey with heavy string at 2-inch intervals.

Combine olive oil and lemon juice; brush over turkey. Combine basil and next 5 ingredients; sprinkle over turkey.

Prepare charcoal fire in one end of grill; let burn 15 to 20 minutes. Place hickory chips on coals. Coat grill rack with cooking spray, and place on grill.

Insert meat thermometer into thickest part of turkey. Place turkey on grill opposite hot coals, and cook, covered, 1½ hours or until meat thermometer registers 170°. Remove string before slicing. Garnish turkey with thyme sprigs, if desired. Yield: 12 servings (143 calories per serving).

Gas Grill Directions: To smoke turkey on gas grill, preheat grill to medium-hot (350° to 400°) using both burners. After preheating, turn left burner off. Place hickory chips in a disposable aluminum foil pan or an aluminum foil packet poked with holes on grill over right burner. Coat grill rack with cooking spray; place on grill. Place turkey on rack over left burner. Grill, covered, 1½ hours or until meat thermometer registers 170°.

Per Serving:		
Protein 25.0g	Fat 3.9g	(Saturated Fat 1.0g)
Carbohydrate 0.3g	Fiber 0g	Cholesterol 58mg
Iron 1.3mg	Sodium 103mg	Calcium 20mg

PUREED ROOT VEGETABLES WITH CARAWAY

8 assorted small gourds (optional)
1 pound baking potatoes, peeled
¾ pound carrots, scraped
¾ pound celeriac, peeled
½ pound parsnips, scraped
2 tablespoons reduced-calorie margarine
1 teaspoon caraway seeds, crushed
¼ teaspoon salt
⅛ teaspoon ground white pepper
⅛ teaspoon ground nutmeg

If desired, cut off top one-fourth of each gourd; discard seeds. Place 4 gourds in a large Dutch oven. Add water to depth of 1½ inches. Bring to a boil. Cover, reduce heat, and simmer 15 minutes or until tender. Remove from Dutch oven; set aside. Repeat procedure with remaining 4 gourds.

Cut potatoes and next 3 ingredients into 2-inch pieces. Cook vegetables in boiling water to cover in a large saucepan 25 minutes or until tender. Drain well. Set aside, and keep warm.

Melt margarine in a small skillet over medium-high heat. Add caraway seeds, and cook, stirring constantly, 1 to 2 minutes or until lightly toasted.

Position knife blade in food processor bowl; add vegetables, caraway mixture, salt, pepper, and nutmeg. Process until smooth.

Spoon ½ cup puree into each gourd or onto each individual serving plate. Yield: 8 servings (84 calories per ½-cup serving).

Per Serving:		
Protein 2.3g	Fat 2.1g	(Saturated Fat 0.3g)
Carbohydrate 15.6g	Fiber 2.7g	Cholesterol 0mg
Iron 2.1mg	Sodium 151mg	Calcium 46mg

SHREDDED BRUSSELS SPROUTS GRATIN

1½ pounds fresh brussels sprouts
3 tablespoons reduced-calorie margarine
3 cloves garlic, minced
1¼ cups evaporated skimmed milk
¼ cup port wine
½ teaspoon salt
½ teaspoon freshly ground pepper
¼ teaspoon freshly grated nutmeg
2 tablespoons all-purpose flour
½ cup water
Vegetable cooking spray
¼ cup grated Parmesan cheese

Wash brussels sprouts thoroughly, and remove discolored leaves. Cut off stem ends. Cut brussels sprouts vertically into very thin shreds. Set aside.

Melt margarine in a large saucepan over medium-high heat; add garlic, and sauté 1 minute. Add brussels sprouts; sauté 6 minutes. Stir in milk and next 4 ingredients; bring to a boil. Cover, reduce heat, and simmer 12 minutes or until brussels sprouts are tender. Combine flour and water in a small bowl, stirring with a wire whisk until smooth. Gradually add flour mixture to brussels sprouts mixture. Cook, stirring constantly, until thickened.

Spoon mixture into a shallow 1½-quart baking dish coated with cooking spray; sprinkle with Parmesan cheese. Bake, uncovered, at 350° for 25 to 30 minutes or until lightly browned and bubbly. Yield: 8 servings (103 calories per ½-cup serving).

Per Serving:		
Protein 6.5g	Fat 3.9g	(Saturated Fat 1.0g)
Carbohydrate 12.3g	Fiber 2.8g	Cholesterol 4mg
Iron 1.2mg	Sodium 297mg	Calcium 181mg

CRANBERRY-PEAR RELISH

1½ cups fresh cranberries
¾ cup peeled, chopped ripe pear
¼ cup sugar
1 teaspoon grated orange rind
¼ cup peeled, chopped orange
¼ cup canned crushed pineapple in juice, drained
¼ teaspoon ground ginger

Position knife blade in food processor bowl. Add cranberries; process 5 seconds or until cranberries are coarsely chopped. Transfer to a bowl. Stir in pear and remaining ingredients. Cover; chill at least 8 hours. Yield: 2 cups (14 calories per tablespoon).

Per Tablespoon:		
Protein 0.1g	Fat 0.0g	(Saturated Fat 0g)
Carbohydrate 3.6g	Fiber 0.3g	Cholesterol 0mg
Iron 0mg	Sodium 0mg	Calcium 2mg

PUMPKIN SPICE CAKE

Applesauce adds flavor and moistness to this cake recipe, reducing the need for added fat.

2¾ cups all-purpose flour
½ teaspoon baking powder
1 teaspoon baking soda
¼ teaspoon salt
1 teaspoon ground cloves
1 teaspoon ground cinnamon
1 teaspoon ground nutmeg
1½ cups sugar
1 (16-ounce) can pumpkin
¾ cup frozen egg substitute, thawed
½ cup unsweetened applesauce
¼ cup vegetable oil
1 cup chopped dates
Vegetable cooking spray
1 teaspoon powdered sugar

Combine first 7 ingredients in a bowl; make a well in center of mixture. Combine 1½ cups sugar and next 4 ingredients; add to dry ingredients, stirring just until dry ingredients are moistened. Fold in dates.

Spoon batter into a 12-cup Bundt pan coated with cooking spray. Bake at 350° for 1 hour and 5 minutes or until a wooden pick inserted in center comes out clean. Cool in pan on a wire rack 10 minutes; remove from pan, and let cool completely on wire rack. Sift powdered sugar over cooled cake. Yield: 16 servings (214 calories per serving).

Per Serving:		
Protein 3.8g	Fat 3.8g	(Saturated Fat 0.7g)
Carbohydrate 42.2g	Fiber 1.6g	Cholesterol 0mg
Iron 1.7mg	Sodium 135mg	Calcium 28mg

Enjoy Strawberry-Chocolate Cheesecake, Chocolate-Raspberry Sauce (page 81), and Irish Coffee Punch (page 81).

The Sweetest Christmas

Strawberry-Chocolate Cheesecake
Cranberry Linzer Squares
Brown-Edge Wafer Cookies
Commercial Fat-Free Pound Cake
Assorted Fresh Fruit
Chocolate-Raspberry Sauce
Strawberry-Lemon Sauce
Irish Coffee Punch

SERVES 12

This is one extravagant end-of-the-year party menu that won't blow your resolve. These desserts have been pared of excess fat, yet remain as flavorful as high-fat creations.

To simplify the affair, make the linzer squares and sauces a couple of days before the party. Store the squares in an airtight container, and refrigerate the sauces. (Let the chocolate sauce come to room temperature before serving.) Prepare the cheesecake a day in advance, but wait until right before the party to add the topping. The cookies are best made the day of the event.

For a special touch, print the recipes on festive note cards for guests to take home.

STRAWBERRY-CHOCOLATE CHEESECAKE

We replaced some of the cream cheese with low-fat cottage cheese to help reduce the fat in this dessert.

Vegetable cooking spray
6 chocolate wafers, crushed
1½ cups light process cream cheese product
1 cup sugar
1 cup 1% low-fat cottage cheese
¼ cup plus 2 tablespoons unsweetened cocoa
¼ cup all-purpose flour
¼ cup strawberry or raspberry schnapps
1 teaspoon vanilla extract
¼ teaspoon salt
1 egg
1½ cups thinly sliced fresh strawberries
¼ cup frozen strawberries in light syrup
1 tablespoon apple jelly, melted

Coat the bottom of an 8-inch springform pan with cooking spray; sprinkle chocolate wafer crumbs evenly over bottom of pan. Set aside.

Position knife blade in food processor bowl. Add cream cheese and next 7 ingredients; process 1 minute or until smooth, scraping sides of processor bowl occasionally. Add egg, and process just until blended.

Pour mixture into prepared pan. Bake at 300° for 1 hour or until set. Remove from oven, and let cool to room temperature on a wire rack. Cover and chill at least 8 hours.

Remove cake from pan, and arrange strawberry slices over cheesecake. Place frozen strawberries in container of an electric blender; cover and process until smooth, stopping once to scrape down sides. Combine pureed strawberries and apple jelly, stirring well.

Brush pureed strawberry mixture over sliced strawberries. Chill at least 30 minutes. Yield: 12 servings (156 calories per serving).

Per Serving:		
Protein 5.4g	Fat 4.9g	(Saturated Fat 2.6g)
Carbohydrate 23.1g	Fiber 0.5g	Cholesterol 28mg
Iron 0.7mg	Sodium 229mg	Calcium 48mg

CRANBERRY LINZER SQUARES

Lining the baking pan with foil makes it a snap to remove these treats from the pan.

2 cups fresh cranberries
½ cup sugar
½ teaspoon ground cinnamon
½ cup plus 2 tablespoons all-purpose flour
½ teaspoon baking powder
¼ teaspoon salt
½ cup plus 2 tablespoons regular oats, uncooked
¼ cup plus 2 tablespoons firmly packed brown sugar
¼ cup toasted wheat germ
½ teaspoon ground cinnamon
2 tablespoons reduced-calorie margarine, melted
1 tablespoon skim milk
2 egg whites, lightly beaten
Vegetable cooking spray

Place cranberries in a 15- x 10- x 1-inch jellyroll pan. Combine ½ cup sugar and ½ teaspoon cinnamon in a small bowl. Sprinkle over cranberries, and toss gently. Bake at 350° for 10 minutes, stirring after 5 minutes. Set aside.

Combine flour and next 6 ingredients in a medium bowl, stirring well. Add margarine, milk, and egg whites; stir just until dry ingredients are moistened.

Line an 8-inch square pan with a large sheet of aluminum foil, allowing foil to extend 1 inch over edges of pan. Coat foil with cooking spray.

Spread three-fourths of oat mixture into prepared pan. Spread cranberry mixture over oat mixture. Sprinkle remaining oat mixture over cranberry mixture. Bake at 375° for 22 minutes or until lightly browned. Let cranberry-oat mixture cool completely in pan.

Carefully lift foil out of pan. Cut baked cranberry-oat mixture into squares, using a sharp knife. Yield: 16 squares (101 calories each).

Per Square:		
Protein 2.1g	Fat 1.5g	(Saturated Fat 0.2g)
Carbohydrate 20.6g	Fiber 1.0g	Cholesterol 0mg
Iron 0.7mg	Sodium 60mg	Calcium 21mg

BROWN-EDGE WAFER COOKIES

⅔ cup sugar
½ cup all-purpose flour
½ cup coarsely ground blanched almonds
¼ cup margarine, melted
1 tablespoon water
2 egg whites, lightly beaten
½ teaspoon vanilla extract
Vegetable cooking spray

Combine sugar, flour, and almonds in a medium bowl. Add margarine, water, egg whites, and vanilla; stir well. Cover and let stand 1 hour. (Batter will be thin.)

Spoon batter by ½ tablespoonfuls, 3 inches apart, onto cookie sheets coated with cooking spray. Bake at 400° for 5 to 6 minutes or until edges of cookies are browned. Remove from cookie sheets, and let cool completely on a wire rack. Yield: 38 cookies (42 calories each).

Per Cookie:		
Protein 0.8g	Fat 2.2g	(Saturated Fat 0.2g)
Carbohydrate 5.0g	Fiber 0.3g	Cholesterol 0mg
Iron 0.2mg	Sodium 17mg	Calcium 5mg

STRAWBERRY-LEMON SAUCE

Serve this sauce as a dip with cubes of fat-free pound cake.

1 (16-ounce) package frozen unsweetened strawberries, thawed
¼ cup lemon marmalade
Fresh mint sprig (optional)

Combine strawberries and marmalade in container of an electric blender; cover and process until smooth. Transfer to a small bowl. Cover and chill thoroughly. Garnish with a mint sprig, if desired. Yield: 2¼ cups (10 calories per tablespoon).

Per Tablespoon:		
Protein 0.1g	Fat 0.0g	(Saturated Fat 0g)
Carbohydrate 2.6g	Fiber 0.1g	Cholesterol 0mg
Iron 0.1mg	Sodium 2mg	Calcium 3mg

CHOCOLATE-RASPBERRY SAUCE

¾ cup frozen unsweetened raspberries, thawed
½ cup sugar
¼ cup plus 2 tablespoons unsweetened cocoa
2 tablespoons cornstarch
1½ cups plus 1 tablespoon evaporated skimmed milk
1 (1-ounce) square unsweetened chocolate

Place raspberries in container of an electric blender; cover and process 1 minute or until smooth, scraping sides of container once. Place puree in a wire-mesh strainer over a bowl; press with back of spoon against the sides of the strainer to squeeze out juice. Discard pulp and seeds remaining in strainer. Set puree aside.

Combine sugar, cocoa, and cornstarch in a saucepan. Add milk; stir with a wire whisk until smooth. Cook over medium heat, stirring constantly, until thickened. Add chocolate; stir until chocolate melts. Cool completely. Stir in raspberry puree. Yield: 2 cups plus 2 tablespoons (32 calories per tablespoon).

Per Tablespoon:		
Protein 1.3g	Fat 0.6g	(Saturated Fat 0.4g)
Carbohydrate 5.8g	Fiber 0.3g	Cholesterol 1mg
Iron 0.3mg	Sodium 14mg	Calcium 37mg

IRISH COFFEE PUNCH

The whiskey mixture can be made up to two days in advance and stored in the refrigerator. Reheat before adding the coffee.

2 cups 1% low-fat milk
⅔ cup Irish whiskey
¼ cup plus 2 tablespoons firmly packed dark brown sugar
2 (3-inch) sticks cinnamon
1 whole nutmeg, quartered
9½ cups warm strong-brewed coffee

Combine milk, whiskey, brown sugar, cinnamon sticks, and nutmeg in a medium saucepan. Cook over medium-high heat, stirring until sugar dissolves and mixture is thoroughly heated.

Pour mixture through a wire-mesh strainer into a serving bowl; discard cinnamon sticks and nutmeg remaining in strainer. Add coffee; stir well. Serve warm. Yield: 3 quarts (47 calories per 1-cup serving).

Per Serving:		
Protein 1.5g	Fat 0.4g	(Saturated Fat 0.3g)
Carbohydrate 9.4g	Fiber 0g	Cholesterol 2mg
Iron 0.9mg	Sodium 27mg	Calcium 60mg

AFTER-WORK STRESS RELIEF

Unwinding after a long day at work is essential, and experts say the mind is the most powerful tool for doing this. These tips tap into that power and let you defuse workday stress quickly and efficiently.

- Before leaving work, set up a schedule for tomorrow. This may help put a concrete end to the workday and allow you to transfer unfinished business to tomorrow's list of concerns.
- On the commute home, listen to a cassette. Experts say that as long as you like what you hear, it will help you relax.
- Once home, change into comfortable clothes immediately. Then grab fresh fruit or fruit juice. Stress experts think that a little natural sugar can help brain metabolism and let you wind down naturally.
- Engage in an activity that is a direct contrast to what you do at work. If your work requires physical labor, make a switch to something that taxes the mind—fill out a crossword puzzle or read a book. If your work is full of mental tasks, do some thing physical—chop vegetables, lift weights, or go for a walk.
- Set aside at least 20 minutes after work for winding down. Walking the dog, meditating, relaxing in a bubble bath, or sipping hot tea can stimulate body changes that bring on relaxation.

Light Recipes

Recipes Your Family Will Love

Welcome to the backbone of *Cooking Light*—hearty, good-for-you recipes that taste and look better than you'd ever dream. That's because we've developed and taste-tested each recipe to merge exceptional flavor with the latest principles of good nutrition. The result? Recipes with more whole grains, fresh fruits and vegetables, lean meats, and low-fat dairy products. We've created satisfying dishes that are higher in nutrient-rich complex carbohydrates and fiber, yet are lower in fat, cholesterol, sugar, and sodium.

Among more than 300 recipes for filling entrées, dazzling salads, flavorful side dishes, and show-stopping desserts, you'll find plenty of additional recipes for your everyday meals or for entertaining. Along with the recipes, look for the following fun and helpful information:

- **Descriptions of unusual ingredients** or cooking terms printed with the recipes they're used in
- **Tips on reducing fat** in traditional recipes without losing flavor
- **Substitution suggestions** for unusual ingredients and even for alcohol and liqueur
- **Information boxes** that fill you in on the latest about topics such as lamb (page 159); tilapia, the new fish on the market, (page 116); and flaxseed, the latest fiber booster, (page 105)
- **Fun facts about food and recipes,** such as Spiral Almond Challah, a Jewish tradition, (page 110), and how to eat spoonbread, an old-time Southern favorite, (page 101)
- **Step-by-step photo instructions** for various techniques, such as making eggplant strips to skewer (page 147)
- **Ideas to save you time**, such as food storage instructions, menu suggestions, and other hints that will help make planning and cooking meals easier and faster

All this and more is waiting for you in the chapters ahead. You're sure to find new recipe favorites that taste just as good as they are good for you.

Overleaf: *A garden of fresh herbs awaits you in such flavorful recipes as Herbed Vinegar (page 206), Basil-Marinated Tomatoes (page 178), Dilled Brown Bread (page 101), and Herbed Chicken and Vegetables (page 168).*

Right: *Eating pizza is fun even when it's served in a different form, as in Layered Pizza Dip (page 87).*

Appetizers & Beverages

PIQUANT CHEESE SPREAD

2/3 cup Chablis or other dry white wine
1/3 cup minced dried apricots
1/3 cup minced sun-dried tomato
1 (7-ounce) jar roasted sweet red pepper in water
1 clove garlic
2 cups (8 ounces) shredded 40% less-fat Cheddar cheese
1 (8-ounce) package nonfat cream cheese product, softened
1/2 teaspoon curry powder

Combine first 3 ingredients in a small saucepan; bring to a boil. Cook, uncovered, over medium-high heat 5 minutes or until liquid evaporates. Let cool.

Drain red pepper, reserving liquid. Chop enough red pepper to measure 1/2 cup. Reserve remaining peppers in liquid for another use.

Position knife blade in food processor bowl. Drop garlic through food chute with processor running; process 3 seconds or until garlic is minced. Add chopped red pepper, Cheddar cheese, cream cheese, and curry powder. Process 1 minute or until smooth, scraping sides of processor bowl once; transfer to a bowl. Stir in apricot mixture. Cover and chill. Serve with unsalted crackers or fresh raw vegetables. Yield: 2 1/2 cups (25 calories per tablespoon).

Per Tablespoon:		
Protein 2.0g	Fat 0.9g	(Saturated Fat 0.5g)
Carbohydrate 2.9g	Fiber 0.1g	Cholesterol 4mg
Iron 0.1mg	Sodium 89mg	Calcium 57mg

TIPSY TUNA SPREAD

1 (8-ounce) carton nonfat sour cream alternative
1/2 (8-ounce) package Neufchâtel cheese, softened
1 (6 1/8-ounce) can 60% less-salt tuna in water, drained
1/4 cup minced purple onion
1/4 cup commercial no-salt-added salsa
2 tablespoons vodka
3/4 teaspoon ground celery seeds
1/2 teaspoon pepper
Vegetable cooking spray (optional)
1 (8-inch) flour tortilla (optional)

Combine sour cream and Neufchâtel cheese in a medium bowl. Beat at medium speed of an electric mixer until smooth. Stir in tuna and next 5 ingredients. Cover and chill.

If desired, place a 10-ounce custard cup upside down on a baking sheet. Coat the outside of cup with cooking spray. Place tortilla over cup; coat tortilla with cooking spray. Bake at 400° for 7 to 9 minutes or until tortilla is crisp and lightly browned. Remove tortilla from cup; let cool completely.

To serve, spoon tuna mixture into tortilla shell or a serving bowl. Serve with unsalted crackers. Yield: 2 1/4 cups (20 calories per tablespoon).

Per Tablespoon:		
Protein 1.7g	Fat 0.8g	(Saturated Fat 0.5g)
Carbohydrate 0.7g	Fiber 0g	Cholesterol 3mg
Iron 0.1mg	Sodium 19mg	Calcium 11mg

HEALTHY PARTNERS FOR DIPS AND SPREADS

Serve low-fat, low-sodium accompaniments with your healthy dips and spreads. Many healthy alternatives are available, making it easy to find low-fat items that suit your fancy.

For Savory Dips and Spreads

Fresh vegetables: broccoli flowerets, cauliflower flowerets, carrot sticks, celery sticks, squash slices, sugar snap peas, cherry tomatoes.

Crackers and chips: fat-free saltines, fat-free potato chips, no-oil baked tortilla chips, water crackers.

For Sweet Dips

Fresh fruit: apple wedges, pear wedges, grapes, strawberries, blackberries, raspberries, pineapple chunks, peach slices, melon cubes.

Cakes or cookies: cubed fat-free pound cake, cubed angel food cake, gingersnaps, fat-free cookies.

CURRIED CRAB DIP

¾ cup nonfat mayonnaise
½ (8-ounce) package Neufchâtel cheese, softened
2 tablespoons commercial mango chutney
1½ teaspoons curry powder
¼ teaspoon dry mustard
Dash of hot sauce
1 (6-ounce) can crabmeat, drained
Vegetable cooking spray
1 tablespoon chopped unsalted dry-roasted peanuts
2 tablespoons sliced green onions

Combine first 6 ingredients in a small bowl; beat at medium speed of an electric mixer until blended. Gently stir in crabmeat. Spoon crabmeat mixture into a 1-quart shallow baking dish coated with cooking spray. Sprinkle with nuts.

Bake, uncovered, at 375° for 15 minutes or until mixture is thoroughly heated. Sprinkle with sliced green onions. Serve warm with endive spears or water crackers. Yield: 1¾ cups (26 calories per tablespoon).

Per Tablespoon:		
Protein 1.4g	Fat 1.2g	(Saturated Fat 0.6g)
Carbohydrate 2.4g	Fiber 0.1g	Cholesterol 7mg
Iron 0.1mg	Sodium 114mg	Calcium 9mg

PIÑA COLADA DIP

Draining the excess liquid from yogurt yields a thicker and creamier low-fat dip or spread.

2 (8-ounce) cartons pineapple low-fat yogurt
¼ cup finely chopped dried apricots
1 tablespoon minced crystallized ginger
1 teaspoon coconut extract
½ teaspoon rum extract

Place a colander in a 2-quart glass measure. Line colander with 4 layers of cheesecloth; allow cheesecloth to extend over edges of colander.

Stir yogurt until smooth. Spoon yogurt into colander, and cover yogurt loosely with plastic wrap; refrigerate 12 hours. Spoon yogurt cheese into a medium bowl; discard liquid.

Add apricots and remaining ingredients to yogurt; stir well. Serve with fresh fruit. Yield: 1¼ cups (29 calories per tablespoon).

Per Tablespoon:		
Protein 1.0g	Fat 0.3g	(Saturated Fat 0.2g)
Carbohydrate 5.6g	Fiber 0.1g	Cholesterol 1mg
Iron 0.2mg	Sodium 13mg	Calcium 33mg

LAYERED PIZZA DIP

1 (8-ounce) package nonfat cream cheese product, softened
½ cup nonfat sour cream alternative
⅛ teaspoon garlic powder
⅛ teaspoon ground red pepper
Vegetable cooking spray
½ cup no-salt-added tomato sauce
¼ teaspoon dried oregano
⅛ teaspoon garlic powder
⅛ teaspoon onion powder
½ cup chopped frozen artichoke hearts, thawed
¼ cup sliced green onions
¼ cup chopped sweet red pepper
¼ cup sliced ripe olives
½ cup (2 ounces) shredded part-skim mozzarella cheese
½ teaspoon dried Italian seasoning

Combine first 4 ingredients in a small bowl; beat at low speed of an electric mixer until smooth. Spread cream cheese mixture in a 9-inch pieplate coated with cooking spray.

Combine tomato sauce and next 3 ingredients in a small bowl, stirring well. Pour tomato sauce mixture over cream cheese mixture. Layer artichokes and remaining ingredients over tomato sauce. Bake, uncovered, at 350° for 15 to 20 minutes or until thoroughly heated. Serve with no-oil baked tortilla chips or melba rounds. Yield: 12 appetizer servings (48 calories per serving).

Per Serving:		
Protein 4.9g	Fat 1.4g	(Saturated Fat 0.6g)
Carbohydrate 3.5g	Fiber 0.5g	Cholesterol 6mg
Iron 0.4mg	Sodium 189mg	Calcium 94mg

BLACK BEAN RELISH

This low-fat relish makes a flavorful accompaniment with grilled beef, chicken, and pork.

1 (15-ounce) can black beans, drained
½ cup seeded, chopped tomato
½ cup diced sweet yellow pepper
½ cup sliced green onions
2 tablespoons chopped fresh cilantro
3 tablespoons red wine vinegar
1 clove garlic, minced
¼ teaspoon salt
¼ teaspoon hot sauce
⅛ teaspoon pepper

Combine all ingredients in a medium bowl; toss well. Cover and chill at least 8 hours. Serve with no-oil baked tortilla chips. Yield: 2¾ cups (10 calories per tablespoon).

Per Tablespoon:		
Protein 0.6g	Fat 0.1g	(Saturated Fat 0.6g)
Carbohydrate 1.9g	Fiber 0.4g	Cholesterol 0mg
Iron 0.2mg	Sodium 32mg	Calcium 4mg

ARTICHOKE PUFFS

1 (9-ounce) package frozen artichoke hearts
½ cup fresh crabmeat, drained and flaked
¼ cup reduced-calorie mayonnaise
2 tablespoons grated Parmesan cheese
1 tablespoon diced pimiento
1 teaspoon low-sodium Worcestershire sauce
¼ teaspoon garlic powder
⅛ teaspoon salt-free lemon-pepper seasoning
Dash of hot sauce
1 cup all-purpose flour
2 tablespoons grated Parmesan cheese
¼ teaspoon salt
1 cup skim milk
¾ cup frozen egg substitute, thawed
1 tablespoon reduced-calorie margarine, melted
Vegetable cooking spray

Cook artichoke hearts according to package directions, omitting salt. Drain and chop. Combine chopped artichoke hearts and next 8 ingredients. Set aside.

Combine flour, 2 tablespoons Parmesan cheese, and salt in a bowl. Combine milk, egg substitute, and margarine in a medium bowl, stirring well. Gradually add flour mixture to milk mixture, stirring with a wire whisk until smooth.

Coat miniature (1¾-inch) muffin pans with cooking spray; spoon batter evenly into muffin cups. Place in a cold oven. Turn oven on to 450°, and bake 5 minutes. Reduce heat to 350°; bake an additional 25 to 30 minutes or until popovers are crusty and brown. Remove popovers from pan, and let cool.

Slice each popover in half horizontally, leaving 1 side intact. Spoon 2 teaspoons artichoke mixture into each popover; place on an ungreased baking sheet. Bake at 400° for 5 minutes or until thoroughly heated. Serve warm. Yield: 3 dozen (32 calories each).

Per Appetizer:		
Protein 2.0g	Fat 1.0g	(Saturated Fat 0.3g)
Carbohydrate 3.9g	Fiber 0.2g	Cholesterol 3mg
Iron 0.3mg	Sodium 64mg	Calcium 22mg

PEPPERED POLENTA STICKS

2 cups water
½ teaspoon cracked black pepper
¼ teaspoon salt
¼ teaspoon dried Italian seasoning
½ cup instant polenta
Olive oil-flavored vegetable cooking spray
Marinara Sauce

Line an 8-inch square pan with heavy-duty plastic wrap; allow plastic wrap to extend over edges of pan. Set aside.

Combine first 4 ingredients in a medium saucepan; bring to a boil. Add polenta in a slow, steady stream, stirring constantly. Reduce heat to medium; cook, stirring constantly, 5 minutes or until mixture pulls away from sides of pan. Press polenta evenly into prepared pan. Fold edges of plastic wrap over to cover polenta; let cool. Chill 1 hour or until firm.

Invert polenta onto a cutting board; remove and discard plastic wrap. Cut polenta in half crosswise; cut each half into 15 (½-inch-wide) strips. Place on a baking sheet coated with cooking spray. Coat polenta strips with cooking spray. Bake at 425° for 25 minutes or until lightly browned. Serve warm with Marinara Sauce. Yield: 6 appetizer servings (78 calories per 5 sticks and ¼ cup sauce).

Marinara Sauce

Olive oil-flavored vegetable cooking spray
1 teaspoon olive oil
2 tablespoons chopped onion
2 tablespoons chopped celery
1 clove garlic, minced
1 (14½-ounce) can no-salt-added whole tomatoes, undrained and chopped
1 teaspoon red wine vinegar
¼ teaspoon salt
¼ teaspoon dried Italian seasoning
¼ teaspoon dried basil

Coat a medium saucepan with cooking spray; add olive oil. Place over medium-high heat until hot. Add onion, celery, and garlic; sauté until vegetables are tender. Add tomato and remaining ingredients. Bring to a boil. Reduce heat, and simmer, uncovered, 10 minutes, stirring occasionally. Yield: 1½ cups.

Per Serving:

Protein 1.9g	Fat 1.3g	(Saturated Fat 0.1g)
Carbohydrate 15.0g	Fiber 1.0g	Cholesterol 0mg
Iron 1.1mg	Sodium 208mg	Calcium 33mg

BROILED PINEAPPLE BITES

By substituting turkey bacon for regular bacon, we reduced the fat in this recipe by half.

1 (15¼-ounce) can pineapple chunks in juice
1 (8-ounce) can sliced water chestnuts
12 slices turkey bacon, cut in half
Vegetable cooking spray
1 tablespoon brown sugar
½ teaspoon cornstarch
¼ teaspoon dry mustard

Drain pineapple chunks; set aside ¼ cup plus 1 tablespoon juice and 24 pineapple chunks. Reserve remaining fruit and juice for another use.

Drain water chestnuts. Set aside 24 slices. Reserve remaining slices for another use.

Place a pineapple chunk and water chestnut slice on each strip of bacon. Roll up, and secure each with a wooden pick. Place on rack of a broiler pan coated with cooking spray. Set aside.

Combine ¼ cup plus 1 tablespoon pineapple juice, brown sugar, cornstarch, and dry mustard in a small saucepan; stir until smooth. Cook over medium heat, stirring constantly, until thickened and bubbly.

Brush pineapple bites evenly with pineapple juice mixture. Broil 5½ inches from heat (with electric oven door partially opened) 6 minutes. Turn pineapple bites, and broil 5 minutes or until bacon is done. Serve immediately. Yield: 2 dozen (23 calories each).

Per Appetizer:

Protein 1.1g	Fat 1.1g	(Saturated Fat 0.3g)
Carbohydrate 2.0g	Fiber 0.1g	Cholesterol 5mg
Iron 0.1mg	Sodium 100mg	Calcium 1mg

SOUTHWESTERN NEW POTATOES

15 small round red potatoes (about 1½ pounds)
½ cup nonfat sour cream alternative
2 tablespoons canned chopped green chiles
1 tablespoon diced pimiento
1 teaspoon ground cumin
¼ teaspoon salt
⅛ teaspoon ground red pepper

Arrange potatoes in a vegetable steamer over boiling water. Cover and steam 15 to 20 minutes or until tender. Remove from steamer; let cool.

Scoop out centers of potatoes with a melon-ball scoop; set aside potato shells. Mash potato pulp at medium speed of an electric mixer until smooth. Stir in sour cream and remaining ingredients. Pipe evenly into potato shells, using a decorating bag fitted with a large round tip.

Place stuffed potatoes on a baking sheet. Bake at 425° for 10 to 15 minutes or until thoroughly heated. Yield: 15 appetizers (39 calories each).

Per Appetizer:

Protein 1.6g	Fat 0.1g	(Saturated Fat 0g)
Carbohydrate 7.9g	Fiber 0.8g	Cholesterol 0mg
Iron 0.7mg	Sodium 58mg	Calcium 8mg

GINGERED POTATO SLICES

2 medium-size sweet potatoes, peeled
Butter-flavored vegetable cooking spray
¼ teaspoon apple pie spice
⅓ cup low-fat sour cream
2½ tablespoons finely chopped crystallized ginger

Cut potatoes into 30 (¼-inch-thick) slices. Arrange potato slices in a single layer on a baking sheet coated with cooking spray. Coat potato slices with cooking spray. Turn slices, and coat again; sprinkle evenly with apple pie spice. Bake at 400° for 15 minutes or until golden on bottom. Turn slices, and bake an additional 10 minutes or until tender.

Arrange slices on a serving platter. Spoon sour cream evenly onto centers of slices; sprinkle with ginger. Yield: 2½ dozen appetizers (23 calories each).

Per Appetizer:		
Protein 0.3g	Fat 0.5g	(Saturated Fat 0.2g)
Carbohydrate 4.5g	Fiber 0.4g	Cholesterol 1mg
Iron 0.4mg	Sodium 4mg	Calcium 9mg

SPINACH-FETA ROLLS

1 (10-ounce) package fresh spinach
Butter-flavored vegetable cooking spray
½ cup minced onion
⅓ cup lite ricotta cheese
¼ cup crumbled feta cheese
1 tablespoon Chablis or other dry white wine
½ teaspoon dried oregano
¼ teaspoon salt
¼ teaspoon garlic powder
¼ teaspoon pepper
18 sheets commercial frozen phyllo pastry, thawed

Trim and chop spinach; place in a large saucepan. Add water to pan to depth of 2 inches; bring to a boil. Cook just until spinach wilts, stirring occasionally. Drain well; press spinach between paper towels until barely moist.

Coat a nonstick skillet with cooking spray. Place over medium-high heat until hot. Add onion, and sauté until tender. Add spinach, ricotta cheese, and next 6 ingredients; stir well. Set aside.

Place 1 sheet of phyllo on a damp towel (keeping remaining phyllo covered). Lightly coat phyllo with cooking spray. Top with another phyllo sheet; lightly coat with cooking spray. Cut stack of phyllo crosswise into 5 strips (each about 3¼ inches wide).

Working with 1 strip at a time, place 2 teaspoons spinach mixture at base of strip (keeping remaining strips covered). Fold lengthwise edges in about ½ inch, and roll up, jellyroll fashion. Place rolls, seam side down, on ungreased baking sheets. (Keep rolls covered before baking.) Repeat procedure with remaining phyllo and spinach mixture. Coat rolls with cooking spray, and bake at 375° for 15 minutes or until golden. Yield: 45 appetizers (30 calories each).

Per Appetizer:		
Protein 1.0g	Fat 0.9g	(Saturated Fat 0.2g)
Carbohydrate 4.5g	Fiber 0.3g	Cholesterol 1mg
Iron 0.4mg	Sodium 63mg	Calcium 13mg

STUFFED CHERRY TOMATOES

20 large cherry tomatoes
½ cup light process cream cheese product
2 tablespoons commercial fat-free Ranch-style dressing
4 (½-ounce) slices Canadian bacon, finely chopped
3 tablespoons minced green onions
¼ teaspoon ground white pepper
⅛ teaspoon garlic powder
⅛ teaspoon hot sauce
Parsley sprigs (optional)

Cut top off each tomato; carefully scoop out pulp. Reserve pulp for another use. Invert tomato shells onto paper towels, and let drain 30 minutes.

Combine cream cheese and Ranch-style dressing, stirring well. Add Canadian bacon and next 4 ingredients; stir well. Spoon mixture evenly into tomato shells, or pipe into shells using a decorating bag fitted with a large round tip. Garnish with parsley, if desired. Yield: 20 appetizers (22 calories each).

Per Appetizer:		
Protein 1.3g	Fat 1.2g	(Saturated Fat 0.6g)
Carbohydrate 1.5g	Fiber 0.2g	Cholesterol 5mg
Iron 0.1mg	Sodium 88mg	Calcium 9mg

MINIATURE EGG FOO YUNG

¾ cup frozen egg substitute, thawed
1 (8-ounce) package frozen cooked salad shrimp, thawed and drained
½ cup chopped canned water chestnuts
½ cup chopped canned bean sprouts
¼ cup chopped green onions
1 teaspoon peeled, minced gingerroot
¼ teaspoon salt
¼ teaspoon hot sauce
Vegetable cooking spray
3 tablespoons plus 2 teaspoons Chinese hot mustard

Beat egg substitute with a wire whisk until foamy. Stir in shrimp and next 6 ingredients.

Coat a nonstick griddle with cooking spray; preheat to 350°. For each pancake, spoon 1 tablespoon shrimp mixture onto hot griddle. Cook 2 to 3 minutes or until browned on bottom; turn and cook an additional 2 to 3 minutes or until browned. Transfer to a serving platter. Top each pancake with ½ teaspoon hot mustard. Serve immediately. Yield: 22 appetizers (20 calories each).

Per Appetizer:		
Protein 2.9g	Fat 0.4g	(Saturated Fat 0g)
Carbohydrate 1.1g	Fiber 0.2g	Cholesterol 16mg
Iron 0.5mg	Sodium 84mg	Calcium 9mg

SALSA MEATBALLS

1 pound freshly ground raw turkey
½ cup commercial no-salt-added salsa, divided
¼ cup fine, dry breadcrumbs
¼ cup (1 ounce) shredded reduced-fat Monterey Jack cheese
2 tablespoons finely chopped green onions
2 cloves garlic, minced
Vegetable cooking spray
¾ cup nonfat sour cream alternative

Combine turkey, ¼ cup salsa, breadcrumbs, and next 3 ingredients in a large bowl; stir well. Shape turkey mixture into 48 (¾-inch) balls. Place meatballs on rack of a broiler pan coated with cooking spray. Bake at 400° for 20 to 25 minutes or until done. Drain on paper towels.

Combine sour cream and remaining ¼ cup salsa, stirring well. Serve meatballs with sour cream sauce mixture. Yield: 4 dozen appetizer servings (19 calories per 1 meatball and 1 teaspoon sauce).

Per Serving:		
Protein 2.6g	Fat 0.4g	(Saturated Fat 0.2g)
Carbohydrate 0.9g	Fiber 0.1g	Cholesterol 7mg
Iron 0.2mg	Sodium 17mg	Calcium 12mg

JERK CHICKEN WINGS

28 chicken wings, skinned (about 2½ pounds)
½ cup canned low-sodium chicken broth, undiluted
2 tablespoons minced fresh jalapeño pepper
2 teaspoons sugar
1 teaspoon onion powder
1 teaspoon pepper
1 teaspoon ground allspice
½ teaspoon dried thyme
¼ teaspoon ground nutmeg
¼ teaspoon ground cinnamon
¼ teaspoon dried crushed red pepper
1 tablespoon low-sodium soy sauce
1 teaspoon cider vinegar
1 teaspoon vegetable oil
Vegetable cooking spray

Cut off and discard chicken wing tips. Cut chicken wings in half at joint; set aside.

Combine chicken broth and next 12 ingredients in a shallow dish, stirring well. Add chicken, and toss well. Cover and marinate in refrigerator at least 8 hours.

Remove chicken from marinade; discard marinade. Place chicken on rack of a broiler pan coated with cooking spray. Bake at 400° for 20 minutes. Turn chicken; bake an additional 15 to 20 minutes or until done. Yield: 28 appetizer servings (47 calories per 1 drummette and 1 wing).

Per Serving:		
Protein 7.0g	Fat 1.8g	(Saturated Fat 0.5g)
Carbohydrate 0.1g	Fiber 0g	Cholesterol 21mg
Iron 0.3mg	Sodium 22mg	Calcium 4mg

Cranberry Chicken Salad Cups whet appetites without adding many calories before dinner.

CRANBERRY CHICKEN SALAD CUPS

1½ cups diced cooked chicken breast (skinned before cooking and cooked without salt)
½ cup canned mandarin oranges in water, drained
¼ cup nonfat mayonnaise
2 tablespoons minced green pepper
3 tablespoons jellied whole-berry cranberry sauce
1 teaspoon minced crystallized ginger
2 teaspoons honey
½ teaspoon prepared horseradish
32 fresh or frozen wonton skins, thawed
Vegetable cooking spray
Fresh parsley sprigs (optional)
Fresh cranberries (optional)

Combine diced chicken, oranges, mayonnaise, green pepper, cranberry sauce, ginger, honey, and horseradish in a small bowl; stir well. Cover and chill thoroughly.

Place 1 wonton skin in each of 32 miniature (1¾-inch) muffin cups coated with cooking spray. Press wontons against bottoms and up sides of cups. Coat wontons with cooking spray. Bake at 350° for 8 minutes or until wontons are crisp and golden. Let cool completely in pans.

Spoon chicken mixture evenly into wonton cups. Remove wonton cups from pans, and serve immediately. If desired, garnish with fresh parsley sprigs and cranberries. Yield: 32 appetizers (42 calories each).

Per Appetizer:

Protein 3.3g	Fat 0.5g	(Saturated Fat 0.1g)
Carbohydrate 5.8g	Fiber 0g	Cholesterol 8mg
Iron 0.4mg	Sodium 72mg	Calcium 7mg

FETA SHRIMP

To make this recipe even speedier, call ahead and ask your grocer to peel, devein, and steam the shrimp.

32 medium-size unpeeled fresh shrimp
3 cups water
16 fresh snow pea pods
¼ cup peeled, shredded cucumber
¼ cup reduced-calorie mayonnaise
¼ cup nonfat sour cream alternative
2 tablespoons grated onion
1 tablespoon lemon juice
2 teaspoons minced fresh dillweed
2 ounces feta cheese, crumbled

Peel and devein shrimp, leaving tails intact. Bring water to a boil in a large saucepan; add shrimp, and cook 3 to 5 minutes or until shrimp turn pink. Drain well; rinse with cold water, and drain again. Chill thoroughly.

Wash snow peas; trim ends, and remove strings. Arrange snow peas in a vegetable steamer over boiling water. Cover and steam 1 minute. Drain well, and chill thoroughly.

Separate each snow pea lengthwise into 2 pieces. Wrap a snow pea half around each shrimp, and secure each with a wooden pick. Cover and chill thoroughly.

Press cucumber between paper towels until barely moist. Combine cucumber, mayonnaise, and remaining ingredients in a small bowl, stirring well. Cover and chill thoroughly.

Arrange shrimp on a serving platter, and serve with mayonnaise mixture. Yield: 32 appetizer servings (20 calories per 1 shrimp and 1½ teaspoons sauce).

Per Serving:		
Protein 1.9g	Fat 1.0g	(Saturated Fat 0.3g)
Carbohydrate 0.7g	Fiber 0.1g	Cholesterol 16mg
Iron 0.3mg	Sodium 51mg	Calcium 15mg

PEACHY BREAKFAST DELIGHT

1½ cups peach nectar, chilled
2 (16-ounce) cans peach slices in juice, drained
1 (8-ounce) carton vanilla low-fat yogurt
⅛ teaspoon almond extract

Combine all ingredients in container of an electric blender; cover and process until smooth. Pour into glasses, and serve immediately. Yield: 5 cups (109 calories per 1-cup serving).

Per Serving:		
Protein 3.0g	Fat 0.8g	(Saturated Fat 0.4g)
Carbohydrate 24.3g	Fiber 0.5g	Cholesterol 2mg
Iron 0.6mg	Sodium 39mg	Calcium 84mg

MAPLE-BANANA FROSTY

Processing frozen banana and partially frozen milk in the blender produces the thick, creamy consistency of this low-fat beverage.

1¼ cups peeled, sliced banana (about 2 medium)
1 cup 1% low-fat milk
1 (8-ounce) carton vanilla low-fat yogurt
1 tablespoon reduced-calorie maple syrup
Ground cinnamon (optional)

Place banana slices in a single layer on a baking sheet. Cover and freeze until firm. Place milk in a shallow container; cover and freeze 25 minutes or until milk is slushy.

Combine frozen banana, milk, yogurt, and syrup in container of an electric blender; cover and process until smooth. Pour into glasses. Sprinkle with cinnamon, if desired. Serve immediately. Yield: 3 cups (153 calories per 1-cup serving).

Per Serving:		
Protein 6.9g	Fat 2.0g	(Saturated Fat 1.3g)
Carbohydrate 28.3g	Fiber 1.7g	Cholesterol 7mg
Iron 0.3mg	Sodium 92mg	Calcium 233mg

CITRUS-MINT COOLER

1 cup loosely packed fresh mint leaves
2 cups unsweetened pink grapefruit juice
1 cup unsweetened orange juice
⅓ cup sugar
1 cup lemon-flavored sparkling water, chilled
Fresh mint sprigs (optional)

Combine first 4 ingredients in a medium bowl, stirring well. Cover and chill at least 8 hours, stirring occasionally. Pour mixture through a wire-mesh strainer into a pitcher, discarding mint. Just before serving, stir in sparkling water. Garnish with mint sprigs, if desired. Yield: 4 cups (139 calories per 1-cup serving).

Per Serving:		
Protein 1.0g	Fat 0.2g	(Saturated Fat 0g)
Carbohydrate 34.3g	Fiber 0.1g	Cholesterol 0mg
Iron 2.5mg	Sodium 14mg	Calcium 14mg

MELON LIME COOLER

4½ cups cubed honeydew melon (about 1 small)
1½ cups lime sherbet
2 tablespoons lime juice
Fresh strawberries (optional)

Place melon cubes in a single layer on a baking sheet. Cover and freeze 30 minutes or until firm.

Position knife blade in food processor bowl; add frozen melon, sherbet, and lime juice. Process until smooth. Pour into glasses. Garnish with strawberries, if desired. Serve immediately. Yield: 5 cups (131 calories per 1-cup serving).

Per Serving:		
Protein 1.5g	Fat 0.7g	(Saturated Fat 0.4g)
Carbohydrate 32.4g	Fiber 1.8g	Cholesterol 0mg
Iron 0.2mg	Sodium 59mg	Calcium 35mg

Invigorate yourself with the fresh taste of mint in Citrus-Mint Cooler, or mellow out with the combination of honeydew melon and lime sherbet in Melon Lime Cooler.

SPICY VEGETABLE SIPPER

2½ cups no-salt-added vegetable juice
1½ cups canned no-salt-added beef broth, undiluted
2 teaspoons sugar
1 teaspoon low-sodium Worcestershire sauce
Dash of hot sauce
Lemon slices (optional)

Combine first 5 ingredients in a medium saucepan; cook over medium heat until thoroughly heated. Pour into individual mugs. Garnish each serving with a lemon slice, if desired. Serve warm. Yield: 4 cups (47 calories per 1-cup serving).

Per Serving:		
Protein 1.7g	Fat 0.2g	(Saturated Fat 0g)
Carbohydrate 9.1g	Fiber 0g	Cholesterol 0mg
Iron 1.1mg	Sodium 38mg	Calcium 21mg

CANDY APPLE CIDER

Red cinnamon candies add a sweet, spicy surprise to this beverage. It's a perfect treat for kids on Halloween night.

4 cups unsweetened apple cider
2 tablespoons red cinnamon candies
1 (1-inch) piece peeled gingerroot
4 (3-inch) sticks cinnamon (optional)

Combine first 3 ingredients in a medium saucepan. Cook over medium heat, stirring constantly, until thoroughly heated and candy melts. Remove and discard gingerroot.

Pour into individual mugs. Garnish each serving with a cinnamon stick, if desired. Serve warm. Yield: 4 cups (156 calories per 1-cup serving).

Per Serving:		
Protein 0.1g	Fat 0.2g	(Saturated Fat 0g)
Carbohydrate 39.4g	Fiber 0.5g	Cholesterol 0mg
Iron 0.9mg	Sodium 11mg	Calcium 18mg

CRANBERRY-ORANGE TEA

3 cups water
2 cranberry-flavored tea bags
2 orange-flavored tea bags
2 tablespoons sugar
2 cups cranberry juice cocktail
1 cup unsweetened orange juice
3 (3-inch) sticks cinnamon
Orange slices (optional)

Bring water to a boil in a medium saucepan. Add tea bags; remove from heat. Cover and steep 10 minutes. Remove and discard tea bags. Add sugar, stirring until sugar dissolves.

Combine cranberry juice, orange juice, and cinnamon sticks in a medium saucepan. Cook over medium heat 5 minutes or until thoroughly heated. Remove and discard cinnamon sticks. Stir in tea, and pour into individual mugs. Garnish each serving with an orange slice, if desired. Serve warm. Yield: 1½ quarts (86 calories per 1-cup serving).

Per Serving:		
Protein 0.3g	Fat 0.1g	(Saturated Fat 0g)
Carbohydrate 21.8g	Fiber 0.1g	Cholesterol 0mg
Iron 0.2mg	Sodium 7mg	Calcium 6mg

FROSTED CAPPUCCINO

The combination of ingredients in this recipe creates the sweet taste and texture of a sinfully rich coffee beverage minus the fat.

2 cups brewed espresso coffee, chilled
2 cups vanilla nonfat frozen dessert
½ teaspoon vanilla extract
Ground cinnamon (optional)

Combine first 3 ingredients in container of an electric blender; cover and process until smooth. Pour into glasses. Sprinkle each serving with cinnamon, if desired. Serve immediately. Yield: 4 cups (104 calories per 1-cup serving).

Per Serving:		
Protein 2.1g	Fat 0.0g	(Saturated Fat 0g)
Carbohydrate 22.7g	Fiber 0g	Cholesterol 0mg
Iron 0.5mg	Sodium 47mg	Calcium 82mg

VANILLA CREAM ALEXANDER

2¾ cups skim milk
1 cup vanilla nonfat frozen dessert
2 tablespoons brandy
2 tablespoons Crème de Cacao
Ground nutmeg (optional)

Combine first 4 ingredients in container of an electric blender; cover and process until smooth. Pour into glasses. Sprinkle with nutmeg, if desired. Serve immediately. Yield: 5¼ cups (88 calories per ¾-cup serving).

Per Serving:		
Protein 3.8g	Fat 0.2g	(Saturated Fat 0.1g)
Carbohydrate 12.7g	Fiber 0g	Cholesterol 2mg
Iron 0mg	Sodium 63mg	Calcium 141mg

The only thing that tops the taste of Spiral Almond Challah (page 110) is its engaging presentation at the table.

Breads

CHILI-CHEESE WAFERS

¾ cup all-purpose flour
¼ cup yellow cornmeal
1 teaspoon baking powder
½ teaspoon baking soda
¼ teaspoon salt
2 teaspoons chili powder
½ teaspoon ground cumin
¼ teaspoon ground red pepper
¼ teaspoon cream of tartar
¼ cup reduced-calorie margarine
¾ cup (3 ounces) finely shredded reduced-fat Cheddar cheese
¼ cup nonfat buttermilk
1 tablespoon all-purpose flour
Vegetable cooking spray

Combine first 9 ingredients in a large bowl; cut in margarine with a pastry blender until mixture resembles coarse meal. Stir in cheese. Sprinkle buttermilk, 1 tablespoon at a time, evenly over surface; stir with a fork just until dry ingredients are moistened. Shape into a ball.

Sprinkle 1 tablespoon flour evenly over work surface. Turn dough out onto floured surface. Roll dough into a 12- x 12-inch square (about ⅛ inch thick). Cut dough into 2-inch squares, using a fluted pastry wheel or a sharp knife.

Place squares on baking sheets coated with cooking spray. Bake at 375° for 12 minutes or until browned. Cool on wire racks. Yield: 36 wafers (37 calories each).

Per Wafer:

Protein 1.2g	Fat 1.4g	(Saturated Fat 0.4g)
Carbohydrate 3.2g	Fiber 0.2g	Cholesterol 2mg
Iron 0.2mg	Sodium 67mg	Calcium 30mg

PEACHES 'N' CREAM PANCAKES

2 cups all-purpose flour
1 tablespoon plus 1 teaspoon baking powder
½ teaspoon salt
2 tablespoons sugar
2 cups skim milk
1 tablespoon vegetable oil
1 egg yolk
½ teaspoon almond extract
1 cup sliced canned peaches in light syrup, drained and chopped
2 egg whites
Vegetable cooking spray
1 tablespoon sifted powdered sugar
1½ cups low-fat sour cream

Combine first 4 ingredients in a large bowl; make a well in center of mixture. Combine milk and next 3 ingredients; stir in peaches. Add peach mixture to dry ingredients, stirring just until dry ingredients are moistened.

Beat egg whites at high speed of an electric mixer until stiff peaks form. Fold egg whites into peach mixture. Let stand 5 minutes.

Coat a nonstick griddle with cooking spray, and preheat to 350°. For each pancake, pour ¼ cup batter onto hot griddle. Cook pancakes until tops are covered with bubbles and edges look cooked; turn pancakes, and cook other side. Sprinkle pancakes evenly with powdered sugar, and top each with 1 tablespoon sour cream. Yield: 24 (4-inch) pancakes (86 calories each).

Per Pancake:

Protein 2.7g	Fat 2.9g	(Saturated Fat 1.3g)
Carbohydrate 12.4g	Fiber 0.3g	Cholesterol 15mg
Iron 0.6mg	Sodium 71mg	Calcium 89mg

BLUEBERRY BRAN MUFFINS

One-half cup unprocessed wheat bran, also called Millers Bran, has 12 grams of fiber.

1½ cups all-purpose flour
½ cup unprocessed wheat bran
2 teaspoons baking powder
¼ teaspoon salt
¾ cup sugar
¾ cup skim milk
2 tablespoons vegetable oil
1 egg, lightly beaten
1 teaspoon vanilla extract
1½ cups fresh or frozen blueberries, thawed
Vegetable cooking spray

Combine first 5 ingredients in a medium bowl; make a well in center of mixture. Combine milk and next 3 ingredients; add to dry ingredients, stirring just until dry ingredients are moistened. Fold in blueberries.

Spoon batter into muffin pans coated with cooking spray, filling two-thirds full. Bake at 400° for 18 to 20 minutes or until golden. Remove from pans immediately. Yield: 16 muffins (118 calories each).

Per Muffin:

Protein 2.4g	Fat 2.5g	(Saturated Fat 0.5g)
Carbohydrate 22.4g	Fiber 1.8g	Cholesterol 14mg
Iron 0.9mg	Sodium 48mg	Calcium 54mg

CHERRY-ALMOND MUFFINS

1 cup dried sweet cherries
½ cup unsweetened apple juice
1¾ cups all-purpose flour
2½ teaspoons baking powder
¼ teaspoon salt
½ cup sugar
1 teaspoon grated lemon rind
½ cup plus 2 tablespoons skim milk
2 tablespoons vegetable oil
1 egg, lightly beaten
1 teaspoon almond extract
Vegetable cooking spray
2 teaspoons sugar

Combine cherries and juice; let stand 30 minutes. Drain; reserve ¼ cup juice. Coarsely chop cherries.

Combine flour and next 4 ingredients; make a well in center of mixture. Combine reserved juice, milk, oil, egg, and extract. Add to dry ingredients, stirring just until moistened. Fold in cherries.

Spoon batter into muffin pans coated with cooking spray, filling two-thirds full; sprinkle with 2 teaspoons sugar. Bake at 400° for 15 to 18 minutes or until golden. Yield: 15 muffins (138 calories each).

Per Muffin:

Protein 2.7g	Fat 2.9g	(Saturated Fat 0.6g)
Carbohydrate 25.7g	Fiber 1.3g	Cholesterol 15mg
Iron 1.0mg	Sodium 49mg	Calcium 68mg

BUCKWHEAT BISCUITS

Toasted kasha adds a slightly nutty flavor to these hearty biscuits.

1¾ cups all-purpose flour
¼ cup kasha (buckwheat groats), toasted
1 tablespoon baking powder
¼ teaspoon baking soda
¼ teaspoon salt
½ teaspoon sugar
3 tablespoons margarine
¾ cup nonfat buttermilk
1 tablespoon all-purpose flour
Vegetable cooking spray

Combine first 6 ingredients in a large bowl; cut in margarine with a pastry blender until mixture resembles coarse meal. Add buttermilk, stirring with a fork just until dry ingredients are moistened.

Sprinkle 1 tablespoon flour evenly over work surface. Turn dough out onto floured surface, and knead 10 to 12 times. Roll dough to ½-inch thickness; cut into rounds with a 2-inch biscuit cutter. Place rounds on a baking sheet coated with cooking spray. Bake at 425° for 10 minutes or until golden. Yield: 16 biscuits (79 calories each).

Per Biscuit:

Protein 2.0g	Fat 2.3g	(Saturated Fat 0.5g)
Carbohydrate 12.5g	Fiber 0.5g	Cholesterol 0mg
Iron 0.8mg	Sodium 94mg	Calcium 68mg

Serve Confetti Scones with low-sugar preserves for a special breakfast or afternoon tea.

CONFETTI SCONES

2 cups all-purpose flour
1 tablespoon baking powder
¼ teaspoon baking soda
¼ teaspoon salt
1 tablespoon sugar
½ teaspoon grated orange rind
3 tablespoons margarine
½ cup diced dried mixed fruit
¾ cup nonfat buttermilk
1 tablespoon all-purpose flour
1 tablespoon skim milk
Vegetable cooking spray
2 teaspoons sugar

Combine first 6 ingredients in a medium bowl; cut in margarine with pastry blender until mixture resembles coarse meal. Stir in dried fruit. Add buttermilk, stirring with a fork just until dry ingredients are moistened.

Sprinkle 1 tablespoon flour evenly over work surface. Turn dough out onto floured surface, and knead 10 to 12 times. Roll dough into an 8-inch circle, and cut into 10 wedges. Brush evenly with skim milk. Transfer wedges to a baking sheet coated with cooking spray. Sprinkle evenly with 2 teaspoons sugar. Bake at 425° for 15 minutes or until golden. Serve warm. Yield: 10 scones (161 calories each).

Per Scone:

Protein 3.6g	Fat 3.8g	(Saturated Fat 0.8g)
Carbohydrate 28.4g	Fiber 0.9g	Cholesterol 1mg
Iron 1.6mg	Sodium 153mg	Calcium 114mg

DILLED BROWN BREAD

½ cup bulgur (cracked wheat), uncooked
½ cup boiling water
1¾ cups all-purpose flour
1 cup whole wheat flour
¼ cup toasted wheat germ
½ teaspoon baking powder
1 teaspoon baking soda
¼ teaspoon salt
2 tablespoons fresh dillweed
1⅔ cups nonfat buttermilk
2 tablespoons vegetable oil
2 tablespoons honey
1 egg, lightly beaten
Vegetable cooking spray

Combine bulgur and boiling water, stirring well. Let stand 5 to 10 minutes or until bulgur is tender and water is absorbed.

Combine all-purpose flour, whole wheat flour, wheat germ, baking powder, baking soda, salt, and dillweed in a medium bowl; make a well in center of mixture. Combine buttermilk and next 3 ingredients, stirring well. Add buttermilk mixture and bulgur to dry ingredients, stirring just until dry ingredients are moistened.

Spoon batter into a 9-inch pieplate coated with cooking spray. Bake at 375° for 45 to 50 minutes or until bread is golden. Let bread cool in pieplate 10 minutes.

Remove bread from pan, and let cool on a wire rack. Cut into wedges. Yield: 16 servings (139 calories per wedge).

Per Wedge:

Protein 4.9g	Fat 2.7g	(Saturated Fat 0.6g)
Carbohydrate 24.2g	Fiber 1.8g	Cholesterol 15mg
Iron 1.4mg	Sodium 149mg	Calcium 50mg

CRANBERRY SPOONBREAD

Spoonbread, a cornmeal-based bread similar to a baked soufflé or stiff pudding, is most commonly served as a side dish in place of rice, pasta, or potatoes and is eaten with a spoon or fork.

1 cup yellow cornmeal
½ cup dried cranberries
3 tablespoons sugar
½ teaspoon grated orange rind
¼ teaspoon salt
¼ teaspoon ground cinnamon
3 cups skim milk
1 tablespoon margarine, melted
½ cup frozen egg substitute, thawed
1½ teaspoons baking powder
4 egg whites
Vegetable cooking spray
2 teaspoons powdered sugar

Combine first 6 ingredients in a saucepan. Add skim milk and margarine; cook over medium heat, stirring constantly, until mixture is thickened and bubbly. Remove mixture from heat, and let cool 5 minutes. Add egg substitute and baking powder, stirring well.

Beat egg whites at high speed of an electric mixer until stiff peaks form. Fold one-third of egg whites into cornmeal mixture; fold in remaining egg whites. Spoon mixture into a 2-quart casserole coated with cooking spray. Bake at 350° for 50 minutes or until puffed and golden. Sprinkle with powdered sugar. Serve immediately. Yield: 9 servings (146 calories per serving).

Per Serving:

Protein 7.1g	Fat 1.8g	(Saturated Fat 0.4g)
Carbohydrate 25.6g	Fiber 1.2g	Cholesterol 2mg
Iron 1.1mg	Sodium 167mg	Calcium 156mg

GRAHAM HONEY ROLLS

Keep variety in the bread basket by shaping the dough differently each time you prepare these rolls.

3 cups bread flour, divided
¼ cup instant nonfat dry milk powder
¼ teaspoon salt
1 package active dry yeast
1½ cups water
2 tablespoons honey
1 tablespoon margarine
1 cup graham flour
1½ tablespoons bread flour
Butter-flavored vegetable cooking spray

Combine 1 cup bread flour and next 3 ingredients in a large mixing bowl, stirring well.

Combine water, honey, and margarine in a saucepan; cook over medium heat until margarine melts, stirring occasionally. Cool to 120° to 130°.

Gradually add liquid mixture to flour mixture, beating well at low speed of an electric mixer. Beat an additional 2 minutes at medium speed. Gradually stir in graham flour and enough of the remaining 2 cups bread flour to make a soft dough.

Sprinkle 1½ tablespoons bread flour evenly over work surface. Turn dough out onto floured surface, and knead until smooth and elastic (about 10 minutes). Place dough in a large bowl coated with cooking spray, turning to coat top. Cover and let rise in a warm place (85°), free from drafts, 45 minutes or until doubled in bulk.

Punch dough down, and divide into 32 equal portions. Roll each portion into a 9-inch rope. Tie each rope in a loose knot, leaving 2 long ends. Place on large baking sheets coated with cooking spray. Cover and let rise in a warm place, free from drafts, 30 minutes or until doubled in bulk.

Bake at 375° for 13 minutes or until golden. Coat rolls lightly with cooking spray. Yield: 32 rolls (74 calories each).

Per Roll:		
Protein 2.6g	Fat 0.7g	(Saturated Fat 0.1g)
Carbohydrate 12.1g	Fiber 0.9g	Cholesterol 0mg
Iron 0.8mg	Sodium 28mg	Calcium 14mg

Cloverleaf Rolls: Coat muffin pans with cooking spray. After first rising, punch dough down, and divide into 4 equal portions. Shape each portion into 21 balls. Place 3 balls in each muffin cup. Cover; let rise until doubled in bulk. Bake as directed. Coat rolls lightly with cooking spray. Yield: 28 rolls (85 calories each).

Per Roll:		
Protein 3.0g	Fat 0.8g	(Saturated Fat 0.1g)
Carbohydrate 13.8g	Fiber 1.0g	Cholesterol 0mg
Iron 0.9mg	Sodium 32mg	Calcium 16mg

Crescent Rolls: After first rising, punch dough down, and divide in half. Place 1 portion of dough on work surface; roll into a 12-inch circle. Cut into 12 wedges; roll each wedge tightly, beginning at wide end. Place rolls, point side down, on a baking sheet coated with cooking spray. Curve into crescent shapes. Repeat procedure with remaining dough. Cover; let rise until doubled in bulk. Bake as directed. Coat rolls lightly with cooking spray. Yield: 24 rolls (99 calories each).

Per Roll:		
Protein 3.5g	Fat 1.0g	(Saturated Fat 0.1g)
Carbohydrate 16.1g	Fiber 1.2g	Cholesterol 0mg
Iron 1.1mg	Sodium 37mg	Calcium 19mg

Spiral Rolls: After first rising, punch dough down, and divide into 32 portions. Roll each portion into a 9-inch rope. Place on baking sheets coated with cooking spray; curl ends in opposite directions. Cover; let rise until doubled in bulk. Bake as directed. Coat rolls lightly with cooking spray. Yield: 32 rolls (74 calories each).

Per Roll:		
Protein 2.6g	Fat 0.7g	(Saturated Fat 0.1g)
Carbohydrate 12.1g	Fiber 0.9g	Cholesterol 0mg
Iron 0.8mg	Sodium 28mg	Calcium 14mg

PARMESAN PAN ROLLS

2¼ cups bread flour, divided
½ cup grated Parmesan cheese, divided
¼ teaspoon salt
2 tablespoons sugar
1½ teaspoons dried Italian seasoning
1 package active dry yeast
1 cup water
⅓ cup skim milk
1 tablespoon vegetable oil
1¼ cups whole wheat flour
1 egg
2 tablespoons bread flour
Butter-flavored vegetable cooking spray

Combine 1 cup bread flour, ¼ cup plus 2 tablespoons Parmesan cheese, and next 4 ingredients in a large mixing bowl, stirring well.

Combine water, milk, and oil in a saucepan; cook over medium heat until very warm (120° to 130°). Gradually add liquid mixture to flour mixture, beating well at low speed of an electric mixer. Beat an additional 2 minutes at medium speed. Add whole wheat flour and egg, beating well. Gradually stir in enough of the remaining 1¼ cups bread flour to make a soft dough.

Sprinkle 2 tablespoons bread flour evenly over work surface. Turn dough out onto floured surface, and knead until smooth and elastic (about 10 minutes). Place dough in a large bowl coated with cooking spray, turning to coat top. Cover and let rise in a warm place (85°), free from drafts, 1 hour or until doubled in bulk.

Punch dough down, and divide into 18 equal portions. Shape each portion into a ball, and place balls in 2 (8-inch) round cakepans coated with cooking spray. Cover and let rise in a warm place, free from drafts, 30 minutes or until doubled in bulk.

Coat tops of rolls with cooking spray; sprinkle evenly with remaining 2 tablespoons Parmesan cheese. Bake at 350° for 20 minutes or until golden. Yield: 1½ dozen (125 calories each).

Per Roll:		
Protein 4.9g	Fat 2.4g	(Saturated Fat 0.7g)
Carbohydrate 21.2g	Fiber 1.2g	Cholesterol 14mg
Iron 1.4mg	Sodium 81mg	Calcium 47mg

CARAWAY-SPINACH TWISTS

3¼ cups bread flour, divided
¼ cup grated Parmesan cheese, divided
2 tablespoons instant nonfat dry milk powder
½ teaspoon salt
1 package active dry yeast
1 (10-ounce) package frozen chopped spinach, thawed
1¼ cups water
1½ tablespoons sugar
1 tablespoon margarine
1 tablespoon caraway seeds
¼ cup bread flour
Vegetable cooking spray

Combine 1 cup flour, 2 tablespoons cheese, and next 3 ingredients in a large bowl, stirring well.

Drain spinach; press between paper towels to remove excess moisture. Combine spinach, water, sugar, and margarine in a saucepan; cook over medium heat until margarine melts, stirring occasionally. Cool to 120° to 130°.

Gradually add spinach mixture to flour mixture, beating well at low speed of an electric mixer. Beat an additional 2 minutes at medium speed. Stir in caraway seeds. Gradually stir in enough of the remaining 2¼ cups flour to make a soft dough.

Sprinkle ¼ cup flour evenly over work surface. Turn dough out onto floured surface, and knead until smooth and elastic (about 10 minutes). Place dough in a large bowl coated with cooking spray, turning to coat top. Cover and let rise in a warm place (85°), free from drafts, 1 hour or until doubled in bulk.

Punch dough down, and divide into 24 equal portions. Roll each portion into a 15-inch rope; fold ropes in half, and twist tightly. Place 2 inches apart on baking sheets coated with cooking spray. Cover and let rise in a warm place, free from drafts, 30 minutes or until doubled in bulk. Coat twists with cooking spray; sprinkle with remaining 2 tablespoons cheese. Bake at 350° for 18 to 20 minutes or until golden. Yield: 2 dozen (92 calories each).

Per Twist:		
Protein 3.5g	Fat 1.4g	(Saturated Fat 0.3g)
Carbohydrate 16.4g	Fiber 0.9g	Cholesterol 1mg
Iron 1.2mg	Sodium 83mg	Calcium 38mg

REUBEN FOCACCIA

2¼ cups bread flour, divided
½ cup rye flour
¼ teaspoon baking soda
¼ teaspoon salt
1 teaspoon dried dillweed
½ teaspoon dry mustard
1 package active dry yeast
1 cup hot water (120° to 130°)
2 tablespoons bread flour
Olive oil-flavored vegetable cooking spray
3 ounces thinly sliced 98% fat-free corned beef, chopped
¾ cup (3 ounces) shredded reduced-fat Swiss cheese
¼ cup sauerkraut, drained
¾ teaspoon caraway seeds

Combine 1 cup bread flour and next 6 ingredients in a large mixing bowl; stir well. Gradually add water to flour mixture, beating well at low speed of an electric mixer. Beat an additional 2 minutes at medium speed. Gradually stir in enough of the remaining 1¼ cups bread flour to make a soft dough.

Sprinkle 2 tablespoons bread flour evenly over work surface. Turn dough out onto floured surface, and knead until smooth and elastic (about 10 minutes). Place dough in a large bowl coated with cooking spray, turning to coat top. Cover and let rise in a warm place (85°), free from drafts, 1 hour or until doubled in bulk.

Punch dough down; turn out onto work surface, and flatten slightly. Sprinkle corned beef and cheese over dough; knead gently to incorporate beef and cheese. Press dough onto a 12-inch pizza pan coated with cooking spray. Coat dough with cooking spray.

Cover dough, and let rise in a warm place, free from drafts, 30 minutes or until doubled in bulk. Sprinkle sauerkraut and caraway seeds over dough. Bake at 375° for 20 to 25 minutes or until golden. Cut into 16 wedges. Yield: 16 servings (110 calories per wedge).

Per Wedge:

Protein 5.9g	Fat 1.6g	(Saturated Fat 0.6g)
Carbohydrate 17.9g	Fiber 0.6g	Cholesterol 6mg
Iron 1.3mg	Sodium 137mg	Calcium 69mg

RYE BEER BREAD

3 cups all-purpose flour, divided
½ cup medium rye flour
2 tablespoons wheat germ
¼ teaspoon salt
1 package active dry yeast
1 cup flat light beer
¼ cup water
2 tablespoons molasses
1 tablespoon vegetable oil
1½ tablespoons caraway seeds
3 tablespoons all-purpose flour
Vegetable cooking spray

Combine 1 cup all-purpose flour and next 4 ingredients in a large mixing bowl, stirring well. Combine beer, water, molasses, and oil in a saucepan; cook over medium heat until mixture is very warm (120° to 130°).

Gradually add warm liquid mixture to flour mixture, beating well at low speed of an electric mixer. Beat an additional 2 minutes at medium speed. Stir in caraway seeds. Gradually stir in enough of the remaining 2 cups all-purpose flour to make a soft dough.

Sprinkle 3 tablespoons all-purpose flour evenly over work surface. Turn dough out onto floured surface, and knead until dough is smooth and elastic (about 10 minutes). Place dough in a large bowl coated with cooking spray, turning to coat top.

Cover and let rise in a warm place (85°), free from drafts, 45 minutes or until dough is doubled in bulk.

Punch dough down, and shape into a 6-inch round loaf. Place loaf on a baking sheet coated with cooking spray. Cover and let rise in a warm place, free from drafts, 25 minutes or until doubled in bulk. Bake at 375° for 15 to 20 minutes or until loaf sounds hollow when tapped.

Remove loaf from baking sheet; cool on a wire rack. Cut into 18 wedges. Yield: 18 servings (114 calories per wedge).

Per Wedge:

Protein 3.0g	Fat 1.3g	(Saturated Fat 0.2g)
Carbohydrate 21.7g	Fiber 1.3g	Cholesterol 0mg
Iron 1.4mg	Sodium 34mg	Calcium 14mg

FLAXSEED BREAD

Beating flaxseeds with a liquid produces a gelatinous mixture that's similar to slightly beaten egg white. A flaxseed mixture replaces an egg in this recipe.

2¾ cups all-purpose flour, divided
½ cup whole wheat flour
3 tablespoons flaxseeds, divided
¼ teaspoon salt
1 package active dry yeast
½ cup unsweetened apple juice
1 cup water
2 tablespoons vegetable oil
1 tablespoon honey
2 tablespoons all-purpose flour
Vegetable cooking spray

Combine 1 cup all-purpose flour, whole wheat flour, 1 tablespoon flaxseeds, salt, and yeast in a large mixing bowl, stirring well. Set aside.

Combine remaining 2 tablespoons flaxseeds and apple juice in container of an electric blender; cover and process until consistency of lightly beaten egg white, stopping once to scrape down sides.

Combine apple juice mixture, water, oil, and honey in a saucepan; cook over medium heat until very warm (120° to 130°), stirring occasionally.

Gradually add liquid mixture to flour mixture, beating well at low speed of an electric mixer. Beat an additional 2 minutes at medium speed. Gradually stir in enough of the remaining 1¾ cups all-purpose flour to make a soft dough.

Sprinkle 2 tablespoons all-purpose flour evenly over work surface. Turn dough out onto floured surface, and knead until smooth and elastic (about 10 minutes). Place dough in a large bowl coated with cooking spray, turning to coat top. Cover and let rise in a warm place (85°), free from drafts, 45 minutes or until doubled in bulk.

Punch dough down; turn out onto work surface, and knead lightly 4 or 5 times. Roll dough into a 14- x 7-inch rectangle. Roll up dough, starting at short side, pressing firmly to eliminate air pockets; pinch ends to seal. Place dough, seam side down, in a 9- x 5- x 3-inch loafpan coated with cooking spray.

Cover and let rise in a warm place, free from drafts, 25 minutes or until doubled in bulk. Bake at 375° for 30 to 35 minutes or until loaf sounds hollow when tapped. (Cover with aluminum foil the last 10 minutes of baking to prevent overbrowning, if necessary.) Remove from pan immediately; cool on a wire rack. Yield: 18 servings (114 calories per ½-inch slice).

Per Slice:

Protein 3.0g	Fat 2.4g	(Saturated Fat 0.4g)
Carbohydrate 20.2g	Fiber 1.4g	Cholesterol 0mg
Iron 1.3mg	Sodium 33mg	Calcium 9mg

FLAX FACTS

Flaxseeds, available in health food stores, are small, shiny, oval-shaped seeds that are rich in oil and high in fiber. Recent research shows that these seeds help lower blood cholesterol levels and may help ward off certain types of cancer. Because of their high oil content, flaxseeds should be stored in the refrigerator or freezer if not used promptly.

Include flaxseeds in your diet by sprinkling them over cereal, into salads, or into casseroles. Add flaxseeds whole to homemade bread and other baked goods, or grind them into a powder to substitute for part of the flour in baked goods. When ground into a paste, flaxseeds work well as a thickening agent for sauces and gravies.

Due to their high fiber content, flaxseeds should be added to your diet slowly. These seeds also are known to thin blood and are not appropriate for hemophiliacs or those scheduled for surgery.

MAPLE SUGAR BREAD

3 cups bread flour, divided
¼ cup instant nonfat dry milk powder
¼ teaspoon salt
1 package active dry yeast
1¼ cups water
⅓ cup firmly packed brown sugar
1 tablespoon vegetable oil
1 teaspoon instant coffee granules
1 teaspoon maple flavoring
½ cup chopped walnuts
½ cup whole wheat flour
1 tablespoon bread flour
Vegetable cooking spray

Combine 1 cup bread flour and next 3 ingredients in a large bowl; stir well. Combine water, brown sugar, oil, and coffee granules in a saucepan; cook over medium heat until very warm (120° to 130°).

Gradually add liquid mixture and flavoring to flour mixture, beating at low speed of an electric mixer. Beat 2 minutes at medium speed. Add walnuts; stir well. Stir in whole wheat flour and enough of the remaining 2 cups bread flour to make a soft dough.

Sprinkle 1 tablespoon bread flour over work surface. Turn dough out onto surface; knead until smooth and elastic (about 10 minutes). Place in a large bowl coated with cooking spray, turning to coat top. Cover and let rise in a warm place (85°), free from drafts, 1 hour or until doubled in bulk.

Punch dough down. Roll into a 14- x 7-inch rectangle. Roll up dough, starting at short side, pressing firmly to eliminate air pockets; pinch ends to seal. Place dough, seam side down, in a 9- x 5- x 3-inch loafpan coated with cooking spray.

Cover and let rise in a warm place, free from drafts, 35 minutes or until doubled in bulk. Bake at 375° for 40 minutes or until loaf sounds hollow when tapped. (Cover with aluminum foil the last 20 minutes of baking to prevent overbrowning, if necessary.) Remove from pan immediately; cool on a wire rack. Yield: 18 servings (147 calories per ½-inch slice).

Per Slice:		
Protein 4.9g	Fat 3.3g	(Saturated Fat 0.3g)
Carbohydrate 24.7g	Fiber 1.4g	Cholesterol 0mg
Iron 1.4mg	Sodium 44mg	Calcium 32mg

BANANA WHEAT BREAD

3¼ cups bread flour, divided
¼ cup instant nonfat dry milk powder
¼ teaspoon salt
1 package active dry yeast
¾ cup water
⅓ cup firmly packed brown sugar
1 cup mashed banana
1 teaspoon vanilla extract
¾ cup plus 1 tablespoon whole wheat flour
3 tablespoons bread flour, divided
Vegetable cooking spray

Combine 1 cup bread flour and next 3 ingredients in a large mixing bowl, stirring well. Combine water and brown sugar in a small saucepan; cook over medium heat until very warm (120° to 130°).

Gradually add liquid mixture to flour mixture, beating well at low speed of an electric mixer. Add banana and vanilla. Beat 2 minutes at medium speed. Stir in whole wheat flour and enough of the remaining 2¼ cups bread flour to make a soft dough.

Sprinkle 1½ tablespoons bread flour over work surface. Turn dough out onto surface; knead until smooth and elastic (about 10 minutes). Place in a large bowl coated with cooking spray, turning to coat top. Cover and let rise in a warm place (85°), free from drafts, 1 hour or until doubled in bulk.

Punch dough down; sprinkle remaining 1½ tablespoons bread flour evenly over work surface. Turn dough out onto floured surface, and knead lightly 4 or 5 times. Roll dough into a 14- x 7-inch rectangle. Roll up dough, starting at short side, pressing firmly to eliminate air pockets; pinch ends to seal. Place dough, seam side down, in a 9- x 5- x 3-inch loafpan coated with cooking spray.

Cover and let rise in a warm place, free from drafts, 1 hour or until doubled in bulk. Bake at 375° for 35 minutes or until loaf sounds hollow when tapped. Remove from pan immediately; cool on a wire rack. Yield: 18 servings (149 calories per ½-inch slice).

Per Slice:		
Protein 4.8g	Fat 0.7g	(Saturated Fat 0.1g)
Carbohydrate 31.1g	Fiber 1.8g	Cholesterol 0mg
Iron 1.6mg	Sodium 44mg	Calcium 31mg

When your main dish can handle extra kick, Taco Bread adds just the right amount of spice to the meal.

TACO BREAD

3¾ cups bread flour, divided
1 teaspoon sugar
1 teaspoon garlic powder
1 teaspoon ground cumin
1 teaspoon chili powder
½ teaspoon salt
¼ teaspoon ground red pepper
1 package active dry yeast
1 cup water
1 tablespoon vegetable oil
1 egg
¾ cup (3 ounces) shredded reduced-fat Cheddar cheese
2 tablespoons bread flour, divided
Vegetable cooking spray

Combine 1 cup flour and next 7 ingredients in a bowl. Combine water and oil in a saucepan; cook over medium heat until very warm (120° to 130°). Add liquid mixture to flour mixture, beating at low speed of an electric mixer. Beat 2 minutes at medium speed. Add egg; beat well. Stir in cheese and enough of the remaining 2¾ cups flour to make a soft dough.

Sprinkle 1 tablespoon flour over work surface. Turn dough out onto floured surface, and knead until smooth and elastic (about 10 minutes). Place in a large bowl coated with cooking spray, turning to coat top. Cover and let rise in a warm place (85°), free from drafts, 45 minutes or until doubled in bulk.

Punch dough down. Sprinkle remaining 1 tablespoon flour over work surface. Turn dough out onto surface, and knead lightly 4 or 5 times; roll into a 14- x 7-inch rectangle. Roll up dough, starting at short side, pressing to eliminate air pockets; pinch ends to seal. Place dough, seam side down, in a 9- x 5- x 3-inch loafpan coated with cooking spray.

Cover and let rise in a warm place, free from drafts, 45 minutes or until doubled in bulk. Bake at 375° for 30 minutes or until loaf sounds hollow when tapped. Remove from pan immediately; cool on a wire rack. Yield: 18 servings (134 calories per ½-inch slice).

Per Slice:

Protein 5.5g	Fat 2.5g	(Saturated Fat 0.8g)
Carbohydrate 21.8g	Fiber 0.9g	Cholesterol 15mg
Iron 1.5mg	Sodium 106mg	Calcium 45mg

PIÑA COLADA BREAD

3 cups bread flour, divided
¼ cup shredded sweetened coconut
¼ teaspoon salt
1 package active dry yeast
¾ cup warm water
1 tablespoon vegetable oil
1 egg
1 teaspoon coconut extract
1 teaspoon pineapple extract
3 tablespoons bread flour, divided
Vegetable cooking spray

Combine 1 cup flour and next 3 ingredients in a large mixing bowl, stirring well. Combine water and oil in a small saucepan; cook over medium heat until very warm (120° to 130°).

Gradually add liquid mixture to flour mixture, beating well at low speed of an electric mixer. Beat 2 minutes at medium speed. Add egg and flavorings; beat well. Gradually stir in enough of the remaining 2 cups flour to make a soft dough.

Sprinkle 1½ tablespoons flour over work surface. Turn dough out onto floured surface; knead until smooth and elastic (about 10 minutes). Place in a large bowl coated with cooking spray, turning to coat top. Cover and let rise in a warm place (85°), free from drafts, 1 hour or until doubled in bulk.

Punch dough down. Sprinkle remaining 1½ tablespoons flour over work surface. Turn dough out onto floured surface, and knead lightly 4 or 5 times; roll into a 14- x 7-inch rectangle.

Roll up dough, starting at short side, pressing to eliminate air pockets; pinch ends to seal. Place dough, seam side down, in a 9- x 5- x 3-inch loafpan coated with cooking spray.

Cover and let rise in a warm place, free from drafts, 1 hour or until doubled in bulk. Bake at 375° for 25 minutes or until loaf sounds hollow when tapped. Remove from pan immediately, and let cool on a wire rack. Yield: 18 servings (109 calories per ½-inch slice).

Per Slice:		
Protein 3.5g	Fat 2.0g	(Saturated Fat 0.7g)
Carbohydrate 18.4g	Fiber 0.8g	Cholesterol 12mg
Iron 1.2mg	Sodium 40mg	Calcium 6mg

HONEY BUTTERMILK BRAID

1 package active dry yeast
½ cup warm water (105° to 115°)
3¼ cups bread flour, divided
¾ cup nonfat buttermilk
3 tablespoons honey
1 tablespoon margarine, melted
¼ teaspoon salt
1½ tablespoons bread flour, divided
Vegetable cooking spray
1 tablespoon skim milk

Combine yeast and warm water in a 1-cup liquid measuring cup; let stand 5 minutes.

Combine yeast mixture, 2 cups flour, buttermilk, honey, melted margarine, and salt in a large mixing bowl, beating at medium speed of an electric mixer until ingredients are well blended. Gradually stir in enough of the remaining 1¼ cups flour to make a soft dough.

Sprinkle 1 tablespoon flour evenly over work surface. Turn dough out onto floured surface, and knead until smooth and elastic (about 10 minutes). Place dough in a large bowl coated with cooking spray, turning to coat top. Cover and let rise in a warm place (85°), free from drafts, 1 hour or until doubled in bulk.

Punch dough down. Sprinkle remaining 1½ teaspoons flour evenly over work surface. Turn dough out onto floured surface, and roll into a 13- x 9-inch rectangle.

Cut rectangle lengthwise into 3 strips. Place strips on a baking sheet coated with cooking spray. Braid strips together, pinching ends to seal; tuck ends under. Coat braid lightly with cooking spray.

Cover braid, and let rise in a warm place, free from drafts, 40 minutes or until doubled in bulk. Brush braid with skim milk. Bake at 350° for 25 to 30 minutes or until loaf sounds hollow when tapped. Remove braid from baking sheet, and let cool on a wire rack. Yield: 18 servings (114 calories per ½-inch slice).

Per Slice:		
Protein 3.6g	Fat 1.2g	(Saturated Fat 0.2g)
Carbohydrate 22.1g	Fiber 0.7g	Cholesterol 0mg
Iron 1.2mg	Sodium 52mg	Calcium 18mg

RICOTTA CASSEROLE BREAD

This no-fuss bread doesn't require kneading and it only rises once, dramatically reducing the preparation time. The texture is slightly coarser than that of kneaded bread dough.

1 cup lite ricotta cheese
2 tablespoons sugar
2 tablespoons instant minced onion
2 tablespoons reduced-calorie margarine, melted
1 teaspoon baking powder
¼ teaspoon salt
2 packages active dry yeast
2 teaspoons sugar
1 cup warm water (105° to 115°)
3¼ cups all-purpose flour, divided
½ cup instant potato flakes
Vegetable cooking spray

Combine first 6 ingredients in a large mixing bowl, stirring well. Set aside.

Combine yeast, 2 teaspoons sugar, and warm water in a 2-cup liquid measuring cup; let stand 5 minutes. Add yeast mixture to ricotta cheese mixture, and stir well.

Add 2 cups flour and instant potato flakes to yeast mixture; beat at low speed of an electric mixer until ingredients are well blended. Beat an additional 2 minutes at medium speed. Gradually stir in remaining 1¼ cups flour.

Place dough in a large bowl coated with cooking spray, turning to coat top. Cover and let rise in a warm place (85°), free from drafts, 40 to 45 minutes or until doubled in bulk.

Punch dough down, and shape into a ball. Place dough in a 2-quart deep casserole coated with cooking spray. Bake at 350° for 50 minutes or until loaf sounds hollow when tapped. Remove from casserole immediately, and let cool on a wire rack. Cut into 18 wedges. Yield: 18 servings (115 calories per wedge).

Per Wedge:		
Protein 4.2g	Fat 1.6g	(Saturated Fat 0.4g)
Carbohydrate 21.5g	Fiber 0.9g	Cholesterol 2mg
Iron 1.3mg	Sodium 58mg	Calcium 37mg

ANISE PANETTONE

3¾ cups bread flour, divided
½ cup diced dried mixed fruit
2 tablespoons sugar
½ teaspoon anise seeds
¼ teaspoon salt
1 package active dry yeast
1 cup skim milk
2 tablespoons vegetable oil
2 tablespoons honey
1 egg
½ teaspoon anise extract
½ teaspoon almond extract
1½ tablespoons bread flour
Vegetable cooking spray

Combine 1 cup flour and next 5 ingredients in a large mixing bowl, stirring well. Combine milk, oil, and honey in a saucepan; cook over medium heat until very warm (120° to 130°).

Gradually add milk mixture to flour mixture, beating well at low speed of an electric mixer. Beat an additional 2 minutes at medium speed. Add egg and flavorings, beating well. Gradually stir in enough of the remaining 2¾ cups flour to make a soft dough.

Sprinkle 1½ tablespoons flour evenly over work surface. Turn dough out onto floured surface, and knead until smooth and elastic (about 10 minutes). Place dough in a large bowl coated with cooking spray, turning to coat top. Cover and let rise in a warm place (85°), free from drafts, 1 hour or until doubled in bulk.

Punch dough down; shape into a ball. Place dough in a 1½-quart soufflé dish coated with cooking spray. Cover and let rise in a warm place, free from drafts, 30 minutes or until doubled in bulk.

Bake at 350° for 1 hour or until loaf sounds hollow when tapped. (Cover with aluminum foil the last 25 minutes of baking to prevent overbrowning, if necessary.) Remove from dish immediately, and let cool on a wire rack. Yield: 18 servings (154 calories per wedge).

Per Wedge:		
Protein 4.6g	Fat 2.4g	(Saturated Fat 0.5g)
Carbohydrate 27.6g	Fiber 0.9g	Cholesterol 13mg
Iron 1.5mg	Sodium 47mg	Calcium 24mg

SPIRAL ALMOND CHALLAH

Challah, a traditional Jewish yeast bread, can be shaped many ways but is most commonly braided. This loaf (pictured on page 97) resembles a turban after the coiled dough is baked.

3½ cups bread flour, divided
2 tablespoons sugar
¼ teaspoon salt
1 package active dry yeast
1 cup skim milk
2 tablespoons vegetable oil
2 tablespoons honey
1 egg
2 teaspoons almond extract
1½ tablespoons bread flour
Vegetable cooking spray
2 tablespoons honey
2 teaspoons skim milk
¼ cup sliced almonds, toasted

Combine 1 cup flour and next 3 ingredients in a large mixing bowl; stir well. Combine 1 cup milk, oil, and 2 tablespoons honey in a saucepan; cook over medium heat until very warm (120° to 130°).

Gradually add liquid mixture to flour mixture, beating well at low speed of an electric mixer. Beat an additional 2 minutes at medium speed. Add egg and extract, beating well. Gradually stir in enough of the remaining 2½ cups flour to make a soft dough.

Sprinkle 1½ tablespoons flour evenly over work surface. Turn dough out onto floured surface, and knead until smooth and elastic (about 10 minutes). Place dough in a large bowl coated with cooking spray, turning to coat top. Cover and let rise in a warm place (85°), free from drafts, 1 hour or until dough is doubled in bulk.

Punch dough down; turn out onto work surface, and knead lightly 4 or 5 times. Roll dough into a 32-inch rope. Form rope into a coil on a baking sheet coated with cooking spray.

Cover and let rise in a warm place, free from drafts, 20 to 25 minutes or until doubled in bulk. Bake at 350° for 25 minutes.

Combine 2 tablespoons honey and 2 teaspoons milk, stirring well. Remove loaf from oven. Brush half of honey mixture over loaf. Add almonds to remaining honey mixture; toss gently. Arrange almonds over loaf.

Return loaf to oven, and bake an additional 5 to 8 minutes or until loaf sounds hollow when tapped. Remove bread from baking sheet immediately, and let cool on a wire rack. Yield: 20 servings (136 calories per wedge).

Per Wedge:		
Protein 4.1g	Fat 2.7g	(Saturated Fat 0.5g)
Carbohydrate 23.6g	Fiber 1.0g	Cholesterol 11mg
Iron 1.2mg	Sodium 40mg	Calcium 24mg

Hickory chips are the secret element that gives Hickory-Grilled Amberjack with Grilled Salsa (page 112) a distinctive smoked flavor.

Fish & Shellfish

HICKORY-GRILLED AMBERJACK WITH GRILLED SALSA

It's important to soak the hickory chips in water before placing them on the grill; this keeps them from burning too quickly.

¼ cup balsamic vinegar
3 tablespoons water
1 teaspoon low-sodium Worcestershire sauce
½ teaspoon chicken-flavored bouillon granules
1 clove garlic, minced
6 (4-ounce) amberjack steaks (¾ inch thick)
Hickory chips
2 ears fresh corn in husks
1½ teaspoons reduced-calorie margarine, melted
1 teaspoon salt-free lemon-pepper seasoning
Vegetable cooking spray
2 small tomatoes
¼ cup chopped onion
1 tablespoon chopped fresh parsley
1 tablespoon balsamic vinegar
1 teaspoon olive oil
½ teaspoon sugar
¼ teaspoon salt
⅛ teaspoon freshly ground pepper
1 clove garlic, minced
Fresh parsley sprigs (optional)

Combine first 5 ingredients in a large heavy-duty, zip-top plastic bag. Add amberjack steaks. Seal bag, and shake gently until steaks are well coated. Marinate in refrigerator 30 minutes.

Soak hickory chips in water 30 minutes.

Carefully peel back husks from corn, leaving husks attached. Remove and discard silks. Brush with margarine, and sprinkle evenly with lemon-pepper seasoning. Return husks to original position, and tie tips with wire twist-ties.

Place hickory chips on medium-hot coals (350° to 400°). Coat grill rack with cooking spray; place on grill over coals. Place corn on rack; grill, covered, 30 minutes or until tender, turning every 5 minutes. Place tomatoes on rack; grill, covered, 5 minutes or until skins split and separate from tomatoes.

Remove steaks from marinade; discard marinade. Place steaks on rack over medium-hot coals; grill, covered, 4 to 6 minutes on each side or until fish flakes easily when tested with a fork. Set fish aside, and keep warm.

Remove husks from corn, and cut corn from cob. Peel tomatoes; seed and chop. Combine corn, tomato, onion, and next 7 ingredients in a medium bowl, stirring well. Transfer steaks to individual serving plates, and top evenly with salsa. Garnish with parsley sprigs, if desired. Yield: 6 servings (159 calories per serving).

Per Serving:		
Protein 22.0g	Fat 3.3g	(Saturated Fat 0.5g)
Carbohydrate 10.6g	Fiber 1.8g	Cholesterol 58mg
Iron 0.8mg	Sodium 225mg	Calcium 23mg

BAKED STRIPED BASS À LA CHESAPEAKE

In ½ teaspoon of Old Bay seasoning, there are only 272 milligrams of sodium compared with 1,172 milligrams of sodium in ½ teaspoon salt.

4 (4-ounce) striped bass steaks (¾ inch thick)
Vegetable cooking spray
2 tablespoons reduced-calorie mayonnaise
1 teaspoon white wine Worcestershire sauce
½ teaspoon Old Bay seasoning
½ teaspoon lemon juice

Place bass steaks in an 8-inch square baking dish coated with cooking spray. Combine mayonnaise and remaining ingredients, stirring well. Brush mayonnaise mixture evenly over steaks.

Bake, uncovered, at 450° for 8 to 10 minutes or until fish flakes easily when tested with a fork. Transfer to a serving platter. Yield: 4 servings (147 calories per serving).

Per Serving:		
Protein 20.7g	Fat 6.2g	(Saturated Fat 1.2g)
Carbohydrate 0.9g	Fiber 0.1g	Cholesterol 77mg
Iron 1.6mg	Sodium 213mg	Calcium 89mg

SPICY PAN-FRIED CATFISH

½ cup yellow cornmeal
1 teaspoon paprika
½ teaspoon pepper
¼ teaspoon salt
¼ teaspoon onion powder
¼ teaspoon ground celery seeds
¼ teaspoon dry mustard
4 (4-ounce) farm-raised catfish fillets
¼ cup skim milk
1 tablespoon vegetable oil

Combine first 7 ingredients. Dip fillets in milk; dredge in cornmeal mixture.

Heat oil in a nonstick skillet over medium-high heat until hot. Add fillets; cook 3 minutes on each side or until fish flakes easily when tested with a fork. Yield: 4 servings (234 calories per serving).

Per Serving:		
Protein 22.8g	Fat 8.7g	(Saturated Fat 1.8g)
Carbohydrate 14.8g	Fiber 1.1g	Cholesterol 66mg
Iron 2.1mg	Sodium 227mg	Calcium 71mg

FLOUNDER ROLLS WITH ROASTED RED PEPPER SAUCE

1 (10-ounce) package frozen chopped spinach, thawed
3 tablespoons grated Parmesan cheese
2 tablespoons minced onion
¼ teaspoon hot sauce
6 (4-ounce) flounder fillets (¼ inch thick)
Vegetable cooking spray
1 tablespoon reduced-calorie margarine, melted
1 clove garlic, crushed
Roasted Red Pepper Sauce

Drain spinach, and press between paper towels to remove excess moisture. Combine spinach and next 3 ingredients, stirring well.

Spoon spinach mixture evenly onto centers of fillets; roll up each fillet, jellyroll fashion, beginning at narrow end. Secure each with a wooden pick. Place rolls, seam side down, in an 11- x 7- x 1½-inch baking dish coated with cooking spray.

Combine margarine and garlic; brush evenly over rolls. Bake, uncovered, at 350° for 20 to 25 minutes or until fish flakes easily when tested with a fork.

Remove picks from rolls. Cut each roll into 4 slices. Spoon Roasted Red Pepper Sauce evenly onto individual serving plates. Arrange fish slices over sauce. Yield: 6 servings (160 calories per serving).

Roasted Red Pepper Sauce

2 medium-size sweet red peppers
2 tablespoons Chablis or other dry white wine
2 tablespoons low-fat sour cream
¼ teaspoon onion powder
¼ teaspoon salt

Cut peppers in half lengthwise; remove and discard seeds and membranes. Place peppers, skin side up, on a baking sheet; flatten with palm of hand. Broil peppers 5½ inches from heat (with electric oven door partially opened) 15 to 20 minutes or until charred. Place peppers in ice water until cool. Remove peppers from water; peel and discard skins. Coarsely chop peppers.

Place chopped pepper and wine in container of an electric blender; cover and process until smooth, stopping once to scrape down sides. Transfer pepper mixture to a small saucepan. Stir in sour cream, onion powder, and salt. Cook over medium heat until thoroughly heated, stirring frequently. Serve warm. Yield: 1 cup.

Per Serving:		
Protein 23.8g	Fat 4.4g	(Saturated Fat 1.4g)
Carbohydrate 6.5g	Fiber 2.7g	Cholesterol 62mg
Iron 2.2mg	Sodium 293mg	Calcium 114mg

In Grilled Grouper with Avocado Aïoli, high-fat avocado in the aïoli is balanced with nonfat mayonnaise.

GRILLED GROUPER WITH AVOCADO AÏOLI

¼ cup low-sodium soy sauce
1 teaspoon grated lemon rind
¼ cup fresh lemon juice
2 tablespoons water
¼ teaspoon chicken-flavored bouillon granules
2 cloves garlic, crushed
8 (4-ounce) grouper fillets
Vegetable cooking spray
Avocado Aïoli
24 (¼-inch-thick) slices avocado (about 2 medium)
8 (⅛-inch-thick) lemon slices, quartered
Fresh cilantro sprigs (optional)

Combine soy sauce, lemon rind, lemon juice, water, bouillon granules, and garlic in a large shallow dish. Place fillets in a single layer in dish, turning to coat. Cover and marinate in refrigerator 30 minutes, turning fillets once.

Remove fillets from marinade, reserving marinade. Coat grill rack with cooking spray; place rack on grill over medium-hot coals (350° to 400°). Place fillets on rack; grill, covered, 4 to 5 minutes on each side or until fish flakes easily when tested with a fork, basting fillets frequently with reserved marinade.

Transfer fillets to a serving platter, and top each fillet with 1 tablespoon Avocado Aïoli. Arrange avocado slices and lemon quarters evenly alongside fillets. Garnish with fresh cilantro sprigs, if desired. Yield: 8 servings (162 calories per serving).

Avocado Aïoli

¼ cup mashed ripe avocado (about 1 small)
1 tablespoon minced fresh cilantro
3 tablespoons nonfat mayonnaise
2 tablespoons lime juice
1 clove garlic, crushed

Combine all ingredients in container of an electric blender; cover and process until smooth, stopping once to scrape down sides. Yield: ½ cup.

Per Serving:

Protein 22.6g	Fat 5.9g	(Saturated Fat 1.0g)
Carbohydrate 4.2g	Fiber 0.7g	Cholesterol 41mg
Iron 1.4mg	Sodium 193mg	Calcium 25mg

ROASTED HALIBUT AND ONIONS

3 medium-size purple onions, sliced
1 tablespoon olive oil
2 teaspoons dried oregano
1 tablespoon balsamic vinegar
½ teaspoon sugar
¼ teaspoon salt
¼ teaspoon pepper
4 (4-ounce) halibut steaks (¾ inch thick)
Fresh oregano sprigs (optional)

Combine first 3 ingredients in a 13- x 9- x 2-inch baking dish; toss to coat. Bake, uncovered, at 400° for 35 minutes, stirring occasionally. Add vinegar and next 3 ingredients; stir well.

Add halibut steaks to onion mixture; spoon onion mixture evenly over each steak. Bake an additional 10 minutes or until fish flakes easily when tested with a fork.

Transfer steaks to a serving platter; top evenly with onion mixture. Garnish with fresh oregano sprigs, if desired. Yield: 4 servings (200 calories per serving).

Per Serving:

Protein 24.9g	Fat 6.2g	(Saturated Fat 0.9g)
Carbohydrate 10.3g	Fiber 2.1g	Cholesterol 53mg
Iron 1.6mg	Sodium 211mg	Calcium 90mg

SEASONED ORANGE ROUGHY IN POTATO CRUST

Frozen hash brown potato makes a crispy, low-fat coating for these seasoned fish fillets.

2⅔ cups frozen hash brown potato, thawed
¼ cup finely chopped onion
¼ cup frozen egg substitute, thawed
¼ teaspoon salt
¼ teaspoon pepper
Butter-flavored vegetable cooking spray
4 (4-ounce) orange roughy fillets
¼ teaspoon dried thyme
¼ teaspoon paprika
⅛ teaspoon salt
⅛ teaspoon garlic powder
⅛ teaspoon ground red pepper
1 tablespoon plus 1 teaspoon margarine, divided

Combine first 5 ingredients in a medium bowl. Coat 4 (12-inch) squares of aluminum foil with cooking spray. Place ⅓ cup potato mixture in center of each foil square, spreading to about ¼-inch thickness; top potato mixture with fillets. Set aside remaining potato mixture.

Combine thyme and next 4 ingredients. Sprinkle evenly over fillets.

Spoon remaining potato mixture evenly over fillets. Press mixture around fillets to seal. Fold foil over potato mixture, and freeze 1 hour or until potato mixture is firm.

Coat a large nonstick skillet with cooking spray; add 2 teaspoons margarine. Place over medium-high heat until margarine melts. Unwrap fillets, and place in skillet. Cook 7 minutes or until browned. Add remaining 2 teaspoons margarine. Turn fillets, and cook an additional 5 minutes or until browned and fish flakes easily when tested with a fork. Yield: 4 servings (181 calories per serving).

Per Serving:

Protein 19.3g	Fat 4.9g	(Saturated Fat 0.8g)
Carbohydrate 14.0g	Fiber 0.5g	Cholesterol 23mg
Iron 1.1mg	Sodium 365mg	Calcium 19mg

TILAPIA WITH CORIANDER SHRIMP SAUCE

Cooking shrimp in their shells enhances the flavor of this sauce. Half the shrimp are peeled and chopped to add to the sauce before serving.

⅔ cup canned no-salt-added chicken broth, undiluted
¼ cup clam juice
½ pound unpeeled small fresh shrimp
¼ cup dry sherry
1 teaspoon coriander seeds, crushed
⅛ teaspoon pepper
¼ cup water
2 tablespoons all-purpose flour
4 (4-ounce) tilapia fillets
Fresh cilantro sprigs (optional)

Bring chicken broth and clam juice to a boil in a small saucepan. Add shrimp, and cook 3 to 5 minutes or until shrimp turn pink. Remove shrimp from liquid using a slotted spoon; reserve liquid. Rinse shrimp with cold water.

Finely chop half of shrimp. (Do not remove shells.) Reserve remaining shrimp. Add finely chopped shrimp, sherry, coriander seeds, and pepper to reserved liquid. Bring to a boil; reduce heat, and simmer, uncovered, 15 minutes or until reduced to ¾ cup. Pour mixture through a wire-mesh strainer into a bowl, discarding solids. Return liquid to pan.

Peel, devein, and chop reserved shrimp; set aside.

Combine water and flour, stirring until smooth. Stir into liquid mixture. Cook, stirring constantly, until thickened and bubbly. Add peeled chopped shrimp; stir well.

Place fillets in a 13- x 9- x 2-inch baking dish; pour shrimp mixture over fillets. Bake, uncovered, at 450° for 10 minutes or until fish flakes easily when tested with a fork.

Transfer fillets to a serving platter; spoon sauce over fillets. Garnish with fresh cilantro sprigs, if desired. Yield: 4 servings (156 calories per serving).

Per Serving:

Protein 26.2g	Fat 3.5g	(Saturated Fat 0.6g)
Carbohydrate 3.7g	Fiber 0.2g	Cholesterol 112mg
Iron 1.9mg	Sodium 146mg	Calcium 86mg

TILAPIA WITH SAFFRON TOMATO SAUCE

2 teaspoons olive oil
¼ cup finely chopped onion
2 cloves garlic, minced
2 cups peeled, seeded, and diced tomato
½ cup unsweetened orange juice
¼ cup Chablis or other dry white wine
¼ teaspoon dried basil
¼ teaspoon dried oregano
¼ teaspoon salt
¼ teaspoon pepper
⅛ teaspoon saffron threads
4 (4-ounce) tilapia fillets
Vegetable cooking spray
2 teaspoons lemon juice

Heat olive oil in a large nonstick skillet over medium heat until hot. Add onion and garlic; sauté until tender. Add tomato and next 7 ingredients; simmer, uncovered, 15 minutes, stirring occasionally.

Place fillets in an 11- x 7- x 1½-inch baking dish coated with cooking spray. Sprinkle with lemon juice; top with tomato mixture. Cover and bake at 450° for 8 minutes or until fish flakes easily when tested with a fork. Yield: 4 servings (184 calories per serving).

Per Serving:

Protein 22.3g	Fat 5.5g	(Saturated Fat 0.9g)
Carbohydrate 9.6g	Fiber 1.6g	Cholesterol 80mg
Iron 1.7mg	Sodium 216mg	Calcium 86mg

TWO THUMBS UP FOR TILAPIA

Tilapia (pronounced ta-LAH-pee-a) is a mild, freshwater fish that recently has made a big splash in the American market, and rightly so. It's low in calories, cholesterol, fat, and sodium, yet rich in protein and essential vitamins and minerals. In addition, tilapia's mild, slightly sweet flavor even appeals to people who don't normally like fish. It has no fishy taste or smell.

Tilapia is sold in 4-ounce and 6-ounce boned, skinned fillets that can be poached, baked, broiled, or sautéed. The fillets are even firm enough to grill.

Broiling instead of frying makes Trout Amandine a healthy, tasty dish. The light seasoning brings on a flood of flavor.

TROUT AMANDINE

¼ cup reduced-calorie margarine
1 tablespoon chopped onion
1 tablespoon lemon juice
¼ cup sliced almonds, lightly toasted
1 tablespoon chopped fresh parsley
4 (4-ounce) rainbow trout fillets
¼ teaspoon salt
⅛ teaspoon pepper
⅛ teaspoon ground red pepper
2 teaspoons lemon juice
Lemon slices (optional)

Combine margarine, chopped onion, and 1 tablespoon lemon juice in a saucepan; cook over medium heat 5 minutes or until margarine melts and onion is tender, stirring occasionally. Stir in toasted almond slices and chopped fresh parsley. Set aside, and keep warm.

Line an 11- x 7- x 1½-inch baking dish with aluminum foil. Place fillets in dish; sprinkle with salt, pepper, ground red pepper, and 2 teaspoons lemon juice. Broil 5½ inches from heat (with electric oven door partially opened) 8 minutes or until fish flakes easily when tested with a fork. Transfer fillets to individual serving plates.

Top fillets with almond mixture. Garnish with lemon slices, if desired. Yield: 4 servings (207 calories per serving).

Per Serving:

Protein 24.1g	Fat 11.6g	(Saturated Fat 1.7g)
Carbohydrate 1.7g	Fiber 0.6g	Cholesterol 64mg
Iron 2.4mg	Sodium 260mg	Calcium 91mg

GRILLED TUNA IN RASPBERRY VINEGAR

Raspberry vinegar adds a pungent flavor to these tuna steaks. But beware—marinating the steaks for more than an hour in the acidic vinegar and lemon juice mixture will "cook" the tuna, resulting in mushy, dry steaks.

¾ cup raspberry vinegar
3 tablespoons fresh lime juice
1 tablespoon vegetable oil
⅛ teaspoon crushed red pepper
2 fresh rosemary sprigs
6 (4-ounce) tuna steaks (1 inch thick)
Vegetable cooking spray
Fresh rosemary sprigs (optional)
Fresh raspberries (optional)

Combine first 5 ingredients in a heavy-duty, zip-top plastic bag. Add tuna steaks. Seal bag; shake gently. Marinate in refrigerator 1 hour, turning once.

Remove steaks from marinade; discard marinade. Coat grill rack with cooking spray; place on grill over medium-hot coals (350° to 400°). Place steaks on rack; grill, uncovered, 4 minutes on each side or until fish flakes easily when tested with a fork. Transfer steaks to a serving platter.

If desired, garnish steaks with rosemary sprigs and fresh raspberries. Yield: 6 servings (166 calories per serving).

Per Serving:

Protein 26.4g	Fat 5.9g	(Saturated Fat 1.5g)
Carbohydrate 0.4g	Fiber 0g	Cholesterol 43mg
Iron 1.2mg	Sodium 44mg	Calcium 0mg

GRILLED TUNA WITH TOMATO SAUCE

For quick accompaniments to this hearty main dish, serve a crisp green salad from your supermarket's salad bar and commercial dinner rolls.

3 tablespoons white vinegar
1½ tablespoons fresh lime juice
1 tablespoon vegetable oil
1 tablespoon low-sodium soy sauce
8 (4-ounce) tuna steaks (1 inch thick)
1 tablespoon reduced-calorie margarine
¼ cup chopped green onions
2 tablespoons chopped onion
2 small cloves garlic, minced
3 (14½-ounce) cans no-salt-added whole tomatoes, undrained and chopped
1½ teaspoons dried oregano
1½ teaspoons dried basil
⅛ teaspoon freshly ground pepper
1 small bay leaf
Vegetable cooking spray
4 cups cooked fettuccine (cooked without salt or fat)

Combine first 4 ingredients in a heavy-duty, zip-top plastic bag. Add tuna steaks. Seal bag, and shake gently until steaks are well coated. Marinate in refrigerator up to 3 hours, turning bag occasionally.

Melt margarine in a large saucepan over medium-high heat; add onions and garlic. Sauté until tender. Add tomato and next 4 ingredients; bring to a boil. Reduce heat, and simmer 30 minutes. Remove and discard bay leaf.

Remove steaks from marinade, discarding marinade. Coat grill rack with cooking spray; place on grill over medium-hot coals (350° to 400°). Place steaks on rack; grill, covered, 3 minutes on each side or until fish flakes easily when tested with a fork.

Place ½ cup pasta on each individual serving plate; spoon sauce evenly over pasta. Top each serving with a tuna steak. Serve immediately. Yield: 8 servings (308 calories per serving).

Per Serving:

Protein 30.2g	Fat 8.0g	(Saturated Fat 1.8g)
Carbohydrate 28.1g	Fiber 2.4g	Cholesterol 42mg
Iron 3.0mg	Sodium 110mg	Calcium 68mg

Garnish Seafood Kabobs, a modern version of the traditional seafood platter, with fresh lime slices.

SEAFOOD KABOBS

½ pound unpeeled medium-size fresh shrimp
½ pound amberjack steaks, cut into 8 pieces
½ pound sea scallops
¼ cup white wine vinegar
2 tablespoons minced green onions
2 tablespoons lime juice
1 tablespoon olive oil
1 tablespoon Dijon mustard
¼ teaspoon pepper
⅛ teaspoon salt
1 (3-pound) spaghetti squash
2 tablespoons chopped fresh parsley
1 tablespoon reduced-calorie margarine
¼ teaspoon garlic powder
¼ teaspoon salt
¼ teaspoon pepper
8 large fresh mushroom caps
1 medium zucchini, cut into ½-inch-thick slices
1 small sweet red pepper, seeded and cut into 1-inch pieces
1 medium onion, cut into 1-inch pieces
Vegetable cooking spray

Peel and devein shrimp; leave tails intact. Place shrimp, amberjack, and scallops in a shallow dish. Combine vinegar and next 6 ingredients; pour over seafood. Cover and marinate in refrigerator 1 hour.

Wash squash. Cut in half lengthwise; discard seeds. Place squash, cut side down, in a Dutch oven; add water to Dutch oven to depth of 2 inches. Bring to a boil; cover, reduce heat, and simmer 20 minutes or until tender. Drain. Using a fork, remove strands from squash; discard shells. Combine strands, parsley, and next 4 ingredients; keep warm.

Remove seafood from marinade; reserve marinade. Thread seafood and vegetables on 4 (16-inch) skewers. Coat grill rack with cooking spray; place on grill over medium-hot coals (350° to 400°). Place kabobs on rack; grill, uncovered, 6 minutes on each side or until fish flakes easily when tested with a fork, basting frequently with marinade. Serve over squash mixture. Yield: 4 servings (283 calories per serving).

Per Serving:

Protein 31.5g	Fat 8.0g	(Saturated Fat 1.2g)
Carbohydrate 21.4g	Fiber 4.3g	Cholesterol 120mg
Iron 3.3mg	Sodium 619mg	Calcium 99mg

SEAFOOD ENCHILADAS

1 pound unpeeled small fresh shrimp
4 cups water
¼ cup reduced-calorie margarine
¼ cup all-purpose flour
1 (10½-ounce) can low-sodium chicken broth
½ cup water
1 cup low-fat sour cream
1 jalapeño pepper, seeded and minced
⅛ teaspoon salt
Vegetable cooking spray
1 cup nonfat cottage cheese
½ pound fresh lump crabmeat, drained
1 (4½-ounce) can chopped green chiles
½ cup (2 ounces) shredded reduced-fat Monterey Jack cheese
10 (6-inch) white corn tortillas
Salsa Cruda
Fresh cilantro sprigs (optional)

Peel and devein shrimp; set aside.

Bring 4 cups water to a boil in a large saucepan; add shrimp, and cook 3 to 5 minutes or until shrimp turn pink. Drain well, and set aside.

Melt margarine in a small saucepan over low heat; add flour, stirring until smooth. Cook, stirring constantly, 1 minute. Gradually add broth and ½ cup water; cook over medium heat, stirring constantly, until mixture is slightly thickened and bubbly. Remove from heat, and let stand 5 minutes.

Gently stir in sour cream, jalapeño pepper, and salt. Pour ¾ cup sauce in bottom of a 13- x 9- x 2-inch baking dish coated with cooking spray. Set remaining sauce aside.

Place cottage cheese in container of an electric blender; cover and process until smooth, stopping once to scrape down sides. Transfer to a medium bowl. Stir in shrimp, crabmeat, chiles, and Monterey Jack cheese.

Spoon ⅓ cup seafood mixture across center of each tortilla. Roll up tortillas; place, seam side down, over sauce in dish. Pour remaining sauce over tortillas. Bake at 350° for 25 minutes or until thoroughly heated. Spoon Salsa Cruda across center of tortillas. Garnish with fresh cilantro sprigs, if desired. Yield: 10 servings (213 calories per serving).

Salsa Cruda

1 cup peeled, seeded, and chopped tomato
½ cup chopped onion
¼ cup no-salt-added tomato juice
2 tablespoons chopped fresh cilantro
⅛ teaspoon salt
1 small jalapeño pepper, seeded and minced

Combine all ingredients in a small bowl, stirring well. Yield: 1½ cups.

Per Serving:

Protein 17.4g	Fat 8.5g	(Saturated Fat 3.0g)
Carbohydrate 17.9g	Fiber 1.9g	Cholesterol 85mg
Iron 1.9mg	Sodium 456mg	Calcium 160mg

MARYLAND SILVER QUEEN CRAB CAKES

If Silver Queen corn isn't available, you may substitute regular white corn.

1¼ cups fresh Silver Queen corn cut from the cob (about 2 ears)
1 egg white
1 pound fresh lump crabmeat, drained
¼ cup plus 2 tablespoons fine, dry breadcrumbs
1 tablespoon dried parsley
1 tablespoon low-sodium Worcestershire sauce
1 teaspoon Dijon mustard
¼ teaspoon Old Bay seasoning
Vegetable cooking spray

Position knife blade in food processor bowl; add corn. Process 8 seconds, scraping sides of processor bowl once. Add egg white; process 2 seconds. Transfer mixture to a bowl; stir in crabmeat and next 5 ingredients. Cover; chill at least 30 minutes.

Shape mixture into 6 patties. Place on a baking sheet coated with cooking spray. Broil 5½ inches from heat (with electric oven door partially opened) 10 minutes on each side or until golden. Yield: 6 servings (137 calories per serving).

Per Serving:

Protein 16.7g	Fat 2.1g	(Saturated Fat 0.3g)
Carbohydrate 13.0g	Fiber 1.4g	Cholesterol 71mg
Iron 1.2mg	Sodium 316mg	Calcium 83mg

LOBSTER RAVIOLI WITH SHRIMP SAUCE

1 cup all-purpose flour
1 egg white
2 tablespoons hot water
2 (8-ounce) fresh or frozen lobster tails, thawed
2 teaspoons vegetable oil
1 tablespoon minced shallots
¼ pound bay scallops
2 tablespoons skim milk
1 egg white
⅛ teaspoon dry mustard
Dash of ground red pepper
4 quarts water
Shrimp Sauce
1 tablespoon chopped fresh parsley

Position knife blade in food processor bowl; add flour and 1 egg white. Process 1 minute or until combined. Slowly add 2 tablespoons hot water through food chute with processor running; process 2 minutes or until dough is smooth and elastic. Remove dough from processor, and shape into a ball. Wrap dough in plastic wrap, and let stand 30 minutes.

Cook lobster tails in boiling water 4 to 6 minutes or until done; drain. Rinse with cold water. Split and clean tails. Reserve shells for sauce. Chop lobster meat, and set aside.

Heat oil in a small nonstick skillet over medium-high heat until hot. Add shallots, and sauté until tender. Set aside.

Position knife blade in processor bowl; add scallops. Process 10 seconds or until smooth. Add sautéed shallots, milk, 1 egg white, dry mustard, and red pepper; process 1 minute or until smooth. Transfer to a bowl, and stir in chopped lobster. Set aside.

Divide dough into fourths. Working with 1 portion at a time (keeping unused portions covered), pass dough through pasta machine, starting at widest setting. Continue moving width gauge to narrower settings, passing dough through twice at each setting until dough is about 1/16 inch thick, 4 inches wide, and 24 inches long.

Place 1 strip of dough in a ravioli form, pressing gently to make an indentation in each square. Place 1 tablespoon lobster mixture in each indentation. Moisten with water around filling; top with another strip of dough. Using a rolling pin, roll across top of ravioli form, cutting into 12 squares. Repeat procedure with remaining 2 strips of dough and filling. Let ravioli dry on a towel 30 minutes, turning once.

Bring 4 quarts water to a boil in a Dutch oven. Add ravioli, and cook 4 minutes. Drain. Place 4 ravioli on each individual serving plate. Spoon Shrimp Sauce evenly over ravioli. Sprinkle evenly with parsley. Yield: 6 servings (190 calories per serving).

Shrimp Sauce

¼ pound unpeeled small fresh shrimp
2 (8-ounce) lobster tail shells (meat removed)
½ cup canned low-sodium chicken broth, undiluted
¼ cup dry sherry
¼ cup clam juice
1 clove garlic, crushed
2 tablespoons reduced-calorie margarine
2 tablespoons all-purpose flour

Finely chop shrimp. (Do not remove shells.) Combine shrimp, lobster shells, and next 4 ingredients in a saucepan. Bring to a boil; reduce heat, and simmer, uncovered, 10 minutes or until liquid is reduced to ¾ cup. Pour mixture through a large wire-mesh strainer into a bowl, discarding solids.

Melt margarine in a small saucepan over medium heat. Add flour. Cook, stirring constantly, until flour mixture is caramel-colored (about 4 minutes). Add strained liquid; cook, stirring constantly, until thickened. Yield: ⅔ cup.

Per Serving:

Protein 15.4g	Fat 4.7g	(Saturated Fat 0.7g)
Carbohydrate 20.7g	Fiber 0.7g	Cholesterol 35mg
Iron 1.5mg	Sodium 267mg	Calcium 44mg

SCALLOPS PESTO

3 tablespoons chopped fresh basil
1 tablespoon chopped fresh parsley
1 teaspoon pine nuts
¼ teaspoon salt
1 large clove garlic
2 teaspoons olive oil
1 cup canned no-salt-added chicken broth, undiluted
1 pound sea scallops
2 tablespoons all-purpose flour
3 tablespoons water
5 ounces fettuccine, uncooked
Fresh basil sprigs (optional)
Fresh parsley sprigs (optional)

Combine first 5 ingredients in a coffee grinder or miniature food processor; process until finely chopped. Add olive oil; process until smooth.

Bring broth to a boil in a large nonstick skillet. Reduce heat, and add scallops; cover and simmer 4 minutes or until scallops are opaque. Remove scallops from broth; set aside. Cook broth, uncovered, over medium heat until reduced to ½ cup.

Combine flour and water, stirring well. Add to broth, stirring well. Cook over medium heat, stirring constantly, until thickened. Stir in herb mixture and scallops; cook until thoroughly heated.

Cook pasta according to package directions, omitting salt and fat; drain. Combine pasta and scallop mixture in a serving bowl; toss gently. If desired, garnish with fresh basil sprigs and fresh parsley sprigs. Serve immediately. Yield: 4 servings (285 calories per serving).

Per Serving:		
Protein 24.8g	Fat 5.3g	(Saturated Fat 0.7g)
Carbohydrate 32.9g	Fiber 1.1g	Cholesterol 37mg
Iron 2.0mg	Sodium 367mg	Calcium 41mg

APRICOT-GINGER SHRIMP STIR-FRY

1½ pounds unpeeled large fresh shrimp
Vegetable cooking spray
1 tablespoon sesame oil
1 cup diagonally sliced carrot
2 teaspoons peeled, minced gingerroot
1 clove garlic, minced
1 cup julienne-sliced green pepper
1 cup julienne-sliced sweet red pepper
1 (8-ounce) can pineapple tidbits in juice
¼ cup no-sugar-added apricot spread
1½ tablespoons low-sodium soy sauce
2 teaspoons cornstarch
½ teaspoon dried crushed red pepper
⅛ teaspoon salt
2½ cups cooked long-grain rice (cooked without salt or fat)

Peel and devein shrimp; set aside.

Coat a wok or large nonstick skillet with cooking spray; drizzle oil around top of wok, coating sides. Heat at medium-high (375°) until hot. Add carrot, gingerroot, and minced garlic; stir-fry 2 minutes. Add julienne-sliced peppers, and stir-fry 2 minutes. Add shrimp, and stir-fry 4 minutes or until shrimp turn pink.

Drain pineapple, reserving juice. Add pineapple to shrimp mixture; stir-fry 30 seconds.

Combine pineapple juice, apricot spread, and next 4 ingredients, stirring well. Add juice mixture to shrimp mixture; stir-fry 1 minute or until thickened. Serve over rice. Yield: 5 servings (334 calories per serving).

Per Serving:		
Protein 23.5g	Fat 5.0g	(Saturated Fat 0.8g)
Carbohydrate 47.0g	Fiber 2.1g	Cholesterol 155mg
Iron 4.2mg	Sodium 335mg	Calcium 81mg

A variety of vegetables makes easy-to-prepare Oriental Wild Rice (page 127) a healthy addition to a meal. The wild rice provides an unusual, hearty base for this typical oriental dish.

Grains & Pastas

VEGETABLE-BARLEY CASSEROLE

Barley is a good source of fiber. Serve it as a side dish, or stir it into soups, stews, and casseroles.

1 tablespoon reduced-calorie margarine
1½ cups sliced fresh mushrooms
¾ cup pearl barley, uncooked
⅓ cup chopped onion
2 tablespoons chopped fresh parsley
1 cup thinly sliced zucchini, halved
½ cup shredded carrot
1 (13¾-ounce) can no-salt-added beef broth
½ teaspoon pepper
¼ teaspoon salt

Melt margarine in a nonstick skillet over medium-high heat. Add mushrooms and next 3 ingredients; sauté 5 minutes or until barley is lightly browned. Place barley mixture, zucchini, and carrot in a 1½-quart casserole.

Bring broth to a boil in a saucepan; pour hot broth over barley mixture, stirring gently. Stir in pepper and salt. Cover and bake at 350° for 45 minutes or until barley is tender and liquid is absorbed. Yield: 8 servings (99 calories per ½-cup serving).

Per Serving:		
Protein 2.9g	Fat 1.3g	(Saturated Fat 0.2g)
Carbohydrate 19.4g	Fiber 4.0g	Cholesterol 0mg
Iron 0.9mg	Sodium 95mg	Calcium 14mg

COUSCOUS WITH VEGETABLES

¾ cup water
¼ teaspoon salt
½ cup couscous, uncooked
10 ounces fresh asparagus
2 teaspoons olive oil
½ cup sliced fresh mushrooms
½ cup finely chopped green onions
⅓ cup chopped sweet red pepper
2 tablespoons chopped fresh parsley
2 tablespoons Chablis or other dry white wine
½ teaspoon dried basil
1 clove garlic, minced
⅓ cup freshly grated Parmesan cheese

Combine water and salt in a small saucepan; bring to a boil. Remove from heat. Add couscous; cover and let stand 5 minutes or until couscous is tender and liquid is absorbed.

Snap off tough ends of asparagus. Remove scales from stalks with a knife or vegetable peeler, if desired. Cut asparagus into 1-inch pieces.

Heat oil in a large nonstick skillet over medium-high heat until hot. Add asparagus, mushrooms, and next 6 ingredients. Sauté 6 minutes or until vegetables are tender.

Fluff couscous with a fork. Add vegetable mixture and cheese; toss gently. Yield: 6 servings (108 calories per ½-cup serving).

Per Serving:		
Protein 5.4g	Fat 3.3g	(Saturated Fat 1.3g)
Carbohydrate 14.9g	Fiber 1.4g	Cholesterol 4mg
Iron 1.0mg	Sodium 203mg	Calcium 98mg

SOUTHERN GRITS

1 (10-ounce) package frozen black-eyed peas
1 (14½-ounce) can no-salt-added stewed tomatoes, drained and chopped
1 cup cubed lean cooked ham
⅛ teaspoon ground red pepper
1 clove garlic, minced
2 cups water
¼ teaspoon salt
½ cup quick-cooking grits, uncooked

Cook peas according to package directions, omitting salt; drain well. Return peas to saucepan; add tomato, ham, red pepper, and garlic. Cook, uncovered, over medium-low heat until thoroughly heated. Set aside, and keep warm.

Combine water and salt in a medium saucepan; bring to a boil. Stir in grits; cover, reduce heat, and simmer 5 minutes or until grits are thickened, stirring frequently. Add pea mixture to grits; stir well. Serve immediately. Yield: 9 servings (108 calories per ½-cup serving).

Per Serving:		
Protein 7.4g	Fat 1.1g	(Saturated Fat 0.4g)
Carbohydrate 17.7g	Fiber 1.1g	Cholesterol 11mg
Iron 1.5mg	Sodium 318mg	Calcium 24mg

HINT-OF-SPICE RICE

1½ cups canned low-sodium chicken broth, undiluted
¾ cup long-grain brown rice, uncooked
1 teaspoon grated orange rind
¼ teaspoon salt
¼ teaspoon ground ginger
¼ teaspoon ground cinnamon
1 medium-size orange, peeled and sectioned
¼ cup sliced almonds, toasted

Combine first 6 ingredients in a large saucepan; bring to a boil. Cover, reduce heat, and simmer 30 minutes or until rice is tender and liquid is absorbed. Gently stir in orange sections and almonds. Yield: 5 servings (143 calories per ½-cup serving).

Per Serving:		
Protein 3.9g	Fat 3.5g	(Saturated Fat 0.5g)
Carbohydrate 24.6g	Fiber 2.0g	Cholesterol 0mg
Iron 1.0mg	Sodium 143mg	Calcium 25mg

TROPICAL RICE

1 (15¼-ounce) can pineapple tidbits in juice, undrained
1½ cups water
1 cup long-grain brown rice, uncooked
¾ cup julienne-sliced carrot
½ cup chopped green pepper
⅓ cup mango nectar
¼ cup unsalted sunflower kernels, toasted
2 tablespoons chopped fresh parsley
¼ teaspoon salt

Drain pineapple, reserving juice. Combine juice, water, and next 4 ingredients in a saucepan. Bring to a boil; cover, reduce heat, and simmer 45 minutes or until rice is tender and liquid is absorbed.

Stir in pineapple, sunflower kernels, parsley, and salt. Serve warm. Yield: 10 servings (131 calories per ½-cup serving).

Per Serving:		
Protein 2.6g	Fat 2.7g	(Saturated Fat 0.3g)
Carbohydrate 24.7g	Fiber 1.8g	Cholesterol 0mg
Iron 0.9mg	Sodium 68mg	Calcium 14mg

MUSHROOM RISOTTO

Arborio rice is a short-grained, starchy rice that develops a distinctive creamy consistency as it cooks, making it the perfect rice for risottos.

1 (13¾-ounce) can no-salt-added chicken broth
1½ cups water
2 teaspoons olive oil
1½ cups sliced fresh mushrooms
¾ cup chopped sweet red pepper
½ cup chopped leeks
2 teaspoons chopped fresh basil
1 clove garlic, minced
1 cup Arborio rice, uncooked
½ cup freshly grated Parmesan cheese
¼ teaspoon salt

Combine broth and water in a saucepan; place over medium heat. Cover and bring to a simmer; reduce heat to low, and keep warm. (Do not boil.)

Heat oil in a medium saucepan over medium-high heat until hot. Add mushrooms and next 4 ingredients; sauté 3 minutes or until tender. Stir in rice; cook, stirring constantly, 2 minutes. Reduce heat to medium-low.

Add 1 cup of simmering broth mixture to rice mixture, stirring constantly until most of liquid is absorbed. Add remaining broth, ½ cup at a time, cooking and stirring constantly until each ½ cup addition is absorbed (about 40 minutes). (Rice will be tender and will have a creamy consistency.) Stir in Parmesan cheese and salt; serve immediately. Yield: 9 servings (127 calories per ½-cup serving).

Per Serving:		
Protein 4.5g	Fat 3.2g	(Saturated Fat 1.2g)
Carbohydrate 19.4g	Fiber 0.7g	Cholesterol 4mg
Iron 1.4mg	Sodium 192mg	Calcium 82mg

Rice with Black Beans and Corn would complement a meal of grilled chicken, mixed green salad, and fresh fruit.

RICE WITH BLACK BEANS AND CORN

1 cup water
½ cup long-grain rice, uncooked
1 cup chopped plum tomato
1 (4½-ounce) can chopped green chiles, drained
1 (15-ounce) can black beans, drained
1 (10-ounce) package frozen whole-kernel corn, thawed
⅓ cup chopped green onions
2 tablespoons chopped fresh cilantro

Bring 1 cup water to a boil in a medium saucepan; stir in long-grain rice. Cover, reduce heat, and simmer 20 minutes or until rice is tender and liquid is absorbed.

Stir in plum tomato, chopped green chiles, black beans, corn, chopped green onions, and chopped fresh cilantro.

Cook over medium heat, stirring constantly, until mixture is thoroughly heated. Yield: 10 servings (100 calories per ½-cup serving).

Per Serving:

Protein 4.1g	Fat 0.5g	(Saturated Fat 0.1g)
Carbohydrate 21.0g	Fiber 2.3g	Cholesterol 0mg
Iron 1.3mg	Sodium 102mg	Calcium 15mg

ITALIAN RICE

1½ cups water
¾ cup long-grain rice, uncooked
1 tablespoon olive oil
1 (9-ounce) package frozen artichoke hearts, thawed and coarsely chopped
⅔ cup sweet red pepper strips
½ cup frozen English peas, thawed
½ cup sliced green onions
1 clove garlic, minced
3 tablespoons commercial oil-free Italian dressing
1 teaspoon dried Italian seasoning

Bring 1½ cups water to a boil in a medium saucepan; stir in long-grain rice. Cover, reduce heat, and simmer 20 minutes or until rice is tender and liquid is absorbed.

Heat olive oil in a large nonstick skillet over medium heat until hot. Add chopped artichoke hearts, red pepper strips, English peas, green onions, and minced garlic. Sauté 5 minutes or until vegetables are crisp-tender.

Combine rice, sautéed vegetables, Italian dressing, and Italian seasoning; toss gently. Yield: 10 servings (85 calories per ½-cup serving).

Per Serving:

Protein 2.3g	Fat 1.7g	(Saturated Fat 0.3g)
Carbohydrate 15.6g	Fiber 1.0g	Cholesterol 0mg
Iron 1.2mg	Sodium 70mg	Calcium 19mg

MEXICAN RICE

Cooking the rice mixture in beef broth instead of water adds flavor without adding fat.

1 cup long-grain rice, uncooked
¾ cup chopped sun-dried tomato
½ cup chopped sweet red pepper
¼ cup chopped green onions
1 (4½-ounce) can chopped green chiles
2 teaspoons cumin seeds
1 clove garlic, minced
Vegetable cooking spray
2½ cups canned no-salt-added beef broth, undiluted

Combine first 7 ingredients in a 2-quart casserole coated with cooking spray. Bring broth to a boil in a medium saucepan. Pour broth over rice mixture. Cover and bake at 350° for 40 minutes or until rice is tender and liquid is absorbed. Yield: 9 servings (108 calories per ½-cup serving).

Per Serving:

Protein 2.9g	Fat 0.6g	(Saturated Fat 0.1g)
Carbohydrate 22.5g	Fiber 1.7g	Cholesterol 0mg
Iron 2.0mg	Sodium 202mg	Calcium 24mg

ORIENTAL WILD RICE

Uncooked wild rice will keep indefinitely if stored in a cool, dry place. (Recipe pictured on page 123.)

2½ cups water
1 cup wild rice, uncooked
Vegetable cooking spray
1 tablespoon dark sesame oil
2 cups broccoli flowerets
1 cup fresh bean sprouts
⅔ cup diagonally sliced carrot
1 small sweet red pepper, seeded and cut into 1-inch pieces
4 green onions, cut into 1-inch pieces
1 tablespoon sesame seeds
1 teaspoon peeled, minced gingerroot
2 teaspoons low-sodium soy sauce

Combine water and rice in a medium saucepan; bring to a boil. Cover, reduce heat, and simmer 40 minutes or until rice is tender. Drain and set aside.

Coat a wok or large nonstick skillet with cooking spray; drizzle oil around top of wok, coating sides. Heat at medium-high (375°) until hot. Add broccoli and remaining ingredients; stir-fry 3 minutes. Cover wok, and allow vegetables to steam 5 to 7 minutes or until crisp-tender. Add rice, and stir-fry until mixture is thoroughly heated. Serve immediately. Yield: 6 servings (137 calories per 1-cup serving).

Per Serving:

Protein 5.3g	Fat 2.9g	(Saturated Fat 0.4g)
Carbohydrate 24.1g	Fiber 2.8g	Cholesterol 0mg
Iron 1.1mg	Sodium 57mg	Calcium 28mg

FARFALLE WITH TOMATO VINAIGRETTE

Farfalle pasta is shaped like small bow ties. If it's unavailable, use any small shaped pasta.

1 cup seeded, chopped plum tomato
⅓ cup red wine vinegar
2 tablespoons water
1 tablespoon olive oil
½ teaspoon sugar
½ teaspoon freshly ground pepper
¼ teaspoon salt
⅛ teaspoon onion powder
1 clove garlic, crushed
6 ounces farfalle pasta, uncooked
½ cup coarsely chopped fresh basil
⅓ cup crumbled feta cheese with basil and tomato

Combine first 9 ingredients in a small bowl.

Cook pasta according to package directions, omitting salt and fat; drain well. Place pasta in a serving bowl. Add tomato mixture, basil, and feta cheese; toss gently. Serve immediately. Yield: 8 servings (121 calories per ½-cup serving).

Per Serving:

Protein 4.0g	Fat 3.6g	(Saturated Fat 1.4g)
Carbohydrate 18.1g	Fiber 1.0g	Cholesterol 6mg
Iron 1.4mg	Sodium 156mg	Calcium 46mg

SUN-DRIED TOMATO PESTO AND LINGUINE

20 sun-dried tomatoes
1½ cups boiling water
½ cup grated Parmesan cheese
½ cup tightly packed fresh parsley sprigs
¼ cup plus 2 tablespoons slivered almonds, toasted
¼ cup chopped fresh basil
2 teaspoons olive oil
⅛ teaspoon salt
6 cloves garlic
1 pound fresh spinach
Vegetable cooking spray
11 ounces linguine, uncooked
Fresh basil sprigs (optional)

Combine tomatoes and boiling water in a small bowl; let stand 5 minutes. Drain, reserving 1 cup liquid.

Position knife blade in food processor bowl; add tomatoes, reserved 1 cup liquid, cheese, and next 6 ingredients. Process until smooth.

Remove and discard stems from spinach; wash leaves thoroughly, and pat dry. Shred spinach.

Coat a large Dutch oven with cooking spray; place over medium heat until hot. Add spinach; cover and cook until spinach wilts, stirring occasionally. Remove from heat, and set aside.

Cook pasta according to package directions, omitting salt and fat; drain well. Combine tomato mixture and pasta; toss gently. Add cooked spinach; toss well. Garnish with basil sprigs, if desired. Yield: 8 servings (229 calories per 1-cup serving).

Per Serving:

Protein 9.6g	Fat 6.3g	(Saturated Fat 1.5g)
Carbohydrate 34.2g	Fiber 3.3g	Cholesterol 4mg
Iron 2.8mg	Sodium 230mg	Calcium 130mg

MACARONI-AND-CHEESE CASSEROLE

6 ounces elbow macaroni, uncooked
Vegetable cooking spray
1 teaspoon vegetable oil
1 cup chopped onion
1 cup chopped green pepper
1 cup (4 ounces) shredded reduced-fat Cheddar cheese
1 cup nonfat mayonnaise
¼ teaspoon pepper
1 (10¾-ounce) can low-fat, one-third-less-salt cream of celery soup, undiluted
1 (4-ounce) can sliced mushrooms, drained
1 (2-ounce) jar diced pimiento, undrained
1 cup corn flakes cereal, crushed

Cook macaroni according to package directions, omitting salt and fat; drain. Place in a large bowl, and set aside.

Coat a large nonstick skillet with cooking spray; add oil. Place over medium heat until hot. Add onion and green pepper; sauté until tender.

Add sautéed vegetables, cheese, and next 5 ingredients to macaroni; stir well. Spoon mixture into a 2-quart casserole coated with cooking spray. Sprinkle crushed cereal over macaroni mixture. Bake, uncovered, at 350° for 40 minutes or until thoroughly heated. Yield: 12 servings (129 calories per serving).

Per Serving:		
Protein 5.3g	Fat 3.0g	(Saturated Fat 1.5g)
Carbohydrate 20.3g	Fiber 1.0g	Cholesterol 7mg
Iron 1.0mg	Sodium 469mg	Calcium 102mg

GARDEN ORZO

Orzo is a small rice-shaped pasta that's not much larger than a pine nut. For a change, cook orzo rather than rice for dinner.

½ pound fresh asparagus
1½ quarts water
1 cup orzo, uncooked
Vegetable cooking spray
1 teaspoon olive oil
¾ cup sliced carrot
1 clove garlic, minced
1 cup sliced fresh mushrooms
¼ cup water
½ teaspoon chicken-flavored bouillon granules
½ teaspoon grated lemon rind
¼ teaspoon salt
¼ teaspoon pepper
¼ cup grated Asiago cheese
Lemon slices (optional)

Snap off tough ends of asparagus. Remove scales from stalks with a knife or vegetable peeler, if desired. Cut asparagus into 1-inch pieces; set aside.

Bring 1½ quarts water to a boil in a large saucepan. Add orzo, and cook 5 minutes. Add asparagus, and cook an additional 4 minutes or until orzo is tender; drain well. Place orzo and asparagus in a serving bowl. Set aside, and keep warm.

Coat a large nonstick skillet with cooking spray; add oil. Place over medium-high heat until hot. Add carrot and garlic; sauté until carrot is crisp-tender. Add mushrooms, and sauté until tender. Combine ¼ cup water and next 4 ingredients; add to carrot mixture. Bring to a boil, and cook 1 minute. Add carrot mixture and cheese to orzo mixture; toss gently. Garnish with lemon slices, if desired. Yield: 9 servings (107 calories per ½-cup serving).

Per Serving:		
Protein 4.5g	Fat 1.7g	(Saturated Fat 0.5g)
Carbohydrate 18.7g	Fiber 1.2g	Cholesterol 2mg
Iron 1.2mg	Sodium 156mg	Calcium 41mg

RATATOUILLE PASTA

Ratatouille usually includes eggplant, tomatoes, and zucchini sautéed in olive oil.

1½ cups coarsely chopped tomato
¼ cup chopped fresh basil
2 tablespoons balsamic vinegar
½ teaspoon freshly ground pepper
¼ teaspoon salt
6 ounces radiatore pasta, uncooked
Vegetable cooking spray
1 tablespoon olive oil
2½ cups coarsely chopped zucchini
4 cups coarsely chopped eggplant
2 teaspoons minced garlic
¼ cup freshly grated Parmesan cheese

Combine first 5 ingredients, stirring well. Cover and let stand 2 hours, stirring occasionally.

Cook pasta according to package directions, omitting salt and fat; drain well. Set pasta aside, and keep warm.

Coat a large nonstick skillet with cooking spray; add oil. Place over medium-high heat until hot. Add zucchini, and sauté 3 minutes. Add eggplant and garlic; sauté an additional 4 minutes or until vegetables are tender. Add tomato mixture and pasta to vegetable mixture. Cook, stirring constantly, until mixture is thoroughly heated. Add cheese, and toss well. Serve warm. Yield: 6 servings (196 calories per 1-cup serving).

Per Serving:		
Protein 8.7g	Fat 5.6g	(Saturated Fat 2.0g)
Carbohydrate 28.9g	Fiber 2.4g	Cholesterol 6mg
Iron 2.1mg	Sodium 259mg	Calcium 150mg

SWEET PEPPER ROTELLE

1 medium-size sweet red pepper
1 medium-size green pepper
¼ cup low-fat sour cream
1 tablespoon Dijon mustard
1 tablespoon lemon juice
½ teaspoon dried Italian seasoning
¼ teaspoon pepper
6 ounces rotelle pasta, uncooked
¼ cup sliced ripe olives

Cut peppers in half lengthwise; remove and discard seeds and membrane. Place peppers, skin side up, on a baking sheet, and flatten with palm of hand. Broil 5½ inches from heat (with electric oven door partially opened) 15 to 20 minutes or until charred. Place in ice water until cool; peel and discard skins. Cut peppers into ¼-inch-wide strips. Set aside.

Combine sour cream and next 4 ingredients in a small bowl, stirring well; set aside.

Cook pasta according to package directions, omitting salt and fat; drain. Place pasta in a serving bowl. Add roasted pepper strips, sour cream mixture, and olives; toss gently. Serve immediately. Yield: 4 servings (211 calories per 1-cup serving).

Per Serving:		
Protein 6.6g	Fat 4.0g	(Saturated Fat 1.4g)
Carbohydrate 37.4g	Fiber 2.5g	Cholesterol 6mg
Iron 3.0mg	Sodium 200mg	Calcium 41mg

FOUR-MUSHROOM SPAGHETTI

You may use one or two types of mushrooms instead of four, just remember to use a total of 12 ounces.

1 (13¾-ounce) can no-salt-added beef broth
Olive oil-flavored vegetable cooking spray
4 ounces fresh crimini mushrooms, sliced
3 ounces fresh oyster mushrooms, sliced
3 ounces fresh shiitake mushrooms, sliced
2 ounces fresh mushrooms, sliced
¼ cup chopped shallots
½ cup Burgundy or other dry red wine
1 teaspoon dried tarragon
¾ teaspoon coarsely ground pepper
¼ teaspoon fines herbes
2 tablespoons cornstarch
4 ounces spaghetti, uncooked
1 tablespoon freshly grated Romano cheese

Bring broth to a boil in a medium saucepan; cook over medium-high heat 5 minutes or until broth is reduced to 1½ cups. Set aside, and let cool.

Coat a large nonstick skillet with cooking spray; place over medium-high heat until hot. Add mushrooms and shallots; sauté until tender. Stir in wine and next 3 ingredients. Cook over medium heat 5 to 6 minutes or until most of liquid evaporates.

Combine broth and cornstarch, stirring until smooth. Add to mushroom mixture, and stir well. Cook over medium heat, stirring constantly, until mixture is thickened. Remove from heat; keep warm.

Cook pasta according to package directions, omitting salt and fat; drain well. Place pasta in a serving bowl. Add mushroom mixture, and toss well. Sprinkle with cheese. Serve immediately. Yield: 4 servings (176 calories per 1-cup serving).

Per Serving:		
Protein 6.5g	Fat 1.4g	(Saturated Fat 0.4g)
Carbohydrate 34.2g	Fiber 2.2g	Cholesterol 2mg
Iron 2.4mg	Sodium 34mg	Calcium 38mg

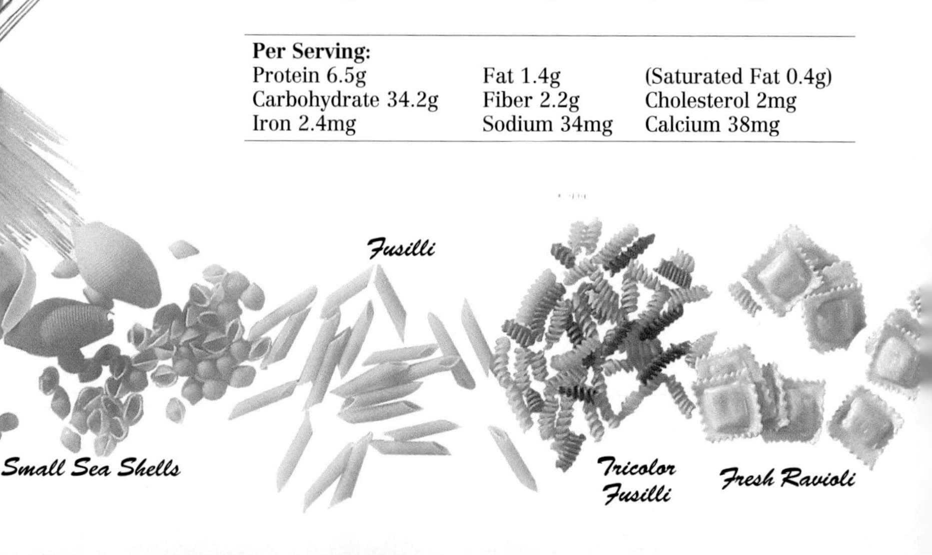

SPINACH-TURKEY CANNELLONI

Compare ground turkey with ground chuck and you'll appreciate the fat savings: 3 ounces of cooked ground turkey has 4 grams less fat and 50 percent less saturated fat.

1 (10-ounce) package frozen chopped spinach
Olive oil-flavored cooking spray
1 pound freshly ground raw turkey
1 cup chopped onion
2 teaspoons minced garlic
½ cup freshly grated Parmesan cheese, divided
½ cup frozen egg substitute, thawed
2 teaspoons dried Italian seasoning
¾ teaspoon pepper
½ teaspoon dried oregano
½ teaspoon dried thyme
¼ teaspoon salt
¼ teaspoon rubbed sage
¼ teaspoon ground cumin
10 cannelloni shells, uncooked
Tomato-Basil Sauce
Creamy White Sauce

Cook spinach according to package directions, omitting salt. Drain spinach, and press gently between paper towels to remove excess moisture. Set spinach aside.

Coat a large nonstick skillet with cooking spray; place over medium-high heat until hot. Add turkey, onion, and garlic; cook until turkey is browned, stirring until it crumbles. Drain turkey mixture, and pat dry with paper towels. Transfer to a large bowl. Add spinach, ¼ cup Parmesan cheese, and next 8 ingredients; stir well. Set aside.

Cook cannelloni shells according to package directions, omitting salt and fat; drain. Stuff turkey mixture evenly into cooked shells.

Spoon 1 cup Tomato-Basil Sauce into a 13- x 9- x 2-inch baking dish coated with cooking spray. Place filled shells over sauce. Pour Creamy White Sauce over shells. Pour remaining Tomato-Basil Sauce over Creamy White Sauce. Cover and bake at 325° for 30 minutes. Uncover and sprinkle with remaining ¼ cup Parmesan cheese. Bake, uncovered, an additional 10 minutes. Yield: 10 servings (255 calories per serving).

Tomato-Basil Sauce

3 cups no-salt-added tomato sauce
1 cup chopped onion
2 teaspoons dried basil
1 teaspoon minced garlic
1 teaspoon sugar
¾ teaspoon pepper
¼ teaspoon salt

Combine all ingredients in a medium saucepan. Cover and cook over medium heat 15 minutes, stirring occasionally. Yield: 3½ cups.

Creamy White Sauce

¼ cup reduced-calorie margarine
¼ cup all-purpose flour
1¾ cups skim milk
¼ teaspoon salt
¼ teaspoon ground white pepper

Melt margarine in a small saucepan over medium heat, and add flour. Cook, stirring constantly with a wire whisk, 1 minute. Gradually add milk, stirring constantly. Cook, stirring constantly, until thickened and bubbly. Stir in salt and pepper. Yield: 2 cups.

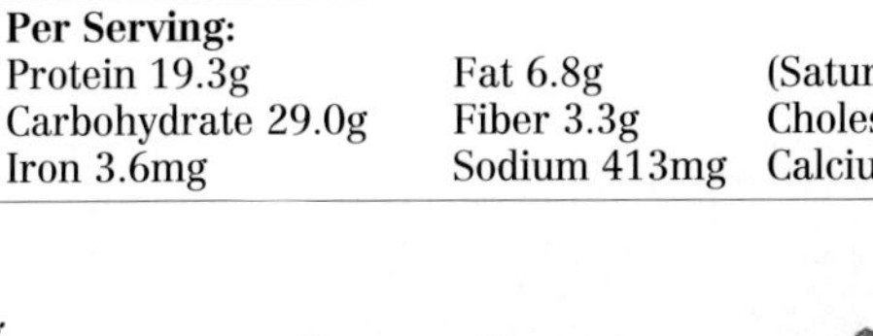

Per Serving:		
Protein 19.3g	Fat 6.8g	(Saturated Fat 2.0g)
Carbohydrate 29.0g	Fiber 3.3g	Cholesterol 31mg
Iron 3.6mg	Sodium 413mg	Calcium 204mg

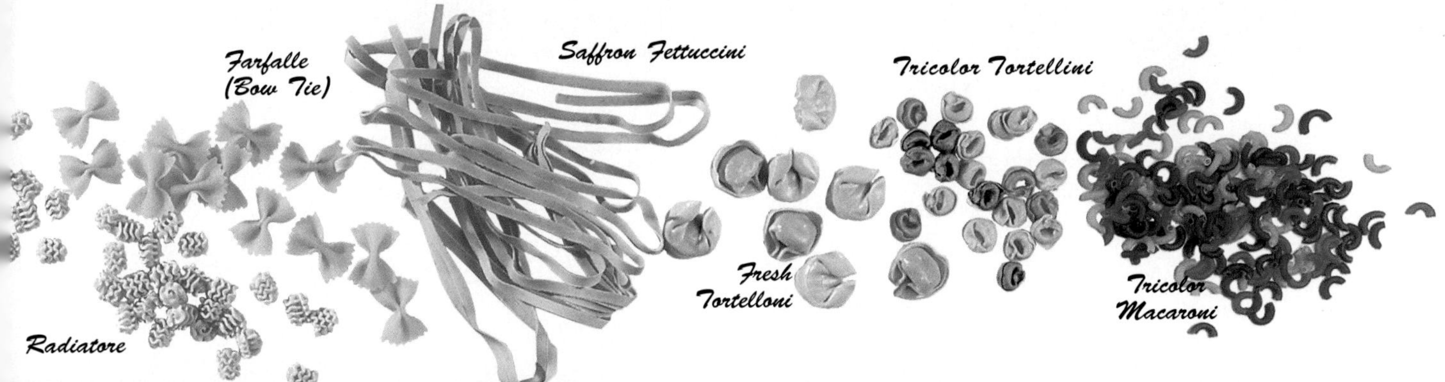

FETTUCCINE ALLA CARBONARA

For this carbonara, we broke tradition to reduce the fat by half by using low-fat milk, egg substitute, and turkey bacon.

1 tablespoon all-purpose flour
1 cup 1% low-fat milk
¼ cup frozen egg substitute, thawed
2 tablespoons chopped fresh parsley
¼ teaspoon dried basil
¼ teaspoon pepper
1 clove garlic, crushed
8 ounces fettuccine, uncooked
1 cup frozen English peas, thawed
⅓ cup freshly grated Parmesan cheese
5 slices turkey bacon, cooked and crumbled

Place flour in a medium saucepan. Gradually add milk, stirring until smooth. Cook over medium heat, stirring constantly, until mixture is slightly thickened. Gradually stir about one-fourth of hot mixture into egg substitute; add to remaining hot mixture, stirring constantly. Cook over medium heat, stirring constantly, until thickened. Stir in parsley and next 3 ingredients.

Cook pasta according to package directions, omitting salt and fat; drain. Combine pasta and sauce in a serving bowl; toss gently. Add English peas, Parmesan cheese, and bacon; toss gently. Serve immediately. Yield: 6 servings (259 calories per 1-cup serving).

Per Serving:

Protein 14.0g	Fat 5.7g	(Saturated Fat 2.1g)
Carbohydrate 35.9g	Fiber 2.3g	Cholesterol 20mg
Iron 2.4mg	Sodium 457mg	Calcium 144mg

GARDEN FETTUCCINE WITH VEAL

½ pound veal cutlets, cut into very thin strips
¼ teaspoon garlic powder
¼ teaspoon dried basil
Olive oil-flavored vegetable cooking spray
1 cup broccoli flowerets
¾ cup sliced yellow squash
¾ cup sliced zucchini
½ cup julienne-sliced sweet red pepper
½ cup julienne-sliced sweet yellow pepper
½ cup sliced green onions
1 cup peeled, chopped tomato
¾ cup sliced fresh mushrooms
1 teaspoon minced garlic
1 cup canned no-salt-added chicken broth, undiluted
1 teaspoon dried Italian seasoning
1 teaspoon dried basil
1 teaspoon coarsely ground pepper
6 ounces fettuccine, uncooked
¼ cup freshly grated Parmesan cheese

Combine first 3 ingredients, tossing gently. Coat a large nonstick skillet with cooking spray; place over medium heat until hot. Add veal; cook 5 minutes or until browned, stirring occasionally. Drain and pat dry with paper towels; set aside. Wipe drippings from skillet with a paper towel.

Coat skillet with cooking spray; place skillet over medium-high heat until hot. Add broccoli and next 5 ingredients; sauté 3 minutes. Add tomato, mushroom slices, and minced garlic; sauté an additional 2 minutes.

Return veal to skillet. Add chicken broth and next 3 ingredients; bring to a boil. Reduce heat, and simmer, uncovered, 15 minutes or until most of liquid evaporates.

Cook pasta according to package directions, omitting salt and fat; drain. Combine pasta and veal mixture in a serving bowl, tossing gently.

Sprinkle pasta and veal mixture with cheese. Serve immediately. Yield: 5 servings (260 calories per 1-cup serving).

Per Serving:

Protein 19.7g	Fat 5.4g	(Saturated Fat 1.8g)
Carbohydrate 33.4g	Fiber 3.3g	Cholesterol 44mg
Iron 3.5mg	Sodium 163mg	Calcium 124mg

Succulent meats from sea and land combine with Chinese noodles to create a light oriental flavor in Noodle Nests with Shrimp and Pork.

NOODLE NESTS WITH SHRIMP AND PORK

6 ounces Chinese egg noodles, uncooked
2 teaspoons light sesame oil
Vegetable cooking spray
½ pound unpeeled small fresh shrimp
½ pound lean boneless pork loin, cut into thin strips
1 tablespoon cornstarch
1 tablespoon dry sherry
½ cup canned no-salt-added beef broth, undiluted
2 teaspoons cornstarch
2 teaspoons low-sodium soy sauce
1 teaspoon oyster sauce
2 teaspoons peanut oil
1 cup sliced green onions
1 cup sliced mushrooms
2 cups julienne-sliced snow pea pods
1 (8-ounce) can sliced water chestnuts, drained
1 teaspoon dried crushed red pepper
Julienne-sliced snow pea pods (optional)
Dried crushed red pepper (optional)

Cook noodles according to package directions, omitting salt and fat; drain. Toss noodles with sesame oil; chill. Shape noodles into 6 (4-inch) rounds on a baking sheet coated with cooking spray; press to make an indentation in center of each round. Bake at 400° for 35 minutes or until golden. Set aside.

Peel and devein shrimp. Place shrimp and pork in a bowl. Combine 1 tablespoon cornstarch and sherry in a bowl; pour over shrimp and pork. Toss gently. Cover and chill 30 minutes.

Combine broth and next 3 ingredients; set aside.

Coat a wok or large nonstick skillet with cooking spray; drizzle peanut oil around top of wok, coating sides. Heat at medium-high (375°) until hot. Add pork mixture; stir-fry 3 minutes or until shrimp turn pink and pork is done. Remove from wok; set aside.

Add onions and mushrooms to wok; stir-fry 2 minutes. Add 2 cups snow peas, water chestnuts, and 1 teaspoon crushed red pepper. Stir-fry 2 minutes or until crisp-tender. Add pork mixture and broth mixture to wok; stir-fry 1 minute or until thickened. Place a noodle nest on each serving plate. Top evenly with pork mixture. If desired, garnish with julienne-sliced snow peas and crushed red pepper. Yield: 6 servings (267 calories per serving).

Per Serving:

Protein 19.0g	Fat 7.9g	(Saturated Fat 1.8g)
Carbohydrate 29.1g	Fiber 2.1g	Cholesterol 93mg
Iron 3.4mg	Sodium 146mg	Calcium 48mg

CHINESE CHICKEN AND NOODLES

4 (4-ounce) skinned, boned chicken breast halves
2 quarts water
4 ounces vermicelli, uncooked
1 tablespoon cornstarch
2 teaspoons low-sodium soy sauce
1 teaspoon light sesame oil
¼ teaspoon ground ginger
¼ teaspoon ground coriander
Vegetable cooking spray
2 teaspoons peanut oil
½ medium onion, cut into thin strips
2¼ cups sliced fresh mushrooms
1 cup frozen English peas, thawed
1 (8-ounce) can sliced water chestnuts, drained
1 (8-ounce) can bamboo shoots, drained and cut into thin strips
1 medium-size sweet red pepper, seeded and cut into thin strips

Place chicken and water in a Dutch oven. Bring to a boil; cover, reduce heat, and simmer 30 minutes or until chicken is done. Remove chicken; reserve broth. Cut chicken into ¾-inch pieces; set aside.

Skim and discard fat from broth. Bring broth to a boil; add vermicelli. Cook 12 minutes or until pasta is tender. Drain pasta, reserving 1 cup broth.

Combine cornstarch, soy sauce, and sesame oil, stirring well. Add cornstarch mixture to reserved broth; stir well. Add ginger and coriander; set aside.

Coat Dutch oven with cooking spray; add peanut oil. Place over medium-high heat until hot. Add onion; sauté 1 minute. Add mushrooms and remaining ingredients, one at a time, sautéing 1 minute after each addition.

Add chicken and cornstarch mixture to vegetable mixture; cook over medium heat, stirring constantly, 1 to 2 minutes or until thickened and bubbly. Add pasta; toss. Cook over medium heat until heated. Yield: 8 servings (200 calories per 1½-cup serving).

Per Serving:

Protein 17.7g	Fat 3.8g	(Saturated Fat 0.8g)
Carbohydrate 22.9g	Fiber 2.5g	Cholesterol 36mg
Iron 2.0mg	Sodium 102mg	Calcium 24mg

PENNE PASTA WITH MUSTARD SAUSAGE SAUCE

1 (8-ounce) carton plain nonfat yogurt
¾ cup evaporated skimmed milk
¼ cup Chablis or other dry white wine
2 tablespoons Dijon mustard
2 tablespoons white wine vinegar
1½ tablespoons coarse-grained mustard
½ teaspoon dried oregano
½ teaspoon dried thyme
½ teaspoon pepper
5 ounces penne pasta, uncooked
Olive oil-flavored vegetable cooking spray
1½ cups chopped onion
1½ cups sliced fresh mushrooms
¼ cup plus 2 tablespoons chopped green pepper
1½ tablespoons minced garlic
3 ounces smoked turkey sausage, sliced

Place a colander in a 2-quart glass measure or medium bowl. Line colander with 4 layers of cheesecloth, allowing cheesecloth to extend over edges. Spoon yogurt into colander. Cover loosely with plastic wrap; refrigerate 12 hours. Combine milk and next 7 ingredients in a bowl. Add ¼ cup yogurt cheese, stirring well; set aside. Reserve remaining yogurt cheese for another use; discard strained liquid.

Cook pasta according to package directions, omitting salt and fat; drain. Set aside; keep warm.

Coat a large nonstick skillet with cooking spray; place over medium-high heat until hot. Add onion and remaining ingredients; sauté until vegetables are tender and sausage is browned.

Add pasta to vegetable mixture. Cook, stirring constantly, until thoroughly heated. Remove from heat. Add yogurt mixture, stirring well. Serve immediately. Yield: 5 servings (246 calories per 1-cup serving).

Per Serving:

Protein 12.1g	Fat 5.2g	(Saturated Fat 1.2g)
Carbohydrate 35.5g	Fiber 2.4g	Cholesterol 22mg
Iron 2.5mg	Sodium 438mg	Calcium 209mg

SALMON WONTONS

Wontons are a Chinese specialty similar to Italian ravioli. This version is filled with seafood and simmered in a seasoned broth.

2 ounces Neufchâtel cheese, softened
2 ounces smoked salmon
1 tablespoon chopped shallots
1 tablespoon chopped fresh dillweed
1 teaspoon lemon juice
¼ teaspoon ground white pepper
20 fresh or frozen wonton skins, thawed
3 (10½-ounce) cans low-sodium chicken broth
¼ cup julienne-sliced carrot
¼ cup julienne-sliced zucchini
¼ cup sliced green onions
1 teaspoon low-sodium soy sauce

Position knife blade in food processor bowl; add first 6 ingredients. Process until smooth, scraping sides of processor bowl once. Spoon mixture evenly onto centers of wonton skins. Brush edges with water; fold each wonton skin over, pressing edges together to seal securely. Set aside.

Bring broth to a boil in a large saucepan; add carrot and remaining ingredients. Reduce heat; simmer 7 minutes or until vegetables are tender. Cook wontons, in batches, in broth mixture 6 minutes or until tender. Remove wontons with a slotted spoon.

Place 5 wontons in each serving bowl. Spoon broth mixture evenly over wontons. Serve immediately. Yield: 4 servings (208 calories per serving).

Per Serving:		
Protein 10.6g	Fat 6.1g	(Saturated Fat 2.8g)
Carbohydrate 27.7g	Fiber 0.4g	Cholesterol 18mg
Iron 3.1mg	Sodium 508mg	Calcium 51mg

MUSTARD-PEPPER ROTELLE

1 (9-ounce) package frozen artichoke hearts
1 cup chopped cooked chicken breast (skinned before cooking and cooked without salt)
¼ cup julienne-sliced onion
¼ cup sliced ripe olives
2 tablespoons chopped fresh basil
1 (7-ounce) jar roasted red peppers in water, drained and cut into very thin strips
6 ounces tricolor rotelle pasta, uncooked
1½ cups plain nonfat yogurt
½ cup reduced-calorie mayonnaise
2 tablespoons fresh lime juice
1 tablespoon Dijon mustard
1 tablespoon coarse-grained mustard
2 teaspoons prepared mustard
¼ teaspoon coarsely ground pepper
Vegetable cooking spray

Arrange artichoke hearts in a vegetable steamer over boiling water. Cover and steam 6 minutes; drain. Transfer to a large bowl. Add chicken and next 4 ingredients, tossing gently; set aside.

Cook pasta according to package directions, omitting salt and fat; drain. Add pasta to vegetable mixture, tossing well.

Combine yogurt and next 6 ingredients, stirring well. Add yogurt mixture to vegetable mixture, and toss well. Spoon into a 2-quart casserole coated with cooking spray. Bake at 350° for 25 to 30 minutes or until thoroughly heated. Yield: 6 servings (285 calories per 1-cup serving).

Per Serving:		
Protein 18.1g	Fat 8.2g	(Saturated Fat 0.6g)
Carbohydrate 34.1g	Fiber 1.3g	Cholesterol 34mg
Iron 2.4mg	Sodium 470mg	Calcium 143mg

TURKEY-EGGPLANT SPAGHETTINI CASSEROLE

Olive oil-flavored vegetable cooking spray
½ pound freshly ground raw turkey breast
1½ cups chopped onion
1½ cups chopped celery
½ cup chopped green pepper
2 teaspoons minced garlic
2⅓ cups cubed eggplant
2 cups seeded, coarsely chopped tomato
½ cup shredded carrot
1 cup water
½ cup Burgundy or other dry red wine
⅓ cup no-salt-added tomato paste
1 (8-ounce) can no-salt-added tomato sauce
1 (6-ounce) jar sliced mushrooms, drained
1½ teaspoons dried basil
1½ teaspoons dried oregano
1 teaspoon sugar
1 teaspoon dried thyme
1 teaspoon pepper
½ teaspoon fennel seeds
¼ teaspoon salt
2 bay leaves
11 ounces spaghettini, uncooked
¾ cup (3 ounces) shredded 50% less-fat mozzarella cheese
½ cup (2 ounces) shredded provolone cheese

Coat a large Dutch oven with cooking spray; place over medium-high heat until hot. Add ground turkey, onion, celery, green pepper, and garlic. Cook over medium heat until turkey is done, stirring until it crumbles. Drain turkey mixture, and pat dry with paper towels. Wipe drippings from pan with a paper towel.

Return turkey mixture to Dutch oven; add eggplant and next 15 ingredients. Bring to a boil; cover, reduce heat, and simmer 25 minutes. Remove and discard bay leaves.

Cook pasta according to package directions, omitting salt and fat; drain.

Place pasta in a large bowl; add turkey mixture, and toss well.

Spoon pasta mixture into a 13- x 9- x 2-inch baking dish coated with cooking spray. Cover and bake at 350° for 25 minutes.

Uncover and sprinkle with cheeses. Bake an additional 5 minutes or until cheeses melt. Serve immediately. Yield: 10 servings (234 calories per 1-cup serving).

Per Serving:

Protein 15.1g	Fat 3.9g	(Saturated Fat 1.7g)
Carbohydrate 35.9g	Fiber 3.3g	Cholesterol 19mg
Iron 2.8mg	Sodium 221g	Calcium 189mg

The dynamic taste and easy preparation will make any pizza-lover a fan of Blue Cheese, Apple, and Spinach Pizza (page 143).

Meatless Main Dishes

CHILE CHEESE PUFF

Vegetable cooking spray
1 (4-ounce) can chopped green chiles, drained
½ cup sliced fresh mushrooms
½ cup chopped onion
2 cups nonfat cottage cheese
1 cup (4 ounces) shredded part-skim mozzarella cheese
1 cup frozen egg substitute, thawed
½ cup (2 ounces) shredded reduced-fat Monterey Jack cheese
¼ cup all-purpose flour
2 tablespoons reduced-calorie margarine, melted
1 teaspoon baking powder
⅛ teaspoon salt
4 egg whites

Coat a 2-quart casserole with cooking spray. Layer green chiles, mushrooms, and onion in casserole; set aside.

Position knife blade in food processor bowl; add cottage cheese and remaining ingredients. Process until smooth, scraping sides of processor bowl once. Spoon cheese mixture over vegetables in prepared casserole.

Bake at 350° for 50 to 55 minutes or until set. Let stand 10 minutes before serving. Yield: 8 servings (151 calories per serving).

Per Serving:		
Protein 18.3g	Fat 5.5g	(Saturated Fat 2.5g)
Carbohydrate 7.4g	Fiber 0.4g	Cholesterol 15mg
Iron 1.0mg	Sodium 509mg	Calcium 226mg

ARTICHOKE-BASIL QUICHE

The rice crust for this quiche offers a low-fat alternative to a standard pastry crust.

2 cups cooked brown rice (cooked without salt or fat)
1¼ cups (5 ounces) shredded part-skim mozzarella cheese, divided
1 egg white, lightly beaten
¼ teaspoon dried dillweed
Vegetable cooking spray
1 teaspoon margarine
½ cup chopped sweet red pepper
¼ cup sliced green onions
1 clove garlic, minced
½ cup shredded fresh basil
1 (14-ounce) can artichoke hearts, drained and sliced
1 cup evaporated skimmed milk
1 teaspoon dried thyme
2 eggs
Fresh basil sprigs (optional)

Combine rice, ¼ cup mozzarella cheese, egg white, and dillweed in a bowl, stirring well. Spread rice mixture in bottom and up sides of a 9-inch pieplate coated with cooking spray. Bake at 350° for 5 minutes. Set aside.

Melt margarine in a small nonstick skillet over medium-high heat. Add red pepper, green onions, and garlic; sauté until vegetables are tender. Stir in shredded basil; spread over prepared crust. Sprinkle with remaining 1 cup cheese. Arrange artichoke slices over cheese.

Combine milk, thyme, and eggs in container of an electric blender; cover and process until smooth. Pour over vegetables.

Bake at 350° for 1 hour or until a knife inserted in center comes out clean. Let stand 10 minutes before serving.

Garnish with fresh basil sprigs, if desired.Yield: 6 servings (224 calories per serving).

Per Serving:		
Protein 14.5g	Fat 7.1g	(Saturated Fat 3.3g)
Carbohydrate 26.0g	Fiber 1.8g	Cholesterol 89mg
Iron 1.7mg	Sodium 324mg	Calcium 320mg

Eggs move into a whole new flavor dimension when served Mexican-style in Huevos Rancheros with Pita Chips.

HUEVOS RANCHEROS WITH PITA CHIPS

1 (8-inch) pita bread round
Butter-flavored vegetable cooking spray
½ teaspoon dried basil
½ teaspoon garlic powder
½ teaspoon ground cumin
1 (16-ounce) can red beans, drained
1 (14½-ounce) can Mexican-style stewed tomatoes
2 tablespoons sliced green onions
4 eggs
¼ cup commercial no-salt-added salsa
¼ cup nonfat sour cream alternative
Fresh cilantro sprigs (optional)

Separate pita bread into 2 rounds; cut each round into 8 wedges. Place wedges on an ungreased baking sheet; coat with cooking spray. Combine basil, garlic powder, and cumin; sprinkle over wedges. Bake at 400° for 5 minutes or until crisp and lightly browned. Remove chips from baking sheet; let cool completely on a wire rack.

Combine beans, tomatoes, and green onions in a saucepan. Cook, uncovered, over medium heat 10 minutes, stirring occasionally. Set aside; keep warm.

Add water to a large saucepan to a depth of 2 inches. Bring to a boil; reduce heat, and maintain at a light simmer. Break eggs, one at a time, into water. Simmer 7 to 9 minutes or until internal temperature of egg reaches 160°. Remove eggs with a slotted spoon.

To serve, arrange 4 pita wedges around edge of each individual serving plate; top evenly with bean mixture. Top each serving with an egg. Spoon 1 tablespoon salsa and 1 tablespoon sour cream over each serving. Garnish each with a cilantro sprig, if desired. Serve immediately. Yield: 4 servings (265 calories per serving).

Per Serving:

Protein 16.2g	Fat 6.4g	(Saturated Fat 1.7g)
Carbohydrate 35.1g	Fiber 4.7g	Cholesterol 221mg
Iron 4.3mg	Sodium 594mg	Calcium 119mg

VEGETABLE LASAGNA

Fresh vegetables add an abundance of color and flavor to this lasagna and keep it high in vitamins and minerals and remarkably low in fat (14 percent fat per serving).

2 cups broccoli flowerets
1 cup thinly sliced zucchini
1 cup thinly sliced yellow squash
1 cup thinly sliced carrot
Vegetable cooking spray
1½ cups thinly sliced fresh mushrooms
1 cup chopped onion
3 cups no-salt-added tomato sauce
1 teaspoon garlic powder
1 teaspoon dried Italian seasoning
1 teaspoon dried basil
¾ to 1 teaspoon pepper
½ teaspoon salt
1 (16-ounce) carton 1% low-fat cottage cheese
½ cup frozen egg substitute, thawed
8 cooked lasagna noodles (cooked without salt or fat)
1 cup (4 ounces) shredded part-skim mozzarella cheese

Arrange first 4 ingredients in a vegetable steamer over boiling water. Cover and steam 4 to 5 minutes or until vegetables are crisp-tender; drain. Transfer to a bowl; set aside.

Coat a nonstick skillet with cooking spray. Place skillet over medium-high heat until hot. Add mushrooms and onion; sauté until tender. Add to broccoli mixture.

Combine tomato sauce and next 5 ingredients in a small bowl, stirring well. Combine cottage cheese and egg substitute, stirring well.

Spread ½ cup tomato sauce mixture over bottom of a 13- x 9- x 2-inch baking dish coated with cooking spray. Place 4 lasagna noodles over sauce; top evenly with vegetable mixture. Spoon cottage cheese mixture evenly over vegetable mixture. Top with remaining 4 noodles and remaining tomato sauce mixture.

Cover and bake at 350° for 40 minutes. Uncover and sprinkle with mozzarella cheese. Bake, uncovered, an additional 10 minutes or until cheese melts. Let lasagna stand 15 minutes before serving. Yield: 8 servings (234 calories per serving).

Per Serving:

Protein 17.7g	Fat 3.6g	(Saturated Fat 1.9g)
Carbohydrate 33.5g	Fiber 3.9g	Cholesterol 10mg
Iron 2.8mg	Sodium 500mg	Calcium 190mg

RATATOUILLE WITH PASTA AND FETA

1 teaspoon olive oil
2 cups sliced leeks
3 cloves garlic, minced
½ teaspoon fennel seeds, crushed
2 cups sliced zucchini
¼ teaspoon salt
2 large sweet red peppers (about 1 pound), seeded and cut into thin strips
1½ cups chopped tomato
½ cup no-salt-added vegetable juice
12 ounces penne pasta, uncooked
½ cup sliced fresh basil
3 ounces feta cheese, crumbled

Heat oil in a large nonstick skillet over medium-high heat until hot. Add leeks, garlic, and fennel seed; sauté 5 minutes or until leeks are tender. Add zucchini and salt; sauté 3 minutes.

Stir in red pepper strips, chopped tomato, and vegetable juice; bring to a boil. Cover, reduce heat, and simmer 15 minutes, stirring occasionally.

Cook pasta according to package directions, omitting salt and fat; drain and place in a large bowl. Add vegetable mixture; toss gently. Sprinkle with basil and feta cheese. Serve immediately. Yield: 6 servings (308 calories per serving).

Per Serving:

Protein 11.4g	Fat 5.2g	(Saturated Fat 2.4g)
Carbohydrate 54.7g	Fiber 3.4g	Cholesterol 13mg
Iron 4.2mg	Sodium 278mg	Calcium 124mg

GARDEN VEGETABLES WITH TORTELLONI

Tortellini, which is similar in shape to tortelloni though smaller, is a suitable substitute in this recipe if tortelloni is not available.

Vegetable cooking spray
1 cup sliced fresh mushrooms
¼ cup sliced green onions
1 clove garlic, minced
¾ pound fresh asparagus
1½ cups sliced carrot
½ cup frozen artichoke hearts, thawed
¼ cup sliced ripe olives
1 (9-ounce) package fresh cheese-and-basil tortelloni
¼ cup cider vinegar
¼ cup unsweetened orange juice
1 tablespoon olive oil
1½ teaspoons Dijon mustard
½ teaspoon pepper
¼ teaspoon dried basil
¼ teaspoon dried oregano
¼ teaspoon sugar
¼ cup grated Parmesan cheese
¼ cup chopped fresh parsley
Fresh parsley sprig (optional)

Coat a nonstick skillet with cooking spray; place over medium-high heat until hot. Add mushrooms, green onions, and garlic; sauté until vegetables are crisp-tender. Set aside, and keep warm.

Snap off tough ends of asparagus. Remove scales from stalks with a knife or vegetable peeler, if desired. Cut spears into 1-inch pieces. Arrange asparagus, carrot, and artichoke hearts in a vegetable steamer over boiling water. Cover and steam 5 minutes or until vegetables are crisp-tender. Drain; place steamed vegetables in a large serving bowl. Add sautéed vegetables and olives to steamed vegetables; toss gently. Set aside, and keep warm.

Cook tortelloni according to package directions, omitting salt and fat; drain. Add to vegetable mixture; toss. Combine vinegar and next 7 ingredients, stirring with a wire whisk. Pour vinegar mixture over pasta mixture; toss. Sprinkle with cheese and chopped parsley. Garnish with a fresh parsley sprig, if desired. Serve immediately. Yield: 5 servings (258 calories per serving).

Per Serving:

Protein 12.0g	Fat 9.1g	(Saturated Fat 2.4g)
Carbohydrate 34.2g	Fiber 3.7g	Cholesterol 28mg
Iron 3.2mg	Sodium 345mg	Calcium 146mg

FOUR-CHEESE STUFFED SHELLS

1½ cups 1% low-fat cottage cheese
1 cup nonfat ricotta cheese
½ cup crumbled blue cheese
2 tablespoons chopped fresh parsley
1 egg, lightly beaten
Vegetable cooking spray
2 teaspoons olive oil
1 cup chopped onion
1 clove garlic, minced
1 (14½-ounce) can no-salt-added stewed tomatoes, undrained and chopped
1 tablespoon dried Italian seasoning
¼ teaspoon salt
16 jumbo pasta shells, uncooked
2 tablespoons freshly grated Parmesan cheese

Combine first 5 ingredients, stirring well; set aside.

Coat a saucepan with cooking spray; add oil. Place over medium-high heat until hot. Add onion and garlic; sauté until tender. Stir in tomato, Italian seasoning, and salt; bring to a boil. Reduce heat, and simmer, uncovered, 15 minutes, stirring occasionally. Set aside.

Cook pasta shells according to package directions, omitting salt and fat; drain well. Spoon cheese mixture evenly into shells. Arrange shells in an 11- x 7- x 1½-inch baking dish coated with cooking spray. Pour tomato mixture over shells.

Cover and bake at 375° for 25 minutes. Uncover; sprinkle with Parmesan cheese. Bake, uncovered, an additional 5 minutes. Let stand 5 minutes before serving. Yield: 8 servings (214 calories per serving).

Per Serving:

Protein 16.2g	Fat 5.2g	(Saturated Fat 2.3g)
Carbohydrate 26.0g	Fiber 1.1g	Cholesterol 39mg
Iron 2.1mg	Sodium 403mg	Calcium 177mg

Each serving of Mediterranean Pita Rounds provides about half of the recommended 20 to 35 grams of fiber per day.

MEDITERRANEAN PITA ROUNDS

2 (15-ounce) cans no-salt-added garbanzo beans, drained
¼ cup skim milk
¼ cup fresh lemon juice
5 cloves garlic
8 (8-inch) pita bread rounds
1 teaspoon olive oil
1 (10-ounce) package frozen chopped spinach, thawed and drained
2 cups chopped tomato
1 cup diced green pepper
1 cup diced sweet red pepper
½ cup crumbled feta cheese
⅓ cup sliced ripe olives

Position knife blade in food processor bowl; add first 4 ingredients. Process until smooth, scraping sides of processor bowl occasionally. Set aside.

Arrange pita bread rounds on ungreased baking sheets; brush with olive oil. Bake at 450° for 6 minutes. Spread bean mixture evenly over pitas, leaving a ½-inch border. Arrange remaining ingredients evenly over pita rounds. Bake at 450° for 5 minutes or until thoroughly heated and crust is crisp. Yield: 8 servings (379 calories per serving).

Per Serving:

Protein 13.5g	Fat 6.6g	(Saturated Fat 1.7g)
Carbohydrate 64.8g	Fiber 11.9g	Cholesterol 6mg
Iron 6.0mg	Sodium 602mg	Calcium 196mg

BLUE CHEESE, APPLE, AND SPINACH PIZZA

Rome apples are excellent for baking because they hold their shape well when baked.

1 (7-ounce) can refrigerated breadstick dough
Vegetable cooking spray
2 cups loosely packed fresh spinach leaves
2 medium Rome apples, thinly sliced
1 cup crumbled blue cheese

Unroll breadstick dough, separating into strips. Working on a flat surface, coil 1 strip of dough into a spiral shape. Add second strip of dough to the end of the first strip, pinching ends together to seal; continue coiling dough in a spiral pattern.

Repeat procedure with remaining dough strips to make an 8-inch circle. Roll coiled dough into a 12-inch circle, and place in a 12-inch pizza pan coated with cooking spray.

Arrange spinach, apple, and cheese over dough. Bake at 450° for 15 minutes or until crust is golden. Yield: 3 servings (347 calories per serving).

Per Serving:		
Protein 12.3g	Fat 12.7g	(Saturated Fat 5.9g)
Carbohydrate 64.3g	Fiber 5.9g	Cholesterol 21mg
Iron 2.6mg	Sodium 801mg	Calcium 189mg

FUELING UP WITH FIBER

To make sure you eat the recommended 20 to 35 grams of fiber a day, eat plenty of whole grains, vegetables, wheat bran, dried beans and peas, oats, and fruits. Remember to add fiber to your diet slowly over a six- to eight-week period, and drink more fluids as you eat more high-fiber foods. Try these easy ways to boost the fiber in your diet:

- Choose fresh fruits and vegetables instead of juice.
- Keep the skin on fruits and vegetables such as apples, peaches, tomatoes, and cooked potatoes.
- Have a high-fiber cereal for breakfast.
- Enjoy sandwiches made with whole grain breads and filled with fresh vegetables.
- Replace your meat entrée with a hearty bean entrée one or two times a week.

FRESH TOMATO AND CHEESE PIZZA

2 thin slices purple onion, cut in half
2 cloves garlic, thinly sliced
Olive oil-flavored vegetable cooking spray
1 (10-ounce) can refrigerated pizza crust dough
1 teaspoon olive oil
1 (15-ounce) carton part-skim ricotta cheese
½ cup (2 ounces) shredded part-skim mozzarella cheese
½ cup freshly grated Parmesan cheese, divided
1 tablespoon chopped fresh basil
4 plum tomatoes, cut into ¼-inch-thick slices
3 yellow tomatoes, cut into ¼-inch-thick slices
3 red teardrop tomatoes, cut in half
8 fresh basil sprigs (optional)

Place onion and garlic on a baking sheet coated with cooking spray. Coat onion and garlic with cooking spray. Broil 5½ inches from heat (with electric oven door partially opened) 8 to 10 minutes or until charred; set aside.

Shape pizza crust dough into a ball, and gently press into a 4-inch circle on a baking sheet coated with cooking spray. Roll dough into a 12-inch circle.

Cut 1-inch-deep slits around edge of dough at ½-inch intervals; fold every other ½-inch-wide piece of dough in toward center. Brush with oil.

Combine ricotta cheese, mozzarella cheese, ¼ cup Parmesan cheese, and chopped basil, stirring well. Spread cheese mixture over pizza dough, leaving a ½-inch border. Arrange tomato slices over cheese mixture; top with roasted onion and garlic. Sprinkle with remaining ¼ cup Parmesan cheese.

Bake at 500° on bottom rack of oven for 12 minutes or until crust is browned. Transfer pizza to a cutting board; top with teardrop tomato halves. Garnish with basil sprigs, if desired. Let stand 5 minutes before cutting. Yield: 6 servings (266 calories per serving).

Per Serving:		
Protein 17.9g	Fat 8.4g	(Saturated Fat 4.1g)
Carbohydrate 32.3g	Fiber 1.9g	Cholesterol 21mg
Iron 1.0mg	Sodium 491mg	Calcium 253mg

Build a vegetable-and-cheese tower of taste sensations with Mile-High Stuffed Potato.

MILE-HIGH STUFFED POTATO

8 (8-ounce) baking potatoes
1 (15-ounce) can no-salt-added pinto beans, drained
1 (8-ounce) can no-salt-added tomato sauce
1 tablespoon taco seasoning mix
1 cup sliced zucchini
1 cup coarsely chopped carrot
1 cup frozen whole-kernel corn
1 cup (4 ounces) shredded part-skim mozzarella cheese
1 cup 1% low-fat cottage cheese
¼ cup sliced green onions
2 tablespoons minced fresh cilantro

Scrub potatoes; prick each several times with a fork. Bake at 400° for 45 minutes or until done. Let cool slightly.

Combine pinto beans, tomato sauce, and taco seasoning mix in a medium saucepan. Bring mixture to a boil; cover, reduce heat, and simmer 15 minutes. Set aside, and keep warm.

Arrange zucchini, carrot, and corn in a vegetable steamer over boiling water. Cover and steam 4 minutes or until crisp-tender. Set aside; keep warm.

Cut a lengthwise slit in top of each potato. Press ends of each potato toward center, pushing pulp up. Sprinkle 2 tablespoons shredded mozzarella cheese over each potato.

Top potatoes evenly with bean mixture and steamed vegetables. Combine cottage cheese and green onions; spoon evenly over potatoes. Sprinkle evenly with cilantro. Yield: 8 servings (285 calories per serving).

Per Serving:

Protein 15.5g	Fat 3.2g	(Saturated Fat 1.7g)
Carbohydrate 53.2g	Fiber 7.3g	Cholesterol 9mg
Iron 3.9mg	Sodium 289mg	Calcium 169mg

BROCCOLI-CHEESE STUFFED POTATOES

6 (8-ounce) baking potatoes
½ (8-ounce) package Neufchâtel cheese
¼ cup crumbled blue cheese
⅓ cup skim milk
2 egg whites
1 cup chopped cooked broccoli
¼ cup sliced green onions
2 tablespoons grated Parmesan cheese
2 tablespoons fine, dry breadcrumbs
2 teaspoons margarine, melted

Scrub potatoes; prick each several times with a fork. Bake at 400° for 45 minutes or until done. Let potatoes cool.

Cut a lengthwise strip from top of each potato; discard strips. Carefully scoop out pulp, leaving ¼-inch-thick shells; set shells aside.

Place potato pulp in a large bowl, and mash; add Neufchâtel cheese, blue cheese, and milk. Beat at medium speed of an electric mixer 2 minutes or until smooth. Add egg whites, and beat at medium speed until smooth. Stir in broccoli and green onions. Spoon mixture evenly into potato shells.

Combine Parmesan cheese, breadcrumbs, and margarine; sprinkle evenly over tops of potatoes. Place potatoes on an ungreased baking sheet. Bake at 350° for 25 minutes or until thoroughly heated. Yield: 6 servings (249 calories per serving).

Per Serving:

Protein 10.4g	Fat 7.9g	(Saturated Fat 4.3g)
Carbohydrate 35.5g	Fiber 3.8g	Cholesterol 20mg
Iron 2.6mg	Sodium 249mg	Calcium 122mg

EGGPLANT ROLL-UPS

Nonfat cottage cheese works best in this recipe because it has a drier texture. Low-fat cottage cheese is creamier and would make the filling too thin.

2 tablespoons all-purpose flour
1 tablespoon chili powder
¼ teaspoon ground oregano
¼ teaspoon salt
Dash of ground cumin
1½ cups water
½ cup no-salt-added tomato sauce
1 (1½ pound) eggplant
½ cup nonfat cottage cheese
½ cup (2 ounces) shredded reduced-fat Monterey Jack cheese
3 tablespoons minced green onions, divided
1 jalapeño pepper, seeded and minced

Combine first 5 ingredients in a medium saucepan, stirring well. Gradually stir in water and tomato sauce. Bring to a boil over medium heat, stirring constantly. Reduce heat, and simmer, uncovered, 15 minutes, stirring frequently. Set tomato sauce mixture aside, and keep warm.

Peel eggplant, and cut lengthwise into 8 (¼-inch-thick) slices. Place eggplant slices in a Dutch oven. Add water to cover. Bring to a boil, and cook 2 to 3 minutes or until eggplant is tender. Press dry between paper towels.

Combine cottage cheese, Monterey Jack cheese, 2 tablespoons onions, and jalapeño pepper. Spoon about 2 tablespoons cheese mixture down center of each eggplant slice; roll up jellyroll fashion.

Spread ½ cup tomato sauce mixture over bottom of an 11- x 7- x 1½-inch baking dish. Place eggplant rolls, seam side down, over sauce. Spoon remaining sauce over rolls. Sprinkle with remaining 1 tablespoon green onions. Bake, uncovered, at 400° for 20 minutes or until thoroughly heated. Yield: 4 servings (130 calories per serving).

Per Serving:

Protein 10.6g	Fat 3.2g	(Saturated Fat 1.7g)
Carbohydrate 17.2g	Fiber 3.5g	Cholesterol 11mg
Iron 1.9mg	Sodium 374mg	Calcium 201mg

ZUCCHINI PARMESAN

Olive oil-flavored vegetable cooking spray
1¾ cups sliced fresh mushrooms
½ cup minced shallots
6 cups peeled, seeded, and chopped tomato
1½ cups no-salt-added tomato juice
1 (6-ounce) can no-salt-added tomato paste
2 tablespoons chopped fresh basil
2 teaspoons chopped fresh oregano
½ teaspoon fennel seeds
¼ teaspoon salt
1 bay leaf
5 large zucchini
1¼ cups (5 ounces) shredded part-skim mozzarella cheese
¼ cup plus 2 tablespoons grated Parmesan cheese

Coat a Dutch oven with cooking spray. Place over medium-high heat until hot. Add mushrooms and shallots; sauté until vegetables are tender.

Add chopped tomato and next 7 ingredients; stir well. Bring to a boil; reduce heat, and simmer, uncovered, 40 minutes, stirring occasionally. Remove and discard bay leaf. Set aside, and keep warm.

Cut each zucchini lengthwise into 5 slices. Cook zucchini slices in boiling water to cover 6 to 8 minutes or until crisp-tender; drain. Rinse with cold water, and drain again. Press slices dry between paper towels.

Spread 2 cups tomato mixture over bottom of a 13- x 9- x 2-inch baking dish. Place half of zucchini slices over sauce, overlapping slices slightly. Sprinkle half of mozzarella cheese and 2 tablespoons Parmesan cheese over zucchini. Repeat layers with 2 cups tomato mixture, remaining zucchini slices, remaining mozzarella cheese, and 2 tablespoons Parmesan cheese. Top with remaining tomato mixture, and sprinkle with remaining 2 tablespoons Parmesan cheese.

Bake, uncovered, at 350° for 30 minutes or until thoroughly heated. Let stand 10 minutes before serving. Yield: 8 servings (156 calories per serving).

Per Serving:

Protein 10.8g	Fat 4.9g	(Saturated Fat 2.7g)
Carbohydrate 21.2g	Fiber 4.1g	Cholesterol 13mg
Iron 2.5mg	Sodium 260mg	Calcium 221mg

CHINESE VEGETABLE STIR-FRY

Tofu is a protein-rich soybean product with a very mild flavor. It absorbs the flavors of the recipe and adds texture.

¼ cup fresh lemon juice
¼ cup low-sodium soy sauce
1 tablespoon peeled, grated gingerroot
2 teaspoons sugar
2 cloves garlic, minced
1 (10-ounce) package firm tofu, drained and cubed
1 cup chopped onion
2 tablespoons vegetable oil
2 cups shredded Chinese cabbage
1 cup fresh bean sprouts
1 cup diced sweet red pepper
1 cup sliced fresh mushrooms
¼ cup sliced green onions
2 teaspoons cornstarch
6 cups cooked brown rice (cooked without salt or fat)

Combine first 5 ingredients in a medium bowl, stirring well. Add tofu and chopped onion. Cover and marinate in refrigerator 2 to 3 hours. Drain tofu and onion, reserving marinade.

Drizzle oil around top of wok, coating sides. Heat at medium (350°) until hot. Add tofu and onion; stir-fry 10 minutes or until tofu starts to brown and onion is tender. Remove tofu mixture from wok; set aside, and keep warm.

Add cabbage, bean sprouts, red pepper, mushrooms, and green onions to wok; stir-fry 2 to 3 minutes or until vegetables are crisp-tender. Combine reserved marinade and cornstarch, stirring well. Add marinade mixture to vegetables; stir-fry 3 minutes or until thickened. Add tofu mixture, and stir-fry 30 seconds or until thoroughly heated. To serve, spoon 1 cup rice onto each individual serving plate. Top evenly with vegetable mixture. Yield: 6 servings (339 calories per serving).

Per Serving:

Protein 10.6g	Fat 8.9g	(Saturated Fat 1.6g)
Carbohydrate 55.3g	Fiber 5.4g	Cholesterol 0mg
Iron 4.3mg	Sodium 291mg	Calcium 107mg

VEGETABLE KABOBS WITH HERBED COUSCOUS

With this recipe, follow the USDA's guideline to eat more complex carbohydrates. The dish is packed with carbohydrate-rich couscous and vegetables.

8 small round red potatoes
1 (1-pound) eggplant
¼ cup plus 2 tablespoons lemon juice
½ cup commercial reduced-calorie Italian dressing
1 tablespoon chopped fresh basil
2 cloves garlic, minced
16 medium-size fresh mushrooms
2 small zucchini, cut into 16 slices
2 small purple onions, quartered
1 small sweet red pepper, cut into 8 pieces
Vegetable cooking spray
1 cup water
1 cup canned vegetable broth, undiluted
1⅔ cups couscous, uncooked
¼ cup minced fresh parsley
2 tablespoons chopped fresh oregano
1 tablespoon chopped fresh thyme

Cook potatoes in boiling water to cover in a medium saucepan 15 minutes or until tender; drain, and set aside.

Trim ends from eggplant. Cut eggplant in half lengthwise. Place 1 half, cut side down, on a cutting board. Cut vertically into ¼-inch-thick strips. Repeat procedure with remaining eggplant half.

Combine lemon juice and next 3 ingredients in a large heavy-duty, zip-top plastic bag. Add potatoes, eggplant strips, mushrooms, and next 3 ingredients; seal bag, and shake until vegetables are well coated. Marinate in refrigerator 1 hour, turning bag occasionally.

Remove vegetables from marinade, reserving marinade. Fold eggplant strips accordian-style, and thread strips alternately with other vegetables on 8 (14-inch) skewers.

Coat grill rack with cooking spray; place on grill over medium-hot coals (350° to 400°). Place kabobs on rack; grill, covered, 10 to 12 minutes or until vegetables are tender, turning and basting occasionally with reserved marinade. Set vegetable kabobs aside, and keep warm.

Bring water and broth to a boil in a medium saucepan. Stir in couscous and remaining ingredients. Remove from heat; cover and let stand 5 minutes. Fluff with a fork. Remove vegetables from skewers, and serve over couscous. Yield: 4 servings (387 calories per serving).

Per Serving:

Protein 14.1g	Fat 2.3g	(Saturated Fat 0.3g)
Carbohydrate 81.6g	Fiber 7.0g	Cholesterol 0mg
Iron 5.6mg	Sodium 627mg	Calcium 126mg

MAKING EGGPLANT STRIPS

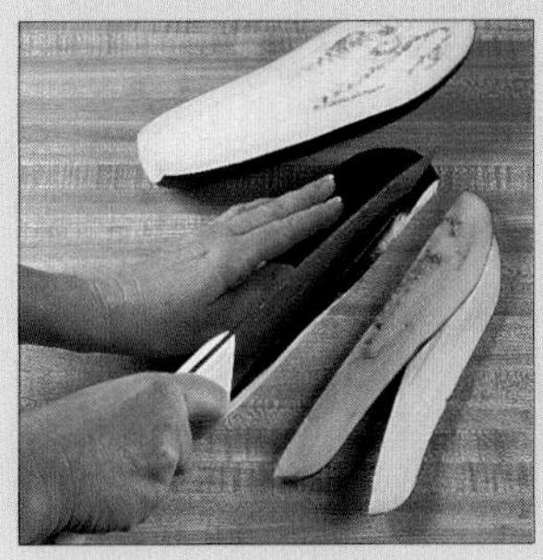

- Cut eggplant in half lengthwise.
- Place one half of eggplant cut side down; cut vertically into ¼-inch-thick strips.
- Repeat procedure with remaining eggplant half.

SKEWERING EGGPLANT STRIPS

- Marinate eggplant strips for one hour to soften and add flavor.
- Thread eggplant strips accordian-style alternately with other vegetables onto skewers.

BULGUR PILAF STUFFED CRÊPES

½ cup all-purpose flour
1 cup skim milk
3 egg whites
1 egg
Vegetable cooking spray
2 teaspoons olive oil
½ cup shredded carrot
¼ cup plus 2 tablespoons finely chopped onion
2 cloves garlic, minced
1⅔ cups water
1 cup canned vegetable broth, undiluted
1⅓ cups bulgur (cracked wheat), uncooked
½ cup freshly grated Parmesan cheese, divided
¼ cup plus 2 tablespoons minced fresh parsley
¼ cup pine nuts, toasted

Position knife blade in food processor bowl; add first 4 ingredients. Process 1 minute or until smooth, scraping sides of processor bowl occasionally. Refrigerate batter 1 hour.

Coat a 7-inch crêpe pan or nonstick skillet with cooking spray; place over medium heat until hot. Pour 2½ tablespoons batter into pan; quickly tilt pan in all directions so batter covers pan in a thin film. Cook 1 minute or until crêpe can be shaken loose from pan. Flip crêpe, and cook about 30 seconds. Remove from pan; place crêpe on a towel to cool. Repeat until all batter is used. Stack cooled crêpes between layers of wax paper to prevent sticking.

Heat oil in a nonstick skillet over medium-high heat until hot. Add carrot, onion, and garlic; sauté 3 minutes. Add water and broth; bring to a boil. Stir in bulgur; cover, reduce heat, and simmer 15 minutes or until bulgur is tender and liquid is absorbed. Stir in ¼ cup cheese, parsley, and pine nuts.

Spoon ⅓ cup bulgur mixture down center of each crêpe. Roll up crêpes; place in a 13- x 9- x 2-inch baking dish coated with cooking spray. Sprinkle with remaining ¼ cup cheese. Bake at 375° for 30 minutes or until thoroughly heated. Yield: 6 servings (286 calories per serving).

Per Serving:
Protein 14.0g	Fat 8.7g	(Saturated Fat 2.6g)
Carbohydrate 41.1g	Fiber 7.6g	Cholesterol 44mg
Iron 2.0mg	Sodium 344mg	Calcium 192mg

BROWN RICE WITH GARDEN VEGETABLES AND BEANS

2 teaspoons olive oil
1 cup chopped onion
3 cloves garlic, minced
⅔ cup water
⅔ cup canned vegetable broth, undiluted
1 cup instant brown rice, uncooked
1 cup sliced carrot
¾ cup chopped tomato
1 teaspoon dried thyme
½ teaspoon dried oregano
¼ teaspoon salt
¼ teaspoon pepper
½ pound fresh asparagus
1 cup sliced zucchini
1 (15-ounce) can no-salt-added garbanzo beans, drained
¼ cup grated Asiago cheese

Heat oil in a large saucepan over medium-high heat until hot. Add onion and garlic; sauté until onion is tender.

Combine water and broth. Add to onion mixture, and bring to a boil. Stir in rice and next 6 ingredients. Cover, reduce heat, and simmer 10 minutes or until rice is tender and liquid is absorbed. Let stand, covered, 5 minutes.

Snap off tough ends of asparagus. Remove scales from stalks with a knife or vegetable peeler, if desired. Cut spears into 1-inch pieces. Arrange asparagus and zucchini in a vegetable steamer over boiling water. Cover and steam 8 minutes or until vegetables are crisp-tender. Drain; add to rice mixture. Add beans and cheese; toss gently. Yield: 4 servings (318 calories per serving).

Per Serving:
Protein 13.9g	Fat 7.3g	(Saturated Fat 1.8g)
Carbohydrate 53.1g	Fiber 7.6g	Cholesterol 5mg
Iron 3.8mg	Sodium 407mg	Calcium 166mg

Fruited Veal Chops Baked in Wine (page 154) may be presented as an elegant feast for a formal dinner party or as a hearty meal for a family dinner.

Meats

CARIBBEAN MEAT LOAF

Using ground round instead of ground chuck in this recipe yields a fat savings of 9 grams per serving.

1½ pounds ground round
½ cup no-salt-added tomato sauce
1 cup soft breadcrumbs
¼ cup frozen egg substitute, thawed
2 tablespoons minced onion
2 teaspoons low-sodium Worcestershire sauce
¼ teaspoon salt
¼ teaspoon pepper
Vegetable cooking spray
½ cup plus 2 tablespoons no-salt-added tomato sauce
¼ cup canned crushed pineapple in juice, drained
2 tablespoons minced onion
1½ teaspoons brown sugar
1½ teaspoons lime juice
1 teaspoon low-sodium Worcestershire sauce
¼ teaspoon ground allspice
⅛ teaspoon salt
⅛ teaspoon ground ginger
⅛ teaspoon dry mustard

Combine first 8 ingredients. Shape mixture into an 8- x 4-inch loaf; place on a rack in a roasting pan coated with cooking spray. Bake at 350° for 1 hour and 5 minutes.

Combine ½ cup plus 2 tablespoons tomato sauce and remaining ingredients. Pour over meat loaf, and bake an additional 5 minutes. Yield: 8 servings (194 calories per serving).

Per Serving:		
Protein 24.4g	Fat 8.8g	(Saturated Fat 0.1g)
Carbohydrate 8.3g	Fiber 0.8g	Cholesterol 55mg
Iron 3.2mg	Sodium 223mg	Calcium 25mg

FLANK STEAK WITH MUSHROOMS

Marinating this cut of beef tenderizes and flavors it.

1 (1-pound) lean flank steak
¼ cup low-sodium soy sauce
2 tablespoons lemon juice
1 teaspoon freeze-dried chives
¼ teaspoon dried marjoram
2 cloves garlic, minced
Vegetable cooking spray
1 teaspoon olive oil
3 cups sliced fresh mushrooms
2 tablespoons minced fresh parsley

Trim fat from steak. Combine soy sauce and next 4 ingredients in a heavy-duty, zip-top plastic bag. Add steak; seal bag, and shake until steak is well coated. Marinate in refrigerator 8 hours, turning bag occasionally.

Remove steak from marinade, reserving marinade. Slice steak diagonally across grain into ¼-inch-wide strips.

Coat a large nonstick skillet with cooking spray; add oil. Place over medium-high heat until hot. Add steak; cook 5 to 6 minutes or until browned on all sides, stirring frequently. Remove steak from skillet. Drain and pat dry with paper towels. Wipe drippings from skillet with a paper towel.

Coat skillet with cooking spray, and place over medium-high heat until hot. Add mushrooms; sauté 3 minutes. Stir in reserved marinade and parsley. Cover, reduce heat to medium, and cook an additional 5 minutes. Return steak to skillet; cook until thoroughly heated. Yield: 4 servings (248 calories per serving).

Per Serving:		
Protein 23.3g	Fat 14.5g	(Saturated Fat 5.6g)
Carbohydrate 4.6g	Fiber 1.0g	Cholesterol 60mg
Iron 3.2mg	Sodium 464mg	Calcium 15mg

BEEF WITH BLACK BEANS

1 pound lean boneless top round steak
¼ cup balsamic vinegar
½ teaspoon ground coriander
½ teaspoon ground cumin
½ teaspoon ground oregano
2 cloves garlic, crushed
Vegetable cooking spray
1 cup chopped onion
½ cup chopped green pepper
½ cup chopped celery
¼ cup chopped carrot
2 cloves garlic, minced
1 jalapeño pepper, seeded and minced
1 (13¾-ounce) can no-salt-added beef broth
1 cup water
2 tablespoons chopped fresh cilantro
2 teaspoons chopped fresh oregano
½ teaspoon ground cumin
¼ teaspoon salt
¼ teaspoon pepper
1 (15-ounce) can black beans, drained
2½ cups cooked orzo (cooked without salt or fat)
2 tablespoons thinly sliced green onions

Trim fat from steak; cut steak into 1-inch pieces. Combine vinegar and next 4 ingredients in a heavy-duty, zip-top plastic bag. Add steak; seal bag, and shake until steak is well coated. Marinate in refrigerator 1 hour, turning bag once.

Remove steak from marinade, reserving marinade. Coat a Dutch oven with cooking spray; place over medium-high heat until hot. Add steak; cook 2 minutes or until browned on all sides, stirring frequently. Drain and pat dry with paper towels. Wipe drippings from Dutch oven with a paper towel.

Coat Dutch oven with cooking spray. Place over medium-high heat until hot. Add onion and next 5 ingredients. Sauté until vegetables are tender.

Add steak, beef broth, and next 6 ingredients; bring to a boil. Cover, reduce heat, and simmer 1 hour. Uncover and simmer an additional hour and 20 minutes or until mixture is thickened and beef is tender. Stir in reserved marinade and black beans; simmer 5 minutes. To serve, spoon ½ cup orzo into each individual serving bowl. Top evenly with beef mixture, and sprinkle with sliced green onions. Yield: 5 servings (350 calories per serving).

Per Serving:		
Protein 30.9g	Fat 5.0g	(Saturated Fat 1.5g)
Carbohydrate 43.9g	Fiber 4.6g	Cholesterol 52mg
Iron 5.4mg	Sodium 340mg	Calcium 57mg

FILET MIGNON WITH BÉARNAISE SAUCE

By using egg substitute, reduced-calorie margarine, and nonfat sour cream alternative, we reduced the fat in this sauce by more than 50 percent.

3 tablespoons Chablis or other dry white wine
2 tablespoons tarragon vinegar
1 tablespoon minced shallots
½ teaspoon dried tarragon
¼ teaspoon freshly ground pepper
¼ cup frozen egg substitute, thawed
3 tablespoons reduced-calorie margarine
1 tablespoon nonfat sour cream alternative
4 (4-ounce) beef tenderloin steaks
Vegetable cooking spray
½ teaspoon salt-free lemon-pepper seasoning

Combine first 5 ingredients in a small skillet. Bring mixture to a boil. Reduce heat, and simmer, uncovered, until mixture is reduced to 2 tablespoons.

Pour mixture through a wire-mesh strainer into the top of a double boiler, discarding shallots. Add egg substitute, and stir well. Bring water to a boil, stirring constantly. Reduce heat to low. Add margarine, 1 tablespoon at a time, stirring constantly with a wire whisk until blended. Cook, stirring constantly, until sauce thickens slightly. Remove from heat; stir in sour cream. Set aside, and keep warm.

Place steaks on rack of a broiler pan coated with cooking spray. Sprinkle steaks with lemon-pepper seasoning. Broil 5½ inches from heat (with electric oven door partially opened) 8 minutes on each side or to desired degree of doneness. Serve with sauce. Yield: 4 servings (232 calories per serving).

Per Serving:		
Protein 25.9g	Fat 13.5g	(Saturated Fat 3.1g)
Carbohydrate 1.0g	Fiber 0.1g	Cholesterol 71mg
Iron 3.5mg	Sodium 162mg	Calcium 14mg

Escape to a world of calypso music and palm trees with the fresh flavors of lemon, lime, and orange in Grilled Sirloin with Citrus Salsa.

GRILLED SIRLOIN WITH CITRUS SALSA

1½ pounds lean boneless top sirloin steak
½ cup low-sodium soy sauce
¼ cup chopped green onions
2 tablespoons dark brown sugar
3 tablespoons fresh lime juice
⅛ teaspoon hot sauce
1 clove garlic, minced
Vegetable cooking spray
Citrus Salsa
Fresh cilantro sprigs (optional)
Lemon slices (optional)
Lime slices (optional)
Orange slices (optional)

Trim fat from steak. Place steak in a shallow dish. Combine soy sauce and next 5 ingredients. Pour over steak; turn steak to coat. Cover and marinate in refrigerator at least 2 hours; turn steak occasionally.

Remove steak from marinade; discard marinade. Coat grill rack with cooking spray; place on grill over medium-hot coals (350° to 400°). Place steak on rack; grill, covered, 5 to 6 minutes on each side or to desired degree of doneness. Let steak stand 5 minutes. Cut diagonally across grain into thin slices; arrange on serving plates. Serve with Citrus Salsa. If desired, garnish with cilantro and fruit slices. Yield: 6 servings (200 calories per serving).

Citrus Salsa

2 oranges, peeled, seeded, and chopped
½ teaspoon grated lemon rind
½ teaspoon grated lime rind
½ small lemon, peeled, seeded, and finely chopped
½ small lime, peeled, seeded, and finely chopped
¼ cup chopped green onions
1 tablespoon sugar
1 tablespoon chopped fresh cilantro
1 teaspoon seeded, minced jalapeño pepper
⅛ teaspoon salt
2 tablespoons unsweetened orange juice
2 tablespoons rice vinegar

Combine all ingredients in a small bowl. Cover and chill at least 2 hours. Yield: 1¼ cups.

Per Serving:		
Protein 26.3g	Fat 6.3g	(Saturated Fat 2.4g)
Carbohydrate 8.1g	Fiber 1.5g	Cholesterol 76mg
Iron 3.0mg	Sodium 179mg	Calcium 29mg

BEEF TENDERLOIN WITH HORSERADISH SAUCE

1 (8-ounce) carton nonfat sour cream alternative
¼ cup minced fresh parsley
¼ cup prepared horseradish
1 teaspoon white wine Worcestershire sauce
⅛ teaspoon pepper
1 (2-pound) beef tenderloin
½ teaspoon salt-free lemon-pepper seasoning
Vegetable cooking spray

Combine first 5 ingredients. Cover and chill.

Trim fat from tenderloin. Sprinkle lemon-pepper seasoning over tenderloin; place on a rack in a roasting pan coated with cooking spray. Insert meat thermometer into thickest part of tenderloin, if desired. Bake at 500° for 35 minutes or until thermometer registers 145° (medium-rare) or 160° (medium).

Let stand 10 minutes before slicing. Serve with sauce. Yield: 8 servings (155 calories per serving).

Per Serving:		
Protein 20.2g	Fat 6.0g	(Saturated Fat 2.3g)
Carbohydrate 3.1g	Fiber 0.2g	Cholesterol 54mg
Iron 2.5mg	Sodium 75mg	Calcium 45mg

GERMAN-STYLE BRISKET

Lean brisket is often referred to as the flat cut. The long cooking time in this recipe tenderizes the beef.

2 (2-pound) lean beef briskets
Vegetable cooking spray
2 (13¾-ounce) cans no-salt-added beef broth
1 (12-ounce) can light beer
2 cups chopped onion
1 cup chopped carrot
1 cup chopped celery
½ cup no-salt-added tomato sauce
¼ cup minced fresh parsley
1 tablespoon sugar
¼ teaspoon salt
¼ teaspoon pepper
¼ teaspoon ground allspice
¼ teaspoon ground cloves
1 bay leaf
¼ cup water
3 tablespoons all-purpose flour

Trim fat from briskets. Coat a large Dutch oven with cooking spray; place over medium-high heat until hot. Add 1 brisket, and cook 8 minutes or until browned on all sides. Remove brisket from Dutch oven. Drain and pat dry with paper towels. Repeat procedure with remaining brisket. Wipe drippings from Dutch oven with a paper towel.

Return meat to Dutch oven; add beef broth and next 12 ingredients. Bring to a boil; cover, reduce heat, and simmer 2½ hours or until meat is tender. Transfer meat to a serving platter, and keep warm.

Skim fat from broth. Remove and discard bay leaf. Set aside 4 cups broth for sauce. Reserve remaining broth for another use. Return 4 cups broth to Dutch oven. Combine water and flour, stirring until smooth; add flour mixture to broth. Cook over medium heat, stirring constantly, until thickened.

Cut meat diagonally across grain into ¼-inch-thick slices. Serve with sauce. Yield: 16 servings (170 calories per serving).

Per Serving:		
Protein 24.7g	Fat 5.6g	(Saturated Fat 1.8g)
Carbohydrate 3.3g	Fiber 0.4g	Cholesterol 67mg
Iron 2.3mg	Sodium 105mg	Calcium 11mg

FRUITED VEAL CHOPS BAKED IN WINE

If you prefer, substitute 1 cup apple juice for the wine in this recipe (pictured on page 149).

¼ teaspoon salt
¼ teaspoon pepper
4 (6-ounce) lean veal loin chops (1 inch thick)
Vegetable cooking spray
1 cup chopped onion
1 cup Riesling wine
½ cup canned low-sodium chicken broth, undiluted
¼ cup raisins
1 tablespoon grated orange rind
¼ teaspoon ground sage
¼ teaspoon dried thyme
1 medium Granny Smith apple, peeled and cut into thin wedges
1 medium orange, peeled and sectioned
Fresh sage sprigs (optional)

Sprinkle salt and pepper over chops. Coat a nonstick skillet with cooking spray; place over medium heat until hot. Add chops; cook 2 minutes on each side or until browned. Remove chops from skillet. Drain and pat dry with paper towels.

Place chops in an 11- x 7- x 1½-inch baking dish coated with cooking spray; set aside. Wipe drippings from skillet with a paper towel.

Coat skillet with cooking spray, and place over medium-high heat until hot. Add onion, and sauté until tender. Add wine and next 5 ingredients. Bring to a boil; cover, reduce heat, and simmer 10 minutes. Uncover and simmer 10 minutes.

Arrange apple wedges and orange sections over chops; pour wine mixture over fruit. Bake, uncovered, at 325° for 50 minutes or until chops are tender, basting occasionally with pan juices. To serve, place chops on individual serving plates. Spoon apple mixture over chops. Garnish with sage sprigs, if desired. Yield: 4 servings (196 calories per serving).

Per Serving:

Protein 24.0g	Fat 4.7g	(Saturated Fat 1.2g)
Carbohydrate 14.7g	Fiber 2.5g	Cholesterol 91mg
Iron 1.6mg	Sodium 266mg	Calcium 47mg

VEAL SHANKS WITH SUN-DRIED TOMATO SAUCE

Serve this soul-satisfying dish with brown rice, steamed broccoli, and commercial multi-grain rolls for a low-fat, high-fiber meal.

4 (5-ounce) veal shanks
Vegetable cooking spray
1 teaspoon olive oil
1½ cups canned no-salt-added beef broth, undiluted
1¼ cups diced carrot
1¼ cups diced celery
1¼ cups diced onion
½ cup Chablis or other dry white wine
½ teaspoon dried basil
½ teaspoon dried thyme
¼ teaspoon salt
¼ teaspoon pepper
5 sun-dried tomatoes, quartered
3 cloves garlic, crushed
1 bay leaf
1 (15-ounce) can garbanzo beans, drained
⅓ cup minced fresh parsley

Trim fat from veal shanks. Coat a Dutch oven with cooking spray; add oil, and place over medium-high heat until hot. Add veal shanks, and cook until browned on all sides. Add beef broth and next 11 ingredients. Bring to a boil; cover, reduce heat, and simmer 2 hours.

Add garbanzo beans and parsley; cover and simmer an additional 10 minutes. Remove and discard bay leaf. Yield: 4 servings (316 calories per serving).

Per Serving:

Protein 27.9g	Fat 8.7g	(Saturated Fat 2.5g)
Carbohydrate 31.2g	Fiber 11.5g	Cholesterol 91mg
Iron 4.0mg	Sodium 474mg	Calcium 112mg

Veal Primavera combines tender veal cutlets with a colorful layer of fresh garden vegetables.

VEAL PRIMAVERA

1 pound veal cutlets (1/4 inch thick)
2 tablespoons all-purpose flour
Olive oil-flavored vegetable cooking spray
2 teaspoons olive oil
1 1/2 cups sliced fresh mushrooms
1 cup Sugar Snap peas
1 cup julienne-sliced carrot
1 cup julienne-sliced fennel
1/2 cup canned low-sodium chicken broth, undiluted
1/3 cup minced shallot
1 teaspoon dried Italian seasoning
1/4 teaspoon salt
1/4 teaspoon pepper
1 clove garlic, minced
8 pear-shaped cherry tomatoes, halved
Fresh fennel leaves (optional)

Trim fat from cutlets. Place cutlets between 2 sheets of heavy-duty plastic wrap; flatten to 1/8-inch thickness, using a meat mallet or rolling pin. Sprinkle cutlets evenly with flour.

Coat a large nonstick skillet with cooking spray; add oil. Place over medium-high heat until hot. Add veal, and cook 3 minutes on each side or until done; remove from skillet. Drain and pat dry with paper towels. Set aside, and keep warm. Wipe drippings from skillet with a paper towel.

Add mushrooms and next 9 ingredients to skillet; bring to a boil. Cover, reduce heat, and simmer 2 to 3 minutes or until vegetables are crisp-tender. Add tomatoes, and cook an additional 30 seconds.

Place veal on individual serving plates; spoon vegetable mixture over veal. Garnish with fennel leaves, if desired. Yield: 4 servings (264 calories per serving).

Per Serving:		
Protein 31.1g	Fat 8.8g	(Saturated Fat 2.0g)
Carbohydrate 15.0g	Fiber 3.0g	Cholesterol 100mg
Iron 3.8mg	Sodium 252mg	Calcium 87mg

ROAST VEAL WITH MUSHROOM SAUCE

Crimini mushrooms are the brown cousins to white button mushrooms. Substitute white button mushrooms if crimini are not available.

1 (2-pound) boneless veal round roast
½ teaspoon salt-free lemon-pepper seasoning
Vegetable cooking spray
1 teaspoon olive oil
½ cup diced shallots (about 4 medium)
1 (8-ounce) package fresh crimini mushrooms, sliced
4 ounces fresh shiitake mushroom caps, sliced
4 ounces sliced fresh mushrooms
1 cup canned no-salt-added beef broth, undiluted
½ cup dry sherry
¼ cup minced fresh parsley
¾ teaspoon dried tarragon
¼ teaspoon salt
Fresh parsley sprigs (optional)

Trim fat from roast. Sprinkle lemon-pepper seasoning over entire surface of roast. Place roast on a rack in a roasting pan coated with cooking spray. Insert meat thermometer into thickest part of roast, if desired. Bake at 450° for 40 minutes or until meat thermometer registers 160°.

Let roast stand 10 minutes; cut into thin slices. Arrange slices on a serving platter, and keep warm.

Coat a large nonstick skillet with cooking spray; add olive oil. Place over medium-high heat until hot. Add shallots and next 3 ingredients; sauté until tender.

Add beef broth, sherry, minced parsley, tarragon, and salt to mushroom mixture. Bring mixture to a boil; reduce heat, and simmer, uncovered, 20 minutes, stirring frequently. Spoon mushroom mixture over veal. Garnish with fresh parsley sprigs, if desired. Yield: 8 servings (202 calories per serving).

Per Serving:

Protein 28.6g	Fat 6.5g	(Saturated Fat 1.7g)
Carbohydrate 6.1g	Fiber 1.0g	Cholesterol 100mg
Iron 1.9mg	Sodium 155mg	Calcium 31mg

MOUSSAKA

2 medium eggplants (about 2 pounds)
½ teaspoon salt
Olive oil-flavored vegetable cooking spray
1½ pounds lean ground lamb
1¼ cups chopped onion
2 cloves garlic, minced
1 (14½-ounce) can no-salt-added whole tomatoes, undrained and chopped
1 (8-ounce) can no-salt-added tomato sauce
½ cup chopped fresh parsley
1 tablespoon chopped fresh basil
2 teaspoons chopped fresh oregano
¼ teaspoon ground nutmeg
½ cup fine, dry breadcrumbs, divided
¼ cup all-purpose flour
2 cups 1% low-fat milk
1 egg yolk, beaten
3 tablespoons grated Romano cheese
¼ teaspoon salt

Peel eggplant, and cut lengthwise into ¼-inch-thick slices. Place slices on wire racks; place racks on large baking sheets. Sprinkle slices evenly with ½ teaspoon salt. Bake at 350° for 22 to 24 minutes or until lightly browned, turning slices once. Let cool slightly. Press eggplant firmly between paper towels to remove excess moisture; set aside.

Coat a large nonstick skillet with cooking spray; place over medium-high heat until hot. Add lamb, onion, and garlic; cook until lamb is browned, stirring until it crumbles. Drain lamb mixture, and pat dry with paper towels. Wipe drippings from skillet with a paper towel.

Return lamb mixture to skillet; add chopped tomato and next 5 ingredients. Bring to a boil; reduce heat, and simmer, uncovered, 20 minutes or until mixture is thickened, stirring occasionally. Stir in ¼ cup breadcrumbs.

Place flour in a medium saucepan. Gradually add milk, stirring until smooth. Cook over medium heat, stirring constantly, until mixture is thickened and bubbly. Gradually stir about one-fourth of hot mixture into egg yolk; add to remaining hot mixture, stirring constantly. Add cheese and ¼ teaspoon salt; stir well, and set aside.

Coat a 13- x 9- x 2-inch baking dish with cooking spray; sprinkle remaining ¼ cup breadcrumbs over bottom of dish. Place half of eggplant slices in dish; top with half of lamb mixture. Repeat layers with remaining eggplant slices and remaining lamb mixture. Pour cheese sauce over lamb mixture. Bake, uncovered, at 350° for 25 minutes or until hot and bubbly. Yield: 8 servings (258 calories per serving).

Per Serving:		
Protein 25.1g	Fat 8.9g	(Saturated Fat 3.5g)
Carbohydrate 18.9g	Fiber 2.3g	Cholesterol 94mg
Iron 2.6mg	Sodium 390mg	Calcium 185mg

LAMB STROGANOFF

Lamb creates a flavorful variation of the traditional beef stroganoff. For this light version, we used a mere teaspoon of oil for sautéing and used low-fat sour cream.

Olive oil-flavored vegetable cooking spray
1½ pounds lean boneless lamb, cut into 1½-inch cubes
4½ cups sliced fresh mushrooms
1 teaspoon olive oil
1 cup sliced green onions
1 clove garlic, minced
1½ tablespoons all-purpose flour
1 tablespoon no-salt-added tomato paste
1 (13¾-ounce) can no-salt-added beef broth, divided
4 thin lemon slices
½ cup low-fat sour cream
2 teaspoons all-purpose flour
¼ teaspoon salt
¾ cup chopped fresh parsley
3 cups cooked wide egg noodles (cooked without salt or fat)

Coat a large nonstick skillet with cooking spray; place over medium-high heat until hot. Add lamb; cook 5 minutes or until browned on all sides, stirring frequently. Drain and pat dry with paper towels. Wipe drippings from skillet with a paper towel.

Coat skillet with cooking spray, and place over medium-high heat until hot. Add mushrooms; sauté 5 minutes. Remove from skillet, and set aside.

Add oil to skillet; place over medium-high heat until hot. Add green onions; sauté 2 minutes. Add garlic; sauté 30 seconds.

Combine 1½ tablespoons flour, tomato paste, and 2 tablespoons beef broth in a medium bowl, stirring well with a wire whisk. Add remaining broth, stirring until smooth.

Add broth mixture to onion mixture. Cook over medium heat, stirring constantly, until slightly thickened. Return lamb to skillet; cover, reduce heat, and simmer 45 minutes, stirring occasionally. Add lemon slices; cook, uncovered, 15 minutes. Add sautéed mushrooms; cook an additional 10 minutes. Remove from heat; remove and discard lemon slices.

Combine sour cream, 2 teaspoons flour, and salt, stirring well. Stir sour cream mixture and parsley into lamb mixture. Serve over cooked noodles. Yield: 6 servings (324 calories per serving).

Per Serving:		
Protein 29.7g	Fat 9.9g	(Saturated Fat 3.7g)
Carbohydrate 27.6g	Fiber 3.1g	Cholesterol 107mg
Iron 4.6mg	Sodium 190mg	Calcium 54mg

WATER WORKOUTS

If you are overweight or have a medical problem that forces you to limit high-impact sports, you may find water workouts to be the answer to your need for total fitness.

In addition to being an excellent workout for the heart, the water's natural resistance creates a good workout for the muscles. The risk of injury is less than that from regular aerobics because the water acts as a cushion. For an optimal water workout, the water temperature should be comfortable (about 82° to 86°). If it's too hot, you may feel drained of energy or possibly even pass out. If the water's too cool, stiff or arthritic joints may begin to ache.

An aerobic workout in the water doesn't have to mean swimming. Many public pools sponsor water aerobic exercise classes. Regular exercises such as jumping jacks, scissor kicks, and upper-body twists are done to music while you enjoy the cool comfort of the water. But be sure to check with your physician before starting this or any other fitness program.

In Lamb Shish Kabobs, the lamb is marinated before grilling and, with the vegetables, is basted during grilling.

LAMB SHISH KABOBS

1 pound lean boneless lamb
⅓ cup lime juice
1 tablespoon grated onion
1½ teaspoons chili powder
1 teaspoon ground ginger
1 teaspoon ground turmeric
1 teaspoon minced garlic
2 tablespoons water
1½ teaspoons olive oil
2 medium onions
1 large green pepper, cut into 1-inch pieces
12 medium-size fresh mushrooms
Vegetable cooking spray

Trim fat from lamb; cut lamb into 1¼-inch cubes. Place lamb in a shallow dish. Combine lime juice and next 7 ingredients, stirring well. Pour over lamb, stirring to coat. Cover and marinate in refrigerator 4 hours, stirring occasionally.

Cook 2 onions in boiling water to cover in a saucepan 10 minutes. Drain; cut each onion into 4 wedges.

Remove lamb from marinade, reserving marinade. Thread lamb, onion, green pepper, and mushrooms alternately onto 8 (10-inch) skewers.

Coat grill rack with cooking spray; place on grill over medium-hot coals (350° to 400°). Place kabobs on rack; grill, covered, 13 to 15 minutes or until lamb is done, turning and basting frequently with reserved marinade. Serve immediately. Yield: 4 servings (250 calories per serving).

Per Serving:

Protein 26.8g	Fat 9.2g	(Saturated Fat 2.7g)
Carbohydrate 15.8g	Fiber 3.4g	Cholesterol 76mg
Iron 3.5mg	Sodium 74mg	Calcium 38mg

LAMB CHOPS WITH APPLES AND PRUNES

Nafplion olives are small green olives marinated in brine. Substitute any Greek olive if Nafplion are not available.

8 (5-ounce) lean lamb loin chops (1 inch thick)
Butter-flavored vegetable cooking spray
2 teaspoons reduced-calorie margarine
1 cup peeled, finely chopped Granny Smith apple
¾ cup chopped onion
1 cup water
1 (8-ounce) can no-salt-added tomato sauce
1 tablespoon all-purpose flour
1 tablespoon chopped fresh rosemary
1½ teaspoons chopped fresh oregano
1½ teaspoons chopped fresh marjoram
1 teaspoon coarsely ground pepper
16 Nafplion olives
16 pitted prunes
2 tablespoons dry sherry
Fresh rosemary sprigs (optional)

Trim fat from chops. Coat a large nonstick skillet with cooking spray; place over medium-high heat until hot. Add chops; cook 2 to 3 minutes on each side or until browned.

Remove chops from skillet. Drain and pat dry with paper towels. Place chops in an ovenproof Dutch oven; set aside. Wipe drippings from skillet.

Melt margarine in skillet over medium-high heat. Add apple and onion; sauté 3 minutes or until tender. Combine water and next 6 ingredients, stirring well; add to apple mixture in skillet. Bring to a boil, stirring constantly. Pour over lamb.

Cover and bake at 350° for 30 minutes. Add olives, prunes, and sherry. Cover and bake an additional 25 minutes or to desired degree of doneness.

To serve, place a chop on each individual serving plate. Spoon sauce mixture evenly over chops. Garnish with fresh rosemary sprigs, if desired. Yield: 8 servings (259 calories per serving).

Per Serving:

Protein 25.1g	Fat 8.5g	(Saturated Fat 2.6g)
Carbohydrate 20.4g	Fiber 1.5g	Cholesterol 76mg
Iron 3.2mg	Sodium 191mg	Calcium 35mg

GRILLED LEG OF LAMB

1 (3½-pound) lean boneless leg of lamb
¼ cup low-sodium soy sauce
3 tablespoons water
3 tablespoons Dijon mustard
2 tablespoons vegetable oil
2 teaspoons dried rosemary
2 teaspoons finely chopped garlic
1 teaspoon ground ginger
Vegetable cooking spray

Trim fat from lamb. Combine soy sauce and next 6 ingredients in a large heavy-duty, zip-top plastic bag. Add lamb; seal bag, and shake until lamb is well coated. Marinate in refrigerator 8 hours, turning bag occasionally.

Remove lamb from marinade, reserving marinade. Coat grill rack with cooking spray; place on grill over medium-hot coals (350° to 400°). Place lamb on rack; grill, covered, 15 minutes on each side or until meat thermometer registers 150° (medium-rare) to 160° (medium), turning and basting occasionally with reserved marinade. Yield: 14 servings (188 calories per serving).

Per Serving:

Protein 24.2g	Fat 8.8g	(Saturated Fat 2.8g)
Carbohydrate 0.7g	Fiber 0.1g	Cholesterol 76mg
Iron 1.9mg	Sodium 265mg	Calcium 11mg

THE LOWDOWN ON LAMB

Expand your menu by including lamb, a versatile meat that can be a healthy addition to any meal. Lamb is succulent and tender, and its calorie, fat, and cholesterol content is similar to that of other lean cuts of meat. Following today's trend with other meats, lamb is being bred to be increasingly leaner.

Try using ground lamb instead of beef in lasagna, meat loaf, or hamburger patties (see page 72). Or stir-fry lamb strips with a combination of vegetables, or toss lamb cubes in stews or casseroles. You can even use lamb instead of beef for stroganoff (see page 157).

PORK-FILLED CABBAGE LEAVES

2 quarts water
8 large cabbage leaves
1 pound lean ground pork
1 cup cooked long-grain rice (cooked without salt or fat)
½ cup minced onion
¼ cup finely chopped green pepper
1 egg, lightly beaten
½ teaspoon dried thyme
¼ teaspoon salt
¼ teaspoon pepper
Vegetable cooking spray
1 (14½-ounce) can no-salt-added stewed tomatoes, undrained
½ cup canned no-salt-added beef broth, undiluted
1 tablespoon brown sugar
2 tablespoons lemon juice

Bring water to a boil in a large saucepan. Add cabbage leaves to water, one at a time. Cover, reduce heat, and simmer 4 minutes. Drain and rinse under cold water; drain again. Cut a small V-shape in the base of each leaf to remove thick center core; discard cores.

Combine pork and next 7 ingredients. Spoon pork mixture evenly in centers of cabbage leaves; fold ends over, and roll up.

Coat a large nonstick skillet with cooking spray. Place cabbage rolls in skillet, seam side down. Combine tomatoes and remaining ingredients; pour over cabbage rolls. Bring to a boil; cover, reduce heat, and simmer 1 hour. Serve warm. Yield: 8 servings (164 calories per serving).

Per Serving:		
Protein 14.3g	Fat 5.1g	(Saturated Fat 1.7g)
Carbohydrate 15.0g	Fiber 1.7g	Cholesterol 62mg
Iron 1.6mg	Sodium 137mg	Calcium 52mg

PORK SATAY WITH PEANUT SAUCE

2 pounds lean boneless pork loin
½ cup chopped onion
½ cup rice wine vinegar
1 tablespoon chopped fresh cilantro
2 tablespoons water
1 teaspoon minced garlic
1 teaspoon peeled, minced gingerroot
1 teaspoon hot oriental chili sauce
1 teaspoon vegetable oil
¼ cup plus 2 tablespoons water
3 tablespoons reduced-fat creamy peanut butter
2 tablespoons low-sodium soy sauce
1½ tablespoons prepared mustard
1 teaspoon ground turmeric
1 teaspoon hot oriental chili sauce
Vegetable cooking spray

Trim fat from pork; cut pork into ¾-inch cubes. Combine onion and next 7 ingredients in a large heavy-duty, zip-top plastic bag. Add pork; seal bag, and shake until pork is well coated. Marinate pork in refrigerator 8 hours, turning bag occasionally.

Soak 8 (10-inch) wooden skewers in water for at least 30 minutes.

Combine ¼ cup plus 2 tablespoons water and next 5 ingredients in a small bowl, stirring well with a wire whisk. Set aside.

Remove pork from marinade; discard marinade. Thread pork onto skewers. Coat grill rack with cooking spray; place on grill over medium-hot coals (350° to 400°). Place skewers on rack; grill, covered, 10 to 12 minutes or until pork is done, turning occasionally. Serve warm with peanut sauce. Yield: 8 servings (239 calories per serving).

Per Serving:		
Protein 22.9g	Fat 14.1g	(Saturated Fat 4.3g)
Carbohydrate 3.5g	Fiber 0.3g	Cholesterol 71mg
Iron 1.2mg	Sodium 239mg	Calcium 11mg

Pork and Sauerkraut Casserole provides a healthy serving of protein for a hearty family meal.

PORK AND SAUERKRAUT CASSEROLE

Vegetable cooking spray
6 (4-ounce) boneless center-cut pork loin chops
1 teaspoon vegetable oil
1 cup chopped onion
½ cup thinly sliced carrot
2 cups sauerkraut
½ cup Chablis or other dry white wine
½ cup canned low-sodium chicken broth, undiluted
1 teaspoon freshly ground pepper
¼ cup chopped fresh parsley

Coat a large nonstick skillet with cooking spray; place over medium-high heat until hot. Add chops, and cook 6 minutes on each side or until browned. Remove chops from skillet. Drain and pat dry with paper towels. Wipe drippings from skillet with a paper towel.

Coat skillet with cooking spray; add oil. Place over medium-high heat until hot. Add onion and carrot; sauté 4 minutes or until tender. Add sauerkraut and next 3 ingredients; cook over medium heat 8 minutes. Place sauerkraut mixture in a 13- x 9- x 2-inch baking dish coated with cooking spray. Arrange pork chops over sauerkraut mixture. Cover and bake at 350° for 1 hour and 15 minutes or until chops are tender. Sprinkle evenly with parsley. Serve immediately. Yield: 6 servings (215 calories per serving).

Per Serving:

Protein 26.5g	Fat 10.0g	(Saturated Fat 2.9g)
Carbohydrate 5.1g	Fiber 2.1g	Cholesterol 71mg
Iron 3.6mg	Sodium 422mg	Calcium 19mg

PORK MEDAILLONS WITH ARTICHOKE CREAM SAUCE

Asiago cheese is an Italian cheese with a rich, nutty flavor. If it's not available, you can substitute Parmesan or Romano cheese.

1 (9-ounce) package frozen artichoke hearts
1 cup canned no-salt-added chicken broth, undiluted
Olive oil-flavored vegetable cooking spray
2 (¾-pound) pork tenderloins, cut into ½-inch-thick slices
1 teaspoon olive oil
1 cup sliced fresh mushrooms
2 tablespoons chopped shallots
2½ tablespoons all-purpose flour
1½ cups skim milk
¼ cup grated Asiago cheese
¼ teaspoon salt
¼ teaspoon pepper
¼ teaspoon dry mustard

Cook artichoke hearts in chicken broth according to package directions, omitting salt; drain well. Coarsely chop artichoke hearts, and set aside.

Coat a large nonstick skillet with cooking spray, and place over medium-high heat until hot. Add pork slices, and cook until browned on both sides, turning once. Drain and pat dry with paper towels. Wipe drippings from skillet. Set pork aside.

Coat skillet with cooking spray; add oil. Place over medium-high heat until hot. Add mushrooms and shallots; sauté until tender. Remove mushroom mixture from skillet. Wipe drippings from skillet with a paper towel.

Combine flour and milk in skillet, stirring with a wire whisk until smooth. Cook over medium heat, stirring constantly, until thickened. Stir in chopped artichoke, mushroom mixture, cheese, salt, pepper, and mustard; add pork. Cover and cook over medium heat 10 minutes or until pork is tender. Yield: 6 servings (226 calories per serving).

Per Serving:

Protein 30.9g	Fat 6.5g	(Saturated Fat 2.5g)
Carbohydrate 10.2g	Fiber 0.6g	Cholesterol 87mg
Iron 2.0mg	Sodium 267mg	Calcium 137mg

ORANGE-GINGER PORK

1 (2½-pound) lean boneless double pork loin roast, tied
⅓ cup low-sodium soy sauce
⅓ cup Chablis or other dry white wine
1½ tablespoons peeled, grated gingerroot
3 tablespoons honey
2 cloves garlic, minced
⅔ cup low-sugar orange marmalade
Vegetable cooking spray

Untie roast, and trim fat. Retie roast. Place roast in a heavy-duty, zip-top plastic bag. Combine soy sauce and next 4 ingredients. Reserve 3 tablespoons soy sauce mixture; pour remaining mixture evenly over meat. Seal bag, and shake well. Marinate in refrigerator 8 hours, turning bag occasionally.

Combine reserved 3 tablespoons marinade and orange marmalade in a small saucepan. Cook over medium heat, until marmalade melts, stirring frequently. Set aside.

Remove roast from marinade, and discard marinade. Place roast on a rack in a roasting pan coated with cooking spray. Insert meat thermometer into thickest part of roast, if desired. Place roast in a 450° oven. Reduce heat to 350°, and bake roast 1 hour and 15 minutes.

Brush roast with half of marmalade mixture. Bake an additional 40 minutes or until meat thermometer registers 160°, basting frequently with remaining marmalade mixture. Yield: 10 servings (204 calories per serving).

Per Serving:

Protein 21.3g	Fat 11.0g	(Saturated Fat 3.8g)
Carbohydrate 2.9g	Fiber 0g	Cholesterol 71mg
Iron 0.9mg	Sodium 136mg	Calcium 16mg

Roasted Orange Chicken (page 170) uses the juice of the orange to tantalize the taste buds. Along with the orange-date sauce, the chicken is made even more appealing when served on a bed of fresh fruit and herb sprigs.

Poultry

CHERRY-SAUCED CHICKEN PATTIES

If prepackaged ground chicken breast isn't available at your supermarket, ask your butcher to grind some for you.

1 pound freshly ground raw chicken breast
1/2 cup soft whole wheat breadcrumbs
1/4 cup chopped green onions
2 tablespoons frozen egg substitute, thawed
1/8 teaspoon salt
1/8 teaspoon pepper
Vegetable cooking spray
1 (16-ounce) can unsweetened pitted dark sweet cherries, undrained
1 tablespoon cornstarch
2 tablespoons sugar
2 tablespoons minced crystallized ginger
1 tablespoon low-sodium soy sauce

Combine first 6 ingredients in a medium bowl, stirring well. Shape mixture into 6 (1/2-inch-thick) patties.

Coat a large nonstick skillet with cooking spray; place over medium-high heat until hot. Add patties, and cook 1 1/2 minutes on each side or until browned. Remove patties from skillet. Drain and pat dry with paper towels; set aside. Wipe drippings from skillet with a paper towel.

Drain cherries, reserving liquid. Combine liquid and cornstarch in skillet, stirring well. Add cherries, sugar, ginger, and soy sauce. Bring mixture to a boil over medium heat, stirring constantly. Cook, stirring constantly, 1 minute or until mixture is slightly thickened.

Return patties to skillet; cover, reduce heat, and simmer 5 minutes or until patties are done. Transfer patties to a serving platter, and spoon cherry mixture over patties. Yield: 6 servings (179 calories per serving).

Per Serving:

Protein 19.2g	Fat 1.2g	(Saturated Fat 0.3g)
Carbohydrate 20.9g	Fiber 0.4g	Cholesterol 44mg
Iron 2.7mg	Sodium 206mg	Calcium 28mg

CHICKEN AND WILD RICE CASSEROLE

3 cups canned no-salt-added chicken broth, undiluted
1 cup wild rice, uncooked
3 cups diced cooked chicken breast (skinned before cooking and cooked without salt)
1 cup chopped pear
3/4 cup jellied whole-berry cranberry sauce
1/2 cup pear nectar
1/4 cup chopped pecans, toasted
1/2 teaspoon dried thyme
1/4 teaspoon salt
1/4 teaspoon pepper
Vegetable cooking spray

Bring chicken broth to a boil in a medium saucepan; stir in rice. Cover, reduce heat, and simmer 1 hour or until rice is tender and liquid is absorbed. Stir in chicken and next 7 ingredients.

Spoon mixture into an 11- x 7- x 1 1/2-inch baking dish coated with cooking spray. Cover and bake at 350° for 30 minutes or until liquid is absorbed and mixture is thoroughly heated. Yield: 6 servings (337 calories per serving).

Per Serving:

Protein 27.0g	Fat 6.3g	(Saturated Fat 1.0g)
Carbohydrate 42.5g	Fiber 2.6g	Cholesterol 60mg
Iron 1.7mg	Sodium 165mg	Calcium 26mg

SOUPED UP BROTH

If you like to make your own chicken broth or beef broth instead of using canned, here's a tip for adding extra flavor to homemade broths: Pan-roast the meat pieces and bones first.

Simply broil the meat pieces and bones on the rack of a broiler pan, turning them occasionally until browned on all sides. Wipe excess fat from the pieces by patting dry with a paper towel, and proceed with your broth recipe.

PEPPERY CHICKEN AND PASTA

Round out this one-dish meal with a crisp green salad and commercial whole wheat dinner rolls.

12 ounces penne pasta, uncooked
1 teaspoon dried Italian seasoning
1½ pounds skinned, boned chicken breast halves, cut into 1-inch-wide strips
1 teaspoon coarsely ground pepper
1 (12-ounce) jar roasted red peppers in water
½ cup pepperoncini peppers, drained and sliced
3½ cups boiling water
1 cup skim milk
2 tablespoons all-purpose flour
2 tablespoons freshly grated Parmesan cheese

Place pasta in a large Dutch oven, and sprinkle with Italian seasoning. Top with chicken strips, and sprinkle with ground pepper.

Drain red peppers, reserving liquid. Cut enough peppers into strips to measure 1 cup. Place pepper strips over chicken. Reserve remaining roasted peppers in liquid for another use. Add pepperoncini peppers to Dutch oven. Pour boiling water over pasta mixture; bring to a boil. Cover, reduce heat, and simmer 10 minutes or until pasta is tender. Uncover and cook an additional 10 minutes or until liquid evaporates.

Combine milk and flour; pour over pasta mixture. Cook over medium heat, stirring constantly, until thickened. Sprinkle with Parmesan cheese. Yield: 8 servings (291 calories per serving).

Per Serving:		
Protein 27.1g	Fat 2.3g	(Saturated Fat 0.7g)
Carbohydrate 35.6g	Fiber 1.4g	Cholesterol 51mg
Iron 3.3mg	Sodium 295mg	Calcium 85mg

CHICKEN AU POIVRE

Flattening the chicken breasts tenderizes them and shortens their cooking time. This recipe goes from stove top to table in about 15 minutes.

4 (4-ounce) skinned, boned chicken breast halves
2 teaspoons assorted whole peppercorns, coarsely crushed
1 tablespoon reduced-calorie margarine
¼ cup canned no-salt-added chicken broth, undiluted
¼ cup Madeira
¼ cup low-fat sour cream
2 teaspoons all-purpose flour
Assorted whole peppercorns (optional)

Place chicken between 2 sheets of heavy-duty plastic wrap, and flatten to ¼-inch thickness, using a meat mallet or rolling pin. Sprinkle both sides of each chicken breast half evenly with crushed peppercorns, pressing pepper into chicken.

Melt margarine in a large nonstick skillet over medium-high heat; add chicken, and sauté 2 to 3 minutes on each side or until chicken is done. Transfer chicken to a serving platter, and keep warm.

Add chicken broth and Madeira to skillet. Bring to a boil; reduce heat, and simmer, uncovered, 2 to 3 minutes or until reduced to ¼ cup. Remove from heat. Combine sour cream and flour; add to broth mixture, stirring constantly. Spoon over chicken. Garnish with assorted whole peppercorns, if desired. Yield: 4 servings (174 calories per serving).

Per Serving:		
Protein 27.0g	Fat 5.1g	(Saturated Fat 1.8g)
Carbohydrate 3.5g	Fiber 0.3g	Cholesterol 71mg
Iron 1.4mg	Sodium 110mg	Calcium 37mg

Grilled Chicken with Roasted Vegetables provides a satisfying meal with its robust flavors and ample portions.

GRILLED CHICKEN WITH ROASTED VEGETABLES

2 tablespoons peeled, grated gingerroot
1 tablespoon minced garlic
½ cup balsamic vinegar
¼ cup plus 2 tablespoons low-sodium teriyaki sauce
2 tablespoons water
1½ tablespoons olive oil
¼ cup nonfat mayonnaise
4 (4-ounce) skinned, boned chicken breast halves
4 small round red potatoes, quartered
Vegetable cooking spray
2 ears yellow corn, each cut into 4 pieces
8 cloves garlic, peeled
2 small yellow squash, cut into 1-inch pieces
2 small onions, quartered
1 medium zucchini, cut into 1-inch pieces
1 medium-size sweet red pepper, seeded and cut into 1-inch pieces

Combine first 6 ingredients in a jar; cover tightly, and shake vigorously. Add 1 tablespoon teriyaki mixture to mayonnaise; stir well. Cover and chill mayonnaise mixture.

Pour ¼ cup teriyaki mixture into a heavy-duty, zip-top plastic bag. Set aside remaining teriyaki mixture. Add chicken to bag; seal bag, and shake until chicken is well coated. Marinate in refrigerator at least 8 hours, turning bag occasionally.

Place potato in a large bowl; add 1 tablespoon reserved teriyaki mixture, tossing well. Place potato in a large roasting pan coated with cooking spray. Bake at 400° for 5 minutes. Place corn in bowl; add 2 tablespoons reserved teriyaki mixture, tossing well. Add to potato, and bake 10 minutes.

Place garlic cloves and remaining ingredients in bowl; add remaining teriyaki mixture, and toss well. Add squash mixture to potato mixture, and bake an additional 35 minutes or until vegetables are tender, stirring frequently. Set aside, and keep warm.

Coat grill rack with cooking spray; place on grill over medium-hot coals (350° to 400°). Remove chicken from marinade, discarding marinade. Place chicken on rack; grill, covered, 4 minutes on each side or until done. Arrange chicken and vegetables evenly on individual serving plates. Serve with mayonnaise mixture. Yield: 4 servings (358 calories per serving).

Per Serving:		
Protein 32.8g	Fat 7.5g	(Saturated Fat 1.5g)
Carbohydrate 41.6g	Fiber 5.3g	Cholesterol 72mg
Iron 3.7mg	Sodium 592mg	Calcium 80mg

CRISPY MEXICAN CHICKEN

A shredded baking potato creates a crispy, lowfat coating for these chicken breasts.

1 (8-ounce) baking potato, peeled and shredded
¼ cup nonfat buttermilk
1 teaspoon chili powder
1 teaspoon dried oregano
½ teaspoon ground cumin
¼ teaspoon ground red pepper
4 (6-ounce) skinned chicken breast halves
Vegetable cooking spray
1 teaspoon vegetable oil

Place potato in ice water; let stand 5 minutes.

Combine buttermilk and next 4 ingredients; brush over both sides of chicken. Line a 15- x 10- x 1-inch jellyroll pan with aluminum foil; coat foil with cooking spray. Place chicken in prepared pan.

Drain potato; pat dry with paper towels. Place in a small bowl; add oil, and toss gently. Spoon ⅓ cup potato mixture over each chicken breast half; spread evenly over top of chicken. Bake at 425° for 35 to 40 minutes or until chicken is done and potato is golden. Serve immediately. Yield: 4 servings (189 calories per serving).

Per Serving:		
Protein 31.1g	Fat 3.2g	(Saturated Fat 0.7g)
Carbohydrate 7.7g	Fiber 1.2g	Cholesterol 74mg
Iron 2.9mg	Sodium 110mg	Calcium 58mg

STEWED CHICKEN AND OKRA

Vegetable cooking spray
½ cup chopped onion
½ cup sliced celery
2 cloves garlic, minced
1 teaspoon vegetable oil
2 (6-ounce) skinned chicken breast halves
½ teaspoon sweet Hungarian paprika
1½ cups sliced fresh okra
1 (5½-ounce) can no-salt-added vegetable juice
¼ teaspoon hot sauce
3 tablespoons plain nonfat yogurt

Coat a large nonstick skillet with cooking spray; place over medium-high heat until hot. Add onion, celery, and garlic; sauté 4 minutes or until vegetables are tender. Remove vegetable mixture from skillet.

Add oil to skillet; place over medium heat until hot. Add chicken, and cook 2 minutes on each side or until lightly browned. Sprinkle chicken with paprika; reduce heat, and cook, uncovered, 1 minute. Combine sautéed vegetable mixture, okra, vegetable juice, and hot sauce, stirring well. Pour over chicken. Cover and cook 40 minutes or until chicken is done and okra is tender.

Transfer chicken to a serving platter, and keep warm. Spoon vegetables around chicken, using a slotted spoon; reserve liquid in skillet. Add yogurt to liquid, stirring with a wire whisk until smooth. Drizzle over chicken and vegetables. Yield: 2 servings (231 calories per serving).

Per Serving:		
Protein 30.7g	Fat 4.4g	(Saturated Fat 0.9g)
Carbohydrate 16.5g	Fiber 2.1g	Cholesterol 66mg
Iron 2.3mg	Sodium 143mg	Calcium 152mg

SKILLET CHICKEN WITH TROPICAL FRUIT SAUCE

6 (6-ounce) skinned chicken breast halves
½ teaspoon pumpkin pie spice
Vegetable cooking spray
1 cup cranberry-apple drink
½ cup dried tropical fruit bits
½ teaspoon ground ginger
⅛ teaspoon ground cloves
1 tablespoon brown sugar
1 tablespoon water
2 teaspoons cornstarch

Sprinkle chicken with pumpkin pie spice.

Coat a large nonstick skillet with cooking spray; place over medium heat until hot. Add chicken, and cook 3 minutes on each side or until browned. Remove chicken from skillet. Drain and pat dry with paper towels. Wipe drippings from skillet with a paper towel.

Return chicken to skillet. Combine cranberry-apple drink and next 3 ingredients; pour over chicken. Bring to a boil; cover, reduce heat, and simmer 20 minutes or until chicken is tender.

Transfer chicken to a serving platter, using a slotted spoon; keep warm. Combine brown sugar, water, and cornstarch, stirring until smooth. Add to fruit mixture. Cook over medium heat, stirring constantly, until thickened. Spoon fruit sauce over chicken. Yield: 6 servings (222 calories per serving).

Per Serving:		
Protein 30.3g	Fat 2.2g	(Saturated Fat 0.6g)
Carbohydrate 18.6g	Fiber 0.4g	Cholesterol 75mg
Iron 1.1mg	Sodium 90mg	Calcium 17mg

HERBED CHICKEN AND VEGETABLES

Serve this chicken and vegetable dish with brown rice and fresh fruit for an easy, tasty, low-fat meal. *(Recipe pictured on page 83.)*

1½ pounds chicken thighs, skinned
1 medium zucchini, sliced
1 medium-size yellow squash, sliced
¾ cup diced sweet red pepper
¼ cup fresh lemon juice
2 tablespoons low-sodium Worcestershire sauce
1½ teaspoons coarsely ground pepper
1 teaspoon chopped fresh oregano
1 teaspoon chopped fresh thyme
1 teaspoon chopped fresh chives
1 teaspoon garlic powder
Vegetable cooking spray
Fresh chive blossoms (optional)
Fresh oregano sprigs (optional)
Fresh thyme sprigs (optional)

Place first 4 ingredients in a heavy-duty, zip-top plastic bag. Combine lemon juice and next 6 ingredients; pour over chicken and vegetables. Seal bag, and shake until chicken and vegetables are well coated. Marinate in refrigerator 2 hours, turning bag occasionally.

Remove chicken from marinade, reserving vegetables and marinade. Place chicken in a 13- x 9- x 2-inch baking dish coated with cooking spray. Bake, uncovered, at 450° for 10 minutes. Cover, reduce heat to 350°, and bake 20 minutes.

Add vegetables and marinade to chicken. Cover; bake an additional 15 minutes or until chicken is done and vegetables are crisp-tender. Transfer chicken and vegetables to a serving platter, using a slotted spoon.

If desired, garnish with chive blossoms, oregano sprigs, and thyme sprigs. Yield: 4 servings (172 calories per serving).

Per Serving:		
Protein 23.8g	Fat 4.9g	(Saturated Fat 1.2g)
Carbohydrate 8.4g	Fiber 1.6g	Cholesterol 94mg
Iron 2.1mg	Sodium 130mg	Calcium 34mg

Try Spicy Peanut Chicken as a low-fat alternative to fried chicken. Pureed Winter Vegetables (page 214) make a warming accompaniment.

SPICY PEANUT CHICKEN

- 1½ cups soft whole wheat breadcrumbs
- 2 tablespoons minced fresh cilantro
- 1½ teaspoons grated lime rind
- 1 teaspoon garlic powder
- ½ teaspoon pepper
- ½ teaspoon ground red pepper
- 3 tablespoons evaporated skimmed milk
- 2 tablespoons no-salt-added creamy peanut butter
- ¾ teaspoon coconut extract
- 1 (3-pound) broiler-fryer, cut up and skinned
- Vegetable cooking spray
- Lime slices (optional)
- Fresh cilantro sprigs (optional)

Combine first 6 ingredients in a heavy-duty, zip-top plastic bag. Seal bag; shake well. Combine milk, peanut butter, and coconut extract in a bowl, stirring with a wire whisk until blended. Brush chicken with milk mixture; add chicken to breadcrumb mixture in bag. Seal bag; shake until chicken is coated.

Place chicken on a rack in a roasting pan coated with cooking spray. Bake, uncovered, at 400° for 45 minutes or until done. Transfer to individual serving plates. If desired, garnish with lime and cilantro. Yield: 6 servings (186 calories per serving).

Per Serving:

Protein 21.7g	Fat 6.0g	(Saturated Fat 1.2g)
Carbohydrate 11.5g	Fiber 1.1g	Cholesterol 58mg
Iron 1.4mg	Sodium 174mg	Calcium 58mg

CHICKEN WITH TOMATOES AND LEEKS

Rinse leeks thoroughly before using to remove any excess dirt trapped between the leaf layers.

Vegetable cooking spray
1½ cups sliced leeks
1 cup sliced fresh mushrooms
1 clove garlic, minced
4 cups peeled, seeded, and chopped tomato
¾ cup no-salt-added tomato juice
¼ cup no-salt-added tomato paste
2 tablespoons chopped fresh basil
1½ teaspoons chopped fresh oregano
½ teaspoon salt
1 bay leaf
1 (3-pound) broiler-fryer, cut up and skinned

Coat a large nonstick skillet with cooking spray; place over medium-high heat until hot. Add leeks, mushrooms, and garlic; sauté 5 minutes or until vegetables are tender. Transfer vegetable mixture to a large bowl. Add tomato and next 6 ingredients; stir well, and set aside.

Coat skillet with cooking spray; place over medium heat until hot. Add chicken, and cook 3 to 5 minutes on each side or until browned. Remove chicken from skillet, and place in a 13- x 9- x 2-inch baking dish. Pour tomato mixture over chicken. Cover and bake at 350° for 30 minutes. Uncover and bake an additional 20 minutes or until chicken is tender. Remove and discard bay leaf. Yield: 6 servings (185 calories per serving).

Per Serving:		
Protein 25.5g	Fat 3.9g	(Saturated Fat 0.9g)
Carbohydrate 12.4g	Fiber 2.6g	Cholesterol 76mg
Iron 2.6mg	Sodium 302mg	Calcium 43mg

ROASTED ORANGE CHICKEN

To keep the skinned chicken from becoming dry, baste it during baking. (Pictured on page 163.)

1 (3-pound) broiler-fryer, skinned
½ small onion, cut into wedges
½ small orange, cut into wedges
Vegetable cooking spray
2 cups unsweetened orange juice
½ cup low-sugar orange marmalade
2 tablespoons Grand Marnier or other orange-flavored liqueur
1 tablespoon grated orange rind
1 tablespoon commercial honey mustard
¼ teaspoon salt
¼ teaspoon pepper
1 tablespoon cornstarch
2 tablespoons water
2 large oranges, peeled and sectioned
½ cup pitted dates, sliced
Orange slices (optional)
Red and green grapes (optional)
Fresh oregano sprigs (optional)
Fresh sage sprigs (optional)
Fresh thyme sprigs (optional)

Trim excess fat from chicken. Remove giblets and neck from chicken; reserve for another use. Rinse chicken under cold water, and pat dry with paper towels. Place onion and orange wedges in cavity of chicken. Truss chicken, and place, breast side up, on a rack in a shallow roasting pan coated with cooking spray. Insert meat thermometer into meaty part of thigh, making sure it does not touch bone.

Combine orange juice and next 6 ingredients. Reserve 1½ cups orange juice mixture for sauce. Brush chicken with some of remaining 1¼ cups orange juice mixture. Bake, uncovered, at 350° for 1½ hours or until meat thermometer registers 180°, basting frequently with orange juice mixture.

Transfer chicken to a serving platter; remove and discard onion and orange wedges from cavity. Set chicken aside, and keep warm.

Place reserved 1½ cups orange juice mixture in a medium saucepan. Combine cornstarch and water;

stir into orange juice mixture. Bring to a boil over medium heat, stirring constantly, and cook 1 minute. Stir in orange sections and dates. Serve sauce with chicken. If desired, garnish with orange slices, red and green grapes, oregano, sage, and thyme. Yield: 6 servings (252 calories per serving).

Per Serving:		
Protein 24.8g	Fat 6.3g	(Saturated Fat 1.7g)
Carbohydrate 24.3g	Fiber 2.6g	Cholesterol 73mg
Iron 1.3mg	Sodium 134mg	Calcium 41mg

WHISKEY-BAKED CORNISH HENS

4 (1-pound) Cornish hens, skinned
Vegetable cooking spray
1 (12-ounce) can frozen pineapple juice concentrate, divided
½ cup bourbon, divided
1 teaspoon low-sodium soy sauce
¼ teaspoon salt
¼ teaspoon coarsely ground pepper
Fresh watercress sprigs (optional)

Remove giblets from hens; reserve for another use. Rinse hens under cold water, and pat dry with paper towels. Split each hen in half lengthwise, using an electric knife.

Place hen halves, cut side down, on a rack in a roasting pan coated with cooking spray.

Combine ¼ cup pineapple juice concentrate, ¼ cup bourbon, and soy sauce, stirring well. Brush hens with bourbon mixture. Bake at 350° for 1 hour or until hens are done, basting frequently with bourbon mixture. Transfer hens to a serving platter, and keep warm.

Place remaining pineapple juice concentrate in a small saucepan. Cook over high heat, stirring constantly, until reduced to 1 cup. Stir in remaining ¼ cup bourbon, salt, and pepper.

Serve hens with sauce. Garnish with watercress sprigs, if desired. Yield: 8 servings (256 calories per serving).

Per Serving:		
Protein 25.1g	Fat 6.4g	(Saturated Fat 1.7g)
Carbohydrate 18.8g	Fiber 0.1g	Cholesterol 76mg
Iron 1.4mg	Sodium 164mg	Calcium 30mg

APPLE BRANDY TURKEY PATTIES

Adding shredded apple to these turkey patties helps keep them moist and tender.

1 pound freshly ground raw turkey breast
½ cup peeled, shredded apple
¼ cup fine, dry breadcrumbs
1 egg white, lightly beaten
¾ teaspoon coarsely ground pepper
¼ teaspoon salt
Vegetable cooking spray
½ cup unsweetened apple juice
¼ cup brandy
2 teaspoons cornstarch
1 tablespoon water
1 tablespoon chopped fresh chives

Combine first 6 ingredients in a medium bowl, stirring well. Shape mixture into 4 (½-inch-thick) patties.

Coat a large nonstick skillet with cooking spray; place over medium heat until hot. Add turkey patties, and cook 4 to 5 minutes on each side or until done. Remove patties from skillet; drain and pat dry with paper towels. Place patties on a serving platter, and keep warm. Wipe drippings from skillet with a paper towel.

Combine apple juice and brandy in skillet; cook over medium heat 2 minutes. Combine cornstarch and water; add to juice mixture. Cook, stirring constantly, until mixture is thickened. Stir in chives. Spoon sauce evenly over patties. Serve immediately. Yield: 4 servings (186 calories per serving).

Per Serving:		
Protein 28.3g	Fat 2.2g	(Saturated Fat 0.6g)
Carbohydrate 11.2	Fiber 0.8g	Cholesterol 68mg
Iron 1.8mg	Sodium 271mg	Calcium 27mg

TURKEY AND BEAN CASSEROLE

This easy-to-fix, hearty main dish is low in fat and high in fiber.

1 pound freshly ground raw turkey breast
2 cups chopped celery
½ cup chopped onion
2 cloves garlic, minced
1 (14½-ounce) can no-salt-added whole tomatoes, drained and chopped
1 (16-ounce) can vegetarian beans in tomato sauce, undrained
1 (15-ounce) can red kidney beans, drained
½ cup reduced-calorie catsup
2 tablespoons molasses
½ teaspoon rubbed sage
½ teaspoon dry mustard
½ teaspoon pepper
¼ teaspoon dried crushed red pepper
Vegetable cooking spray

Combine first 4 ingredients in a nonstick skillet. Cook over medium-high heat until turkey is browned, stirring until it crumbles. Drain and pat dry with paper towels. Place turkey mixture in a large bowl.

Stir in tomato and next 8 ingredients. Spoon into a 13- x 9- x 2-inch baking dish coated with cooking spray. Bake at 350° for 45 minutes; stir after 20 minutes. Yield: 6 servings (252 calories per serving).

Per Serving:		
Protein 23.6g	Fat 2.6g	(Saturated Fat 0.6g)
Carbohydrate 35.1g	Fiber 7.2g	Cholesterol 39mg
Iron 3.1mg	Sodium 488mg	Calcium 107mg

GLAZED TURKEY KABOBS

1 (15¼-ounce) can pineapple chunks in juice, undrained
1 pound boneless turkey breast, skinned and cut into 1-inch pieces
2 medium-size green peppers, seeded and cut into 1-inch pieces
1 (8-ounce) can jellied cranberry sauce
2 teaspoons prepared horseradish
Vegetable cooking spray

Drain pineapple, reserving ¼ cup juice. Thread pineapple, turkey, and green pepper evenly onto 8 (10-inch) skewers; set aside.

Combine cranberry sauce and horseradish in a small saucepan. Add reserved ¼ cup pineapple juice, and cook over low heat, stirring constantly, until smooth.

Coat grill rack with cooking spray; place on grill over medium-hot coals (350° to 400°). Place kabobs on rack; grill, covered, 12 to 15 minutes or until turkey is done, turning and basting frequently with warm cranberry mixture. Yield: 4 servings (283 calories per serving).

Per Serving:		
Protein 26.1g	Fat 4.4g	(Saturated Fat 0.9g)
Carbohydrate 34.3g	Fiber 1.9g	Cholesterol 59mg
Iron 2.2mg	Sodium 85mg	Calcium 40mg

ARTICHOKE-STUFFED TURKEY ROLLS

½ cup frozen artichoke hearts, thawed and finely chopped
¼ cup finely chopped fresh mushrooms
¼ cup (1 ounce) shredded reduced-fat Swiss cheese
2 tablespoons finely chopped sweet red pepper
4 (4-ounce) turkey breast cutlets
Vegetable cooking spray
¾ cup plus 2 tablespoons canned no-salt-added chicken broth, undiluted and divided
¼ cup Chablis or other dry white wine
½ teaspoon dried dillweed
¼ teaspoon salt
1 tablespoon cornstarch
4 ounces capellini (angel hair pasta), uncooked
Fresh dillweed sprigs (optional)

Combine first 4 ingredients in a small bowl, stirring well. Set aside.

Place turkey cutlets between 2 sheets of heavy-duty plastic wrap; flatten to ¼-inch thickness, using a meat mallet or rolling pin. Spoon artichoke mixture evenly onto centers of turkey cutlets. Roll up cutlets lengthwise, tucking ends under. Secure cutlets with wooden picks.

Artichoke-Stuffed Turkey Rolls make a heavenly presentation when served on a bed of angel hair pasta.

Coat a nonstick skillet with cooking spray; place over medium-high heat until hot. Add turkey rolls; cook until browned on all sides. Add ¾ cup broth, wine, dillweed, and salt; cover and cook 10 minutes or until turkey is tender. Remove turkey from skillet, using a slotted spoon; set aside, and keep warm.

Combine cornstarch and remaining 2 tablespoons broth. Add cornstarch mixture to liquid in skillet, stirring constantly. Bring to a boil over medium heat; cook, stirring constantly, 1 minute.

Cook pasta according to package directions, omitting salt and fat; drain. Place ½ cup pasta on each plate. Remove picks from turkey rolls. Cut each roll into 8 (¼-inch-thick) slices; arrange over pasta, and drizzle with sauce. Garnish with dillweed sprigs, if desired. Yield: 4 servings (288 calories per serving).

Per Serving:

Protein 33.9g	Fat 3.8g	(Saturated Fat 1.4g)
Carbohydrate 27.0g	Fiber 1.2g	Cholesterol 72mg
Iron 2.9mg	Sodium 249mg	Calcium 114mg

MAPLE-GLAZED TURKEY BREAST

Break from tradition this Thanksgiving and serve a stuffed turkey breast instead of a whole turkey. Offer it with spinach salad, Raspberry-Glazed Sweet Potatoes (page 213), steamed green beans, and, of course, cranberry relish.

Vegetable cooking spray
½ cup sliced green onions
⅓ cup diced celery
2 cups cooked couscous (cooked without salt or fat)
½ cup chopped dried pitted prunes
⅓ cup unsweetened applesauce
2 tablespoons chopped fresh parsley
½ teaspoon salt
½ teaspoon imitation maple flavoring
¼ teaspoon pepper
¼ teaspoon pumpkin pie spice
¼ teaspoon poultry seasoning
1 (3-pound) boneless turkey breast, skinned
¾ cup unsweetened apple cider
¼ cup reduced-calorie maple syrup
¾ teaspoon cornstarch
¼ teaspoon pumpkin pie spice
Spinach leaves (optional)

Coat a small nonstick skillet with cooking spray; place over medium-high heat until hot. Add green onions and celery; sauté until tender. Combine onion mixture, couscous, and next 8 ingredients in a medium bowl, stirring well; set aside.

Trim fat from turkey; remove tendons. Place turkey, boned side up, on heavy-duty plastic wrap. From center, slice horizontally through thickest part of each side of breast almost to outer edge; flip each cut piece over to enlarge turkey breast. Place heavy-duty plastic wrap over turkey, and flatten to ½-inch thickness, using a meat mallet or rolling pin.

Spoon couscous mixture onto center of turkey, leaving a 2-inch border at sides; roll up, jellyroll fashion, starting with short side. Tie turkey securely at 2-inch intervals with string. Place turkey, seam side down, on a rack in a roasting pan coated with cooking spray.

Combine apple cider and next 3 ingredients in a small saucepan; bring to a boil over medium heat, stirring constantly. Cook 1 minute; brush apple cider mixture over turkey. Insert meat thermometer into turkey. Bake at 325° for 1 hour and 30 minutes or until meat thermometer registers 170°, basting frequently with remaining cider mixture. Transfer turkey to a large serving platter lined with spinach leaves, if desired. Remove string. Let stand 10 minutes before serving. Yield: 12 servings (202 calories per serving).

Per Serving:		
Protein 28.2g	Fat 2.1g	(Saturated Fat 0.6g)
Carbohydrate 16.5g	Fiber 0.7g	Cholesterol 68mg
Iron 1.9mg	Sodium 180mg	Calcium 28mg

Smoked Turkey and Blackberry Salad (page 183) contains a variety of lettuces combined with the sweet taste of blackberries and tender strips of turkey breast.

Salads & Salad Dressings

FRESH FRUIT SALAD WITH LIME CREAM

1½ cups peeled, sliced banana (about 2 medium)
3 tablespoons lime juice, divided
2 kiwifruit, peeled and cut into ½-inch-thick slices
2 cups fresh pineapple chunks
2 tablespoons sugar, divided
1 teaspoon grated lime rind, divided
⅓ cup nonfat mayonnaise
⅓ cup nonfat sour cream alternative
⅛ teaspoon ground mace

Combine banana and 1 tablespoon lime juice in a medium bowl; toss gently. Cut kiwifruit slices in half. Add to banana mixture; toss gently. Add pineapple, 1 tablespoon sugar, and ½ teaspoon lime rind; toss gently. Cover and chill up to 8 hours.

Combine mayonnaise and sour cream; add remaining 2 tablespoons lime juice, remaining 1 tablespoon sugar, remaining ½ teaspoon lime rind, and mace, stirring well. Spoon fruit mixture into individual serving bowls; top evenly with sour cream mixture. Yield: 8 servings (82 calories per ½-cup fruit and 1½ tablespoons sour cream mixture).

Per Serving:

Protein 1.3g	Fat 0.4g	(Saturated Fat 0.1g)
Carbohydrate 19.3g	Fiber 2.0g	Cholesterol 0mg
Iron 0.3mg	Sodium 135mg	Calcium 21mg

MELON SALAD WITH PEPPERCORN-FRUIT DRESSING

Peppercorns add just a hint of spice to this recipe, creating a nice flavor contrast to the sweet fruit.

¾ cup frozen sliced peaches, thawed
½ cup sliced strawberries
1 tablespoon minced fresh mint
1 teaspoon sugar
½ teaspoon green peppercorns
1½ teaspoons olive oil
½ teaspoon red wine vinegar
21 (¼-inch-thick) slices honeydew (about 1 small)
14 (¼-inch-thick) slices cantaloupe (about 1 small)
Fresh mint sprigs (optional)

Combine first 7 ingredients in container of an electric blender or food processor; cover and process until smooth. Pour mixture through a wire-mesh strainer into a bowl; press mixture with back of a spoon against sides of strainer to squeeze out liquid. Discard solids remaining in stainer. Cover and chill dressing mixture thoroughly.

Arrange melon slices on individual salad plates; drizzle dressing mixture evenly over melon. Garnish with mint sprigs, if desired. Yield: 7 servings (81 calories per serving).

Per Serving:

Protein 1.2g	Fat 1.3g	(Saturated Fat 0.3g)
Carbohydrate 18.4g	Fiber 2.3g	Cholesterol 0mg
Iron 0.4mg	Sodium 16mg	Calcium 18mg

MARINATED GREEN BEAN SALAD

1 pound fresh green beans
8 cherry tomatoes, halved
¾ teaspoon dill seeds
½ teaspoon sugar
½ teaspoon dried crushed red pepper
¼ teaspoon salt
2 cloves garlic, sliced
⅓ cup water
⅓ cup white wine vinegar

Wash beans; trim ends, and remove strings. Cut beans into 1½-inch pieces, and arrange in a vegetable steamer over boiling water. Cover and steam 3 minutes or until crisp-tender. Plunge beans into ice water; drain well. Combine beans and tomatoes in a large shallow dish. Combine dill seeds, sugar, crushed red pepper, and salt; sprinkle over bean mixture. Add garlic slices, and toss gently.

Combine water and vinegar in a small saucepan; bring to a boil. Pour vinegar mixture over bean mixture, and toss gently. Cover and marinate in refrigerator at least 8 hours, stirring occasionally. Serve chilled, using a slotted spoon. Yield: 8 servings (25 calories per ½-cup serving).

Per Serving:

Protein 1.2g	Fat 0.2g	(Saturated Fat 0g)
Carbohydrate 5.9g	Fiber 1.4g	Cholesterol 0mg
Iron 0.7mg	Sodium 78mg	Calcium 26mg

Fresh, tangy vegetables lie in a nest of crisp, colorful cabbage leaves in Southwestern Succotash Salad.

SOUTHWESTERN SUCCOTASH SALAD

1 (10-ounce) package frozen baby lima beans
1¾ cups frozen whole-kernel corn, thawed
1 cup quartered cherry tomatoes
½ cup diced green pepper
½ cup thinly sliced celery
½ cup thinly sliced green onions
¼ cup minced fresh cilantro
2 tablespoons finely chopped jalapeño pepper
⅓ cup commercial nonfat Ranch-style dressing
2 tablespoons lime juice
½ teaspoon ground cumin
½ teaspoon ground oregano
¼ teaspoon garlic powder
¼ teaspoon ground red pepper
Red cabbage leaves (optional)

Cook lima beans in boiling water to cover 5 to 6 minutes or until crisp-tender. Drain well.

Combine lima beans, corn, tomatoes, green pepper, celery, green onions, cilantro, and jalapeño pepper in a large bowl; toss gently, and set aside.

Combine Ranch-style dressing and next 5 ingredients in a small bowl; pour over vegetable mixture, and toss gently. Cover and chill 2 hours, stirring occasionally.

To serve, spoon vegetable mixture into a cabbage leaf-lined serving bowl, if desired. Yield: 11 servings (70 calories per ½-cup serving).

Per Serving:

Protein 3.1g	Fat 0.4g	(Saturated Fat 0.1g)
Carbohydrate 14.5g	Fiber 1.7g	Cholesterol 0mg
Iron 1.3mg	Sodium 119mg	Calcium 31mg

POTATO, RADISH, AND WATERCRESS SALAD

If you prefer not to use wine, substitute undiluted low-sodium chicken broth for the Chablis.

3 cups cubed red potato
¼ cup Chablis or other dry white wine
2 tablespoons white wine vinegar
½ teaspoon freshly ground pepper
¼ teaspoon garlic powder
⅛ teaspoon salt
¼ cup reduced-calorie mayonnaise
2 tablespoons nonfat sour cream alternative
1 cup loosely packed watercress leaves
1 cup thinly sliced radishes

Cook potato in a medium saucepan in boiling water to cover 8 to 10 minutes or until tender. Drain well, and place in a medium bowl.

Combine wine and next 4 ingredients in a small saucepan. Bring to a boil; cook 30 seconds. Pour over potato; toss well. Cool slightly. Cover and chill.

Combine mayonnaise and sour cream in a small bowl, stirring well with a wire whisk. Cover and chill.

Add mayonnaise mixture, watercress, and radishes to potato mixture; toss gently. Serve immediately. Yield: 4 servings (159 calories per 1-cup serving).

Per Serving:		
Protein 3.3g	Fat 4.3g	(Saturated Fat 0g)
Carbohydrate 27.4g	Fiber 2.2g	Cholesterol 5mg
Iron 0.6mg	Sodium 206mg	Calcium 24mg

BASIL-MARINATED TOMATOES

¼ cup minced fresh basil
2 teaspoons capers
2 teaspoons olive oil
½ teaspoon freshly ground pepper
¼ teaspoon salt
4 small cloves garlic, minced
6 medium plum tomatoes, quartered lengthwise
1 tablespoon white wine vinegar
Fresh basil sprigs (optional)

Combine minced basil, capers, olive oil, pepper, salt, and garlic in a heavy-duty, zip-top plastic bag. Add tomato; seal bag, and shake gently until tomato is well coated. Marinate in refrigerator at least 8 hours, turning bag occasionally.

Just before serving, add vinegar to tomato mixture. Spoon tomato mixture onto a serving platter. Garnish with basil sprigs, if desired. Yield: 4 servings (57 calories per ½-cup serving).

Per Serving:		
Protein 1.6g	Fat 2.8g	(Saturated Fat 0.4g)
Carbohydrate 8.0g	Fiber 2.0g	Cholesterol 0mg
Iron 0.9mg	Sodium 272mg	Calcium 19mg

GREENS WITH PEARS AND WALNUTS

Watercress has small, crisp, dark green leaves with a slightly bitter, peppery taste. If it's unavailable, simply increase the Bibb lettuce to 3 cups.

¼ cup plus 2 tablespoons plain nonfat yogurt
1 tablespoon sherry vinegar
1 tablespoon honey
¼ teaspoon salt
¼ teaspoon ground mace
1 head Belgian endive
2 cups torn Bibb lettuce
1 cup loosely packed watercress leaves
3 Seckel pears, cored and thinly sliced
2½ tablespoons finely chopped walnuts, toasted

Combine first 5 ingredients in a small bowl, stirring well. Cover and chill 1 hour.

Core endive, and separate into spears. Arrange endive, lettuce, and watercress evenly on individual salad plates.

Arrange pear slices over greens. Top each serving with 2 tablespoons yogurt mixture; sprinkle with toasted walnuts. Yield: 4 servings (101 calories per serving).

Per Serving:		
Protein 3.3g	Fat 3.2g	(Saturated Fat 0.2g)
Carbohydrate 16.2g	Fiber 2.0g	Cholesterol 0mg
Iron 0.5mg	Sodium 190mg	Calcium 59mg

Tangelos, in season from November through March, add tartness to Mixed Greens with Tangelo Vinaigrette.

MIXED GREENS WITH TANGELO VINAIGRETTE

2 teaspoons coarse-grained mustard
2 teaspoons sherry vinegar
1 teaspoon grated tangelo rind
5 tangelos
1 tablespoon honey
1½ cups loosely packed watercress leaves
1½ cups arugula
1 cup thinly sliced Belgian endive
1 pint fresh strawberries, sliced

Combine first 3 ingredients in a small jar, and set aside.

Peel and section 2 tangelos; set aside. Squeeze juice from remaining 3 tangelos to measure ½ cup juice. Combine juice and honey in a small saucepan, stirring well. Bring juice mixture to a boil; cook, uncovered, until reduced to ⅓ cup, stirring occasionally. Remove from heat, and cool completely. Add juice mixture to mustard mixture in jar; cover tightly, and shake vigorously.

Combine watercress, arugula, and endive in a bowl; add mustard mixture, and toss gently. Place lettuce mixture evenly on chilled individual salad plates; top evenly with tangelo sections and strawberry slices. Yield: 4 servings (115 calories per serving).

Per Serving:

Protein 2.5g	Fat 0.7g	(Saturated Fat 0g)
Carbohydrate 27.0g	Fiber 7.5g	Cholesterol 0mg
Iron 0.9mg	Sodium 58mg	Calcium 86mg

ORIENTAL GARDEN SALAD

¾ cup plain nonfat yogurt
2 tablespoons reduced-calorie mayonnaise
1½ tablespoons white wine vinegar
2 teaspoons sesame oil
½ teaspoon wasabi
½ teaspoon ground ginger
¼ teaspoon salt
1 clove garlic, crushed
3 cups torn romaine lettuce
3 cups torn red leaf lettuce
1½ cups fresh bean sprouts
⅔ cup chopped fresh chives
½ cup chopped fresh cilantro
1 cup julienne-sliced snow pea pods
1 cup julienne-sliced carrot
1 cup julienne-sliced daikon (oriental radish)

Combine first 8 ingredients in a small bowl, stirring well with a wire whisk. Cover yogurt mixture, and chill thoroughly.

Combine romaine lettuce and next 4 ingredients in a bowl; toss well. Place lettuce mixture evenly on individual salad plates. Arrange snow peas, carrot, and radishes over lettuce mixture. Drizzle yogurt mixture evenly over salads. Yield: 8 servings (64 calories per serving).

Per Serving:		
Protein 3.3g	Fat 2.4g	(Saturated Fat 0.4g)
Carbohydrate 8.2g	Fiber 2.1g	Cholesterol 2mg
Iron 1.3mg	Sodium 133mg	Calcium 86mg

SPINACH SALAD WITH WARM RASPBERRY VINAIGRETTE

¼ cup raspberry wine vinegar
½ teaspoon grated orange rind
2 tablespoons fresh orange juice
2 tablespoons honey
2 teaspoons vegetable oil
¼ teaspoon salt
Dash of pepper
4 cups torn fresh spinach
1 cup fresh raspberries
½ cup frozen English peas, thawed

Combine first 7 ingredients in a small saucepan. Bring mixture to a boil. Remove from heat.

Arrange spinach on individual salad plates. Top evenly with raspberries and peas; drizzle vinegar mixture evenly over salads. Yield: 4 servings (97 calories per serving).

Per Serving:		
Protein 2.1g	Fat 2.6g	(Saturated Fat 0.4g)
Carbohydrate 17.6g	Fiber 4.6g	Cholesterol 0mg
Iron 1.2mg	Sodium 187mg	Calcium 37mg

SOUTHWESTERN TABBOULEH

Jicama is a root vegetable with crunchy flesh and a thin brown skin that must be removed before using. If jicama isn't available, substitute chopped water chestnuts.

1 cup bulgur (cracked wheat), uncooked
2 cups boiling water
3 tablespoons low-sodium soy sauce
2 tablespoons lemon juice
1 tablespoon olive oil
1 cup seeded, diced tomato
1 cup peeled, minced jicama
½ cup minced fresh cilantro
3 tablespoons minced fresh chives
2 tablespoons minced fresh mint
1 tablespoon peeled, grated gingerroot
2 teaspoons minced garlic

Combine bulgur and water in a large bowl; let stand 1 hour or until bulgur is tender and liquid is absorbed.

Combine soy sauce, lemon juice, and oil, stirring well. Add to bulgur; toss well. Add tomato and remaining ingredients; toss. Cover and chill at least 4 hours. Yield: 5 servings (153 calories per 1-cup serving).

Per Serving:		
Protein 4.7g	Fat 3.4g	(Saturated Fat 0.5g)
Carbohydrate 27.8g	Fiber 6.6g	Cholesterol 0mg
Iron 2.3mg	Sodium 254mg	Calcium 47mg

SUMMER COUSCOUS SALAD

1 cup plus 2 tablespoons water
¾ cup couscous, uncooked
6 ounces fresh asparagus
½ cup diced sweet yellow pepper
½ cup cherry tomatoes, quartered and seeded
¼ cup thinly sliced green onions
1½ tablespoons canned no-salt-added chicken broth, undiluted
1 tablespoon frozen orange juice concentrate, thawed and undiluted
1 tablespoon balsamic vinegar
1 teaspoon grated orange rind
1½ teaspoons olive oil
½ teaspoon ground cumin
¼ teaspoon salt
4 romaine lettuce leaves

Bring water to a boil in a medium saucepan. Remove from heat. Add couscous; cover and let stand 5 minutes or until couscous is tender and liquid is absorbed. Fluff couscous with a fork, and transfer to a serving bowl.

Snap off tough ends of asparagus. Remove scales from stalks with a knife or vegetable peeler, if desired. Cut spears into 1-inch pieces. Cook asparagus in boiling water 1 minute or until crisp-tender. Drain and rinse under cold water until cool; drain again. Add asparagus, yellow pepper, tomatoes, and green onions to couscous; toss gently.

Combine broth and next 6 ingredients in a small bowl, stirring well with a wire whisk. Pour over couscous mixture, and toss gently. Cover and chill at least 8 hours.

Spoon 1 cup couscous mixture onto each individual lettuce-lined salad plate. Yield: 4 servings (174 calories per 1-cup serving).

Per Serving:		
Protein 6.1g	Fat 2.0g	(Saturated Fat 0.3g)
Carbohydrate 33.4g	Fiber 2.0g	Cholesterol 0mg
Iron 1.7mg	Sodium 9mg	Calcium 36mg

CURRIED JASMINE RICE SALAD

Jasmine rice has snowy white kernels with a soft texture when cooked. If it isn't available, substitute regular long-grain rice.

2 cups water
1 cup Jasmine rice, uncooked
1¼ cups shredded red cabbage
1¼ cups grated carrot
⅓ cup minced fresh chives
2 tablespoons minced pickled ginger
1 teaspoon curry powder
⅓ cup unsweetened orange juice
1 tablespoon lime juice
1 tablespoon white wine vinegar
2 teaspoons olive oil
1 teaspoon sesame oil
¼ teaspoon salt
¼ teaspoon freshly ground pepper
Red cabbage leaves (optional)
3 tablespoons pine nuts, toasted
3 tablespoons flaked coconut, toasted

Bring water to a boil in a medium saucepan; stir in rice. Cover, reduce heat, and simmer 20 minutes or until rice is tender and liquid is absorbed. Remove from heat; fluff rice with a fork, and let cool.

Arrange shredded cabbage and carrot in a vegetable steamer over boiling water. Cover and steam 5 minutes or until crisp-tender. Transfer vegetables to a large bowl; stir in chives and ginger. Add rice; toss gently. Set aside.

Cook curry powder in a small skillet over medium heat, stirring constantly, 2 minutes or until fragrant. Remove from heat. Add orange juice and next 6 ingredients to curry powder; stir well. Pour curry mixture over rice; toss gently. Cover and let stand 30 minutes, stirring occasionally.

Spoon ½ cup rice mixture onto each individual cabbage leaf-lined salad plate, if desired. Sprinkle evenly with pine nuts and coconut. Yield: 11 servings (116 calories per ½-cup serving).

Per Serving:		
Protein 2.0g	Fat 3.9g	(Saturated Fat 1.3g)
Carbohydrate 18.8g	Fiber 1.2g	Cholesterol 0mg
Iron 1.1mg	Sodium 95mg	Calcium 18mg

ANTIPASTO RICE SALAD

1 cup long-grain rice, uncooked
1 cup frozen artichoke hearts, cooked and quartered
1 cup drained canned kidney beans
1 cup sliced fresh mushrooms
¾ cup diced turkey salami
½ cup finely chopped purple onion
½ cup commercial oil-free Italian dressing
1 teaspoon dried oregano
Lettuce leaves (optional)

Cook rice according to package directions, omitting salt and fat. Rinse with cold water; drain.

Combine rice, artichoke, and next 6 ingredients, stirring well. Cover and chill; stir occasionally. Serve on individual lettuce-lined salad plates, if desired. Yield: 7 servings (179 calories per 1-cup serving).

Per Serving:		
Protein 7.3g	Fat 2.4g	(Saturated Fat 0.7g)
Carbohydrate 31.8g	Fiber 1.6g	Cholesterol 12mg
Iron 2.4mg	Sodium 390mg	Calcium 28mg

PASTA SALAD WITH MARINATED OYSTERS

1 (16-ounce) container fresh oysters, drained
1 cup commercial reduced-calorie Italian dressing
2 ounces rotini pasta, uncooked
2 ounces elbow macaroni, uncooked
2 ounces spinach egg noodles, uncooked
½ cup broccoli flowerets
½ cup diagonally sliced celery
½ cup thinly sliced carrot
½ cup thinly sliced radishes
½ cup julienne-sliced green pepper
¼ cup chopped fresh parsley
6 green leaf lettuce leaves

Place oysters in a medium saucepan; add water to cover. Cook over medium-high heat 6 minutes or until done. Drain well. Combine oysters and Italian dressing. Marinate oysters in refrigerator at least 8 hours. Drain oysters, reserving ½ cup dressing; set aside.

Cook rotini, macaroni, and egg noodles according to package directions, omitting salt and fat. Drain; rinse under cold water, and drain again.

Place pastas in a large bowl. Add oysters, reserved dressing, broccoli, and next 5 ingredients; toss well. Cover and chill at least 1 hour.

Spoon 1 cup pasta mixture onto each individual lettuce-lined salad plate. Yield: 6 servings (208 calories per 1-cup serving).

Per Serving:		
Protein 13.0g	Fat 4.5g	(Saturated Fat 1.0g)
Carbohydrate 28.6g	Fiber 2.2g	Cholesterol 83mg
Iron 9.5mg	Sodium 447mg	Calcium 91mg

GRILLED FLANK STEAK SALAD

1 (1-pound) lean flank steak
¼ cup Chablis or other dry white wine
2 tablespoons peeled, grated gingerroot
3 tablespoons low-sodium soy sauce
2 tablespoons honey
½ teaspoon garlic powder
Vegetable cooking spray
4 cups shredded romaine lettuce
2 cups sliced fresh mushrooms
1½ cups cherry tomato halves
1 cup thinly sliced purple onion
Zesty Cucumber Dressing

Trim fat from steak. Combine wine and next 4 ingredients in a large heavy-duty, zip-top plastic bag; add steak. Seal bag, and shake until steak is well coated. Marinate in refrigerator at least 4 hours, turning bag occasionally.

Remove steak from marinade, discarding marinade. Coat grill rack with cooking spray; place on grill over medium-hot coals (350° to 400°). Place steak on rack; grill, covered, 5 to 6 minutes on each side or to desired degree of doneness. Remove steak from grill; let stand 5 minutes. Slice steak diagonally across the grain into ¼-inch-thick strips.

Place ⅔ cup lettuce on each individual salad plate. Arrange mushrooms, tomato halves, onion slices, and steak evenly over lettuce. Spoon 2 tablespoons Zesty Cucumber Dressing over each salad. Yield: 6 servings (210 calories per serving).

Zesty Cucumber Dressing

1/3 cup peeled, seeded, and diced cucumber
1/4 cup nonfat sour cream alternative
2 1/2 tablespoons nonfat buttermilk
1 1/2 tablespoons prepared horseradish
1 teaspoon minced fresh tarragon
1 teaspoon white wine vinegar
1/8 teaspoon garlic powder

Combine all ingredients in a small bowl, stirring well. Cover and chill 1 hour. Yield: 3/4 cup.

Per Serving:		
Protein 17.8g	Fat 9.0g	(Saturated Fat 3.7g)
Carbohydrate 14.9g	Fiber 2.0g	Cholesterol 40mg
Iron 2.8mg	Sodium 317mg	Calcium 55mg

WARM PORK AND APPLE SALAD

1 (1/2-pound) pork tenderloin
3 tablespoons Dijon mustard
3 tablespoons bourbon
3 tablespoons dark corn syrup
2 teaspoons peanut oil
3 tablespoons frozen apple juice concentrate, thawed and undiluted
3 tablespoons cider vinegar
2 medium Granny Smith apples, cored and sliced
3 cups thinly sliced cabbage
1 cup thinly sliced purple onion
Curly endive leaves (optional)

Partially freeze tenderloin. Trim fat; cut tenderloin into 1/8-inch-thick slices. Place slices in a bowl.

Combine mustard, bourbon, and corn syrup in a bowl. Add 1/4 cup mustard mixture to pork; toss to coat. Reserve remaining mustard mixture. Cover pork, and marinate in refrigerator 30 minutes.

Place oil in a large nonstick skillet over high heat until hot; add pork, and cook 2 minutes or until done. Remove pork from skillet; set aside, and keep warm.

Add reserved mustard mixture, apple juice concentrate, vinegar, and apple to skillet; bring to a boil over medium-high heat, stirring constantly. Cook 1 minute. Add pork, cabbage, and onion; cook, stirring constantly, 1 minute. Spoon evenly onto individual endive leaf-lined salad plates, if desired. Serve warm. Yield: 4 servings (234 calories per 1 1/2-cup serving).

Per Serving:		
Protein 13.3g	Fat 4.9g	(Saturated Fat 1.0g)
Carbohydrate 35.9g	Fiber 4.4g	Cholesterol 37mg
Iron 1.5mg	Sodium 397mg	Calcium 50mg

SMOKED TURKEY AND BLACKBERRY SALAD

2 teaspoons olive oil
3 tablespoons minced shallots
1 teaspoon dried thyme
2 cups fresh or frozen blackberries, thawed and divided
1/4 cup ruby port
1/4 cup canned low-sodium chicken broth, undiluted
1 tablespoon sugar
1 tablespoon balsamic vinegar
1 1/2 cups torn romaine lettuce
1 1/2 cups torn red leaf lettuce
1 cup torn radicchio
1 cup torn curly endive
6 ounces thinly sliced smoked turkey breast, cut into thin strips
3 tablespoons chopped walnuts, toasted

Place olive oil in a nonstick skillet over medium-high heat until hot. Add shallots and thyme; sauté 2 minutes. Add 1 cup blackberries and ruby port; cook 2 minutes. Mash blackberry mixture; cook, stirring constantly, 2 minutes or until liquid evaporates. Add broth, sugar, and vinegar; cook 2 minutes.

Pour mixture through a wire-mesh strainer into a bowl; press mixture with back of a spoon against sides of the strainer to squeeze out liquid. Discard solids remaining in strainer.

Combine romaine lettuce and next 3 ingredients in a bowl; add blackberry mixture, and toss. Arrange lettuce mixture on salad plates; top evenly with turkey strips and remaining blackberries. Sprinkle with walnuts. Yield: 4 servings (154 calories per serving).

Per Serving:		
Protein 12.3g	Fat 6.9g	(Saturated Fat 0.5g)
Carbohydrate 12.6g	Fiber 4.8g	Cholesterol 24mg
Iron 1.6mg	Sodium 338mg	Calcium 46mg

Pickled ginger is the secret ingredient that gives Imperial Crab Salad a sweet, spicy flavor.

IMPERIAL CRAB SALAD

1 (6-ounce) jar pickled ginger
2 tablespoons rice wine vinegar
2 tablespoons commercial no-salt-added chili sauce
1 tablespoon vegetable oil
2 teaspoons peeled, grated gingerroot
2 teaspoons grated orange rind
¼ teaspoon salt
3 cups shredded Bibb lettuce
3 cups shredded fresh spinach
1 cup alfalfa sprouts
¾ pound fresh lump crabmeat, drained
2 banana peppers, sliced crosswise into rings
2 medium oranges, peeled and sectioned
Coarsely chopped fresh chives (optional)

Drain pickled ginger, reserving 2 tablespoons juice. Slice enough ginger into strips to measure ¼ cup. Reserve remaining pickled ginger and juice for another use.

Combine 2 tablespoons ginger juice, rice wine vinegar, and next 5 ingredients in a small jar; cover tightly, and shake vigorously. Cover and chill at least 1 hour.

Combine lettuce, spinach, and alfalfa sprouts in a large bowl; toss gently. Pour vinegar mixture over lettuce mixture; toss gently. Place lettuce mixture evenly on individual salad plates. Arrange crabmeat, ginger strips, banana pepper, and orange sections over spinach mixture. Garnish with chives, if desired. Yield: 6 servings (115 calories per serving).

Per Serving:		
Protein 12.0g	Fat 3.4g	(Saturated Fat 0.6g)
Carbohydrate 10.0g	Fiber 3.3g	Cholesterol 51mg
Iron 1.2mg	Sodium 306mg	Calcium 94mg

GRILLED TERIYAKI CORN AND SHRIMP SALAD

This salad is refreshing and light. Add commercial French rolls and iced tea to round out this low-fat summer meal.

3 ears fresh corn
1 pound unpeeled medium-size fresh shrimp
3 tablespoons low-sodium teriyaki sauce, divided
Vegetable cooking spray
½ cup sliced green onions
½ cup finely diced sweet red pepper
⅓ cup minced fresh cilantro
¼ cup reduced-calorie mayonnaise
¼ cup nonfat sour cream alternative
½ teaspoon ground cumin
4 green leaf lettuce leaves

Remove and discard husks and silks from corn; set corn aside. Peel and devein shrimp. Thread shrimp onto 4 (10-inch) skewers.

Brush 2 tablespoons teriyaki sauce over corn and shrimp. Coat grill rack with cooking spray, and place on grill over hot coals (400° to 500°). Place corn on rack; grill, covered, 20 minutes or until tender and slightly charred, turning frequently. Place shrimp on rack; grill, covered, 3 to 4 minutes on each side or until done.

Let corn cool slightly. Cut corn from cobs, and place in a medium bowl; discard cobs. Add shrimp, green onions, sweet red pepper, and cilantro. Combine remaining 1 tablespoon teriyaki sauce, mayonnaise, sour cream, and cumin; stir into shrimp mixture. Spoon 1 cup shrimp mixture onto each individual lettuce-lined salad plate. Yield: 4 servings (185 calories per 1-cup serving).

Per Serving:		
Protein 18.1g	Fat 5.7g	(Saturated Fat 0.9g)
Carbohydrate 16.3g	Fiber 2.7g	Cholesterol 136mg
Iron 3.3mg	Sodium 479mg	Calcium 65mg

SHRIMP AND LOBSTER SALAD

When buying frozen lobster tails, make sure the packaging is intact with no evidence of juices or ice. Don't buy tails that have dry or frosty spots.

½ cup reduced-calorie mayonnaise
2 tablespoons no-salt-added catsup
1 teaspoon white wine Worcestershire sauce
½ teaspoon dry mustard
½ teaspoon celery seeds
⅛ teaspoon Old Bay seasoning
⅛ teaspoon garlic powder
⅛ teaspoon hot sauce
6 cups water
1 (8-ounce) fresh or frozen lobster tail, thawed
½ pound unpeeled medium-size fresh shrimp
¼ cup minced celery
¼ cup minced onion
1½ tablespoons minced ripe olives
2 teaspoons minced green pepper
Green leaf lettuce (optional)

Combine first 8 ingredients in a small bowl, stirring well; set aside.

Bring 6 cups water to a boil in a medium saucepan; add lobster, and cook 3 minutes. Add shrimp; cook an additional 3 to 5 minutes or until lobster is done and shrimp turn pink. Drain well; rinse with cold water. Split and clean lobster tail; discard shell. Chop lobster meat. Peel, devein, and chop shrimp.

Combine lobster, shrimp, celery, and next 3 ingredients in a medium bowl. Add mayonnaise mixture, and toss gently. Cover and chill.

To serve, spoon ½ cup lobster mixture onto each individual lettuce-lined salad plate, if desired. Yield: 4 servings (174 calories per ½-cup serving).

Per Serving:		
Protein 16.1g	Fat 9.2g	(Saturated Fat 1.4g)
Carbohydrate 6.6g	Fiber 0.6g	Cholesterol 103mg
Iron 1.5mg	Sodium 527mg	Calcium 53mg

SEAFOOD AND FUSILLI SALAD

1 cup peeled, diced papaya
1½ tablespoons lemon juice
1½ tablespoons white wine vinegar
1 tablespoon olive oil
1 tablespoon chopped fresh dillweed
1 tablespoon chopped fresh tarragon
2 ounces fusilli pasta, uncooked
1 pound unpeeled medium-size fresh shrimp
1 cup white Zinfandel
4 cloves garlic, minced
½ pound bay scallops
1 cup thinly sliced sweet red pepper
1 cup diced celery
1 cup tightly packed watercress leaves
4 cups shredded romaine lettuce

Combine papaya, lemon juice, vinegar, and olive oil in container of an electric blender; cover and process until smooth. Add dillweed and tarragon; process until herbs are minced. Cover and chill at least 1 hour.

Cook pasta according to package directions, omitting salt and fat. Set aside.

Peel and devein shrimp; set aside.

Combine Zinfandel and garlic in a large saucepan; bring to a boil. Cook 1 minute. Add scallops; cook 1 minute or until scallops are opaque, stirring frequently. Remove from heat. Transfer scallops to a large bowl, using a slotted spoon; reserve wine mixture in saucepan.

Return saucepan to heat; bring wine mixture to a boil. Add shrimp; cook 3 to 5 minutes or until shrimp turn pink. Drain well.

Add pasta, shrimp, sweet red pepper, celery, and watercress to scallops; toss gently. Cover and chill thoroughly.

Just before serving, add papaya mixture to seafood mixture; toss gently. Place shredded romaine lettuce evenly on individual salad plates. Top evenly with seafood mixture. Yield: 5 servings (186 calories per serving).

Per Serving:

Protein 21.0g	Fat 4.0g	(Saturated Fat 0.6g)
Carbohydrate 16.0g	Fiber 2.2g	Cholesterol 114mg
Iron 3.1mg	Sodium 218mg	Calcium 78mg

SCANDINAVIAN POTATO-SALMON SALAD

2 tablespoons minced fresh dillweed
3 tablespoons canned low-sodium chicken broth, undiluted
1 tablespoon white wine vinegar
1 tablespoon lemon juice
2 teaspoons olive oil
2 teaspoons Dijon mustard
¼ teaspoon salt
¼ teaspoon ground white pepper
¼ pound fresh green beans
¾ pound small round red potatoes
1 (12-ounce) salmon fillet
1 tablespoon capers
10 Boston lettuce leaves
¼ cup plus 2 tablespoons nonfat sour cream alternative

Combine first 8 ingredients in a small bowl, stirring well with a wire whisk; set aside.

Wash beans; trim ends, and remove strings. Arrange beans in a vegetable steamer over boiling water. Cover and steam 4 to 6 minutes or until crisp-tender; cut into ½-inch pieces. Place in a large bowl; set aside.

Cook potatoes in a medium saucepan in boiling water to cover 15 to 17 minutes or just until tender. Remove potatoes from water, using a slotted spoon; reserve water in pan. Cut potatoes into ¼-inch-thick slices. Cut slices in half; add to beans.

Bring water in saucepan to a boil; add fillet. Cover, reduce heat, and simmer 6 to 8 minutes or until fish flakes easily when tested with a fork. Drain; remove skin from fillet. Flake fish into bite-size pieces. Add salmon and capers to potato mixture; toss gently.

Pour broth mixture over salmon mixture, and toss gently. Spoon 1 cup salmon mixture onto each individual lettuce-lined salad plate. Top each serving with 1 tablespoon sour cream. Yield: 5 servings (204 calories per 1-cup serving).

Per Serving:

Protein 17.5g	Fat 7.8g	(Saturated Fat 1.3g)
Carbohydrate 15.1g	Fiber 1.8g	Cholesterol 44mg
Iron 1.6mg	Sodium 367mg	Calcium 23mg

MANGO-CHILI LIME DRESSING

The pureed fruit adds an abundance of flavor, body, and color to this sweet-hot dressing.

1 cup peeled, diced ripe mango
3 tablespoons lime juice
2 tablespoons white wine vinegar
1 tablespoon vegetable oil
2 teaspoons peeled, grated gingerroot
1 teaspoon chili powder
½ teaspoon ground cumin
¼ teaspoon garlic powder
⅛ teaspoon salt

Combine all ingredients in container of an electric blender; cover and process until smooth. Transfer to a bowl. Cover and chill thoroughly. Serve with salad greens or chicken salad. Yield: 1¼ cups (15 calories per tablespoon).

Per Tablespoon:		
Protein 0.1g	Fat 0.8g	(Saturated Fat 0.1g)
Carbohydrate 2.4g	Fiber 0.2g	Cholesterol 0mg
Iron 0.1mg	Sodium 16mg	Calcium 2mg

ORANGE CURRY DRESSING

Enjoy this sweet, creamy, fat-free dressing with your favorite combination of fresh fruit.

1 (8-ounce) carton plain nonfat yogurt
¼ cup low-sugar orange marmalade
1 teaspoon lemon juice
½ teaspoon curry powder
¼ teaspoon ground ginger

Combine all ingredients in a bowl, stirring well. Cover; chill thoroughly. Serve with fresh fruit. Yield: 1 cup plus 2 tablespoons (8 calories per tablespoon).

Per Tablespoon:		
Protein 0.8g	Fat 0.0g	(Saturated Fat 0g)
Carbohydrate 1.2g	Fiber 0g	Cholesterol 0mg
Iron 0mg	Sodium 10mg	Calcium 27mg

CELERY BUTTERMILK DRESSING

2 cups thinly sliced celery
¾ cup nonfat buttermilk
¼ cup reduced-calorie mayonnaise
1 teaspoon dried oregano
½ teaspoon freshly ground pepper
1 clove garlic

Combine all ingredients in container of an electric blender; cover and process until smooth, stopping once to scrape down sides. Cover and chill.

Pour celery mixture through a wire-mesh strainer into a bowl; press with back of a spoon against the sides of strainer to squeeze out liquid. Discard solids remaining in strainer. Cover celery mixture, and chill thoroughly. Serve with salad greens. Yield: 1¾ cups (10 calories per tablespoon).

Per Tablespoon:		
Protein 0.3g	Fat 0.6g	(Saturated Fat 0.1g)
Carbohydrate 0.8g	Fiber 0.1g	Cholesterol 1mg
Iron 0.1mg	Sodium 30mg	Calcium 12mg

CREAMY CAESAR DRESSING

¼ teaspoon salt
1 large clove garlic
½ cup nonfat sour cream alternative
2 tablespoons lemon juice
2 tablespoons skim milk
1 tablespoon low-sodium Worcestershire sauce
2 teaspoons olive oil
1 teaspoon Dijon mustard
½ teaspoon freshly ground pepper

Mash salt and garlic to a paste; place in a bowl. Add sour cream and remaining ingredients; stir with a wire whisk. Cover and chill. Serve with salad greens. Yield: ¾ cup (17 calories per tablespoon).

Per Tablespoon:		
Protein 0.8g	Fat 0.8g	(Saturated Fat 0.1g)
Carbohydrate 1.4g	Fiber 0g	Cholesterol 0mg
Iron 0mg	Sodium 74mg	Calcium 10mg

ROASTED GARLIC DRESSING

Roasted garlic adds a mildly sweet, mellow flavor to this dressing without adding fat.

2 large heads garlic, unpeeled
1 cup plain nonfat yogurt
2 tablespoons red wine vinegar
2 tablespoons Dijon mustard
2 teaspoons olive oil
½ teaspoon freshly ground pepper

Peel outer skins from garlic; cut off top one-fourth of each head, and discard. Place garlic, cut side up, in center of a piece of heavy-duty aluminum foil. Fold foil over garlic, sealing tightly. Bake at 350° for 1 hour or until garlic is soft. Remove from oven; cool.

Remove papery skin from garlic. Scoop out soft garlic with a spoon. Combine garlic, yogurt, and remaining ingredients in container of an electric blender. Cover and process on high speed 1 minute or until smooth, stopping once to scrape down sides.

Cover and chill thoroughly. Serve with potato salad or other vegetable salads. Yield: 1½ cups (15 calories per tablespoon).

Per Tablespoon:		
Protein 0.7g	Fat 0.5g	(Saturated Fat 0.1g)
Carbohydrate 1.9g	Fiber 0.1g	Cholesterol 0mg
Iron 0.1mg	Sodium 45mg	Calcium 24mg

RASPBERRY-WALNUT DRESSING

1 cup frozen unsweetened raspberries, thawed
1 tablespoon minced fresh thyme
2 tablespoons raspberry vinegar
2 tablespoons commercial honey mustard
2 teaspoons walnut oil
½ teaspoon freshly ground pepper

Combine all ingredients in container of an electric blender; cover and process until smooth. Chill thoroughly. Serve with bitter greens. Yield: ¾ cup (19 calories per tablespoon).

Per Tablespoon:		
Protein 0.2g	Fat 0.9g	(Saturated Fat 0.1g)
Carbohydrate 2.9g	Fiber 0.7g	Cholesterol 0mg
Iron 0.2mg	Sodium 17mg	Calcium 5mg

ORIENTAL SALAD DRESSING

2 tablespoons brown sugar
1 tablespoon chopped fresh parsley
2½ tablespoons red wine vinegar
2½ tablespoons water
2 teaspoons low-sodium soy sauce
1 teaspoon vegetable oil
1 teaspoon dark sesame oil

Combine all ingredients in a small jar; cover tightly, and shake vigorously. Serve at room temperature with salad greens. Yield: ½ cup (20 calories per tablespoon).

Per Tablespoon:		
Protein 0.0g	Fat 1.1g	(Saturated Fat 0.2g)
Carbohydrate 2.4g	Fiber 0g	Cholesterol 0mg
Iron 0.1mg	Sodium 34mg	Calcium 3mg

CRANBERRY-HONEY VINAIGRETTE

½ cup cranberry juice cocktail
2 tablespoons balsamic vinegar
1 tablespoon honey
1 tablespoon Dijon mustard
2 teaspoons minced fresh thyme
2 teaspoons walnut oil
¼ teaspoon freshly ground pepper

Combine all ingredients in a small jar; cover tightly, and shake vigorously. Chill thoroughly. Serve with salad greens. Yield: ¾ cup plus 2 tablespoons (17 calories per tablespoon).

Per Tablespoon:		
Protein 0.0g	Fat 0.7g	(Saturated Fat 0.1g)
Carbohydrate 2.8g	Fiber 0g	Cholesterol 0mg
Iron 0.1mg	Sodium 32mg	Calcium 1mg

Fruit and Cheese Subs (page 190) offer a healthy way to enjoy a favorite sandwich. The combination of fresh fruit, creamy cheese, and a hint of spices makes them irresistible.

Sandwiches & Snacks

FRUIT AND CHEESE SUBS

¾ cup plus 2 tablespoons nonfat herb-and-garlic cream cheese product, divided
1 tablespoon minced fresh dillweed
1 tablespoon commercial nonfat creamy cucumber dressing
1 cup peeled, finely chopped fresh peaches
1 cup seeded, finely chopped cucumber
3 tablespoons chopped almonds, toasted
1 (16-ounce) loaf Italian bread
6 green leaf lettuce leaves
5 ounces reduced-fat Havarti cheese, thinly sliced

Combine ¼ cup cream cheese, dillweed, and dressing, stirring well. Add peaches, cucumber, and almonds; stir well. Set aside.

Slice bread in half horizontally. Hollow out center of each half, leaving 1-inch-thick shells. Reserve inside of bread for another use.

Spread remaining ½ cup plus 2 tablespoons cream cheese over cut sides of bread. Place lettuce leaves on bottom half of bread. Spoon peach mixture evenly over lettuce. Place cheese slices over peach mixture, and top with remaining bread half. Cut loaf into 8 slices. Yield: 8 servings (229 calories per serving).

Per Serving:

Protein 13.0g	Fat 6.0g	(Saturated Fat 2.7g)
Carbohydrate 30.7g	Fiber 2.5g	Cholesterol 17mg
Iron 1.3mg	Sodium 563mg	Calcium 306mg

THE SECRETS TO LONG LIFE

To find the formula for long life, University of Georgia researchers compared the diets of 24 centenarians (people aged 100 years and older) with those of 60- and 80-year-olds. The centenarians ate more vegetables, drank less alcohol, and were more likely to eat breakfast than the younger people. Also, their weight had remained stable over the years, suggesting they had avoided weight-loss diets.

Compared with the younger folks, the centenarians did include more fat in their diet (at the maximum, about 9 grams more per day) and were less likely to follow a diet geared to lower the risk of chronic diseases such as cancer.

CRISPY POTATO, TOMATO, AND MOZZARELLA SQUARES

This sandwich is worth the little extra time it takes to prepare.

Vegetable cooking spray
1 (10-ounce) can refrigerated pizza crust dough
1 teaspoon dried rosemary, crushed
½ teaspoon dried crushed red pepper
2 large cloves garlic, minced
¾ pound round red potatoes, cut into ¼-inch-thick slices
2 tablespoons balsamic vinegar
¼ teaspoon salt
3 plum tomatoes, sliced
18 basil leaves
6 ounces part-skim mozzarella cheese, thinly sliced

Coat a 13- x 9- x 2-inch baking dish with cooking spray. Unroll dough, and press into bottom of dish. Spray dough with cooking spray; sprinkle with rosemary, red pepper, and garlic. Bake at 400° for 15 minutes or until lightly browned. Let cool on a wire rack.

Place potato slices in a medium saucepan; add water to cover. Bring to a boil; boil 5 minutes or until potato is crisp-tender. Drain; pat dry with paper towels. Place potato slices in a shallow dish. Combine vinegar and salt; pour over potato slices, tossing to coat. Arrange potato slices in a single layer on a baking sheet coated with cooking spray. Bake at 450° for 18 to 20 minutes or until browned, turning after 10 minutes.

Cut crust into 12 squares. Arrange potato slices evenly over 6 squares. Top potato evenly with tomato slices, basil, and cheese. Top with remaining crust squares, garlic side down. Wrap each sandwich in heavy-duty plastic wrap. Place a pan holding 2 or 3 (1-pound) cans on top of sandwiches to flatten, and refrigerate up to 4 hours. Yield: 6 servings (256 calories per serving).

Per Serving:

Protein 12.6g	Fat 6.5g	(Saturated Fat 3.2g)
Carbohydrate 35.4g	Fiber 1.5g	Cholesterol 16mg
Iron 0.8mg	Sodium 498mg	Calcium 201mg

GRILLED RATATOUILLE GYROS

1 (¾-pound) eggplant
2 small zucchini
1 large sweet red pepper
½ cup no-salt-added tomato juice
¼ cup commercial oil-free Italian dressing
¼ cup white wine vinegar
2 tablespoons minced fresh basil
1 tablespoon minced garlic
½ teaspoon freshly ground pepper
3 (6-inch) pita bread rounds
Vegetable cooking spray
4 ounces feta cheese with basil and tomato, crumbled

Cut eggplant, zucchini, and sweet red pepper into 1-inch pieces. Thread vegetable pieces onto 10 (10-inch) skewers, keeping eggplant pieces on separate skewers; set aside.

Combine tomato juice and next 5 ingredients in a small bowl, stirring well. Set aside.

Separate each pita bread into 2 rounds; wrap pita rounds in aluminum foil. Set aside.

Coat grill rack with cooking spray; place on grill over medium-hot coals (350° to 400°). Place zucchini and sweet red pepper skewers on rack; grill, covered, 5 minutes, brushing frequently with tomato juice mixture. Place eggplant skewers on rack with zucchini and sweet red pepper; grill, covered, 15 minutes or until vegetables are tender, brushing frequently with remaining tomato juice mixture. Set aside, and keep warm.

Place foil-wrapped pita bread rounds on rack; grill, covered, 2 minutes, turning once.

Remove vegetables from skewers. Arrange vegetables evenly down centers of pita bread rounds; sprinkle evenly with cheese. Roll up pitas; place each on a piece of heavy-duty aluminum foil. Wrap securely in foil. Place on rack; grill, covered, 4 minutes or until sandwiches are thoroughly heated. Serve immediately. Yield: 6 servings (173 calories per serving).

Per Serving:		
Protein 5.9g	Fat 5.1g	(Saturated Fat 2.9g)
Carbohydrate 25.3g	Fiber 4.4g	Cholesterol 17mg
Iron 1.9mg	Sodium 506mg	Calcium 151mg

SPICY CATFISH SANDWICHES WITH TROPICAL TARTAR SAUCE

The fat-free tartar sauce also complements grilled fish or chicken.

4 (4-ounce) farm-raised catfish fillets
¼ cup hot sauce
¾ cup cornmeal
⅛ teaspoon salt
Butter-flavored vegetable cooking spray
2 teaspoons reduced-calorie margarine
4 green leaf lettuce leaves
4 reduced-calorie whole wheat hamburger buns
Tropical Tartar Sauce

Place fillets in a shallow dish; pour hot sauce over fillets, turning to coat. Cover and marinate in refrigerator 30 minutes.

Combine cornmeal and salt in a shallow container; dredge fillets in cornmeal mixture, shaking off excess.

Coat a large nonstick skillet with cooking spray; add margarine. Place over medium-high heat until margarine melts. Add fillets, and cook 3 to 4 minutes on each side or until fish flakes easily when tested with a fork.

Place a lettuce leaf on bottom half of each bun; top each with a fillet. Spoon 2 tablespoons Tropical Tartar Sauce over each fillet; top with remaining bun halves. Yield: 4 servings (301 calories per serving).

Tropical Tartar Sauce

2 tablespoons nonfat mayonnaise
2 tablespoons nonfat sour cream alternative
1 tablespoon crushed pineapple in juice
2 teaspoons diced pimiento
2 teaspoons minced green onions
2 teaspoons finely chopped sweet pickle

Combine all ingredients in a small bowl, stirring well. Cover and chill thoroughly. Yield: ½ cup.

Per Serving:		
Protein 24.7g	Fat 7.6g	(Saturated Fat 1.5g)
Carbohydrate 31.4g	Fiber 2.5g	Cholesterol 66mg
Iron 3.4mg	Sodium 537mg	Calcium 70mg

Niçoise Loaf, a meal in itself, is brimming with robust Mediterranean flavors.

NIÇOISE LOAF

- 2 large sweet red peppers
- 1 (16-ounce) round loaf sourdough bread
- 8 large basil leaves
- 2 (6⅛-ounce) cans 60%-less-salt tuna in water, drained
- 1 tablespoon balsamic vinegar
- 4 thin slices purple onion, separated into rings
- 4 canned artichoke hearts, drained and quartered
- ¼ cup sliced ripe olives
- 8 thin slices plum tomato
- Fresh basil sprigs (optional)

Cut peppers in half lengthwise; remove and discard seeds and membrane. Place peppers, skin side up, on a baking sheet; flatten with palm of hand. Broil 5½ inches from heat (with electric oven door partially opened) 15 to 20 minutes or until charred. Place in ice water until cool; peel and discard skins. Dice peppers, and set aside.

Slice bread in half horizontally. Hollow out center of each half, leaving 1-inch-thick shells. Reserve inside of bread for another use.

Place basil leaves over bottom half of bread. Combine tuna and vinegar; toss well. Spoon tuna mixture over basil leaves. Top with diced pepper, onion, and next 3 ingredients. Top with remaining bread half.

Wrap sandwich in heavy-duty plastic wrap. Place a pan holding 2 or 3 (1-pound) cans on top of sandwich to flatten, and refrigerate up to 8 hours.

To serve, slice sandwich into 6 wedges. Garnish with fresh basil sprigs, if desired. Yield: 6 servings (238 calories per serving).

Per Serving:		
Protein 18.8g	Fat 2.4g	(Saturated Fat 0.3g)
Carbohydrate 36.0g	Fiber 2.4g	Cholesterol 14mg
Iron 3.3mg	Sodium 511mg	Calcium 91mg

BUFFALO CHICKEN SANDWICHES

¼ cup hot sauce
2 tablespoons reduced-calorie margarine, melted
4 (4-ounce) skinned, boned chicken breast halves
1 medium-size purple onion, thinly sliced and separated into rings
2 cups finely shredded cabbage
1 cup finely shredded carrot
¼ cup commercial nonfat blue cheese dressing, divided
Vegetable cooking spray
4 reduced-calorie hamburger buns, split and toasted
4 green leaf lettuce leaves

Combine hot sauce and margarine in a shallow dish; add chicken and onion, turning to coat. Cover and marinate in refrigerator up to 1 hour.

Combine cabbage, carrot, and 2½ tablespoons blue cheese dressing; toss well, and set aside.

Remove chicken and onion from marinade, reserving marinade. Place chicken and onion on rack of broiler pan coated with cooking spray; brush with half of reserved marinade. Broil 5½ inches from heat (with electric oven door partially opened) 4 minutes. Turn chicken and onion; brush with remaining marinade. Broil an additional 6 to 8 minutes or until chicken is done and onion is browned.

Spread remaining 1½ tablespoons blue cheese dressing over bottom halves of buns. Top each with a lettuce leaf. Spoon cabbage mixture evenly over lettuce leaves; top each with a chicken breast. Place onion evenly over chicken; top with remaining bun halves. Serve immediately. Yield: 4 servings (308 calories per serving).

Per Serving:		
Protein 29.1g	Fat 8.0g	(Saturated Fat 1.4g)
Carbohydrate 24.9g	Fiber 4g	Cholesterol 70mg
Iron 1.4mg	Sodium 583mg	Calcium 51mg

SOUTHWESTERN CHICKEN SALAD SANDWICHES

This chicken salad is much lower in fat than is traditional chicken salad. Salsa, cumin, and ground red pepper give it a spicy flair.

4 ounces nonfat cream cheese product, softened
⅓ cup nonfat sour cream alternative
2 tablespoons commercial no-salt-added mild salsa
½ teaspoon ground cumin
¼ teaspoon salt
¼ teaspoon ground red pepper
1½ cups shredded cooked chicken
⅓ cup finely chopped sweet red pepper
⅓ cup minced green onions
8 (¾-ounce) slices reduced-calorie whole wheat bread, toasted
16 medium-size fresh spinach leaves
1 cup alfalfa sprouts

Combine first 6 ingredients in a small bowl. Stir in chicken, sweet red pepper, and green onions. Spread mixture evenly over 4 slices of bread; top evenly with spinach leaves. Place alfalfa sprouts evenly over spinach; top with remaining 4 bread slices. Yield: 4 servings (225 calories per serving).

Per Serving:		
Protein 25.3g	Fat 6.0g	(Saturated Fat 1.4g)
Carbohydrate 17.6g	Fiber 6g	Cholesterol 52mg
Iron 2.7mg	Sodium 595mg	Calcium 149mg

BLACKENED LAMB POCKETS WITH WHITE BEAN SALSA

This bean salsa will also enhance the taste of roasted or grilled beef or pork.

¾ pound lean boneless lamb
1 teaspoon ground cumin
1 teaspoon chili powder
¼ teaspoon garlic powder
⅛ teaspoon salt
Vegetable cooking spray
¼ cup plus 2 tablespoons plain nonfat yogurt, divided
3 (6-inch) pita bread rounds, cut in half crosswise
24 peeled cucumber slices (⅛ inch thick)
White Bean Salsa

Cut lamb into ¼-inch-wide strips. Combine cumin, chili powder, garlic powder, and salt, stirring well. Sprinkle evenly over lamb. Coat a large nonstick skillet with cooking spray; place over high heat until hot. Add lamb, and cook until browned on all sides, stirring frequently.

Spread 1 tablespoon yogurt in each pita half; place 4 cucumber slices over yogurt in each pita. Spoon lamb mixture evenly into pita halves. Top lamb evenly with White Bean Salsa. Yield: 6 servings (213 calories per serving).

White Bean Salsa

½ cup drained canned navy beans
¼ cup seeded, diced tomato
¼ cup diced green pepper
¼ cup minced purple onion
2 tablespoons minced fresh cilantro
1 tablespoon seeded, minced jalapeño pepper
1 tablespoon lime juice
¼ teaspoon ground cumin
¼ teaspoon chili powder

Combine all ingredients in a small bowl, stirring well. Cover and let stand 2 hours. Yield: 1⅓ cups.

Per Serving:

Protein 17.2g	Fat 5.2g	(Saturated Fat 1.6g)
Carbohydrate 22.7g	Fiber 4.1g	Cholesterol 41mg
Iron 2.8mg	Sodium 301mg	Calcium 83mg

PORK FAJITAS WITH AVOCADO-CORN SALSA

2 (½-pound) pork tenderloins
¾ cup commercial no-salt-added chunky salsa, divided
½ cup light beer
½ cup lime juice, divided
2 teaspoons ground cumin
½ teaspoon garlic powder
1 teaspoon hot sauce
¾ cup frozen whole-kernel corn, thawed
¾ cup peeled, diced avocado
¼ cup finely chopped sweet red pepper
3 tablespoons minced fresh cilantro
¼ teaspoon garlic powder
6 (7-inch) flour tortillas
Vegetable cooking spray
Fresh cilantro sprigs (optional)

Partially freeze pork; cut into ¼-inch-thick slices. Place pork slices in a heavy-duty, zip-top plastic bag. Combine ½ cup salsa, beer, ¼ cup plus 2 tablespoons lime juice, ground cumin, ½ teaspoon garlic powder, and hot sauce; pour over pork. Seal bag, and shake until pork slices are well coated. Marinate pork slices in refrigerator at least 3 hours, turning bag occasionally.

Combine remaining ¼ cup salsa, remaining 2 tablespoons lime juice, corn, avocado, sweet red pepper, minced cilantro, and ¼ teaspoon garlic powder in a small bowl. Set aside.

Wrap tortillas in heavy-duty aluminum foil. Bake at 350° for 5 minutes or until thoroughly heated. Set aside, and keep warm.

Remove pork from marinade, discarding marinade. Coat a large nonstick skillet with cooking spray; place over medium-high heat until hot. Add pork, and cook 4 minutes or until done, stirring frequently. Place pork evenly down centers of tortillas. Top each with ¼ cup corn mixture; roll up tortillas. Garnish with fresh cilantro sprigs, if desired. Serve immediately. Yield: 6 servings (275 calories per serving).

Per Serving:

Protein 21.7g	Fat 8.7g	(Saturated Fat 1.9g)
Carbohydrate 27.6g	Fiber 2.2g	Cholesterol 56mg
Iron 2.8mg	Sodium 252mg	Calcium 68mg

Serve Firecracker Sandwiches wrapped in plastic wrap and tied with colorful streamers for a festive addition to your next Fourth of July celebration.

FIRECRACKER SANDWICHES

¼ cup nonfat cream cheese product, softened
2 tablespoons reduced-calorie mayonnaise
2 teaspoons minced onion
1 teaspoon white vinegar
½ teaspoon sugar
1 cup minced reduced-fat, low-salt ham
½ cup grated carrot
¼ cup raisins
8 (1-ounce) slices white bread

Combine softened cream cheese, mayonnaise, minced onion, white vinegar, and sugar in a medium bowl, stirring well. Add minced ham, grated carrot, and raisins; stir well.

Using a rolling pin, roll bread slices until flat. Spread ham mixture evenly over bread slices, spreading to edges. Roll up sandwiches, jellyroll fashion.

If desired, wrap each sandwich in plastic wrap, twisting ends; secure ends of plastic wrap with decorative ribbon.

Store wrapped sandwiches in refrigerator up to 4 hours. Yield: 8 servings (124 calories per serving).

Per Serving:

Protein 6.8g	Fat 2.8g	(Saturated Fat 0.9g)
Carbohydrate 17.7g	Fiber 0.9g	Cholesterol 12mg
Iron 0.8mg	Sodium 354mg	Calcium 43mg

FRUIT SALSA WITH GRANOLA TOPPING

If covered tightly, this fruit mixture will keep in the refrigerator up to three days.

3 medium plums, pitted and diced
2 medium navel oranges, peeled, sectioned, and chopped
1 medium peach, pitted and diced
1 cup fresh raspberries
1 tablespoon minced fresh mint
1 tablespoon minced crystallized ginger
1 tablespoon fresh lime juice
2 teaspoons sugar
1 teaspoon grated orange rind
⅔ cup fresh orange juice
1 cup low-fat granola without raisins

Combine first 10 ingredients in a large bowl; toss gently. Cover and chill thoroughly.

To serve, spoon ½ cup fruit mixture into each individual serving bowl; top each with 2 tablespoons granola. Yield: 8 servings (116 calories per serving).

Per Serving:

Protein 2.0g	Fat 1.2g	(Saturated Fat 0g)
Carbohydrate 27.2g	Fiber 4.9g	Cholesterol 0mg
Iron 1.1mg	Sodium 14mg	Calcium 27mg

BERRY POPS

Each of these frozen strawberry pops has less than 1 gram of fat.

1 envelope unflavored gelatin
1 cup peach nectar
2 cups vanilla low-fat yogurt
1 teaspoon vanilla extract
2½ cups frozen unsweetened strawberries, thawed
8 (3-ounce) paper cups
8 wooden sticks

Sprinkle gelatin over peach nectar in a small saucepan; let stand 1 minute. Cook over low heat, stirring until gelatin dissolves, about 2 minutes. Remove from heat; add yogurt and vanilla, stirring with a wire whisk until smooth.

Mash strawberries; add to yogurt mixture. Spoon strawberry mixture evenly into paper cups. Cover tops of cups with aluminum foil, and insert a wooden stick through foil into center of each cup. Freeze until firm. To serve, remove aluminum foil; peel cup from pop. Yield: 8 pops (86 calories each).

Per Pop:

Protein 3.8g	Fat 0.8g	(Saturated Fat 0.5g)
Carbohydrate 16.4g	Fiber 0.4g	Cholesterol 3mg
Iron 0.4mg	Sodium 42mg	Calcium 106mg

LAYERED FRUIT POPS

1½ cups fresh orange juice
¼ cup sugar
¼ cup plus 2 tablespoons fresh lemon juice
¼ teaspoon ground cinnamon
4 cups fresh strawberries, hulled and sliced
4 cups chopped fresh peaches
14 (6-ounce) paper cups
14 wooden sticks

Combine first 4 ingredients in container of an electric blender; cover and process until combined, stopping once to scrape down sides. Reserve 1 cup orange juice mixture; set aside. Add strawberries to remaining juice in blender; process until smooth. Transfer strawberry mixture to a bowl, and set aside.

Combine reserved 1 cup orange juice mixture and peaches in blender; cover and process until smooth. Transfer mixture to a bowl.

Spoon 2 tablespoons strawberry mixture into each paper cup. Cover tops of cups with aluminum foil, and insert a wooden stick through foil into center of each cup. Freeze until firm. Pour 2 tablespoons peach mixture over frozen strawberry mixture in each cup. Freeze until firm. Repeat procedure with remaining strawberry and peach mixtures. To serve, remove aluminum foil; peel cup from pop. Yield: 14 pops (56 calories each).

Per Pop:

Protein 0.7g	Fat 0.2g	(Saturated Fat 0g)
Carbohydrate 14.1g	Fiber 1.6g	Cholesterol 0mg
Iron 0.2mg	Sodium 1mg	Calcium 10mg

CHOCOLATE YOGURT CHEESE

4 (8-ounce) cartons plain nonfat yogurt
½ cup sifted powdered sugar
3 tablespoons unsweetened cocoa
¾ teaspoon ground cinnamon
2 teaspoons vanilla extract

Place a colander in a bowl. Line colander with 4 layers of cheesecloth, allowing cheesecloth to extend over outside edges. Spoon yogurt into colander. Cover with plastic wrap; refrigerate 12 hours.

Spoon yogurt cheese into a bowl; discard liquid. Combine sugar, cocoa, and cinnamon, stirring well. Add cocoa mixture to yogurt cheese; stir well. Add vanilla, and beat at low speed of an electric mixer until combined. Cover and chill. Serve with fresh fruit. Yield: 1½ cups (35 calories per tablespoon).

Per Tablespoon:		
Protein 2.4g	Fat 0.2g	(Saturated Fat 0.1g)
Carbohydrate 5.9g	Fiber 0g	Cholesterol 1mg
Iron 0.2mg	Sodium 29mg	Calcium 77mg

CREAM CHEESE AND OLIVE SPREAD

By using low-fat cottage cheese and light process cream cheese instead of regular cream cheese, we cut the fat in this recipe by half.

¼ cup plus 2 tablespoons low-fat cottage cheese
¼ cup plus 2 tablespoons light process cream cheese product
1 teaspoon lemon juice
¼ cup diced pimiento-stuffed olives
¼ cup nonfat sour cream alternative
1 (2-ounce) jar diced pimiento, drained

Position knife blade in food processor bowl; add first 3 ingredients, and process until smooth. Transfer mixture to a bowl; stir in olives, sour cream, and pimiento. Yield: 1¼ cups (16 calories per tablespoon).

Per Tablespoon:		
Protein 1.2g	Fat 0.9g	(Saturated Fat 0.9g)
Carbohydrate 0.8g	Fiber 0.1g	Cholesterol 3mg
Iron 0.1mg	Sodium 146mg	Calcium 12mg

CINNAMON TORTILLA CHIPS WITH COFFEE DIP

It's hard to believe that this sweet snack is low in fat. Best of all, the chips and dip are easy to make, so you can enjoy this snack often.

6 (6-inch) flour tortillas
Vegetable cooking spray
2 tablespoons sugar
1 teaspoon unsweetened cocoa
¼ teaspoon ground cinnamon
1 cup reduced-calorie frozen whipped topping, thawed
½ cup coffee-flavored low-fat yogurt

Cut each tortilla into 6 wedges, and arrange in a single layer on a large baking sheet coated with cooking spray. Combine sugar, cocoa, and ground cinnamon, stirring well. Coat wedges with cooking spray; sprinkle half of sugar mixture over wedges. Turn wedges over, and coat again; sprinkle remaining sugar mixture over wedges. Bake at 350° for 15 minutes or until crisp.

Combine whipped topping and yogurt, stirring well. Serve with tortilla wedges. Yield: 12 servings (76 calories per 3 wedges and 2 tablespoons dip).

Per Serving:		
Protein 1.9g	Fat 2.0g	(Saturated Fat 0.7g)
Carbohydrate 12.7g	Fiber 0.5g	Cholesterol 1mg
Iron 0.5mg	Sodium 78mg	Calcium 39mg

PARMESAN-GARLIC BAGEL CHIPS

These flavorful bagel chips are lower in fat than commercial ones because they aren't heavily coated with oil or shortening before baking.

4 plain bagels
Butter-flavored vegetable cooking spray
¼ cup grated Parmesan cheese
1½ teaspoons dried Italian seasoning
½ teaspoon garlic powder

Cut each bagel into 2 half-circles using a serrated knife. Cut each half-circle horizontally into ¼-inch-thick slices. Place slices on a wire rack; place rack on a baking sheet. Coat slices with cooking spray.

Combine cheese, Italian seasoning, and garlic powder; sprinkle evenly over bagel slices. Bake at 325° for 12 to 15 minutes or until lightly browned and crisp; let cool. Store in an airtight container. Yield: 4 dozen chips (19 calories per chip).

Per Chip:		
Protein 0.8g	Fat 0.3g	(Saturated Fat 0.1g)
Carbohydrate 3.2g	Fiber 0.1g	Cholesterol 0mg
Iron 0.3mg	Sodium 39mg	Calcium 11mg

HAM BAGEL BITES

3 ounces Neufchâtel cheese, softened
½ cup shredded baking apple
2 tablespoons chopped onion
2 teaspoons Dijon mustard
1 cup finely chopped reduced-fat, low-salt ham
12 miniature bagels, split
¼ cup (1 ounce) finely shredded smoked Gouda cheese

Combine first 4 ingredients. Stir in ham. Spread ham mixture evenly over bagel halves. Place on an ungreased baking sheet. Bake at 375° for 10 minutes. Sprinkle bagels with Gouda cheese; bake 5 minutes or until cheese melts. Yield: 2 dozen snacks (59 calories each).

Per Snack:		
Protein 3.1g	Fat 1.7g	(Saturated Fat 0.9g)
Carbohydrate 7.7g	Fiber 0.4g	Cholesterol 7mg
Iron 0.5mg	Sodium 150mg	Calcium 21mg

GREEK PITA SNACKS

⅔ cup drained canned no-salt-added garbanzo beans (chickpeas)
2½ tablespoons skim milk
1½ teaspoons reduced-calorie Ranch-style dressing mix
⅛ teaspoon ground red pepper
1 clove garlic, minced
8 (3-inch) miniature pita bread rounds, cut in half crosswise
16 cucumber slices, cut in half
½ cup alfalfa sprouts
⅓ cup seeded, chopped tomato
2 ounces feta cheese, crumbled
1½ tablespoons chopped ripe olives

Mash beans slightly with a potato masher. Add milk; mash until smooth. Stir in dressing mix, red pepper, and garlic.

Spread bean mixture evenly in pita halves; place 2 cucumber slices over bean mixture in each pita half. Place alfalfa sprouts and remaining ingredients evenly in pita halves. Yield: 16 snacks (42 calories each).

Per Snack:		
Protein 1.7g	Fat 1.2g	(Saturated Fat 0.6g)
Carbohydrate 5.9g	Fiber 1.0g	Cholesterol 3mg
Iron 0.5mg	Sodium 89mg	Calcium 32mg

Spicy Mixed Fruit Chutney (page 203) will heighten the flavor of chicken or pork at dinner. Or serve it as a zesty appetizer with crackers or bread.

Sauces & Condiments

AMARETTO SYRUP

½ cup unsweetened apple juice
¼ cup firmly packed brown sugar
¼ cup amaretto
2 tablespoons margarine
1 tablespoon cornstarch
¼ cup plus 2 tablespoons water

Combine first 4 ingredients in a small saucepan. Cook over medium heat, stirring constantly, until sugar dissolves and margarine melts.

Combine cornstarch and water, stirring until smooth. Add to juice mixture. Bring to a boil, and cook, stirring constantly, 1 minute.

Serve warm over angel food cake, ice milk, or nonfat frozen yogurt. Yield: 1¼ cups (32 calories per tablespoon).

Per Tablespoon:		
Protein 0.1g	Fat 1.6g	(Saturated Fat 0.5g)
Carbohydrate 4.4g	Fiber 0g	Cholesterol 0mg
Iron 0.1mg	Sodium 17mg	Calcium 4mg

BROWN SUGAR-ALMOND SAUCE

2 tablespoons reduced-calorie margarine
1½ tablespoons all-purpose flour
1¼ cups evaporated skimmed milk
⅓ cup firmly packed brown sugar
¼ cup slivered almonds, toasted
1 teaspoon vanilla extract

Melt margarine in a medium saucepan over medium heat; add flour. Cook, stirring constantly with a wire whisk, 1 minute.

Gradually add milk and brown sugar, stirring constantly. Cook over medium heat, stirring constantly, until thickened.

Stir in almonds and vanilla. Serve warm or at room temperature over fat-free pound cake, ice milk, or nonfat frozen yogurt. Yield: 1½ cups (37 calories per tablespoon).

Per Tablespoon:		
Protein 1.3g	Fat 1.3g	(Saturated Fat 0.2g)
Carbohydrate 5.2g	Fiber 0.2g	Cholesterol 1mg
Iron 0.2mg	Sodium 26mg	Calcium 45mg

CHOCOLATE-RUM SAUCE

3 tablespoons sugar
3 tablespoons unsweetened cocoa
1 tablespoon cornstarch
1 cup skim milk
2 tablespoons light-colored corn syrup
1 tablespoon rum
1 teaspoon vanilla extract

Combine first 3 ingredients in a small saucepan. Gradually stir in milk and corn syrup. Cook over medium heat, stirring constantly, until thickened. Remove from heat; stir in rum and vanilla. Serve warm over angel food cake, ice milk, or nonfat frozen yogurt. Yield: 1¼ cups (26 calories per tablespoon).

Per Tablespoon:		
Protein 0.7g	Fat 0.1g	(Saturated Fat 0.1g)
Carbohydrate 4.8g	Fiber 0g	Cholesterol 0mg
Iron 0.1mg	Sodium 9mg	Calcium 16mg

CHAMBORD-CHOCOLATE SAUCE

Corn syrup helps give this sauce its thick consistency. Raspberries add an extra flavor burst without adding fat.

1½ cups fresh or frozen unsweetened raspberries, thawed
⅓ cup sifted powdered sugar
3 tablespoons unsweetened cocoa
1 tablespoon cornstarch
¼ cup light-colored corn syrup
2 tablespoons water
1 tablespoon Chambord or other raspberry-flavored liqueur
1 teaspoon vanilla extract

Place raspberries in a wire-mesh strainer over a bowl; press with back of a spoon against the sides of the strainer to squeeze out juice. Discard pulp and seeds remaining in strainer.

Combine powdered sugar, cocoa, and cornstarch in a small saucepan. Gradually add raspberry juice, corn syrup, and water to sugar mixture. Cook over medium heat, stirring constantly, until mixture begins to boil. Cook, stirring constantly, 1 minute. Remove from heat. Stir in liqueur and vanilla.

Transfer to a bowl; cover and chill thoroughly. Serve over angel food cake, ice milk, or nonfat frozen yogurt. Yield: 1 cup plus 1 tablespoon (37 calories per tablespoon).

Per Tablespoon:		
Protein 0.4g	Fat 0.3g	(Saturated Fat 0.2g)
Carbohydrate 8.2g	Fiber 0.7g	Cholesterol 0mg
Iron 0.2mg	Sodium 7mg	Calcium 4mg

CREAMY SPINACH SAUCE

1 (10-ounce) package frozen chopped spinach, thawed
Vegetable cooking spray
1 tablespoon reduced-calorie margarine
¾ cup chopped sweet red pepper
½ cup chopped onion
2 cloves garlic, minced
¼ cup all-purpose flour
2 cups 1% low-fat milk
⅓ cup grated Parmesan cheese
2 teaspoons dried basil
¼ teaspoon pepper
⅛ teaspoon salt
⅛ teaspoon hot sauce

Drain spinach, and press between paper towels to remove excess moisture. Set aside.

Coat a nonstick skillet with cooking spray; add margarine. Place over medium-high heat until margarine melts. Add sweet red pepper, onion, and garlic; sauté until vegetables are tender. Add spinach; cook until thoroughly heated, stirring occasionally. Set aside.

Place flour in a large saucepan; gradually add milk, stirring until smooth. Cook over medium heat, stirring constantly, until thickened. Stir in spinach mixture, Parmesan cheese, and remaining ingredients; cook 1 minute or until thoroughly heated. Serve over pasta. Yield: 3¼ cups (12 calories per tablespoon).

Per Tablespoon:		
Protein 0.8g	Fat 0.4g	(Saturated Fat 0.2g)
Carbohydrate 1.4g	Fiber 0.3g	Cholesterol 1mg
Iron 0.2mg	Sodium 26mg	Calcium 26mg

CREOLE MUSTARD

This mustard is delicious and fiery hot. A little goes a long way!

¾ cup flat dark beer
½ cup firmly packed brown sugar
½ cup finely chopped green pepper
1 (2-ounce) can dry mustard
1 tablespoon dried onion flakes
1 tablespoon cider vinegar
1½ teaspoons garlic powder
1½ teaspoons no-salt-added tomato paste
½ teaspoon pepper
⅛ teaspoon salt

Combine all ingredients in a medium saucepan. Bring to a boil over medium-high heat, stirring constantly. Remove from heat, and cool completely. Serve as a sandwich spread or with chicken or pork. Yield: 1½ cups (35 calories per tablespoon).

Per Tablespoon:		
Protein 0.9g	Fat 1.0g	(Saturated Fat 0g)
Carbohydrate 5.8g	Fiber 0.1g	Cholesterol 0mg
Iron 0.4mg	Sodium 16mg	Calcium 13mg

CURRIED PEPPERCORN MUSTARD

½ cup Dijon mustard
½ cup nonfat sour cream alternative
1 tablespoon black peppercorns, crushed
1 teaspoon curry powder
½ teaspoon dried tarragon, crushed
¼ teaspoon ground allspice

Combine all ingredients in a small bowl, stirring well. Cover and chill at least 8 hours. Serve as a sandwich spread or with chicken or pork. Yield: 1 cup (17 calories per tablespoon).

Per Tablespoon:		
Protein 0.6g	Fat 0.6g	(Saturated Fat 0g)
Carbohydrate 1.7g	Fiber 0.2g	Cholesterol 0mg
Iron 0.3mg	Sodium 228mg	Calcium 13mg

SWEET POTATO BUTTER

4⅓ cups mashed, cooked sweet potato
1½ cups sugar
3 cups unsweetened apple cider
2 teaspoons ground cinnamon
½ teaspoon ground cloves

Combine first 3 ingredients in a large saucepan; bring to a boil, and cook, stirring constantly, until sugar dissolves. Reduce heat; add cinnamon and cloves. Simmer, uncovered, 1½ hours, stirring frequently.

Spoon mixture into hot sterilized jars, leaving ½-inch headspace; wipe jar rims. Cover at once with metal lids, and screw on bands. Refrigerate at least 24 hours before serving. Serve with toast or English muffins. Store in refrigerator. Yield: 6½ cups (27 calories per tablespoon).

Per Tablespoon:		
Protein 0.2g	Fat 0.0g	(Saturated Fat 0g)
Carbohydrate 6.6g	Fiber 0.4g	Cholesterol 0mg
Iron 0.1mg	Sodium 2mg	Calcium 4mg

REFRIGERATOR PLUM PRESERVES

2 envelopes unflavored gelatin
⅔ cup grape juice
6 cups pitted, chopped plums (about 10 plums)
½ cup sugar
2 teaspoons lemon juice

Sprinkle gelatin over grape juice in a large saucepan; let stand 1 minute. Cook over low heat, stirring until gelatin dissolves, about 2 minutes. Add plums, sugar, and lemon juice; bring to a boil. Reduce heat; simmer 6 minutes, stirring frequently.

Spoon mixture into hot sterilized jars, leaving ½-inch headspace; wipe jar rims. Cover at once with metal lids, and screw on bands. Refrigerate until preserves are set. Serve with toast or English muffins. Store in refrigerator. Yield: 2½ pints (14 calories per tablespoon).

Per Tablespoon:		
Protein 0.3g	Fat 0.1g	(Saturated Fat 0g)
Carbohydrate 3.2g	Fiber 0.3g	Cholesterol 0mg
Iron 0mg	Sodium 0mg	Calcium 1mg

BREAD SPREADS

Instead of spreading butter or margarine on your bread, slather on one of these low-fat options.

Fruit or vegetable butter: moderately thick fruit or vegetable puree usually flavored with sugar and spices.

Preserves: fruit cooked with sugar and sometimes pectin. Preserves are similar to jams but usually have larger pieces of fruit.

Chutney: spicy condiment containing fruit (and sometimes vegetables), vinegar, sugar, and spices. The texture ranges from chunky to smooth. Sweet chutney also makes a delicious accompaniment to cheese.

SPICY MIXED FRUIT CHUTNEY

1 cup coarsely chopped dried apricots
½ cup golden raisins
3 tablespoons dark brown sugar
1 tablespoon minced crystallized ginger
¾ cup water
⅓ cup white wine vinegar
½ teaspoon dry mustard
¼ teaspoon chili powder
⅓ cup fresh cranberries

Combine first 8 ingredients in a saucepan; bring to a boil. Cover, reduce heat, and simmer 20 minutes, stirring occasionally. Stir in cranberries; cover and cook 7 minutes. Uncover and cook 5 minutes, stirring frequently. Serve with French bread, chicken, or pork. Yield: 1½ cups (36 calories per tablespoon).

Per Tablespoon:		
Protein 0.4g	Fat 0.1g	(Saturated Fat 0g)
Carbohydrate 9.2g	Fiber 0.4g	Cholesterol 0mg
Iron 0.6mg	Sodium 7mg	Calcium 8mg

Perk up your breakfast with spiced Sweet Potato Butter.

Liven up any meal with the hot mixture of vegetables in Cilantro-Jalapeño Corn Relish.

CILANTRO-JALAPEÑO CORN RELISH

1 cup finely chopped tomato
½ cup frozen whole-kernel corn, thawed
½ cup finely chopped zucchini
½ cup finely chopped onion
½ cup chopped fresh cilantro
3 tablespoons red wine vinegar
1½ tablespoons lime juice
1½ teaspoons vegetable oil
1 jalapeño pepper, seeded and chopped
½ teaspoon ground cumin
½ teaspoon pepper
¼ teaspoon salt
¼ teaspoon celery seeds
Fresh cilantro sprigs (optional)
Lime wedges (optional)

Combine first 5 ingredients in a medium saucepan; set aside.

Combine vinegar and next 7 ingredients in container of an electric blender; cover and process until smooth. Pour over tomato mixture, and bring to a boil. Remove from heat, and transfer to a bowl.

Cover and chill at least 8 hours. Garnish with cilantro sprigs and lime wedges, if desired.

Serve relish with beef, chicken, or pork, using a slotted spoon. Yield: 2¼ cups (7 calories per tablespoon).

Per Tablespoon:

Protein 0.2g	Fat 0.2g	(Saturated Fat 0g)
Carbohydrate 1.3g	Fiber 0.2g	Cholesterol 0mg
Iron 0.1mg	Sodium 18mg	Calcium 3mg

TOMATO-CUMIN RELISH

2 cups seeded, chopped tomato
1 cup chopped onion
¼ cup red wine vinegar
1½ teaspoons olive oil
1½ teaspoons no-salt-added tomato paste
½ teaspoon sugar
½ teaspoon ground cumin
½ teaspoon paprika
¼ teaspoon salt
¼ teaspoon garlic powder
¼ teaspoon ground thyme
¼ teaspoon pepper

Combine all ingredients in a large saucepan. Cook over medium-high heat 5 minutes, stirring occasionally. Serve with beef, chicken, or fish. Yield: 2 cups (7 calories per tablespoon).

Per Tablespoon:		
Protein 0.2g	Fat 0.3g	(Saturated Fat 0g)
Carbohydrate 1.1g	Fiber 0.2g	Cholesterol 0mg
Iron 0.1mg	Sodium 20mg	Calcium 2mg

PINEAPPLE SALSA VERDE

Tightly covered, this salsa will keep up to one week. If you want a smaller amount, the recipe can be easily cut in half.

2 (14½-ounce) cans no-salt-added stewed tomatoes, undrained and chopped
1 cup chopped onion
½ cup chopped fresh cilantro
½ cup canned crushed pineapple in juice, drained
3 cloves garlic, minced
1 jalapeño pepper, seeded and chopped
3 tablespoons lime juice
1 tablespoon red wine vinegar
½ teaspoon ground cumin
½ teaspoon ground oregano
½ teaspoon pepper

Combine first 6 ingredients in a medium bowl; toss well. Combine lime juice and remaining ingredients, stirring well with a wire whisk. Pour over tomato mixture; toss gently.

Cover and chill at least 8 hours. Serve salsa with beef, chicken, or pork. Yield: 4½ cups (6 calories per tablespoon).

Per Tablespoon:		
Protein 0.2g	Fat 0.0g	(Saturated Fat 0g)
Carbohydrate 1.3g	Fiber 0.2g	Cholesterol 0mg
Iron 0.1mg	Sodium 2mg	Calcium 5mg

FIRECRACKER MEAT MARINADE

¼ cup low-sodium Worcestershire sauce
¼ cup dry sherry
¼ cup lime juice
1 teaspoon dry mustard
1 to 2 teaspoons hot sauce
½ teaspoon dried marjoram
½ teaspoon dried thyme
2 cloves garlic, minced

Combine all ingredients. Use to marinate beef or chicken before grilling. Use remainder to baste while grilling. Yield: ¾ cup (8 calories per tablespoon).

Per Tablespoon:		
Protein 0.1g	Fat 0.1g	(Saturated Fat 0g)
Carbohydrate 1.9g	Fiber 0g	Cholesterol 0mg
Iron 0.1mg	Sodium 23mg	Calcium 4mg

LEMON-PINEAPPLE MARINADE

1½ cups unsweetened pineapple juice
¼ cup plus 2 tablespoons lemon juice
2 tablespoons honey
2 tablespoons balsamic vinegar
2 teaspoons vegetable oil
2 teaspoons garlic powder
1 teaspoon dried basil
1 teaspoon pepper
¼ teaspoon salt

Combine all ingredients. Use to marinate chicken or fish before grilling. Use remainder to baste while grilling. Yield: 2¼ cups (13 calories per tablespoon).

Per Tablespoon:		
Protein 0.1g	Fat 0.3g	(Saturated Fat 0.1g)
Carbohydrate 2.8g	Fiber 0g	Cholesterol 0mg
Iron 0.1mg	Sodium 17mg	Calcium 3mg

CRANBERRY WINE VINEGAR

1 cup white vinegar
½ cup Chablis or other dry white wine
½ cup cranberry juice cocktail
2 cloves garlic, minced
Fresh rosemary sprigs (optional)

Combine first 4 ingredients in a pint jar; cover tightly, and shake vigorously. Chill at least 8 hours. Place rosemary sprigs in vinegar mixture, if desired. Use in salad dressings or vinaigrettes. Yield: 2 cups (6 calories per tablespoon).

Per Tablespoon:		
Protein 0.0g	Fat 0.0g	(Saturated Fat 0g)
Carbohydrate 1.1g	Fiber 0g	Cholesterol 0mg
Iron 0mg	Sodium 0mg	Calcium 1mg

HERBED VINEGAR

5 sprigs fresh dillweed, oregano, or rosemary
3 cups white wine vinegar
Additional sprigs fresh dillweed, oregano, or rosemary

Place 5 dillweed sprigs in a wide-mouth quart glass jar. Place vinegar in a nonaluminum saucepan; bring to a boil. Pour hot vinegar over dillweed in jar; cover with lid. Let stand at room temperature 2 weeks.

Pour mixture through a wire-mesh strainer lined with 2 layers of cheesecloth into decorative bottles or jars; discard herbs remaining in strainer. Add additional sprigs of dillweed. Seal bottles with a cork or other airtight lid. Use in salad dressings or vinaigrettes. Yield: 3 cups (2 calories per tablespoon).

Per Tablespoon:		
Protein 0.0g	Fat 0.0g	(Saturated Fat 0.0g)
Carbohydrate 0.0g	Fiber 0g	Cholesterol 0mg
Iron 0mg	Sodium 1mg	Calcium 0mg

CHILI SEASONING

Try this seasoning blend as a lower-sodium alternative to commercial packaged chili seasoning. It contains about 86 percent less sodium than do commercial varieties.

¼ cup chili powder
2 tablespoons plus 2 teaspoons onion powder
1 tablespoon plus 1 teaspoon sugar
1 tablespoon plus 1 teaspoon garlic powder
1 tablespoon plus 1 teaspoon dry mustard
1 tablespoon plus 1 teaspoon ground cumin
1 tablespoon plus 1 teaspoon paprika
1 tablespoon plus 1 teaspoon ground oregano
¼ teaspoon salt

Combine all ingredients in an airtight container. Cover and store at room temperature.

Use to season ground beef or ground turkey for use in chili or tacos. Yield: ¾ cup plus 2 tablespoons (24 calories per tablespoon).

Note: To make seasoned beef or turkey, brown ¼ pound lean ground beef or turkey in a skillet; drain and pat dry with paper towels. Return beef or turkey to skillet; add 1 tablespoon Chili Seasoning and 2 tablespoons water. Bring to a boil; cover, reduce heat, and simmer 5 minutes.

Per Tablespoon:		
Protein 0.9g	Fat 0.8g	(Saturated Fat 0.1g)
Carbohydrate 4.5g	Fiber 1.0g	Cholesterol 0mg
Iron 1.1mg	Sodium 64mg	Calcium 25mg

A wealth of produce is conveniently packaged in Vegetable-Stuffed Tomatoes (page 214). Asparagus with Raspberry Vinaigrette (page 208) is an easy-to-prepare side dish.

Side Dishes

ASPARAGUS WITH RASPBERRY VINAIGRETTE

Raspberry vinegar and fresh raspberries add a burst of flavor to this recipe without adding fat.

1½ pounds fresh asparagus spears
¼ cup raspberry vinegar
1 tablespoon minced shallots
1 tablespoon Dijon mustard
2 teaspoons olive oil
Fresh raspberries (optional)

Snap off tough ends of asparagus. Remove scales from stalks with a knife or vegetable peeler, if desired. Arrange asparagus in a vegetable steamer over boiling water. Cover and steam 7 minutes or until crisp-tender. Drain; transfer to a serving platter.

Combine raspberry vinegar and next 3 ingredients, stirring well. Pour vinegar mixture over asparagus. Garnish with fresh raspberries, if desired. Yield: 6 servings (35 calories per serving).

Per Serving:		
Protein 1.8g	Fat 1.8g	(Saturated Fat 0.2g)
Carbohydrate 3.9g	Fiber 1.6g	Cholesterol 0mg
Iron 0.8mg	Sodium 76mg	Calcium 16mg

CRANBERRY BAKED BEANS

Omitting the bacon in these baked beans keeps the fat content low. For extra flavor we added whole-berry cranberry sauce.

Vegetable cooking spray
½ cup chopped green onions
½ cup chopped green pepper
2 (16-ounce) cans vegetarian beans in tomato sauce
2 (15-ounce) cans kidney beans, drained
½ (16-ounce) can jellied whole-berry cranberry sauce
1 teaspoon ground ginger
1 teaspoon dry mustard

Coat a Dutch oven with cooking spray; place over medium-high heat until hot. Add green onions and green pepper; sauté until tender. Add vegetarian beans and remaining ingredients; stir well. Bring to a boil; reduce heat, and simmer, uncovered, 20 minutes. Yield: 13 servings (152 calories per ½-cup serving).

Per Serving:		
Protein 7.0g	Fat 0.6g	(Saturated Fat 0g)
Carbohydrate 32.6g	Fiber 5.4g	Cholesterol 0mg
Iron 2.3mg	Sodium 305mg	Calcium 45mg

BABY LIMA BEANS WITH BACON

2 (10-ounce) packages frozen baby lima beans
Vegetable cooking spray
4 (½-ounce) slices Canadian bacon, cut into thin strips
2 tablespoons chopped shallots
1¼ cups peeled, seeded, and chopped plum tomato
¼ cup water
½ teaspoon chicken-flavored bouillon granules
½ teaspoon low-sodium Worcestershire sauce
¼ teaspoon pepper
⅛ teaspoon hot sauce

Cook beans according to package directions, omitting salt; drain and set aside.

Coat a large saucepan with cooking spray. Place over medium-high heat until hot. Add bacon and shallots; sauté until shallots are tender. Add lima beans, tomato, and remaining ingredients. Bring to a boil. Reduce heat to medium; cook, uncovered, 2 minutes or until most of liquid evaporates, stirring frequently. Yield: 5 servings (173 calories per 1-cup serving).

Per Serving:		
Protein 11.5g	Fat 1.4g	(Saturated Fat 0.3g)
Carbohydrate 29.6g	Fiber 2.8g	Cholesterol 6mg
Iron 3.5mg	Sodium 418mg	Calcium 49mg

TANGY BROCCOLI-CAULIFLOWER TOSS

This side dish, a new twist on a familiar salad, is served warm.

4 cups small cauliflower flowerets
2 cups small broccoli flowerets
1 (2-ounce) jar diced pimiento, drained
¾ cup plain nonfat yogurt
3 tablespoons minced fresh parsley
2 tablespoons grated Parmesan cheese
1 tablespoon Dijon mustard
¼ teaspoon garlic powder
Dash of ground white pepper

Arrange cauliflower and broccoli in a vegetable steamer over boiling water. Cover and steam 4 minutes or until crisp-tender. Drain well. Transfer to a serving bowl; add pimiento, and toss well. Set aside, and keep warm.

Combine yogurt and remaining ingredients. Pour yogurt mixture over vegetables; toss gently. Yield: 6 servings (52 calories per 1-cup serving).

Per Serving:

Protein 4.5g	Fat 1.1g	(Saturated Fat 0.5g)
Carbohydrate 6.9g	Fiber 2.1g	Cholesterol 2mg
Iron 0.7mg	Sodium 156mg	Calcium 118mg

BROCCOLI-TOMATO STIR-FRY

¼ cup sun-dried tomatoes
½ cup boiling water
Vegetable cooking spray
1 teaspoon olive oil
6½ cups chopped fresh broccoli
1 small onion, cut into wedges
2 cloves garlic, minced
¼ cup plus 2 tablespoons water
1 teaspoon cornstarch
1 teaspoon dried oregano
1 ounce crumbled feta cheese

Combine tomatoes and boiling water in a small bowl; let stand 5 minutes. Drain well, and thinly slice tomatoes. Set aside.

Coat a wok or large nonstick skillet with cooking spray; drizzle oil around top of wok, coating sides. Heat at medium-high (375°) until hot. Add broccoli, onion, and garlic; stir-fry 4 to 5 minutes or until vegetables are crisp-tender.

Combine ¼ cup plus 2 tablespoons water, cornstarch, and oregano; add to vegetable mixture, and stir-fry 30 seconds. Add sliced tomato; stir-fry until mixture is thoroughly heated. Transfer to a serving bowl, and sprinkle with cheese. Yield: 5 servings (75 calories per 1-cup serving).

Per Serving:

Protein 4.5g	Fat 2.7g	(Saturated Fat 1.1g)
Carbohydrate 10.7g	Fiber 3.6g	Cholesterol 5mg
Iron 1.1mg	Sodium 149mg	Calcium 90mg

GINGER-MINT CARROTS

Serve these spiced carrots with baked chicken or roasted pork, a steamed green vegetable, and whole wheat dinner rolls for a quick meal.

4½ cups diagonally sliced carrot (about 1½ pounds)
1 tablespoon minced crystallized ginger
1 tablespoon mint jelly
1 teaspoon minced fresh mint

Arrange carrot in a vegetable steamer over boiling water. Cover and steam 8 minutes or until crisp-tender. Transfer to a serving bowl; keep warm.

Combine ginger, jelly, and mint in a small saucepan, stirring well. Cook over medium heat 1 minute or until jelly melts. Pour over carrot; toss well. Yield: 7 servings (45 calories per ½-cup serving).

Per Serving:

Protein 0.8g	Fat 0.1g	(Saturated Fat 0.1g)
Carbohydrate 10.8g	Fiber 2.5g	Cholesterol 0mg
Iron 0.6mg	Sodium 29mg	Calcium 24mg

Hearty Corn Casserole boasts a flavorful blend of vegetables nestled in a creamy custard.

HEARTY CORN CASSEROLE

1 (16½-ounce) can no-salt-added cream-style corn
½ cup frozen egg substitute, thawed
½ cup sliced green onions
½ cup chopped green pepper
¼ cup cornmeal
2 tablespoons all-purpose flour
¼ teaspoon salt
1 (17-ounce) can no-salt-added whole-kernel corn, drained
1 (8-ounce) carton plain nonfat yogurt
1 (2¼-ounce) can sliced jalapeño-flavored ripe olives, drained
1 (2-ounce) jar diced pimiento, drained
Vegetable cooking spray
Green pepper rings (optional)

Combine cream-style corn and egg substitute in container of an electric blender; cover and process until smooth, stopping once to scrape down sides. Transfer mixture to a bowl; add sliced green onions and next 8 ingredients, stirring well.

Pour mixture into a 2-quart casserole coated with cooking spray. Bake, uncovered, at 350° for 45 minutes. Remove casserole from oven, and stir well. Return to oven, and bake 25 minutes or until set. Garnish with green pepper rings, if desired. Yield: 6 servings (172 calories per serving).

Per Serving:		
Protein 7.4g	Fat 2.6g	(Saturated Fat 0.1g)
Carbohydrate 32.4g	Fiber 2.2g	Cholesterol 1mg
Iron 1.7mg	Sodium 246mg	Calcium 91mg

NUTTY CORN

Try this recipe instead of plain grilled corn. Creamy peanut butter gives the corn a slightly nutty flavor.

6 ears fresh corn
2 tablespoons nonfat margarine
2 tablespoons reduced-fat creamy peanut butter
1/8 teaspoon salt
1/8 teaspoon hot sauce

Remove and discard husks and silks from corn; set corn aside. Combine margarine and peanut butter in a small saucepan. Cook over low heat, stirring constantly, until peanut butter mixture melts. Add salt and hot sauce, stirring well. Brush peanut butter mixture evenly over corn. Wrap each ear of corn in heavy-duty aluminum foil.

Place grill rack on grill over medium-hot coals (350° to 400°). Place corn on rack; grill, covered, 40 minutes or until corn is tender, turning frequently. Yield: 6 servings (116 calories per serving).

Per Serving:		
Protein 3.8g	Fat 3.0g	(Saturated Fat 0.5g)
Carbohydrate 22.1g	Fiber 3.1g	Cholesterol 0mg
Iron 0.6mg	Sodium 114mg	Calcium 2mg

BASIL-LEMON SNAP PEAS

Sugar Snap peas are best served crisp-tender, so be careful not to overcook them.

2 teaspoons olive oil
1 clove garlic, minced
1½ pounds Sugar Snap peas, trimmed
1 cup chopped sweet yellow pepper
1/3 cup chopped fresh basil
1/2 teaspoon sugar
1/2 teaspoon grated lemon rind
1/4 teaspoon salt
1/4 teaspoon pepper
2 tablespoons fresh lemon juice

Place oil in a large nonstick skillet over medium-high heat until hot. Add garlic, and sauté 30 seconds. Add peas and yellow pepper; sauté 2 to 3 minutes or until peas are crisp-tender. Add basil and next 4 ingredients; sauté 30 seconds. Add lemon juice, and sauté 30 seconds. Serve immediately. Yield: 6 servings (65 calories per 1-cup serving).

Per Serving:		
Protein 3.0g	Fat 1.8g	(Saturated Fat 0.3g)
Carbohydrate 9.8g	Fiber 3.0g	Cholesterol 0mg
Iron 2.5mg	Sodium 103mg	Calcium 53mg

FIGURING ON FOLIC ACID

Folic acid, also called folacin, is garnering scientific attention for two new reasons. First, research suggests that folic acid may play a protective role against cervical cancer. Second, overwhelming evidence finds that the vitamin offers protection against birth defects such as spina bifida (incomplete closing of the bony casing around the spinal cord) and anencephaly (parts of brain tissue missing).

The case for folic acid is so strong that the U.S. Public Health Service recommends that women of childbearing age take in at least 0.4 milligrams of folic acid daily, which is about twice the average intake.

Good food sources of folic acid include leafy green vegetables such as kale, dark green lettuces, spinach, and turnip greens; citrus fruits such as grapefruit, oranges, and tangerines; and fortified bread and cereal products.

To consume the recommended amount of folic acid from food, you'd have to eat about 3 cups of greens each day. An alternative is to supplement your diet with an over-the-counter multivitamin. One word of caution: Excessive amounts of folic acid have been known to mask a vitamin B_{12} deficiency, so steer clear of megadose vitamins.

POTATO CROQUETTES

3 medium baking potatoes (about 1½ pounds), peeled and sliced
¼ cup (1 ounce) shredded reduced-fat Swiss cheese
¼ cup nonfat cream cheese product
1 tablespoon chopped fresh chives
2 tablespoons nonfat margarine
1½ teaspoons prepared mustard
¼ teaspoon hot sauce
⅛ teaspoon salt
1 egg white, lightly beaten
1¾ cups corn flakes cereal, coarsely crushed
Vegetable cooking spray

Cook potato in boiling water to cover 20 minutes or until tender; drain. Transfer to a bowl.

Beat potato at medium speed of an electric mixer until smooth. Add Swiss cheese and next 6 ingredients; beat well. Divide mixture into 10 equal portions, and shape into balls. Dip balls in egg white, and roll in cereal. Place on a baking sheet coated with cooking spray. Bake at 400° for 10 to 15 minutes or until crisp and golden. Yield: 5 servings (166 calories per 2 croquettes).

Per Serving:		
Protein 7.5g	Fat 1.3g	(Saturated Fat 0.6g)
Carbohydrate 30.4g	Fiber 2.0g	Cholesterol 6mg
Iron 1.6mg	Sodium 334mg	Calcium 110mg

SCALLOPED POTATOES AND MUSHROOMS

Vegetable cooking spray
3⅔ cups sliced fresh mushrooms
⅓ cup chopped onion
2 cloves garlic, minced
1½ tablespoons all-purpose flour
1 cup plus 2 tablespoons evaporated skimmed milk
1 cup plus 2 tablespoons skim milk
¾ teaspoon salt
¼ teaspoon dried crushed red pepper
¼ teaspoon freshly ground pepper
2 pounds round red potatoes, peeled and cut into ⅛-inch-thick slices
¾ cup (3 ounces) shredded light Jarlsberg cheese
3 tablespoons freshly grated Parmesan cheese

Coat a Dutch oven with cooking spray; place over medium-high heat until hot. Add mushrooms, onion, and garlic; sauté until tender. Set aside.

Place flour in a small saucepan. Gradually add evaporated milk and next 4 ingredients, stirring well. Cook over medium heat, stirring constantly, until mixture boils and is slightly thickened. Add potato, and return to a boil, stirring occasionally. Place half of potato mixture in an 11- x 7- x 1½-inch baking dish coated with cooking spray. Top with half of mushroom mixture and half of each cheese. Repeat layers with remaining potato mixture, mushroom mixture, and cheeses.

Cover and bake at 350° for 45 minutes; uncover and bake an additional 30 minutes or until potato is tender. Let stand 10 minutes before serving. Yield: 8 servings (184 calories per serving).

Per Serving:		
Protein 11.9g	Fat 3.3g	(Saturated Fat 1.8g)
Carbohydrate 27.6g	Fiber 2.3g	Cholesterol 11mg
Iron 1.6mg	Sodium 361mg	Calcium 327mg

SPINACH-ARTICHOKE CASSEROLE

2 (10-ounce) packages frozen chopped spinach, thawed
6 ounces light process cream cheese product, softened
1 tablespoon reduced-calorie margarine, softened
¼ cup skim milk
1 (9-ounce) package frozen artichoke hearts, thawed and chopped
3 tablespoons commercial oil-free Italian dressing
1 (2-ounce) jar diced pimiento, drained
¼ teaspoon pepper
Vegetable cooking spray
2 tablespoons grated fat-free Parmesan Italian Topping

Drain spinach, and press between paper towels to remove excess moisture. Set aside.

Combine cream cheese and margarine in a bowl; beat at medium speed of an electric mixer until creamy. Gradually add milk, beating well. Stir in spinach, artichoke hearts, and next 3 ingredients.

Spoon into a 1-quart casserole coated with cooking spray; sprinkle with Italian topping. Cover; bake at 350° for 30 minutes. Uncover; bake 10 minutes. Yield: 6 servings (126 calories per ½-cup serving).

Per Serving:		
Protein 8.0g	Fat 6.5g	(Saturated Fat 3.1g)
Carbohydrate 11.4g	Fiber 3.4g	Cholesterol 18mg
Iron 2.4mg	Sodium 371mg	Calcium 171mg

FRUITED BUTTERNUT SQUASH CUPS

Try this creamy squash side dish as a low-fat alternative to traditional sweet potato casserole.

1 (2-pound) butternut squash
½ cup mashed ripe banana (about 2 small)
¼ cup firmly packed brown sugar
1 tablespoon reduced-calorie margarine
½ teaspoon ground cinnamon
¼ teaspoon ground ginger
Vegetable cooking spray
2 tablespoons chopped pecans, toasted

Wash squash; cut in half lengthwise. Remove and discard seeds. Place squash, cut side down, in an 11- x 7- x 1½-inch baking dish. Add water to dish to a depth of ½ inch. Cover and bake at 375° for 35 to 40 minutes or until squash is tender. Drain; let cool slightly. Scoop out pulp, and place in a medium bowl; discard shells. Mash pulp.

Combine squash pulp, banana, and next 4 ingredients; beat at medium speed of an electric mixer until smooth. Spoon mixture into 4 (6-ounce) custard cups or ramekins coated with cooking spray. Sprinkle evenly with chopped pecans. Place cups on a baking sheet. Bake, uncovered, at 350° for 15 minutes or until thoroughly heated. Yield: 4 servings (190 calories per serving).

Per Serving:		
Protein 2.0g	Fat 5.2g	(Saturated Fat 0.6g)
Carbohydrate 38.1g	Fiber 3.1g	Cholesterol 0mg
Iron 1.4mg	Sodium 39mg	Calcium 83mg

RASPBERRY-GLAZED SWEET POTATOES

1½ cups pearl onions
4 cups peeled, cubed sweet potato
1 teaspoon grated orange rind
1 teaspoon vegetable oil
¼ teaspoon salt
2 tablespoons no-sugar-added raspberry spread
1 tablespoon honey

Place onions in a large saucepan; add water to cover. Bring to a boil; cook onions 3 to 5 minutes or until crisp-tender. Drain; peel onions.

Combine onions, sweet potato, and next 3 ingredients in a 2-quart casserole. Bake, uncovered, at 375° for 20 minutes.

Combine raspberry spread and honey; add to sweet potato mixture, tossing gently. Bake an additional 30 minutes or until potato is tender, stirring frequently. Yield: 8 servings (103 calories per ½-cup serving).

Per Serving:		
Protein 1.3g	Fat 0.8g	(Saturated Fat 0.2g)
Carbohydrate 23.7g	Fiber 2.2g	Cholesterol 0mg
Iron 0.5mg	Sodium 84mg	Calcium 23mg

VEGETABLE-STUFFED TOMATOES

6 medium tomatoes
2 tablespoons commercial reduced-calorie Caesar dressing
1 cup fresh corn cut from cob (about 2 ears)
1 cup diced sweet red pepper
½ cup sliced green onions
2 tablespoons minced fresh basil
1 ounce goat cheese, crumbled

Cut top off each tomato. Scoop out pulp, leaving shells intact. Chop 1 cup of pulp; drain and set aside. Reserve remaining pulp for another use. Invert tomato shells on paper towels; let stand 30 minutes.

Pour dressing into a skillet; place over medium-high heat until hot. Add corn, pepper, and onions; sauté 4 minutes or until tender. Stir in 1 cup tomato pulp and basil. Spoon evenly into tomato shells. Place shells in an 11- x 7- x 1½-inch baking dish. Bake, uncovered, at 350° for 10 minutes. Remove from oven. Sprinkle evenly with cheese. Broil 5½ inches from heat (with electric oven door partially opened) 4 minutes or until cheese melts. Serve immediately. Yield: 6 servings (78 calories per serving).

Per Serving:		
Protein 2.7g	Fat 2.8g	(Saturated Fat 0.8g)
Carbohydrate 13.1g	Fiber 2.8g	Cholesterol 5mg
Iron 1.1mg	Sodium 158mg	Calcium 35mg

ZUCCHINI PANCAKES

Serve these pancakes with no-salt-added salsa.

2½ cups shredded zucchini
¾ cup all-purpose flour
¾ teaspoon baking powder
¼ teaspoon baking soda
¼ teaspoon salt
½ cup nonfat buttermilk
¼ cup frozen egg substitute, thawed
2 teaspoons vegetable oil
½ cup shredded carrot
¼ cup finely chopped onion
½ teaspoon dried dillweed
Vegetable cooking spray

Press zucchini between paper towels to remove excess moisture. Set aside.

Combine flour and next 3 ingredients in a medium bowl. Combine buttermilk, egg substitute, and oil; add to dry ingredients, stirring just until dry ingredients are moistened. Stir in zucchini, carrot, onion, and dillweed.

Coat a nonstick griddle with cooking spray; preheat to 350°. For each pancake, pour 1 heaping tablespoon batter onto hot griddle, spreading into a 3-inch circle. Cook 3 minutes or until browned on bottom. Turn; cook an additional 3 minutes or until browned. Yield: 17 (3-inch) pancakes (34 calories each).

Per Pancake:		
Protein 1.4g	Fat 0.7g	(Saturated Fat 0.1g)
Carbohydrate 5.5g	Fiber 0.3g	Cholesterol 0mg
Iron 0.4mg	Sodium 68mg	Calcium 27mg

PUREED WINTER VEGETABLES

For variety, serve this recipe instead of mashed potatoes. The apple adds a hint of sweetness to the puree.

1½ cups peeled, cubed red potato
1 cup sliced parsnips
½ cup peeled, cubed turnip
½ cup peeled, chopped Granny Smith apple
1 tablespoon reduced-calorie margarine
¼ cup low-fat sour cream
2 tablespoons chopped fresh chives
¼ teaspoon salt
⅛ teaspoon pepper

Combine first 4 ingredients in a large saucepan; add water to cover. Bring to a boil; cover, reduce heat, and simmer 10 minutes or until tender. Drain.

Position knife blade in food processor bowl; add vegetable mixture and margarine. Process 1 minute or just until smooth. Transfer to a medium bowl, and stir in sour cream and remaining ingredients. Yield: 5 servings (112 calories per ½-cup serving).

Per Serving:		
Protein 2.2g	Fat 3.2g	(Saturated Fat 1.1g)
Carbohydrate 20.0g	Fiber 2.4g	Cholesterol 5mg
Iron 0.8mg	Sodium 160mg	Calcium 38mg

VEGETABLE CURRY

A "curry" is a dish seasoned with curry powder, which is a combination of several pungent ground spices.

½ cup no-salt-added tomato juice
½ cup vegetable broth, undiluted
1 tablespoon cornstarch
2 teaspoons curry powder
1 teaspoon peeled, minced gingerroot
¼ teaspoon salt
⅛ teaspoon ground red pepper
½ pound fresh green beans
Vegetable cooking spray
1 teaspoon vegetable oil
1 cup diagonally sliced carrot
2 tablespoons water, divided
1 cup broccoli flowerets
½ cup coarsely chopped onion
1 cup coarsely chopped sweet red pepper
1 cup sliced zucchini
1 cup sliced fresh okra

Combine first 7 ingredients in a small bowl, stirring until smooth. Set aside.

Wash beans; trim ends, and remove strings.

Coat a wok or nonstick skillet with cooking spray; drizzle oil around top of wok, coating sides. Heat at medium-high (375°) until hot. Add beans and carrot; stir-fry 2 minutes. Add 1 tablespoon water, broccoli, and onion; stir-fry 4 minutes. Add remaining 1 tablespoon water, sweet red pepper, zucchini, and okra; stir-fry 4 minutes.

Add tomato juice mixture to wok; cook, stirring constantly, 1 to 2 minutes or until mixture is thickened and bubbly. Serve immediately. Yield: 5 servings (72 calories per 1-cup serving).

Per Serving:		
Protein 2.7g	Fat 1.6g	(Saturated Fat 0.2g)
Carbohydrate 13.7g	Fiber 2.9g	Cholesterol 0mg
Iron 1.4mg	Sodium 209mg	Calcium 55mg

SAUTÉED APPLE RINGS WITH ORANGE JUICE

2 small Winesap apples
¼ cup unsweetened orange juice
1 tablespoon brown sugar
1 teaspoon ground cinnamon
1 teaspoon reduced-calorie margarine

Core apples, and slice each crosswise into 6 rings.

Combine orange juice and remaining ingredients in a large nonstick skillet. Bring to a boil over medium heat, stirring until sugar dissolves. Arrange apple rings in skillet in a single layer. Cook 5 to 6 minutes or until tender, turning once. Serve warm. Yield: 4 servings (70 calories per serving).

Per Serving:		
Protein 0.3g	Fat 0.9g	(Saturated Fat 0.1g)
Carbohydrate 16.9g	Fiber 2.4g	Cholesterol 0mg
Iron 0.3	Sodium 10mg	Calcium 14mg

JUICY PROMISES

Americans are extracting liquids from just about every fruit and vegetable in the supermarket produce bin. Proponents of freshly squeezed juices contend that these products give the body something extra. Nutritionists, however, say that although these juices do offer generous amounts of the nutrients needed for disease prevention, the juices are not magical healers.

Probably the best trait of the fresh juices is the good taste. The disadvantage is that juices aren't good sources of fiber, which is a critical component lacking in the diets of many Americans.

Ultimately, the decision comes down to whether it's worth the time and effort to pulverize 4 cups of raw carrots to make 1 cup of fresh carrot juice. The choice should be made because you enjoy the taste, not because you're trying to squeeze all your nutritional needs into a glass.

CRANBERRY APPLESAUCE

Fresh cranberries add a rosy color and slightly tart flavor to this applesauce. It's delicious served with lean pork or reduced-fat, low-salt ham.

5 cups sliced Rome apple
1 cup fresh cranberries
½ cup water
⅓ cup sugar
1 tablespoon lemon juice
½ teaspoon ground cinnamon

Combine apple, cranberries, and water in a large saucepan. Bring mixture to a boil; cover, reduce heat, and simmer 15 minutes or until apple is tender.

Add sugar, lemon juice, and cinnamon; cook, stirring constantly, until sugar dissolves. Remove from heat, and cool slightly.

Position knife blade in food processor bowl; add apple mixture. Process 1½ minutes or until smooth, scraping sides of processor bowl occasionally. Cover and refrigerate at least 8 hours. Yield: 5 servings (124 calories per ½-cup serving).

Per Serving:

Protein 0.3g	Fat 0.4g	(Saturated Fat 0.1g)
Carbohydrate 32.1g	Fiber 3.5g	Cholesterol 0mg
Iron 0.3mg	Sodium 0mg	Calcium 12mg

MANGO-PEPPER MEDLEY

Vegetable cooking spray
2 teaspoons vegetable oil
1 large green pepper, seeded and cut into thin strips
1 medium-size sweet red pepper, seeded and cut into thin strips
2 teaspoons finely chopped purple onion
¼ cup water
2 tablespoons white wine vinegar
1 teaspoon sugar
½ teaspoon dry mustard
2 cups canned mango slices, drained
2 tablespoons chopped fresh cilantro

Coat a large nonstick skillet with cooking spray; add oil. Place over medium-high heat until hot. Add peppers and onion; sauté 1 minute. Combine water and next 3 ingredients; add to vegetable mixture, and sauté 3 minutes. Add mango; sauté 1 minute or until thoroughly heated. Transfer to a serving bowl, and sprinkle with cilantro. Serve immediately. Yield: 4 servings (132 calories per 1-cup serving).

Per Serving:

Protein 1.4g	Fat 2.6g	(Saturated Fat 0.5g)
Carbohydrate 26.2g	Fiber 3.3g	Cholesterol 0mg
Iron 2.7mg	Sodium 139mg	Calcium 7mg

KID-STYLE EXERCISE

People are more likely to follow lifelong physical fitness habits if they develop them early in life—even as early as preschool age. Use the tips below to guide your child to a healthy, active lifestyle.

- **Aerobic activity**—Children need 20 to 30 minutes of vigorous exercise—running, skipping rope, riding a bicycle—every day, according to the American College of Sports Medicine (ACSM).
- **Strength training**—Although lifting too heavy a weight could damage a child's fragile and growing skeletal system, the consensus is that closely supervised weight training (using low resistance and a high number of repetitions) is quite safe for children and adolescents. In fact, it helps build stronger muscles. Just make sure the close supervision you enlist comes from a knowledgeable professional.
- **Flexibility exercises**—Stretching muscles is important for all age groups, but it should never be overlooked in children because their muscles and bones are growing so rapidly. The ACSM states that exercise sessions for a child should contain a warm-up and cool down that include flexibility exercises.
- **Fun factor**—It's true that a child's exercise needs to help meet the physical standards appropriate for the child's age and size, but children need to play. They will be more likely to continue exercising if it's fun. For a lifetime commitment to exercise, emphasize participation and fun instead of competition.

If you're looking for a side dish that has a touch of sweetness yet doesn't go overboard on the sugar, look no further than Poached Pears with Blue Cheese and Toasted Walnuts.

POACHED PEARS WITH BLUE CHEESE AND TOASTED WALNUTS

4 firm ripe Bartlett pears
1 cup water
½ cup Burgundy or other dry red wine
¼ cup lemon juice
2 ounces crumbled blue cheese
2½ tablespoons coarsely chopped walnuts, toasted
Watercress sprigs (optional)
Freshly ground pepper (optional)

Peel and core pears; cut each in half lengthwise. Combine water, wine, and lemon juice in a skillet; bring to a boil. Place pear halves, cut side down, in skillet. Cover, reduce heat, and simmer 20 minutes, turning and basting once with wine mixture.

Remove pears from wine mixture, using a slotted spoon. Place pear halves on a serving platter; sprinkle evenly with cheese and walnuts. If desired, garnish with watercress sprigs, and sprinkle with pepper. Yield: 8 servings (102 calories per serving).

Per Serving:

Protein 2.6g	Fat 4.1g	(Saturated Fat 1.5g)
Carbohydrate 15.7g	Fiber 2.8g	Cholesterol 5mg
Iron 0.4mg	Sodium 99mg	Calcium 50mg

WARM CURRIED FRUIT

1 (8-ounce) can pineapple chunks in juice, undrained
1 (8¼-ounce) can pear halves in juice, drained and cut in half
1 (8¼-ounce) can apricot halves in light syrup, drained
1 (8¼-ounce) can sliced peaches in water, drained
Butter-flavored vegetable cooking spray
1 tablespoon sun-dried cranberries
1 tablespoon reduced-calorie margarine
3 tablespoons brown sugar
2 tablespoons water
1½ teaspoons curry powder
2 teaspoons cornstarch

Drain pineapple, reserving 3 tablespoons juice. Discard remaining juice. Place pineapple, pears, apricots, and peaches on paper towels; pat dry, and place in an 11- x 7- x 1½-inch baking dish coated with cooking spray. Sprinkle fruit with cranberries, and set aside.

Melt margarine in a small saucepan over medium-high heat. Add brown sugar, water, and curry powder, stirring well. Cook over medium heat, stirring until sugar dissolves. Combine reserved pineapple juice and cornstarch, stirring until smooth. Add to margarine mixture. Bring to a boil over medium heat, stirring constantly, and cook 1 minute. Pour margarine mixture over fruit. Cover and refrigerate 8 hours. Bake, uncovered, at 350° for 45 minutes or until thoroughly heated. Yield: 8 servings (71 calories per ½-cup serving).

Per Serving:		
Protein 0.5g	Fat 1.1g	(Saturated Fat 0g)
Carbohydrate 15.8g	Fiber 1.4g	Cholesterol 0mg
Iron 0.5mg	Sodium 16mg	Calcium 11mg

GRILLED PINEAPPLE KABOBS

12 (1½-inch) chunks fresh pineapple
1 tablespoon low-sodium soy sauce
2 teaspoons water
1 teaspoon sesame oil
¼ teaspoon dry mustard
Vegetable cooking spray

Place pineapple in an 11- x 7- x 1½-inch baking dish. Combine soy sauce and next 3 ingredients, stirring well. Pour over pineapple, and toss to coat. Let stand at room temperature 30 minutes.

Soak 4 (6-inch) wooden skewers in water for at least 30 minutes. Drain fruit mixture, reserving marinade. Thread fruit evenly onto skewers.

Coat grill rack with cooking spray; place on grill over medium-hot coals (350° to 400°). Place kabobs on rack. Grill, covered, 6 minutes, turning and basting occasionally with marinade. Yield: 4 servings (80 calories per serving).

Per Serving:		
Protein 0.5g	Fat 1.9g	(Saturated Fat 0.2g)
Carbohydrate 16.7g	Fiber 2.0g	Cholesterol 0mg
Iron 0.5mg	Sodium 99mg	Calcium 10mg

Its elegant simplicity and versatility help make Citrus Cantaloupe Soup (page 220) equally refreshing as an appetizer or a dessert.

Soups & Stews

CITRUS CANTALOUPE SOUP

This soup is refreshing and light. Serve it as an appetizer or dessert.

3 cups cubed cantaloupe (about 1 small)
1 cup unsweetened orange juice
¼ cup vanilla low-fat yogurt
2 teaspoons honey
¼ teaspoon ground ginger
⅛ teaspoon freshly grated nutmeg
1 tablespoon plus 1 teaspoon vanilla low-fat yogurt
Fresh mint leaves (optional)
Edible flowers (optional)

Place first 6 ingredients in container of an electric blender or food processor; cover and process until smooth. Transfer to a bowl. Cover and chill.

To serve, ladle soup into individual bowls. Top each serving with 1 teaspoon yogurt. If desired, garnish with mint leaves and edible flowers. Yield: 4 cups (103 calories per 1-cup serving).

Per Serving:		
Protein 2.6g	Fat 0.7g	(Saturated Fat 0.4g)
Carbohydrate 23.6g	Fiber 1.7g	Cholesterol 1mg
Iron 0.4mg	Sodium 25mg	Calcium 53mg

FRESH ASPARAGUS SOUP

The potato helps give this soup its thick, creamy consistency without adding fat.

1¾ pounds fresh asparagus
1 cup peeled, cubed potato
Vegetable cooking spray
1 tablespoon reduced-calorie margarine
¼ cup finely chopped onion
¼ cup finely chopped celery
¼ cup chopped fresh parsley
1 tablespoon chopped fresh basil
1 tablespoon all-purpose flour
1 (13¾-ounce) can no-salt-added chicken broth
1 cup 1% low-fat milk
2 teaspoons lemon juice
¼ teaspoon salt
Lemon zest (optional)

Snap off tough ends of asparagus. Remove scales from stalks with a knife or vegetable peeler, if desired. Cut asparagus into 2-inch pieces. Place asparagus pieces and cubed potato in a large saucepan. Add water to cover. Bring to a boil. Cover, reduce heat, and simmer 10 minutes or until potato is tender; drain well.

Coat a large saucepan with cooking spray, and add margarine. Place over medium-high heat until margarine melts. Add onion and celery; sauté until vegetables are tender. Reduce heat to low. Add parsley, basil, and flour; cook, stirring constantly, 1 minute. Gradually add chicken broth; cook over medium heat, stirring constantly, 5 minutes. Stir in asparagus mixture.

Pour vegetable mixture into container of an electric blender; cover and process until smooth. Return mixture to saucepan. Add milk, lemon juice, and salt; cook until thoroughly heated, stirring frequently.

To serve, ladle soup into individual bowls. Garnish with lemon zest, if desired. Yield: 1½ quarts (87 calories per 1-cup serving).

Per Serving:		
Protein 4.6g	Fat 2.0g	(Saturated Fat 0.5g)
Carbohydrate 13.8g	Fiber 2.8g	Cholesterol 2mg
Iron 1.3mg	Sodium 146mg	Calcium 79mg

BORSCHT

2 (10½-ounce) cans low-sodium chicken broth
½ cup no-salt-added tomato sauce
1 cup shredded cabbage
½ cup finely chopped onion
½ cup finely chopped carrot
¼ cup finely chopped celery
1 (16-ounce) can diced beets, drained and divided
1½ teaspoons red wine vinegar
½ teaspoon sugar
½ teaspoon dried dillweed
¼ teaspoon dill seeds
¼ teaspoon salt
¼ teaspoon pepper
1 tablespoon plus 2 teaspoons low-fat sour cream

Combine chicken broth and tomato sauce in a large saucepan; bring to a boil. Stir in cabbage, onion, carrot, and celery. Cover, reduce heat, and simmer 30 minutes.

Place half of beets in container of an electric blender or food processor; cover and process until smooth. Add pureed beets, remaining diced beets, vinegar, and next 5 ingredients to vegetable mixture in saucepan. Bring to a boil; cover, reduce heat, and simmer 20 minutes.

To serve, ladle soup into individual bowls. Top each serving with 1 teaspoon sour cream. Yield: 5 cups (70 calories per 1-cup serving).

Per Serving:		
Protein 2.7g	Fat 1.6g	(Saturated Fat 0.6g)
Carbohydrate 12.4g	Fiber 2.0g	Cholesterol 2mg
Iron 1.4mg	Sodium 323mg	Calcium 40mg

FRESH MUSHROOM SOUP

If crimini mushrooms are not available, you may replace them with white button mushrooms in this recipe.

6 cups canned no-salt-added chicken broth, undiluted
1 cup sliced onion, separated into rings
1 cup chopped green onions
4 ounces fresh crimini mushrooms, sliced
2 ounces sliced fresh mushrooms
1 (3½-ounce) package fresh shiitake mushrooms, sliced
1 (3½-ounce) package fresh oyster mushrooms
1 teaspoon dried tarragon
1 teaspoon coarsely ground pepper
2 teaspoons sesame oil
¼ teaspoon salt

Combine all ingredients in a large Dutch oven. Bring to a boil; cover, reduce heat, and simmer 3 minutes or until mushrooms are tender. Ladle soup into individual bowls. Yield: 2 quarts (56 calories per 1-cup serving).

Per Serving:		
Protein 1.6g	Fat 1.3g	(Saturated Fat 0.2g)
Carbohydrate 8.5g	Fiber 1.4g	Cholesterol 0mg
Iron 0.7mg	Sodium 81mg	Calcium 16mg

HERBED NAVY BEAN SOUP

2 (6-inch) corn tortillas
Vegetable cooking spray
½ teaspoon chili powder
½ ounce dried porcini mushrooms
1 cup water
16 fresh asparagus spears
1½ pounds red potatoes, peeled and cut into ½-inch cubes
2 (15-ounce) cans navy beans, drained
1½ cups diced leeks
2½ cups canned low-sodium chicken broth, undiluted
2 cloves garlic, crushed
3 sprigs fresh thyme
1 sprig fresh rosemary
2 tablespoons coarsely chopped fresh chives

Coat tortillas with cooking spray; sprinkle one side of each tortilla with chili powder. Cut tortillas into very thin strips. Arrange strips on an ungreased baking sheet. Bake at 350° for 10 minutes or until crisp. Let cool, and set aside.

Combine mushrooms and water in a small saucepan; bring to a boil. Cover, reduce heat, and simmer 5 minutes. Remove mushrooms from liquid, using a slotted spoon; reserve liquid. Finely chop mushrooms, and set aside. Pour mushroom liquid through a coffee filter into a small bowl, and set liquid aside.

Cut 1½-inch-long tips from asparagus spears. Reserve stalks for another use. Set asparagus tips aside.

Combine reserved mushroom liquid, potato, and next 6 ingredients in a large saucepan. Bring to a boil; cover, reduce heat, and simmer 25 minutes or until potato is tender. Stir in chopped mushrooms and asparagus tips; cook 1 minute. Remove and discard thyme and rosemary sprigs. Ladle soup into individual bowls; sprinkle evenly with chives, and top with tortilla strips. Yield: 2 quarts (148 calories per 1-cup serving).

Per Serving:		
Protein 7.8g	Fat 1.2g	(Saturated Fat 0.2g)
Carbohydrate 27.7g	Fiber 4.0g	Cholesterol 0mg
Iron 4.2mg	Sodium 142mg	Calcium 70mg

A bowl of Cuban Black Bean Soup, filled with lean ham and vegetables, makes a mouth-watering meal.

CUBAN BLACK BEAN SOUP

3 (15-ounce) cans no-salt-added black beans, undrained
2 (13¾-ounce) cans low-sodium beef broth
1½ cups chopped onion
2 cups water
¾ cup chopped green pepper
2 teaspoons minced garlic
1 (14½-ounce) can no-salt-added whole tomatoes, undrained and chopped
1 (4½-ounce) can chopped green chiles, undrained
¼ pound extra-lean cooked ham, diced
½ cup red wine vinegar
1 teaspoon dried oregano
1 teaspoon dried thyme
1 teaspoon ground cumin
½ teaspoon coarsely ground pepper

Combine black beans, beef broth, chopped onion, water, chopped green pepper, and minced garlic in a large Dutch oven; bring mixture to a boil. Cover, reduce heat, and simmer 20 minutes, stirring frequently.

Add tomato, chopped green chiles, diced ham, red wine vinegar, dried oregano, dried thyme, ground cumin, and coarsely ground pepper to bean mixture. Cook, uncovered, over low heat an additional 30 minutes, stirring occasionally.

To serve, ladle soup into individual bowls. Yield: 15 cups (220 calories per 1½-cup serving).

Per Serving:

Protein 14.8g	Fat 1.5g	(Saturated Fat 0.4g)
Carbohydrate 37.4g	Fiber 6.6g	Cholesterol 6mg
Iron 3.8mg	Sodium 192mg	Calcium 66mg

VEGETABLE GUMBO

3½ cups peeled, chopped tomato
3 cups sliced fresh okra
2 cups fresh corn cut from cob (about 3 ears)
1 cup chopped onion
1 teaspoon pepper
2½ cups water
2½ cups canned vegetable broth, undiluted
½ cup long-grain rice, uncooked

Combine first 7 ingredients in a Dutch oven. Bring to a boil; reduce heat, and simmer, uncovered, 20 minutes or until vegetables are tender.

Add rice; cover and cook 20 minutes. Uncover and cook an additional 5 minutes. Yield: 10½ cups (95 calories per 1½-cup serving).

Per Serving:		
Protein 2.9g	Fat 0.9g	(Saturated Fat 0.1g)
Carbohydrate 20.7g	Fiber 2.5g	Cholesterol 0mg
Iron 1.1mg	Sodium 569mg	Calcium 33mg

QUICK-AND-EASY VEGETABLE SOUP

This recipe makes a big batch of soup. Enjoy half now, and freeze half for later. Frozen in an airtight container, the soup will keep up to one month.

1 pound ultra-lean ground beef
1¼ cups chopped onion
8 (5½-ounce) cans low-sodium vegetable juice
2 (14½-ounce) cans no-salt-added whole tomatoes, undrained and coarsely chopped
1 (13¾-ounce) can no-salt-added beef broth
1 (10-ounce) package frozen chopped okra
1 (10-ounce) package frozen baby lima beans
1 (10-ounce) package frozen whole-kernel corn
1 teaspoon coarsely ground pepper
½ teaspoon salt

Cook ground beef and onion in a Dutch oven over medium-high heat until beef is browned, stirring until it crumbles. Drain beef mixture, and pat dry with paper towels. Wipe drippings from Dutch oven with a paper towel.

Return beef mixture to Dutch oven. Stir in vegetable juice and remaining ingredients. Bring to a boil; cover, reduce heat, and simmer 1 hour. Ladle soup into individual bowls. Yield: 18 cups (143 calories per 1½-cup serving).

Per Serving:		
Protein 11.1g	Fat 2.6g	(Saturated Fat 0.9g)
Carbohydrate 21.0g	Fiber 2.0g	Cholesterol 22mg
Iron 2.5mg	Sodium 238mg	Calcium 70mg

TORTILLA SOUP

The tortillas absorb some of the soup's liquid and become tender, similar to cooked noodles.

2 (7-inch) flour tortillas
4 (4-ounce) skinned, boned chicken breast halves
5 cups canned no-salt-added chicken broth, undiluted
1 cup chopped onion
2 teaspoons minced garlic
2 cups frozen corn with red and green peppers, thawed
¼ cup chopped green chiles, drained
¼ cup chopped ripe olives
½ teaspoon coarsely ground pepper
¼ teaspoon salt
¼ teaspoon ground cumin
¼ cup chopped fresh cilantro

Cut tortillas into 2- x 1-inch strips. Set aside.

Combine chicken and broth in a large saucepan. Bring to a boil. Cover, reduce heat, and simmer 20 minutes or until chicken is tender. Remove chicken from broth, reserving broth. Let chicken cool slightly. Shred chicken; set aside.

Skim fat from broth; add onion and garlic to broth. Bring to a boil. Cover, reduce heat, and simmer 10 minutes. Add shredded chicken, corn and peppers, and next 5 ingredients. Cook, uncovered, 15 minutes. Add tortilla strips and cilantro; cook an additional 5 minutes. Ladle soup into individual bowls. Yield: 2 quarts (149 calories per 1-cup serving).

Per Serving:		
Protein 15.4g	Fat 2.9g	(Saturated Fat 0.7g)
Carbohydrate 13.8g	Fiber 1.7g	Cholesterol 36mg
Iron 1.3mg	Sodium 218mg	Calcium 30mg

GREEK CHICKEN AND RICE SOUP

2 (4-ounce) skinned, boned chicken breast halves
4½ cups canned low-sodium chicken broth, undiluted
½ cup Chablis or other dry white wine
½ cup long-grain rice, uncooked
½ cup wild rice, uncooked
½ cup chopped onion
1 tablespoon minced garlic
2 tablespoons chopped ripe olives
1 teaspoon dried dillweed
½ teaspoon coarsely ground pepper
¼ teaspoon salt
¼ cup frozen egg substitute, thawed
2 tablespoons lemon juice

Combine chicken, chicken broth, and wine in a large Dutch oven. Bring to a boil; cover, reduce heat, and simmer 20 minutes or until chicken is tender. Remove chicken from broth, reserving broth. Let chicken cool slightly. Shred chicken.

Skim fat from broth; add rices, onion, and garlic. Bring to a boil; cover, reduce heat, and simmer 30 minutes. Add shredded chicken, olives, and next 3 ingredients; cover and cook an additional 20 minutes or until wild rice is tender. Combine egg substitute and lemon juice; add to soup, stirring well. Yield: 1½ quarts (277 calories per 1½-cup serving).

Per Serving:		
Protein 20.4g	Fat 2.3g	(Saturated Fat 0.6g)
Carbohydrate 39.8g	Fiber 1.9g	Cholesterol 36mg
Iron 2.6mg	Sodium 243mg	Calcium 42mg

CHICKEN-CRABMEAT PEPPERPOT

4 (4-ounce) skinned, boned chicken breast halves
5 (10½-ounce) cans low-sodium chicken broth
1 cup chopped onion
1 teaspoon minced garlic
3 cups fresh corn cut from cob (about 5 ears)
½ pound fresh lump crabmeat, drained
1 medium-size sweet red pepper, cut into 1-inch pieces
1 medium-size green pepper, cut into 1-inch pieces
½ cup chopped green onions
½ cup chopped fresh cilantro
1 teaspoon coarsely ground pepper
¼ teaspoon salt

Combine chicken, chicken broth, chopped onion, and minced garlic in a large Dutch oven. Bring to a boil; cover, reduce heat, and simmer 20 minutes or until chicken is tender. Remove chicken from broth, reserving broth. Let chicken cool slightly. Shred chicken.

Skim fat from broth; add shredded chicken and corn to broth. Bring to a boil; cover, reduce heat, and simmer 10 minutes. Stir in crabmeat and remaining ingredients; cover and cook an additional 10 minutes or until vegetables are tender. Yield: 11 cups (143 calories per 1-cup serving).

Per Serving:		
Protein 16.5g	Fat 3.0g	(Saturated Fat 0.8g)
Carbohydrate 13.8g	Fiber 2.1g	Cholesterol 46mg
Iron 1.8mg	Sodium 184mg	Calcium 34mg

EATING WELL ON THE ROAD

A car trip doesn't have to be a dietary disaster. With a little planning and careful menu reading, you can eat nutritiously almost anywhere.

Diners are good choices because their menus are extensive and they often honor special requests. You can probably get a baked potato instead of French fries, for example. Stick with bean or vegetable soups, spaghetti with tomato sauce, or sandwiches and salads without mayonnaise. Choose vegetables, or check the salad section of the menu for fresh fruit.

Fast-food restaurants usually offer healthy choices such as salads, grilled chicken sandwiches, and baked potatoes. Otherwise, a plain burger will do.

Convenience stores can be a good place to stock up for a roadside picnic. Have a sandwich made to order (extra lettuce and tomato but hold the mayonnaise), or buy whole wheat bread, mustard, and sliced turkey to make your own. Buy fresh fruit and juices, pretzels, and skim milk for healthy snacking.

Ladle up a hearty, warming meal with Chicken-Crabmeat Pepperpot.

CIOPPINO

4 (14½-ounce) cans no-salt-added whole tomatoes, undrained and chopped
¾ cup Chablis or other dry white wine
1 cup chopped green pepper
1 cup chopped onion
2 teaspoons minced garlic
2 teaspoons chopped fresh oregano
1 teaspoon chopped fresh rosemary
1 teaspoon chopped fresh thyme
1 teaspoon chopped fresh basil
1 teaspoon freshly ground pepper
1 teaspoon grated lemon rind
¼ teaspoon salt
1 bay leaf
1½ pounds unpeeled medium-size fresh shrimp
1 pound grouper, cut into 1-inch pieces
½ pound bay scallops
½ pound lump crabmeat, drained
6½ cups cooked long-grain rice (cooked without salt or fat)
Fresh oregano sprigs (optional)
Fresh thyme sprigs (optional)

Combine tomato and wine in a large Dutch oven. Bring to a boil; add chopped green pepper and next 10 ingredients. Cover, reduce heat, and simmer 30 minutes.

Peel and devein shrimp. Add shrimp and grouper to tomato mixture. Cover and cook 10 minutes. Stir in scallops and crabmeat; cook an additional 10 minutes or until fish flakes easily when tested with a fork and shrimp and scallops are done. Remove and discard bay leaf.

To serve, place ½ cup rice in each individual bowl. Ladle soup over rice. If desired, garnish with fresh oregano and thyme sprigs. Yield: 13 servings (249 calories per 1-cup soup and ½-cup rice).

Per Serving:

Protein 24.4g	Fat 1.7g	(Saturated Fat 0.3g)
Carbohydrate 33.0g	Fiber 1.8g	Cholesterol 95mg
Iron 3.3mg	Sodium 214mg	Calcium 115mg

SAUSAGE AND BEAN SOUP

Tying the onion and herbs in a cheesecloth bag allows their flavors to seep into the soup and makes it easy to remove them before serving.

½ pound dried navy beans
½ pound smoked turkey sausage, sliced
2 cups chopped reduced-fat, low-salt ham
1 cup chopped onion
1 cup chopped celery
½ cup chopped carrot
3½ cups canned no-salt-added beef broth, undiluted
1 (14½-ounce) can no-salt-added whole tomatoes, undrained and chopped
1 teaspoon dried thyme
½ teaspoon pepper
3 bay leaves
½ small onion
8 black peppercorns
6 whole cloves
2 cloves garlic
1 fresh thyme sprig
1 fresh rosemary sprig
1 fresh oregano sprig

Sort and wash beans; place beans in a large Dutch oven. Cover with water to a depth of 2 inches above beans. Bring to a boil; cover, remove from heat, and let stand for 1 hour. Drain beans, and return to Dutch oven. Set aside.

Cook sausage in a large nonstick skillet over medium heat until browned, stirring frequently. Drain and pat dry with paper towels. Add sausage, ham, and next 8 ingredients to beans.

Place onion half and remaining ingredients on a large piece of cheesecloth; tie ends of cheesecloth securely. Add to bean mixture. Bring to a boil; cover, reduce heat, and simmer 1½ hours or until beans are tender. Remove and discard bay leaves and cheesecloth bag. Ladle soup into individual bowls. Yield: 9 cups (218 calories per 1-cup serving).

Per Serving:

Protein 16.4g	Fat 7.2g	(Saturated Fat 1.9g)
Carbohydrate 21.8g	Fiber 3.6g	Cholesterol 46mg
Iron 2.7mg	Sodium 482mg	Calcium 97mg

Eggplant chunks absorb the flavors in the broth, giving Vegetable Chili as much body and taste as beef chili.

VEGETABLE CHILI

2 cups chopped onion
1 cup chopped green pepper
1 (13¾-ounce) can no-salt-added beef broth
1 (2-pound) eggplant, cubed
2 (15-ounce) cans kidney beans, drained
2 (10¾-ounce) cans low-sodium tomato soup
¼ cup sliced ripe olives
2 tablespoons chili powder
1 teaspoon ground coriander
1 teaspoon dried oregano
1 teaspoon pepper
½ cup (2 ounces) finely shredded reduced-fat sharp Cheddar cheese

Combine first 3 ingredients in a Dutch oven. Bring broth to a boil; cover, reduce heat, and simmer 15 minutes.

Add eggplant and next 7 ingredients; cover and cook an additional 50 minutes or until vegetables are tender, stirring occasionally. Ladle chili into individual bowls. Sprinkle 1 tablespoon Cheddar cheese over each serving. Yield: 3 quarts (195 calories per 1½-cup serving).

Per Serving:

Protein 10.2g	Fat 3.5g	(Saturated Fat 1.2g)
Carbohydrate 33.5g	Fiber 5.5g	Cholesterol 5mg
Iron 3.2mg	Sodium 456mg	Calcium 137mg

BURGUNDY BEEF STEW

Baking the stew slowly in the oven allows the flavors to blend, creating a thick, rich-tasting beef broth.

2 teaspoons garlic powder
2 teaspoons dried thyme
1 teaspoon pepper
2 pounds lean boneless beef sirloin steak, cut into 1-inch pieces
Vegetable cooking spray
3 cups canned no-salt-added beef broth, undiluted and divided
2 cups Burgundy or other dry red wine
¼ cup all-purpose flour
3 cups sliced carrot
2 tablespoons no-salt-added tomato paste
1 tablespoon plus 1 teaspoon minced garlic
2 teaspoons minced fresh rosemary
2 cups frozen pearl onions
4 cups small fresh mushrooms

Combine first 3 ingredients, and sprinkle evenly over beef.

Coat a large nonstick skillet with cooking spray; place over medium-high heat until hot. Add beef, and cook until beef is browned on all sides, stirring frequently. Transfer to a 4-quart casserole. Set aside.

Add 2¾ cups broth and wine to skillet; cook over high heat, deglazing skillet by scraping particles that cling to bottom.

Combine flour and remaining ¼ cup broth, stirring with a wire whisk until smooth. Reduce heat to medium; add flour mixture to wine mixture, stirring constantly. Cook, stirring constantly, until mixture is thickened. Add carrot, tomato paste, garlic, and rosemary; stir well. Bring to a boil; pour wine mixture over beef. Cover and bake at 350° for 1½ hours, stirring occasionally. Add onions, and bake 30 minutes. Add mushrooms, and bake an additional 30 minutes. Ladle stew into individual bowls. Yield: 9 cups (214 calories per 1-cup serving).

Per Serving:

Protein 24.2g	Fat 5.5g	(Saturated Fat 1.9g)
Carbohydrate 16.2g	Fiber 2.8g	Cholesterol 61mg
Iron 4.6mg	Sodium 90mg	Calcium 51mg

ZESTY PORK STEW

Toasting the cumin seeds intensifies their flavor; they add a hearty, nutlike flavor to this stew.

2 pounds lean boneless pork loin
Olive oil-flavored vegetable cooking spray
1 (14½-ounce) can no-salt-added stewed tomatoes, undrained and chopped
1½ cups water
3 cups peeled, cubed red potato
2 cups thinly sliced onion
2 cups sliced carrot
1 teaspoon dried crushed red pepper
1 teaspoon dried oregano
1 teaspoon cumin seeds, toasted
¼ teaspoon salt

Trim fat from pork; cut pork into 1-inch cubes. Coat a large Dutch oven with cooking spray; place over medium heat until hot. Add pork, and cook until browned on all sides, stirring frequently. Drain and pat dry with paper towels. Wipe drippings from Dutch oven with a paper towel.

Return pork to Dutch oven; stir in tomato and water. Bring to a boil; cover, reduce heat, and simmer 45 minutes. Add potato and remaining ingredients; cover and cook 30 minutes. Uncover and cook an additional 25 minutes or until vegetables are tender. Ladle stew into individual bowls. Yield: 2 quarts (262 calories per 1-cup serving).

Per Serving:

Protein 25.9g	Fat 8.9g	(Saturated Fat 3.0g)
Carbohydrate 19.3g	Fiber 2.9g	Cholesterol 68mg
Iron 2.2mg	Sodium 172mg	Calcium 47mg

Fresh Raspberry Tart (page 242) makes such a lovely presentation you may be reluctant to cut into it. But once you taste it, all regrets will be cast aside.

Desserts

APPLE-PECAN CRÊPES WITH BOURBON SAUCE

Butter-flavored vegetable cooking spray
1 tablespoon reduced-calorie margarine
3 cups peeled, chopped Granny Smith apple
¼ cup firmly packed brown sugar
¼ cup chopped pecans
1 teaspoon ground cinnamon
½ teaspoon ground allspice
¼ teaspoon ground nutmeg
1 (8-ounce) package Neufchâtel cheese, softened
3 tablespoons honey
1 tablespoon skim milk
Crêpes
Bourbon Sauce
1 cup reduced-calorie frozen whipped topping, thawed

Coat a large nonstick skillet with cooking spray; add margarine. Place over medium-high heat until margarine melts. Add apple and brown sugar; cook, stirring constantly, 3 minutes. Stir in pecans and next 3 ingredients; cook, stirring constantly, an additional 3 minutes or until apple is tender. Remove from heat, and let cool completely.

Beat Neufchâtel cheese at medium speed of an electric mixer until smooth. Gradually add honey and milk, beating well. Stir in apple mixture.

Spoon 2 tablespoons apple mixture down center of each crêpe. Fold right and left sides of each crêpe over filling.

To serve, place a filled crêpe, seam side down, on each individual serving plate. Top each with about 2 tablespoons Bourbon Sauce. Spoon 1 tablespoon whipped topping over each serving. Yield: 16 servings (169 calories per serving).

Crêpes

½ cup plus 2 tablespoons all-purpose flour
1⅓ cups skim milk
4 egg whites
Vegetable cooking spray

Combine flour, milk, and egg whites in container of an electric blender or food processor. Cover and process 30 seconds, scraping sides of container once; process an additional 30 seconds. Refrigerate batter at least 1 hour.

Coat a 6-inch crêpe pan or nonstick skillet with cooking spray; place over medium heat until hot. Pour 2 tablespoons batter into pan, and quickly tilt pan in all directions so batter covers pan in a thin film. Cook 1 minute or until crêpe can be shaken loose from pan. Flip crêpe, and cook about 30 seconds. Place crêpe on a towel to cool. Repeat procedure until all batter is used. Stack crêpes between layers of wax paper to prevent sticking. Yield: 16 (6-inch) crêpes.

Bourbon Sauce

1½ cups unsweetened apple juice
⅓ cup firmly packed brown sugar
¼ cup bourbon
2 tablespoons cornstarch
1½ tablespoons reduced-calorie margarine

Combine all ingredients in a medium saucepan. Cook over medium heat, stirring constantly, until mixture comes to a boil; boil, stirring constantly, 1 minute. Remove from heat, and let cool slightly. Yield: 1¾ cups plus 3 tablespoons.

Per Serving:

Protein 3.8g	Fat 6.7g	(Saturated Fat 2.8g)
Carbohydrate 24.8g	Fiber 1.0g	Cholesterol 11mg
Iron 0.7mg	Sodium 105mg	Calcium 53mg

TROPICAL BANANAS FOSTER

2 medium bananas
⅓ cup firmly packed brown sugar
3 tablespoons reduced-calorie margarine
1 (8-ounce) can pineapple chunks in juice, drained
¼ teaspoon ground cinnamon
2 tablespoons Crème de Bananes
3 tablespoons light rum
3 cups vanilla nonfat frozen yogurt

Peel bananas; cut each banana in half lengthwise. Cut each half into 6 pieces.

Place brown sugar and margarine in a large skillet. Cook over medium heat, stirring until margarine melts. Add banana, pineapple, and cinnamon. Cook until banana is slightly soft, stirring and basting frequently with cooking liquid. Stir in Crème de Bananes.

Place rum in a small, long-handled pan; heat just until warm. Ignite with a long match; pour over banana mixture. Stir gently until flame dies down. Scoop ½ cup yogurt into each individual dessert bowl. Spoon banana mixture evenly over yogurt. Serve immediately. Yield: 6 servings (223 calories per serving).

Per Serving:		
Protein 4.1g	Fat 4.8g	(Saturated Fat 1.1g)
Carbohydrate 44.6g	Fiber 1.7g	Cholesterol 0mg
Iron 0.5mg	Sodium 126mg	Calcium 146mg

TANGERINES AND SAMBUCA

Sambuca tastes similar to licorice candy. If it isn't available, substitute Anisette or another anise-flavored liqueur.

6 tangerines, peeled and cut crosswise into ¼-inch-thick slices
⅓ cup finely chopped fresh mint
2 tablespoons honey
1 tablespoon Sambuca or other anise-flavored liqueur
Fresh mint sprigs (optional)
Lemon rind curls (optional)

Combine tangerine slices and chopped mint in a medium bowl. Combine honey and liqueur, stirring well. Pour honey mixture over tangerine mixture; toss gently.

Spoon tangerine mixture evenly into individual dessert bowls. If desired, garnish with mint sprigs and lemon rind curls. Yield: 4 servings (96 calories per serving).

Per Serving:		
Protein 1.1g	Fat 0.3g	(Saturated Fat 0g)
Carbohydrate 22.3g	Fiber 1.9g	Cholesterol 0mg
Iron 0.8mg	Sodium 2g	Calcium 46g

MOCHA PUDDING PARFAITS

For a milder coffee flavor, substitute instant coffee granules for the espresso powder.

1 (8-ounce) carton light process cream cheese product, softened
1 (8-ounce) carton vanilla low-fat yogurt
1 cup nonfat sour cream alternative
1 cup nonfat cottage cheese
½ cup sugar
1 tablespoon instant espresso powder
2 tablespoons amaretto
¾ cup chocolate wafer crumbs, divided
½ cup reduced-calorie frozen whipped topping, thawed
Candied coffee beans (optional)

Position knife blade in food processor bowl; add first 7 ingredients. Process until smooth, scraping sides of processor bowl occasionally.

Spoon 3 tablespoons yogurt mixture into each of 8 (6-ounce) parfait glasses. Top each with 2 teaspoons chocolate wafer crumbs. Repeat layers with 1½ cups yogurt mixture and ⅓ cup chocolate wafer crumbs. Top evenly with remaining yogurt mixture. Cover and chill 3 hours.

Top each serving with 1 tablespoon whipped topping. Sprinkle evenly with remaining 1 tablespoon plus 1 teaspoon chocolate crumbs. Garnish with candied coffee beans, if desired. Yield: 8 servings (235 calories per serving).

Per Serving:		
Protein 10.9g	Fat 7.6g	(Saturated Fat 4.0g)
Carbohydrate 28.3g	Fiber 0g	Cholesterol 26mg
Iron 0.3mg	Sodium 342mg	Calcium 132mg

End a festive occasion with Black Forest Trifle—a spectacular low-fat dessert that tastes as grand as it looks.

BLACK FOREST TRIFLE

¼ cup plus 2 tablespoons sugar
¼ cup unsweetened cocoa
3½ tablespoons cornstarch
2 cups 1% low-fat milk
1 tablespoon margarine
¾ teaspoon vanilla extract
1 (15-ounce) loaf fat-free chocolate pound cake
¼ cup Kirsch or other cherry-flavored liqueur
1 (20-ounce) can lite cherry pie filling
2 cups reduced-calorie frozen whipped topping, thawed
Fresh cherries (optional)
Chocolate curls (optional)

Combine first 3 ingredients in a saucepan. Gradually add milk, stirring with a wire whisk until smooth. Cook over medium heat, stirring constantly, 5 to 8 minutes until mixture is thickened. Remove from heat. Add margarine and vanilla, stirring until margarine melts. Cover and chill.

Cut cake into 1-inch cubes. Arrange half of cake cubes in a 3-quart trifle bowl; brush with 2 tablespoons liqueur. Spoon half of cherry filling over cake. Spread half of chocolate mixture over cherry filling. Top with half of whipped topping. Repeat layers with remaining cake, liqueur, cherry filling, chocolate mixture, and whipped topping. Cover and chill at least 8 hours. If desired, garnish with fresh cherries and chocolate curls. Yield: 12 servings (234 calories per serving).

Per Serving:

Protein 3.9g	Fat 3.0g	(Saturated Fat 1.6g)
Carbohydrate 41.3g	Fiber 1.4g	Cholesterol 2mg
Iron 1.0mg	Sodium 220mg	Calcium 68mg

PEACH MELBA TRIFLE

1 (5.1-ounce) package vanilla instant pudding mix
2 cups skim milk
½ cup light process cream cheese product, softened
1 (8-ounce) carton raspberry low-fat yogurt
1 (10½-ounce) loaf commercial angel food cake
3 cups sliced fresh peaches
2 cups fresh raspberries
Raspberry Sauce

Combine pudding mix and milk; beat at low speed of an electric mixer until smooth. Set aside.

Beat cream cheese at medium speed until creamy. Add yogurt, beating until well blended. Stir in pudding mixture. Cover and chill at least 30 minutes.

Cut cake into 1-inch cubes. Arrange 2 cups cake cubes in a 3-quart trifle bowl. Spread 1⅓ cups pudding mixture over cake cubes. Arrange 1 cup peaches over pudding mixture; top with ⅔ cup raspberries. Repeat layers twice with remaining cake, pudding mixture, peaches, and raspberries. Cover; chill at least 3 hours. Serve with Raspberry Sauce. Yield: 12 servings (217 calories per serving).

Raspberry Sauce

3 cups fresh raspberries
2 tablespoons Chambord or other raspberry-flavored liqueur
1 tablespoon sugar
2 teaspoons cornstarch

Combine raspberries and liqueur in container of an electric blender; cover and process until smooth. Place raspberry mixture in a wire-mesh strainer over a bowl; press with back of spoon against the sides of the strainer to squeeze out juice. Discard pulp and seeds remaining in strainer.

Combine raspberry puree, sugar, and cornstarch in a saucepan, stirring until smooth. Cook over medium heat, stirring constantly, until thickened. Remove from heat; cool completely. Yield: 1½ cups.

Per Serving:

Protein 5.3g	Fat 2.3g	(Saturated Fat 1.2g)
Carbohydrate 45.6g	Fiber 4.7g	Cholesterol 7mg
Iron 0.5mg	Sodium 205mg	Calcium 127mg

APRICOT MOUSSE

We reduced the fat in this mousse by more than 90 percent and earned a calorie savings of 363 calories per serving.

1 (15-ounce) can apricot halves in juice, drained
2 tablespoons lemon juice
½ cup 1% low-fat cottage cheese
½ cup plain nonfat yogurt
1 envelope unflavored gelatin
½ cup cold water
½ cup apricot nectar
½ cup sugar
1 teaspoon almond extract
1 cup reduced-calorie frozen whipped topping, thawed
Fresh mint sprigs (optional)

If desired, cut 1 apricot half into 8 slices for garnish, and set aside.

Position knife blade in food processor bowl; add remaining apricots and lemon juice. Process until apricots are finely chopped. Add cottage cheese and yogurt; process until smooth, scraping sides of processor bowl once.

Sprinkle gelatin over ½ cup cold water in a small saucepan; let stand 1 minute. Cook over low heat, stirring until gelatin dissolves, about 2 minutes. Add apricot nectar, sugar, and almond extract, stirring until sugar dissolves.

Combine yogurt mixture and gelatin mixture in a large bowl; chill 30 minutes or until consistency of unbeaten egg white. Gently fold in whipped topping. Spoon evenly into individual dessert dishes. Cover and chill until firm. If desired, garnish with reserved apricot slices and mint sprigs. Yield: 8 servings (110 calories per serving).

Per Serving:

Protein 4.0g	Fat 1.2g	(Saturated Fat 0.8g)
Carbohydrate 21.4g	Fiber 0.9g	Cholesterol 1mg
Iron 0.4mg	Sodium 81mg	Calcium 48mg

CANTALOUPE-CHAMPAGNE SORBET

Unlike many sherbets, sorbet is made with water or juice instead of milk.

3½ cups chopped cantaloupe (about 1 small)
½ cup sugar
⅔ cup champagne
2 teaspoons grated lemon rind

Position knife blade in food processor bowl; add all ingredients. Process until smooth. Pour mixture into an 8-inch square pan. Cover; freeze until firm.

Remove from freezer, and let stand 5 minutes. Break cantaloupe mixture into chunks using a fork, and place in a medium bowl. Beat cantaloupe mixture at medium speed of an electric mixer until smooth. Return mixture to pan. Cover and freeze at least 2 hours. Scoop sorbet into individual dessert bowls. Serve immediately. Yield: 4 cups (93 calories per ½-cup serving).

Per Serving:		
Protein 0.8g	Fat 0.2g	(Saturated Fat 0.1g)
Carbohydrate 19.8g	Fiber 1.0g	Cholesterol 0mg
Iron 0.3mg	Sodium 8mg	Calcium 11mg

REFRESHING LIME SHERBET

¼ cup plain nonfat yogurt
¼ cup nonfat cottage cheese
1½ cups sugar
3½ cups water
1 teaspoon grated lime rind
½ cup fresh lime juice
1 drop green food coloring (optional)
Lime wedges (optional)
Edible flowers (optional)

Combine yogurt and cottage cheese in container of an electric blender; cover and process until smooth. Set aside.

Combine sugar, 3½ cups water, and grated lime rind in a medium saucepan; bring to a boil. Cover, reduce heat, and simmer 10 minutes. Remove from heat, and stir in lime juice. Let mixture cool to room temperature.

Combine yogurt mixture and lime mixture in a bowl, stirring well. Stir in green food coloring, if desired. Pour lime mixture into freezer can of a 2-quart hand-turned or electric freezer. Freeze according to manufacturer's instructions. Pack freezer with additional ice and rock salt, and let stand 1 hour before serving. Scoop sherbet into individual dessert bowls. If desired, garnish with lime wedges and edible flowers. Serve immediately. Yield: 5 cups (126 calories per ½-cup serving).

Per Serving:		
Protein 1.1g	Fat 0.0g	(Saturated Fat 0g)
Carbohydrate 31.7g	Fiber 0g	Cholesterol 0mg
Iron 0mg	Sodium 26mg	Calcium 16mg

In Refreshing Lime Sherbet, cottage cheese helps create an extra-creamy texture.

CHOCOLATE MINT ICE MILK

½ cup sugar
¼ cup instant nonfat dry milk powder
¼ cup unsweetened cocoa
2 tablespoons cornstarch
2 cups 1% low-fat milk
1 (12-ounce) can evaporated skimmed milk
1 egg yolk, lightly beaten
2 teaspoons vanilla extract
¼ teaspoon imitation peppermint extract

Combine first 4 ingredients in a medium saucepan, stirring well. Gradually stir in low-fat milk and evaporated milk.

Cook over medium heat, stirring constantly, until mixture is slightly thickened. Gradually stir about one-fourth of hot mixture into egg yolk; add to remaining hot mixture, stirring constantly. Cook over low heat, stirring constantly, 1 minute or until thickened. Remove from heat; stir in flavorings. Cover and chill thoroughly.

Pour mixture into freezer can of a 2-quart hand-turned or electric freezer. Freeze according to manufacturer's instructions. Pack freezer with additional ice and rock salt, and let stand 1 hour before serving.

Scoop ice milk into individual dessert bowls. Serve immediately. Yield: 3½ cups (174 calories per ½-cup serving).

Per Serving:

Protein 8.8g	Fat 2.0g	(Saturated Fat 1.0g)
Carbohydrate 29.4g	Fiber 0g	Cholesterol 37mg
Iron 0.8mg	Sodium 116mg	Calcium 289mg

TROPICAL FROZEN YOGURT

2 cups fresh strawberry halves
2 cups peeled, sliced banana
¼ cup sugar
¾ cup frozen pineapple juice concentrate, thawed and undiluted
½ cup plain low-fat yogurt

Position knife blade in food processor bowl; add first 4 ingredients. Process until smooth, scraping sides of processor bowl once. Add yogurt, and pulse 3 or 4 times or until combined.

Pour mixture into freezer can of a 2-quart hand-turned or electric freezer. Freeze according to manufacturer's instructions. Pack freezer with additional ice and rock salt, and let stand 1 hour before serving. Scoop frozen yogurt into individual dessert bowls. Serve immediately. Yield: 5½ cups (97 calories per ½-cup serving).

Per Serving:

Protein 1.3g	Fat 0.4g	(Saturated Fat 0.2g)
Carbohydrate 23.3g	Fiber 1.7g	Cholesterol 1mg
Iron 0.4mg	Sodium 8mg	Calcium 33mg

FROZEN PUMPKIN DESSERT

¾ cup graham cracker crumbs
¼ cup sugar
3 tablespoons reduced-calorie margarine, melted
Vegetable cooking spray
1½ cups canned pumpkin
¾ cup sifted powdered sugar
1 teaspoon ground cinnamon
¼ teaspoon ground cloves
¼ teaspoon ground nutmeg
¼ teaspoon salt
4 cups vanilla nonfat frozen dessert, softened
2 tablespoons graham cracker crumbs

Combine first 3 ingredients, stirring well. Press mixture into bottom of an 11- x 7- x 1½-inch baking dish coated with cooking spray. Bake at 350° for 8 minutes. Let cool completely on a wire rack.

Combine pumpkin and next 5 ingredients in a large bowl, stirring well. Add frozen dessert, and beat at low speed of an electric mixer 1 minute or until smooth.

Spoon into prepared dish. Sprinkle 2 tablespoons graham cracker crumbs over pumpkin mixture. Cover and freeze until firm. Yield: 10 servings (209 calories per serving).

Per Serving:

Protein 2.6g	Fat 3.4g	(Saturated Fat 0.6g)
Carbohydrate 42.3g	Fiber 1.0g	Cholesterol 0mg
Iron 1.0mg	Sodium 194mg	Calcium 81mg

APPLE-RAISIN RICE PUDDING

We reduced the fat and cholesterol in this recipe by more than half by using skim milk and egg substitute instead of their higher-fat counterparts.

Vegetable cooking spray
½ cup chopped cooking apple
½ cup raisins
3 cups plus 2 teaspoons skim milk, divided
½ cup plus 1 tablespoon sugar, divided
⅓ cup short-grain rice, uncooked
1 tablespoon cornstarch
1 egg, lightly beaten
1 teaspoon vanilla extract
¼ teaspoon ground cinnamon

Coat a medium nonstick skillet with cooking spray; place over medium-high heat until hot. Add apple and raisins; sauté 1 minute. Set aside.

Combine 3 cups milk, ½ cup sugar, and rice in a large saucepan; bring to a boil. Cover, reduce heat, and simmer 15 minutes. Combine cornstarch and remaining 2 teaspoons milk, stirring well; add to rice mixture. Bring to a boil; cook 1 minute, stirring occasionally. Remove from heat.

Gradually stir about one-fourth of hot rice mixture into egg; add to remaining hot mixture, stirring constantly. Stir in apple mixture and vanilla.

Pour rice mixture into a 1-quart baking dish coated with cooking spray. Combine remaining 1 tablespoon sugar and cinnamon; sprinkle over rice mixture. Place baking dish in a large shallow pan; add hot water to pan to a depth of 1 inch. Bake at 325° for 1 hour and 15 minutes. Remove dish from water; let cool 30 minutes before serving. Yield: 6 servings (228 calories per serving).

Per Serving:		
Protein 6.5g	Fat 1.5g	(Saturated Fat 0.5g)
Carbohydrate 48.1g	Fiber 1.3g	Cholesterol 39mg
Iron 1.0mg	Sodium 78mg	Calcium 167mg

ORANGE FLAN

¾ cup sugar, divided
½ teaspoon grated orange rind
1 (12-ounce) can evaporated skimmed milk
⅔ cup 1% low-fat milk
¼ cup unsweetened orange juice
1 tablespoon Triple Sec or other orange-flavored liqueur
1 cup frozen egg substitute, thawed
1 teaspoon vanilla extract
⅛ teaspoon salt

Place ½ cup sugar in a medium saucepan. Cook over medium heat, stirring constantly, until sugar melts and is light brown. Pour melted sugar evenly into 8 (6-ounce) custard cups, tilting to coat bottoms of cups. Sprinkle grated orange rind evenly over bottoms of cups.

Combine evaporated milk and next 3 ingredients in a medium saucepan. Cook over medium heat, stirring constantly, until mixture is thoroughly heated.

Combine remaining ¼ cup sugar, egg substitute, vanilla, and salt in a medium bowl. Beat at medium speed of an electric mixer until blended. Gradually stir 1 cup hot milk mixture into egg substitute mixture; add to remaining hot mixture, stirring constantly. Pour evenly into prepared custard cups.

Place custard cups in 2 (9-inch) square pans; pour hot water into pans to a depth of 1 inch. Bake at 350° for 55 minutes or until a knife inserted in center comes out clean. Remove cups from water, and let cool on wire racks.

Cover and chill at least 4 hours. Loosen edges of custards with a knife; invert onto individual serving plates. Yield: 8 servings (139 calories per serving).

Per Serving:		
Protein 7.0g	Fat 0.6g	(Saturated Fat 0.4g)
Carbohydrate 26.5g	Fiber 0g	Cholesterol 3mg
Iron 0.7mg	Sodium 143mg	Calcium 160mg

FRESH APPLE CAKE WITH RUM RAISIN SAUCE

4 cups peeled, diced Granny Smith apple
1½ cups sugar
¼ cup plus 2 tablespoons vegetable oil
2 teaspoons vanilla extract
3 egg whites, lightly beaten
2½ cups whole wheat flour
2 teaspoons baking soda
½ teaspoon salt
2 teaspoons ground cinnamon
½ cup chopped walnuts
Vegetable cooking spray
Rum Raisin Sauce

Combine first 4 ingredients in a large bowl, stirring well. Add egg whites; stir well. Combine flour, soda, salt, and cinnamon; add to apple mixture, stirring well. Stir in walnuts.

Spread batter in a 13- x 9- x 2-inch pan coated with cooking spray. Bake at 350° for 45 to 50 minutes or until a wooden pick inserted in center comes out clean.

Remove from oven, and let cool completely on a wire rack. Serve with Rum Raisin Sauce. Yield: 24 servings (178 calories per serving).

Rum Raisin Sauce

½ cup raisins
2 tablespoons dark rum
1 tablespoon water
¼ cup sugar
1 tablespoon cornstarch
1¼ cups skim milk
1 egg yolk, lightly beaten
1 teaspoon vanilla extract

Combine first 3 ingredients in a zip-top plastic bag. Seal bag, and shake until raisins are coated. Let stand at least 4 hours, turning bag occasionally.

Combine sugar and cornstarch in a medium saucepan. Gradually stir in milk. Cook over medium heat, stirring constantly, until mixture comes to a boil; boil 1 minute. Gradually stir about one-fourth of hot mixture into egg yolk; add to remaining hot mixture, stirring constantly. Cook over low heat, stirring constantly, 1 minute or until slightly thickened. Remove from heat. Stir in raisin mixture and vanilla. Yield: 1¾ cups.

Per Serving:

Protein 3.3g	Fat 5.2g	(Saturated Fat 0.8g)
Carbohydrate 30.2g	Fiber 2.5g	Cholesterol 9mg
Iron 0.7mg	Sodium 168mg	Calcium 27mg

HONEY-LEMON CAKE

Vegetable cooking spray
1¾ cups plus 1 teaspoon all-purpose flour, divided
2 teaspoons baking powder
¼ teaspoon salt
¾ cup sugar
1 teaspoon grated lemon rind
½ cup plus 2 tablespoons skim milk
¼ cup vegetable oil
¼ cup nonfat sour cream alternative
3 tablespoons honey
1 teaspoon lemon extract
3 egg whites
¼ cup sifted powdered sugar
1¼ teaspoons lemon juice

Coat an 8½- x 4½- x 3-inch loafpan with cooking spray; dust pan with 1 teaspoon flour. Set aside.

Combine remaining 1¾ cups flour and next 4 ingredients in a large bowl. Combine milk and next 4 ingredients in a small bowl, stirring well. Add to flour mixture, and beat at medium speed of an electric mixer until smooth.

Beat egg whites at high speed of an electric mixer until stiff peaks form. Fold beaten egg whites into batter. Pour batter into prepared pan. Bake at 350° for 55 minutes or until a wooden pick inserted in center comes out clean. Cool in pan on a wire rack 10 minutes. Remove from pan, and let cool completely on wire rack.

Combine powdered sugar and lemon juice, stirring until smooth. Drizzle over cake. Yield: 12 servings (197 calories per serving).

Per Serving:

Protein 3.5g	Fat 4.8g	(Saturated Fat 0.9g)
Carbohydrate 34.7g	Fiber 0.5g	Cholesterol 0mg
Iron 1.0mg	Sodium 73mg	Calcium 68mg

Sour Cream-Lemon Pound Cake offers slices of sun-colored sweetness and the tangy taste of lemon.

SOUR CREAM-LEMON POUND CAKE

⅔ cup margarine, softened
2⅔ cups sugar
1¼ cups frozen egg substitute, thawed
1½ cups low-fat sour cream
1 teaspoon baking soda
4½ cups sifted cake flour
¼ teaspoon salt
2 teaspoons vanilla extract
Vegetable cooking spray
½ cup sifted powdered sugar
1 teaspoon grated lemon rind
1 tablespoon fresh lemon juice
Lemon slices (optional)
Lemon rind curls (optional)

Beat margarine at medium speed of an electric mixer until creamy; gradually add 2⅔ cups sugar, beating well. Add egg substitute, and beat well.

Combine sour cream and soda, stirring well. Combine flour and salt; add to margarine mixture alternately with sour cream mixture, beginning and ending with flour mixture. Mix after each addition. Stir in vanilla. Spoon batter into a 10-inch tube pan coated with cooking spray. Bake at 325° for 1 hour and 20 minutes or until a wooden pick inserted in center comes out clean. Cool in pan 10 minutes.

Remove cake from pan. Combine powdered sugar, grated lemon rind, and fresh lemon juice; drizzle over top of cake. Let cake cool completely on a wire rack. If desired, garnish with lemon slices and lemon rind curls. Yield: 24 servings (242 calories per serving).

Per Serving:

Protein 3.4g	Fat 7.0g	(Saturated Fat 2.1g)
Carbohydrate 41.7g	Fiber 0.4g	Cholesterol 6mg
Iron 1.8mg	Sodium 161mg	Calcium 25mg

KAHLÚA SPONGE CAKE

Egg whites whip to maximum volume when at room temperature. Place them in a bowl within a larger bowl of warm water, and stir until warm.

3 egg yolks
½ cup sugar
¼ cup Kahlúa or other coffee-flavored liqueur
6 egg whites
1 teaspoon cream of tartar
½ teaspoon salt
½ cup sugar
1 cup sifted cake flour
Kahlúa Sauce

Beat egg yolks at high speed of an electric mixer until foamy (about 3 minutes). Gradually add ½ cup sugar, beating until yolks are thick and pale (about 2 minutes). Add liqueur; beat well. Set aside.

Beat egg whites at medium speed of an electric mixer until foamy. Add cream of tartar and salt; beat just until soft peaks form. Increase mixer speed to high; gradually add ½ cup sugar, 1 tablespoon at a time, beating until stiff peaks form and sugar dissolves (2 to 4 minutes).

Gently fold flour into yolk mixture using a large wire whisk. Stir one-fourth of egg white mixture into yolk mixture. Gently fold remaining egg white mixture into yolk mixture.

Spoon batter into an ungreased 10-inch tube pan. Break large air pockets by cutting through batter with a knife. Bake at 350° for 45 to 50 minutes or until cake springs back when lightly touched. Invert pan; cool completely. Loosen cake from sides of pan, using a metal spatula; remove cake from pan. Serve with Kahlúa Sauce. Yield: 12 servings (203 calories per serving).

Kahlúa Sauce

½ cup sugar
¼ cup plus 2 tablespoons unsweetened cocoa
1 tablespoon cornstarch
2 teaspoons instant coffee granules
1¼ cups water
⅓ cup Kahlúa or other coffee-flavored liqueur
2 teaspoons vanilla extract

Combine first 5 ingredients in a medium saucepan, stirring until smooth. Cook over medium heat, stirring constantly, until thickened. Stir in liqueur and vanilla. Serve warm. Yield: 2 cups.

Per Serving:

Protein 4.0g	Fat 1.8g	(Saturated Fat 0.7g)
Carbohydrate 39.3g	Fiber 0.2g	Cholesterol 55mg
Iron 1.3mg	Sodium 128mg	Calcium 14mg

KEY LIME CHEESECAKE

Compared with a traditional lime cheesecake, this one has 77 percent less fat and 57 percent fewer calories.

Vegetable cooking spray
¼ cup graham cracker crumbs
1 (24-ounce) carton 1% low-fat cottage cheese
2 (8-ounce) cartons light process cream cheese product, softened
1 cup sugar
3 eggs
2 egg whites
1 teaspoon grated Key lime rind
⅓ cup fresh Key lime juice
Key lime slices (optional)

Coat a 9-inch springform pan with cooking spray. Sprinkle graham cracker crumbs evenly over bottom of pan. Set aside.

Position knife blade in food processor bowl. Add cottage cheese and cream cheese; process until smooth, scraping sides of processor bowl once. Add sugar and next 4 ingredients; process until smooth. Spoon mixture over graham cracker crumbs.

Bake at 300° for 48 to 50 minutes or until almost set (center will be soft but will firm when chilled). Turn off oven; partially open oven door. Leave cheesecake in oven 30 minutes. Remove from oven, and let cool on a wire rack. Cover and chill 8 hours. Garnish with lime slices, if desired. Yield: 14 servings (190 calories per serving).

Per Serving:

Protein 11.4g	Fat 7.3g	(Saturated Fat 3.9g)
Carbohydrate 19.9g	Fiber 0.1g	Cholesterol 68mg
Iron 0.4mg	Sodium 415mg	Calcium 81mg

BUTTERSCOTCH PEACH COBBLER

1 cup sifted cake flour
1 tablespoon sugar
1 teaspoon baking powder
3 tablespoons margarine
1 to 2 tablespoons ice water
½ cup sugar
½ cup water
1 tablespoon cornstarch
4 cups peeled, sliced fresh peaches
⅓ cup butterscotch morsels
1 teaspoon lemon juice
½ teaspoon vanilla extract
Butter-flavored vegetable cooking spray
1 teaspoon sugar

Position knife blade in food processor bowl; add first 3 ingredients. Cover and process, pulsing 3 or 4 times or until combined. Add margarine to flour mixture. Process, pulsing 5 or 6 times or until mixture resembles coarse meal and is pale yellow. With processor running, slowly add ice water, 1 tablespoon at a time; process only until dough begins to form a ball and leaves sides of bowl. Gently press dough into a 4-inch square between 2 sheets of heavy-duty plastic wrap. Chill 30 minutes.

Combine ½ cup sugar, ½ cup water, and cornstarch in a large saucepan. Add peaches; cook, stirring constantly, 5 to 6 minutes or until thickened. Stir in butterscotch morsels, lemon juice, and vanilla. Spoon mixture into an 8-inch square pan coated with cooking spray. Let cool.

Roll dough, still covered, into an 8-inch square. Place dough in freezer 10 minutes or until plastic wrap can easily be removed.

Remove plastic wrap; cut dough into strips, and place in a lattice-design over filling. Coat strips with cooking spray. Sprinkle 1 teaspoon sugar over pastry.

Bake at 350° for 40 to 45 minutes or until filling is bubbly and crust is golden. Yield: 8 servings (215 calories per serving).

Per Serving:		
Protein 1.9g	Fat 6.3g	(Saturated Fat 2.6g)
Carbohydrate 38.4g	Fiber 1.3g	Cholesterol 0mg
Iron 1.1mg	Sodium 56mg	Calcium 51mg

ALMOND PEACH TARTS

2 tablespoons sugar
1½ tablespoons cornstarch
1 cup 1% low-fat milk
1 teaspoon reduced-calorie margarine
½ teaspoon vanilla extract
1 cup sifted cake flour
2 tablespoons ground almonds
3 tablespoons reduced-calorie margarine, cut into small pieces and chilled
2 to 3 tablespoons ice water
1 cup peeled, sliced fresh peaches
2 tablespoons sliced almonds, toasted
2 tablespoons low-sugar peach spread, melted

Combine sugar and cornstarch in a small saucepan. Gradually stir in milk. Cook over medium heat, stirring constantly, until mixture is thickened and bubbly. Remove from heat; stir in 1 teaspoon margarine and vanilla. Let cool. Cover and chill.

Combine flour and ground almonds in a bowl; cut in 3 tablespoons margarine with a pastry blender until mixture resembles coarse meal and is pale yellow (about 3½ minutes). Sprinkle ice water, 1 tablespoon at a time, over surface; toss with a fork until dry ingredients are moistened and mixture is crumbly. (Do not form a ball.)

Divide dough into 8 equal portions. Gently press each portion into a 2-inch circle on heavy-duty plastic wrap; cover with additional heavy-duty plastic wrap. Roll each portion of dough, still covered, into a 4-inch circle. Remove top sheets of plastic wrap. Invert and fit dough into 3-inch tart pans; remove remaining sheets of plastic wrap.

Prick bottom of pastry shells with a fork. Bake at 375° for 15 to 18 minutes or until lightly browned. Let cool in pans 5 minutes. Remove from pans, and cool completely on a wire rack.

Stir filling with a wire whisk. Spoon 2 tablespoons filling into each pastry shell. Arrange peaches over filling; sprinkle with sliced almonds. Brush peach spread over tarts. Yield: 8 tarts (154 calories each).

Per Tart:		
Protein 4.0g	Fat 6.3g	(Saturated Fat 0.9g)
Carbohydrate 21.4g	Fiber 1.4g	Cholesterol 1mg
Iron 1.0mg	Sodium 62mg	Calcium 54mg

FRESH RASPBERRY TART

1 (8-ounce) carton red raspberry low-fat yogurt
1 cup sifted cake flour
1 teaspoon baking powder
2 tablespoons sugar
3 tablespoons margarine, cut into small pieces and chilled
2 to 3 tablespoons ice water
½ cup light process cream cheese product, softened
⅓ cup sifted powdered sugar
2 tablespoons Chambord or other raspberry-flavored liqueur, divided
1 cup fresh raspberries
1 cup fresh blueberries
¾ cup fresh strawberries
½ cup low-sugar apple jelly
Fresh strawberry fan (optional)
Edible strawberry blossom (optional)
Fresh mint sprig (optional)

Stir yogurt, and spoon onto several layers of heavy-duty paper towels; spread to ½-inch thickness. Cover with additional paper towels, and let stand 15 minutes. Scrape yogurt into a bowl, using a rubber spatula; set aside.

Combine flour, baking powder, and 2 tablespoons sugar in a bowl. Cut in margarine with a pastry blender until mixture resembles coarse meal and is pale yellow (about 3½ minutes). Sprinkle ice water, 1 tablespoon at a time, over surface; toss with a fork until dry ingredients are moistened and mixture is crumbly. (Do not form a ball.)

Gently press mixture into a 4-inch circle on heavy-duty plastic wrap; cover with additional heavy-duty plastic wrap, and chill 1 hour. Roll dough, still covered, into an 11-inch circle. Place dough in freezer 5 minutes or until plastic wrap can easily be removed. Remove top sheet of plastic wrap. Invert and fit dough into a 9-inch tart pan; remove remaining sheet of plastic wrap. Prick bottom and sides of pastry with a fork. Bake at 350° for 20 minutes or until lightly browned. Cool completely on a wire rack.

Combine drained yogurt, cream cheese, powdered sugar, and 1 tablespoon liqueur. Spoon mixture into bottom of tart shell, spreading to edges. Arrange raspberries, blueberries, and strawberries over yogurt mixture.

Combine jelly and remaining 1 tablespoon liqueur in a small saucepan. Cook over medium heat until jelly melts, stirring occasionally. Brush jelly mixture over berries. Cover and chill at least 1 hour. If desired, garnish with a strawberry fan, a strawberry blossom, and a fresh mint sprig. Yield: 10 servings (191 calories per serving).

Per Serving:		
Protein 3.4g	Fat 6.0g	(Saturated Fat 2.1g)
Carbohydrate 31.1g	Fiber 2.1g	Cholesterol 7mg
Iron 1.0mg	Sodium 131mg	Calcium 82mg

CREAMY PEANUT BUTTER PIE

1 cup sifted cake flour
3 tablespoons brown sugar
2 tablespoons unsweetened cocoa
⅛ teaspoon salt
¼ cup margarine, cut into small pieces and chilled
2 to 3 tablespoons ice water
½ cup sugar
2 tablespoons all-purpose flour
1 tablespoon cornstarch
¼ teaspoon salt
2½ cups 1% low-fat milk
¼ cup frozen egg substitute, thawed
¼ cup reduced-fat creamy peanut butter
½ teaspoon vanilla extract
¾ cup reduced-calorie frozen whipped topping, thawed

Combine first 4 ingredients in a large bowl; cut in margarine with a pastry blender until mixture resembles coarse meal and is pale yellow (about 3½ minutes). Sprinkle ice water, 1 tablespoon at a time, over surface; toss with a fork until dry ingredients are moistened and mixture is crumbly. (Do not form a ball.)

Gently press mixture into a 4-inch circle on heavy-duty plastic wrap; cover with additional plastic wrap, and chill 15 minutes. Roll dough, still covered, into a 12-inch circle. Place dough in freezer 5 minutes or until plastic wrap can easily be removed. Remove top sheet of plastic wrap. Invert and fit dough into a 9-inch pieplate; remove remaining sheet of plastic wrap. Fold edges under and flute. Prick bottom of pastry with a fork. Bake at 450° for 8 minutes or until browned. Let cool completely on a wire rack.

Combine ½ cup sugar and next 3 ingredients in a saucepan. Gradually add milk, stirring with a wire whisk until blended. Cook over medium heat, stirring constantly, until mixture is thickened and bubbly. Gradually stir about one-fourth of hot mixture into egg substitute; add to remaining hot mixture, stirring constantly. Cook over low heat, stirring constantly, 1 minute. Stir in peanut butter and vanilla. Let cool, stirring occasionally. Pour mixture into prepared crust. Cover and chill thoroughly.

Just before serving, pipe whipped topping around edge of pie, using a pastry bag fitted with a medium star tip. Yield: 10 servings (219 calories per serving).

Per Serving:		
Protein 5.8g	Fat 8.5g	(Saturated Fat 2.2g)
Carbohydrate 30.9g	Fiber 0.5g	Cholesterol 3mg
Iron 1.4mg	Sodium 214mg	Calcium 89mg

RAISIN CIDER PIE

Using only one crust in this pie keeps the fat to 16 percent per serving.

1 cup sifted cake flour
1 tablespoon sugar
½ teaspoon baking powder
3 tablespoons margarine, cut into small pieces and chilled
2 tablespoons ice water
Vegetable cooking spray
4 cups peeled, coarsely chopped Granny Smith apple (about 3 large)
1 cup raisins
½ cup sugar
1½ cups unsweetened apple cider
½ teaspoon grated lemon rind
1 tablespoon lemon juice
½ teaspoon ground cinnamon
¼ teaspoon salt
2 tablespoons cornstarch
2 tablespoons water

Combine first 3 ingredients in a bowl; cut in margarine with a pastry blender until mixture resembles coarse meal and is pale yellow (about 3½ minutes). Sprinkle 2 tablespoons ice water, 1 tablespoon at a time, over surface; toss with a fork until dry ingredients are moistened. (Do not form a ball.)

Gently press mixture into a 4-inch circle on heavy-duty plastic wrap; cover with additional heavy-duty plastic wrap, and chill 15 minutes. Roll dough, still covered, into an 11-inch circle. Place dough in freezer 5 minutes or until plastic wrap can easily be removed. Remove top sheet of plastic wrap. Invert and fit dough into a 9-inch pieplate coated with cooking spray. Remove remaining sheet of plastic wrap. Fold edges under and flute.

Combine apple and next 7 ingredients in a saucepan; bring to a boil. Combine cornstarch and 2 tablespoons water in a bowl, stirring well. Add cornstarch mixture to apple mixture, stirring constantly. Cook, stirring constantly, until mixture thickens and begins to boil. Pour hot mixture into prepared pastry shell. Bake at 400° for 10 minutes. Reduce heat to 350°; bake 40 to 45 minutes or until filling is hot and bubbly. Let cool completely on a wire rack. Yield: 10 servings (213 calories per serving).

Per Serving:		
Protein 1.5g	Fat 3.8g	(Saturated Fat 0.7g)
Carbohydrate 45.5g	Fiber 2.4g	Cholesterol 0mg
Iron 1.4mg	Sodium 102mg	Calcium 31mg

SKIP THAT MIDNIGHT SNACK

The time of day or night that you eat a snack affects how your body responds to the calories. And munching even a small snack late at night may add up to unwanted pounds as time goes by.

French researchers have found that the body burns calories more slowly in the late evening hours than it does earlier in the day. Although your metabolism typically speeds up after a meal to burn the new fuel, the participants in the French study burned calories more slowly when they ate a snack at midnight than when they ate the same snack earlier in the day.

The reason the body burns calories more slowly at night may be tied to the body's internal clock.

A glass of cool milk and freshly baked Chocolate Peppermint Cookies make an unbeatable afternoon snack.

CHOCOLATE PEPPERMINT COOKIES

½ cup margarine, softened
½ cup sugar
½ cup firmly packed brown sugar
½ cup frozen egg substitute, thawed
1 teaspoon vanilla extract
2¼ cups all-purpose flour
1 teaspoon baking powder
¾ teaspoon baking soda
¼ teaspoon salt
¼ cup plus 1 tablespoon unsweetened cocoa
⅔ cup finely crushed peppermint candies (about 30 candies)
Vegetable cooking spray

Beat margarine at medium speed of an electric mixer until creamy; gradually add sugars, beating well. Add egg substitute and vanilla; beat well.

Combine flour and next 4 ingredients. Add to margarine mixture, stirring just until blended. Stir in crushed candy. Drop dough by level tablespoonfuls, 2 inches apart, onto cookie sheets coated with cooking spray. Bake at 350° for 10 to 12 minutes. Remove from cookie sheets, and let cool on wire racks. Yield: 44 cookies (75 calories each).

Per Cookie:

Protein 1.1g	Fat 2.2g	(Saturated Fat 0.5g)
Carbohydrate 12.9g	Fiber 0.2g	Cholesterol 0mg
Iron 0.5mg	Sodium 66mg	Calcium 12mg

GRANOLA MERINGUE COOKIES

Store these sweet treats in an airtight container to keep them crisp.

3 egg whites
½ teaspoon cream of tartar
¼ cup plus 2 tablespoons sugar
¾ cup low-fat granola cereal without raisins
¼ teaspoon vanilla extract
¼ teaspoon almond extract

Line 2 large baking sheets with parchment or heavy brown paper; set aside.

Beat egg whites and cream of tartar at high speed of an electric mixer until foamy. Gradually add sugar, 1 tablespoon at a time, beating until stiff peaks form and sugar dissolves (2 to 4 minutes). Fold in cereal and flavorings.

Drop egg white mixture by level tablespoonfuls, 2 inches apart, onto prepared baking sheets. Bake at 225° for 1 hour and 10 minutes. Turn oven off. Cool in oven 2 hours with oven door closed. Carefully remove cookies from paper; let cool completely on wire racks. Yield: 4 dozen (12 calories each).

Per Cookie:		
Protein 0.3g	Fat 0.1g	(Saturated Fat 0g)
Carbohydrate 2.7g	Fiber 0.1g	Cholesterol 0mg
Iron 0.1mg	Sodium 5mg	Calcium 0mg

GRANOLA APRICOT BARS

½ cup diced dried apricots
½ cup peeled, grated Granny Smith apple (about 1 medium)
½ cup low-sugar apricot spread
¼ cup currants
2 cups regular oats, uncooked
1 cup all-purpose flour
1½ teaspoons baking soda
1 cup firmly packed brown sugar
½ cup low-fat granola cereal without raisins
1 teaspoon ground cinnamon
½ cup reduced-calorie margarine, melted
1½ tablespoons skim milk
Vegetable cooking spray

Combine first 4 ingredients; set aside.

Combine oats and next 5 ingredients in a large bowl, stirring well. Add margarine and milk, stirring just until dry ingredients are moistened.

Press two-thirds (about 2 cups) of oat mixture into bottom of a 13- x 9- x 2-inch pan coated with cooking spray. Spread apricot mixture over oat mixture, and sprinkle remaining oat mixture over apricot mixture. Bake at 325° for 25 minutes. Let cool completely in pan on a wire rack. Cut into bars. Yield: 32 bars (98 calories each).

Per Bar:		
Protein 1.5g	Fat 2.4g	(Saturated Fat 0.3g)
Carbohydrate 18.8g	Fiber 0.9g	Cholesterol 0mg
Iron 0.8mg	Sodium 94mg	Calcium 14mg

FUDGY MINT BROWNIES

¼ cup margarine, softened
⅔ cup sugar
2 egg whites, divided
2 tablespoons water
2 teaspoons vanilla extract
¾ cup all-purpose flour
¼ teaspoon baking powder
⅓ cup unsweetened cocoa
8 peppermint candy pieces, finely crushed
Vegetable cooking spray

Beat margarine at medium speed of an electric mixer until creamy; gradually add sugar, beating well. Add 1 egg white, water, and vanilla; beat well.

Combine flour and next 3 ingredients; add to margarine mixture, stirring just until dry ingredients are moistened. Set aside.

Beat remaining egg white at high speed of an electric mixer until stiff peaks form; gently fold into cocoa mixture.

Pour into an 8-inch square pan coated with cooking spray. Bake at 350° for 22 to 24 minutes or until edges pull away from pan slightly. Cool in pan on a wire rack. Yield: 16 brownies (101 calories each).

Per Brownie:		
Protein 1.6g	Fat 3.2g	(Saturated Fat 0.7g)
Carbohydrate 16.5g	Fiber 0.2g	Cholesterol 0mg
Iron 0.6mg	Sodium 42mg	Calcium 9mg

Cooking Light 1995 Menu Plans

Here is an entire week's worth of menus designed to take the guesswork out of planning calorie-controlled meals.

So you want to lose weight. Or maybe you just want a few menus on hand so you don't have to decide which foods go together. Either way, these 21 preplanned menus will help you eat healthy without even thinking about it. The menus are designed around recipes in this book. (Those recipes are noted with an asterisk. Page numbers are included for your convenience.) Other items are foods you can prepare practically blindfolded—such as baked potatoes.

If you're trying to lose weight or just want to consume a steady calorie level, you'll love the way each menu is adjusted to fit a 1,200-calorie and a 1,600-calorie eating plan. And substituting food that's not on the menu (for example, baked sweet potato instead of steamed carrots), is no problem. Just check the "Calorie/Nutrient Chart" on pages 250 through 261 to find out how many calories the substitution contains.

Most women can safely lose weight by eating 1,200 calories a day, and most men can do the same at 1,600 a day. But you can continue to use these menus after you've lost weight—just alter them to include the number of calories you need to maintain your desired weight.

If you get impatient should the weight come off slowly, resist the urge to cut more calories to try to lose weight faster. Increase your exercise time instead. Severely restricting your calories may rob your body of the nutrients you need to stay healthy. And it can cause your metabolism to slow down to accommodate a limited food supply, which means you're more likely to put back on the weight you've lost (and more) when you go back to a normal diet.

For more information about safe weight loss and diet planning, see "Nutrition Basics for *Cooking Light*" on pages 12 and 13.

Breakfast

Day 1

1200 CALORIES			1600 CALORIES	
		BREAKFAST		
2 servings	172	*Peaches 'n' Cream Pancakes (p. 98)	3 servings	258
1 slice	30	Turkey Bacon	2 slices	60
½ cup	30	Honeydew Melon	½ cup	30
½ cup	23	Strawberry Halves	½ cup	23
1 cup	86	Skim Milk	1 cup	86
	341			**457**
		LUNCH		
1½ cups	143	*Quick-and-Easy Vegetable Soup (p. 223)	1½ cups	143
1 each	106	*Buttermilk Corn Muffins (p. 46)	1 each	106
1 each	101	*Fudgy Mint Brownies (p. 245)	1 each	101
	350			**350**
		DINNER		
1 serving	137	*Maryland Silver Queen Crab Cakes (p. 120)	2 servings	274
1 cup	75	*Broccoli-Tomato Stir-Fry (p. 209)	1 cup	75
1 medium	218	Baked Potato	1 medium	218
—	—	Reduced-Calorie Margarine	1 teaspoon	17
1 tablespoon	10	Nonfat Sour Cream Alternative	1 tablespoon	10
	440			**594**
		SNACK		
1 each	42	*Greek Pita Snacks (p. 198)	2 each	84
—	—	Green Grapes	¾ cup	86
	42			**170**
	Total 1173			**Total 1571**
	(Calories from Fat: 17%)			(Calories from Fat: 19%)

Lunch

Dinner

Day 2

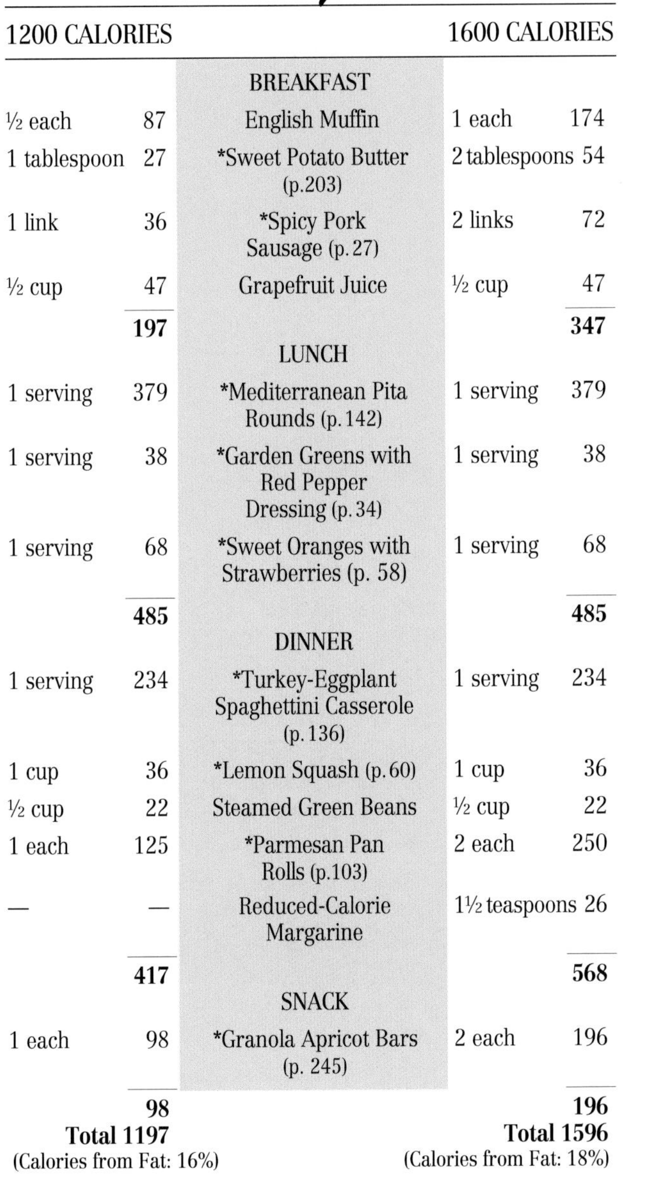

1200 CALORIES			1600 CALORIES	
		BREAKFAST		
½ each	87	English Muffin	1 each	174
1 tablespoon	27	*Sweet Potato Butter (p.203)	2 tablespoons	54
1 link	36	*Spicy Pork Sausage (p. 27)	2 links	72
½ cup	47	Grapefruit Juice	½ cup	47
	197			**347**
		LUNCH		
1 serving	379	*Mediterranean Pita Rounds (p. 142)	1 serving	379
1 serving	38	*Garden Greens with Red Pepper Dressing (p. 34)	1 serving	38
1 serving	68	*Sweet Oranges with Strawberries (p. 58)	1 serving	68
	485			**485**
		DINNER		
1 serving	234	*Turkey-Eggplant Spaghettini Casserole (p. 136)	1 serving	234
1 cup	36	*Lemon Squash (p. 60)	1 cup	36
½ cup	22	Steamed Green Beans	½ cup	22
1 each	125	*Parmesan Pan Rolls (p.103)	2 each	250
—	—	Reduced-Calorie Margarine	1½ teaspoons	26
	417			**568**
		SNACK		
1 each	98	*Granola Apricot Bars (p. 245)	2 each	196
	98			**196**
	Total 1197			**Total 1596**
	(Calories from Fat: 16%)			(Calories from Fat: 18%)

Day 3

1200 CALORIES			1600 CALORIES	
		BREAKFAST		
1 cup	109	*Peachy Breakfast Delight (p. 93)	1 cup	109
1 each	77	Poached Egg	1 each	77
1 slice	56	Whole Wheat Toast	2 slices	112
2 teaspoons	19	Reduced-Calorie Blackberry Jam	2 teaspoons	19
	261			**317**
		LUNCH		
1 serving	213	*Blackened Lamb Pockets with White Bean Salsa (p.194)	1 serving	213
½ each	13	Medium Tomato	1 each	26
4 each	76	*Parmesan-Garlic Bagel Chips (p. 198)	6 each	114
1 cup	139	*Citrus-Mint Cooler (p. 95)	1 cup	139
	441			**492**
		DINNER		
1 serving	189	*Crispy Mexican Chicken (p. 167)	1 serving	189
½ cup	118	*Fiesta Rice (p. 64)	1 cup	236
½ cup	17	Steamed Zucchini	1 cup	34
—	—	*Taco Bread (p. 107)	1 slice	134
½ cup	127	*Papaya Sorbet (p. 74)	½ cup	127
	451			**720**
		SNACK		
1 cup	47	*Spicy Vegetable Sipper (p. 95)	1 cup	47
—	—	Popcorn, popped	1 cup	31
	47			**78**
	Total 1200			**Total 1607**
	(Calories from Fat: 14%)			(Calories from Fat: 13%)

Breakfast

Day 4

1200 CALORIES			1600 CALORIES	
		BREAKFAST		
1 slice	98	*Zucchini-Orange Bread (p. 34)	1 slice	98
1 ounce	24	Nonfat Cream Cheese	1 ounce	24
2 teaspoons	19	Reduced-Calorie Jam	2 teaspoons	19
½ cup	41	Blueberries	1 cup	82
1 cup	86	Skim Milk	1 cup	86
	268			**309**
		LUNCH		
1 serving	256	*Crispy Potato, Tomato, and Mozzarella Squares (p. 190)	1 serving	256
1 serving	81	*Melon Salad with Peppercorn-Fruit Dressing (p. 176)	1 serving	81
—	—	*Cream Cheese and Olive Spread (p. 197)	2 tablespoons	32
—	—	Melba Rounds	6 each	60
	337			**429**
		DINNER		
1 serving	164	*Pork-Filled Cabbage Leaves (p. 160)	1 serving	164
1 cup	65	Steamed Carrots	1 cup	65
½ cup	112	*Pureed Winter Vegetables (p. 214)	1 cup	224
1 each	92	*Caraway-Spinach Twists (p. 103)	2 each	184
	433			**637**
		SNACK		
1 cup	153	*Maple-Banana Frosty (p. 93)	1 cup	153
—	—	Graham Crackers	2 each	54
	153			**207**
	Total 1191			**Total 1582**
	(Calories from Fat: 17%)			(Calories from Fat: 19%)

Lunch

1200 CALORIES			1600 CALORIES	
		BREAKFAST		
1 each	161	*Confetti Scones (p. 100)	1 each	161
½ cup	97	Vanilla Low-Fat Yogurt	1 cup	193
½ cup	23	Fresh Strawberries	1 cup	45
1 cup	2	Hot Tea	1 cup	2
	283			**401**
		LUNCH		
1 serving	185	*Grilled Teriyaki Corn and Shrimp Salad (p. 185)	1 serving	185
1 each	139	*Golden Honey Crescent Rolls (p. 52)	1 each	139
½ each	22	Kiwifruit	1 each	44
	346			**368**
		DINNER		
1 serving	174	*Chicken au Poivre (p. 165)	1 serving	174
1 serving	35	*Asparagus with Raspberry Vinaigrette (p. 208)	1 serving	35
1 cup	137	*Oriental Wild Rice (p. 127)	1 cup	137
1 cup	86	*Cranberry-Orange Tea (p. 96)	1 cup	86
—	—	*Kalhúa Sponge Cake (p. 240)	1 slice	203
	432			**635**
		SNACK		
2 each	140	*Orange Marmalade Tea Cakes (p. 61)	2 each	140
—	—	*Hazelnut Café au Lait (p. 32)	1 cup	45
	140			**185**
	Total 1201			**Total 1589**
	(Calories from Fat: 22%)			(Calories from Fat: 19%)

Lunch

Day 6

1200 CALORIES			1600 CALORIES	
		BREAKFAST		
1 each	138	*Cherry-Almond Muffins (p. 99)	2 each	276
1 cup	86	Skim Milk	1 cup	86
½ cup	56	Orange Juice	½ cup	56
	280			**418**
		LUNCH		
1 serving	225	*Southwestern Chicken Salad Sandwiches (p. 193)	1 serving	225
½ cup	38	*Vegetable Coleslaw (p. 55)	1 cup	76
1 each	81	Apple	1 each	81
	344			**382**
		DINNER		
1 serving	200	*Grilled Sirloin with Citrus Salsa (p. 152)	1 serving	200
½ cup	100	*Rice with Black Beans and Corn (p. 126)	1 cup	200
¾ cup	32	Steamed Spinach	¾ cup	32
½ cup	174	*Chocolate Mint Ice Milk (p. 236)	½ cup	174
	506			**606**
		SNACK		
1 tablespoon	25	*Piquant Cheese Spread (p. 86)	2 tablespoons	50
3 each	39	Unsalted Crackers	6 each	78
—	—	Pineapple Juice	½ cup	70
	64			**198**
	Total 1194 (Calories from Fat: 16%)			**Total 1604** (Calories from Fat: 15%)

Dinner

Day 7

1200 CALORIES			1600 CALORIES	
		BREAKFAST		
1 serving	151	*Chile Cheese Puff (p. 138)	1 serving	151
½ cup	73	Grits	½ cup	73
1 serving	70	*Sautéed Apple Rings with Orange Juice (p. 215)	1 serving	70
¾ cup	38	*Cinnamon-Chocolate Coffee (p. 30)	¾ cup	38
—	—	Reduced-Calorie Margarine	1 teaspoon	17
	332			**349**
		LUNCH		
1 serving	249	*Broccoli-Cheese Stuffed Potatoes (p. 145)	1 serving	249
1 serving	115	*Mixed Greens with Tangelo Vinaigrette (p. 179)	1 serving	115
—	—	Whole Wheat Roll	1 each	72
—	—	*Honey-Lemon Cake (p. 238)	1 slice	197
	364			**633**
		DINNER		
1 serving	260	*Garden Fettuccine with Veal (p. 132)	1 serving	260
1 cup	121	*Melon with Sweet Onion Dressing (p. 34)	1 cup	121
1 each	74	*Graham Honey Rolls (p. 102)	1 each	74
	455			**455**
		SNACK		
4 each	48	*Granola Meringue Cookies (p. 245)	6 each	72
—	—	Skim milk	1 cup	86
	48			**158**
	Total 1199 (Calories from Fat: 18%)			**Total 1595** (Calories from Fat: 19%)

Calorie/Nutrient Chart

FOOD	APPROXIMATE MEASURE	FOOD ENERGY (CALORIES)	PROTEIN (GRAMS)	FAT (GRAMS)	SATURATED FAT (GRAMS)	CARBOHYDRATE (GRAMS)	FIBER (GRAMS)	CHOLESTEROL (MILLIGRAMS)	IRON (MILLIGRAMS)	SODIUM (MILLIGRAMS)	CALCIUM (MILLIGRAMS)
Alfalfa sprouts	½ cup	8	1.1	0.2	0.02	1.1	0.6	0	0.3	2	9
Apple											
Fresh, with skin	1 medium	81	0.2	0.5	0.08	21.0	4.3	0	0.2	0	10
Juice, unsweetened	½ cup	58	0.1	0.1	0.02	14.5	0.2	0	0.5	4	9
Applesauce, unsweetened	½ cup	52	0.2	0.1	0.01	13.8	1.8	0	0.1	2	4
Apricot											
Fresh	1 each	18	0.4	0.1	0.01	4.1	0.8	0	0.2	0	5
Canned, in juice	½ cup	58	0.8	0.0	0.00	15.0	0.5	0	0.4	5	15
Canned, in light syrup	½ cup	75	0.7	0.1	—	19.0	0.5	—	0.3	1	12
Canned, peeled, in water	½ cup	25	0.8	0.0	0.00	6.2	1.7	0	0.6	12	9
Dried, uncooked	1 each	17	0.3	0.0	0.00	4.3	0.5	0	0.3	1	3
Nectar	½ cup	70	0.5	0.1	0.01	18.0	0.8	0	0.5	4	9
Artichoke											
Whole, cooked	1 each	53	2.6	0.2	0.04	12.4	1.1	0	1.6	79	47
Hearts, cooked	½ cup	37	1.8	0.1	0.03	8.7	0.8	0	1.1	55	33
Arugula	3 ounces	21	2.2	0.5	—	3.1	—	0	—	23	136
Asparagus, fresh, cooked	½ cup	23	2.3	0.3	0.06	4.0	0.9	0	0.6	4	22
Avocado	1 medium	322	3.9	30.6	4.88	14.8	4.2	0	2.0	20	22
Bacon											
Canadian-style	1 ounce	45	5.8	2.0	0.63	0.5	0.0	14	0.2	399	2
Cured, broiled	1 ounce	163	8.6	14.0	4.93	0.2	0.0	24	0.5	452	3
Turkey, cooked	1 ounce	60	4.0	4.0	—	8.0	—	20	—	400	—
Bamboo shoots, cooked	½ cup	7	0.9	0.1	0.03	1.1	0.4	0	0.1	2	7
Banana											
Mashed	½ cup	101	1.1	0.5	0.20	25.8	3.2	0	0.3	1	7
Whole	1 medium	109	1.2	0.5	0.22	27.6	3.5	0	0.4	1	7
Barley											
Dry	½ cup	352	9.9	1.2	0.24	77.7	15.6	0	2.5	9	29
Cooked	½ cup	97	1.8	0.3	0.07	22.2	—	0	1.0	2	9
Basil, fresh, raw	¼ cup	1	0.1	0.0	—	0.1	—	0	0.1	0	3
Bean sprouts, raw	½ cup	16	1.6	0.1	0.01	3.1	0.6	0	0.5	3	7
Beans, cooked and drained											
Black	½ cup	114	7.6	0.5	0.12	20.4	3.6	0	1.8	1	23
Black, canned, no-salt-added	½ cup	100	7.0	0.0	0.00	17.0	6.0	0	1.5	15	48
Cannellini	½ cup	112	7.7	0.4	0.06	20.2	3.2	0	2.6	2	25
Garbanzo (chickpeas)	½ cup	134	7.3	2.1	0.22	22.5	2.9	0	2.4	6	40
Great Northern	½ cup	132	9.3	0.5	0.16	23.7	3.8	0	2.4	2	76
Green, fresh	½ cup	22	1.2	0.2	0.40	4.9	1.1	0	0.8	2	29
Green, canned, regular pack	½ cup	14	0.8	0.1	0.01	3.1	0.9	0	0.5	171	18
Kidney or red	½ cup	112	7.7	0.4	0.06	20.2	3.2	0	2.6	2	25
Lima, frozen, baby	½ cup	94	6.0	0.3	0.06	17.5	4.8	0	1.8	26	25
Pinto, canned	½ cup	94	5.5	0.4	0.08	17.5	2.6	0	1.9	184	44
Pinto, canned, no-salt-added	½ cup	90	5.0	0.5	0.00	17.0	6.0	0	1.5	15	32
Wax, canned	½ cup	14	0.8	0.1	0.01	3.1	0.8	0	0.5	171	18
White	½ cup	127	8.0	0.6	0.15	23.2	3.9	0	2.5	2	65
Beef, trimmed of fat											
Flank steak, broiled	3 ounces	207	21.6	12.7	5.43	0.0	0.0	60	2.2	71	5
Ground, extra-lean, broiled	3 ounces	218	21.5	13.9	5.46	0.0	0.0	71	2.0	60	6
Ground, ultra-lean, broiled	3 ounces	146	20.8	7.0	2.75	1.5	—	72	—	238	—
Liver, braised	3 ounces	137	20.7	4.2	1.62	2.9	0.0	331	5.7	60	6

Dash (—) indicates insufficient data available

FOOD	APPROXIMATE MEASURE	FOOD ENERGY (CALORIES)	PROTEIN (GRAMS)	FAT (GRAMS)	SATURATED FAT (GRAMS)	CARBOHYDRATE (GRAMS)	FIBER (GRAMS)	CHOLESTEROL (MILLIGRAMS)	IRON (MILLIGRAMS)	SODIUM (MILLIGRAMS)	CALCIUM (MILLIGRAMS)
Beef *(continued)*											
Round, bottom, braised	3 ounces	189	26.9	8.2	2.92	0.0	0.0	82	2.9	43	4
Round, eye of, cooked	3 ounces	156	24.7	5.5	2.12	0.0	0.0	59	1.7	53	4
Round, top, lean, broiled	3 ounces	162	27.0	5.3	1.84	0.0	0.0	71	2.4	52	5
Sirloin, broiled	3 ounces	177	25.8	7.4	3.03	0.0	0.0	76	2.9	56	9
Tenderloin, roasted	3 ounces	173	24.0	7.9	3.09	0.0	0.0	71	3.0	54	6
Beets											
Fresh, diced, cooked	½ cup	26	0.9	0.4	0.01	5.7	0.8	0	0.5	42	9
Canned, regular pack	½ cup	31	0.8	0.1	0.02	7.5	0.7	0	0.5	201	16
Beverages											
Beer	12 fluid ounces	146	1.1	0.0	0.00	13.1	0.7	0	0.1	18	18
Beer, light	12 fluid ounces	95	0.7	0.0	0.00	4.4	—	0	0.1	10	17
Bourbon, brandy, gin, rum, vodka, or whiskey, 80 proof	1 fluid ounce	65	0.0	0.0	0.00	0.0	0.0	0	0.0	0	0
Champagne	6 fluid ounces	135	0.5	0.0	0.00	2.1	0.0	0	0.9	7	5
Club soda	8 fluid ounces	0	0.0	0.0	0.00	0.0	0.0	0	—	48	11
Coffee, black	1 cup	5	0.2	0.0	0.00	0.9	—	0	1.0	5	5
Coffee liqueur	1 fluid ounce	99	0.0	0.1	0.03	13.9	—	0	0.0	2	0
Cognac brandy	1 fluid ounce	69	—	—	—	—	—	—	—	—	—
Crème de menthe liqueur	1 tablespoon	110	0.0	0.1	0.00	12.3	—	0	0.0	1	0
Sherry, sweet	1 fluid ounce	39	0.1	0.0	—	2.0	0.0	0	0.1	4	2
Vermouth, dry	1 fluid ounce	35	0.0	0.0	0.00	1.6	0.0	0	0.1	5	2
Vermouth, sweet	1 fluid ounce	45	0.0	0.0	0.00	4.7	0.0	0	0.1	8	2
Wine, port	6 fluid ounces	279	0.2	0.0	0.00	21.3	0.0	0	0.7	7	7
Wine, red	6 fluid ounces	121	0.4	0.0	0.00	0.5	0.0	0	1.4	18	12
Wine, white, dry	6 fluid ounces	117	0.2	0.0	0.00	1.1	0.0	0	0.9	7	16
Wine cooler											
Berry	12 fluid ounces	210	0.0	0.0	0.00	32.0	0.0	0	—	5	—
Original	12 fluid ounces	180	0.0	0.0	0.00	27.0	0.0	0	—	0	—
Biscuit and baking mix, low-fat	¼ cup	140	3.0	0.5	0.00	40.0	0.0	0	1.1	510	0
Blackberries, fresh	½ cup	37	0.5	0.3	0.01	9.2	5.3	0	0.4	0	23
Blueberries, fresh	½ cup	41	0.5	0.3	0.02	10.2	3.3	0	0.1	4	4
Bouillon, dry											
Beef-flavored cubes	1 cube	3	0.1	0.0	—	0.2	—	—	—	400	—
Beef-flavored granules	1 teaspoon	10	0.5	1.1	0.30	0.5	—	—	—	945	—
Chicken-flavored cubes	1 cube	10	0.2	0.2	—	1.1	—	1	0.1	1152	—
Chicken-flavored granules	1 teaspoon	10	0.5	1.1	0.30	0.5	—	—	—	819	—
Bran											
Oat, dry, uncooked	½ cup	153	8.0	3.0	0.28	23.5	6.0	0	2.6	1	31
Oat, unprocessed	½ cup	114	8.0	3.3	0.62	30.8	7.4	0	2.5	2	27
Wheat, crude	½ cup	65	4.7	1.3	0.19	19.4	12.7	0	3.2	1	22
Bread											
Bagel, miniature, plain	1 each	70	3.0	0.0	0.00	14.0	—	0	0.9	130	—
Bagel, regular-size, plain	1 each	161	5.9	1.5	0.21	30.5	1.2	—	1.4	196	23
Biscuit, homemade	1 each	127	2.3	6.4	1.74	14.9	0.6	2	0.6	224	65
Bun, hamburger or hot dog	1 each	136	3.2	3.4	0.52	22.4	0.1	13	0.8	112	19
Bun, hamburger, reduced-calorie, whole wheat	1 each	80	2.0	1.0	0.00	15.0	1.4	0	—	220	1
Cornbread	2-ounce square	154	3.5	6.0	3.36	21.1	1.2	56	0.7	273	96
English muffin	1 each	182	5.9	3.6	1.93	30.9	0.8	32	1.5	234	41
French	1 slice	73	2.3	0.5	0.16	13.9	0.6	1	0.6	145	11
Light, Italian	1 slice	40	2.0	0.0	0.00	10.0	2.0	0	0.6	120	0
Light, wheatberry or 7-grain	1 slice	40	2.0	1.0	—	7.0	2.8	0	0.7	105	20
Pita, whole wheat	1 medium	122	2.4	0.9	0.10	23.5	4.4	0	4.4	—	39
Pumpernickel	1 slice	76	2.8	0.4	0.05	16.4	1.8	0	0.7	176	26
Raisin	1 slice	66	1.6	0.7	0.16	13.4	0.9	1	0.3	91	18
Rye	1 slice	61	2.3	0.3	0.04	13.0	1.5	0	0.4	139	19
White	1 slice	67	2.2	0.8	0.19	12.6	0.5	1	0.6	127	18
Whole wheat	1 slice	56	2.4	0.7	0.12	11.0	2.1	1	0.5	121	23

FOOD	APPROXIMATE MEASURE	FOOD ENERGY (CALORIES)	PROTEIN (GRAMS)	FAT (GRAMS)	SATURATED FAT (GRAMS)	CARBOHYDRATE (GRAMS)	FIBER (GRAMS)	CHOLESTEROL (MILLIGRAMS)	IRON (MILLIGRAMS)	SODIUM (MILLIGRAMS)	CALCIUM (MILLIGRAMS)
Breadcrumbs											
Fine, dry	½ cup	196	6.3	2.2	0.52	36.7	2.1	2	1.7	368	61
Seasoned	½ cup	214	8.4	1.5	—	41.5	0.3	—	1.9	1590	59
Breadstick, plain	1 each	17	0.4	0.5	—	2.7	—	—	0.2	20	1
Broccoli, fresh, chopped, cooked or raw	½ cup	12	1.3	0.1	0.02	2.3	1.4	0	0.4	12	21
Broth											
Beef, canned, diluted	1 cup	31	4.8	0.7	0.34	2.6	0.0	24	0.5	782	0
Beef, no-salt-added	1 cup	22	0.5	0.0	0.00	1.9	0.0	0	0.0	7	0
Chicken, low-sodium	1 cup	22	0.4	0.0	—	2.0	0.0	0	0.0	4	0
Chicken, no-salt-added	1 cup	16	1.0	1.0	—	0.0	—	—	—	67	—
Vegetable	1 cup	22	0.0	1.1	—	3.3	—	—	0.3	1015	—
Brussels sprouts, fresh, cooked	½ cup	30	2.0	0.4	0.08	6.8	3.4	0	0.9	16	28
Bulgur, uncooked	½ cup	239	8.6	0.9	0.16	53.1	12.8	0	1.7	12	24
Butter											
Regular	1 tablespoon	102	0.1	11.5	7.17	0.0	0.0	31	0.0	117	3
Whipped	1 tablespoon	68	0.1	7.7	4.78	0.0	0.0	21	0.0	78	2
Cabbage											
Bok choy	1 cup	9	1.0	0.1	0.02	1.5	0.7	0	0.6	45	73
Common varieties, raw, shredded	½ cup	8	0.4	0.1	0.01	1.9	0.8	0	0.2	6	16
Cake, without frosting											
Angel food	2-ounce slice	147	3.2	0.1	—	33.7	0.0	0	0.2	83	54
Pound	1-ounce slice	305	3.6	17.5	10.19	33.7	0.4	134	0.5	245	27
Pound, fat-free	2-ounce slice	147	3.3	0.0	0.00	32.7	0.3	0	0.0	193	21
Pound, chocolate, fat-free	2-ounce slice	140	2.7	0.0	0.00	32.7	1.3	0	0.8	273	11
Sponge, cut into 12 slices	1 slice	183	3.6	5.0	1.48	30.8	0.3	221	0.8	99	44
Yellow, cut into 12 slices	1 slice	190	2.8	7.5	1.92	28.0	0.3	40	0.2	157	79
Candy											
Caramels	1 ounce	108	1.3	2.3	1.87	21.8	0.3	2	0.0	69	39
Fudge, chocolate	1 ounce	113	0.8	3.4	—	21.3	0.1	0	0.3	54	22
Gumdrops	1 ounce	98	0.0	0.2	0.03	24.8	0.0	0	0.1	10	2
Hard	1 each	27	0.0	0.0	0.00	6.8	0.0	0	0.1	2	1
Jelly beans	1 ounce	104	0.0	0.1	0.09	26.4	0.0	0	0.3	3	3
Milk chocolate	1 ounce	153	2.4	8.7	5.13	16.4	—	7	0.4	23	58
Cantaloupe, raw, diced	½ cup	28	0.7	0.2	0.12	6.7	0.9	0	0.2	7	9
Capers	1 tablespoon	4	0.4	0.0	—	0.6	—	0	—	670	—
Carambola (starfruit)	1 medium	42	0.7	0.4	—	9.9	1.5	0	0.3	3	5
Carrot											
Raw	1 medium	31	0.7	0.1	0.02	7.3	2.3	0	0.4	25	19
Cooked, sliced	½ cup	33	0.8	0.1	0.22	7.6	1.4	0	0.4	48	22
Juice, canned	½ cup	66	1.6	0.2	0.05	15.3	1.6	0	0.8	48	40
Catsup											
Regular	1 tablespoon	18	0.3	0.1	0.01	4.3	0.3	0	0.1	178	4
No-salt-added	1 tablespoon	15	0.0	0.0	—	4.0	—	—	—	6	—
Reduced-calorie	1 tablespoon	7	0.0	0.0	—	1.2	—	—	0.0	3	0
Cauliflower											
Raw, flowerets	½ cup	12	1.0	0.1	0.01	2.5	1.2	0	0.3	7	14
Cooked, flowerets	½ cup	15	1.2	0.1	0.02	2.8	1.4	0	0.2	4	17
Caviar	1 tablespoon	40	3.9	2.9	0.07	0.6	0.0	94	—	240	—
Celeriac, raw, shredded	½ cup	30	1.2	0.2	0.06	7.2	1.0	0	0.5	78	34
Celery, raw, diced	½ cup	10	0.4	0.1	0.02	2.2	1.0	0	0.2	52	24
Cereal											
Bran flakes	½ cup	64	2.5	0.4	0.06	15.3	2.7	0	5.6	182	10
Bran, whole	½ cup	104	6.0	1.5	0.12	32.7	14.9	0	6.7	387	30
Corn flakes	½ cup	44	0.9	0.0	0.00	9.8	0.1	0	0.7	140	0
Crispy rice	½ cup	55	0.9	0.1	—	12.4	0.2	0	0.3	103	3
Granola	½ cup	242	5.8	8.9	—	34.7	—	—	1.8	66	29

Dash (—) indicates insufficient data available

FOOD	APPROXIMATE MEASURE	FOOD ENERGY (CALORIES)	PROTEIN (GRAMS)	FAT (GRAMS)	SATURATED FAT (GRAMS)	CARBOHYDRATE (GRAMS)	FIBER (GRAMS)	CHOLESTEROL (MILLIGRAMS)	IRON (MILLIGRAMS)	SODIUM (MILLIGRAMS)	CALCIUM (MILLIGRAMS)
Cereal *(continued)*											
Granola, with raisins, low-fat	½ cup	181	4.5	3.0	0.00	38.0	3.0	0	2.7	91	—
Granola, without raisins, low-fat	½ cup	165	3.0	2.2	0.00	34.5	3.0	0	2.7	53	—
Puffed wheat	½ cup	22	0.9	0.1	0.01	4.8	0.2	0	0.3	0	2
Raisin bran	½ cup	77	2.7	0.5	—	18.6	3.4	0	3.0	179	9
Shredded wheat miniatures	½ cup	76	2.3	0.5	0.08	17.0	2.0	0	0.9	2	8
Toasted oat	½ cup	44	1.7	0.7	0.13	7.8	0.4	0	1.8	123	19
Whole-grain wheat flakes	½ cup	79	1.9	0.2	0.04	18.6	1.4	0	0.6	150	6
Cheese											
American, processed	1 ounce	106	6.3	8.9	5.58	0.5	0.0	27	0.1	405	175
American, processed, fat-free	¾ ounce	30	5.0	0.0	0.00	3.0	0.0	3	0.0	320	120
American, processed, light	1 ounce	50	6.9	2.0	—	1.0	0.0	—	—	407	198
American, processed, skim	1 ounce	69	6.0	4.0	—	2.0	0.0	15	—	407	198
Asiago	1 ounce	101	7.0	8.0	5.00	0.5	0.0	25	—	342	168
Blue	1 ounce	100	6.1	8.1	5.30	0.7	0.0	21	0.1	395	150
Brie	1 ounce	95	5.9	7.8	4.94	0.1	0.0	28	0.1	178	52
Camembert	1 ounce	85	5.6	6.9	4.33	0.1	0.0	20	0.1	239	110
Cheddar	1 ounce	114	7.0	9.4	5.98	0.4	0.0	30	0.2	176	204
Cheddar, fat-free	1 ounce	40	9.0	0.0	0.00	1.0	0.0	5	0.0	200	200
Cheddar, 40% less-fat	1 ounce	71	5.0	4.1	2.40	6.0	—	15	0.1	195	192
Cheddar, light, processed	1 ounce	50	6.9	2.0	—	1.0	0.0	—	—	442	198
Cheddar, reduced-fat, sharp	1 ounce	86	8.3	5.4	3.15	1.2	—	19	0.1	205	251
Colby, reduced-fat	1 ounce	85	8.2	5.5	3.23	0.7	—	19	0.1	163	223
Cottage, dry curd, no-salt-added	½ cup	62	12.5	0.3	0.20	1.3	0.0	5	0.2	9	23
Cottage, nonfat	½ cup	70	15.0	0.0	0.00	3.0	—	5	—	419	60
Cottage, low-fat (1% milkfat)	½ cup	81	14.0	1.1	0.72	3.1	0.0	5	0.2	459	69
Cottage, low-fat (2% milkfat)	½ cup	102	15.5	2.2	1.38	4.1		9	0.2	459	77
Cottage (4% milkfat)	½ cup	108	13.1	4.7	2.99	2.8	0.0	16	0.1	425	63
Cream, light	1 ounce	62	2.9	4.8	2.86	1.8	—	16	0.0	160	38
Cream, nonfat	1 ounce	24	4.0	0.0	—	1.0	0.0	5	0.0	170	80
Farmer	1 ounce	40	4.0	3.0	—	1.0	—	—	—	—	30
Feta	1 ounce	75	4.0	6.0	4.24	1.2	0.0	25	0.2	316	139
Fontina	1 ounce	110	7.3	8.8	5.44	0.4	0.0	33	0.1	—	156
Goat, semisoft	1 ounce	103	6.1	8.5	5.85	0.7	0.0	22	0.5	146	84
Gouda	1 ounce	101	7.1	7.8	4.99	0.6	0.0	32	0.1	232	198
Gruyère	1 ounce	117	8.4	9.2	5.36	0.1	0.0	31	—	95	287
Monterey Jack	1 ounce	106	6.9	8.6	5.41	0.2	0.0	22	0.2	152	211
Monterey Jack, fat-free	1 ounce	40	9.0	0.0	0.00	1.0	0.0	5	0.0	200	200
Monterey Jack, reduced-fat	1 ounce	83	8.4	5.4	3.15	0.5	—	19	0.1	181	227
Mozzarella, part-skim	1 ounce	72	6.9	4.5	2.86	0.8	0.0	16	0.1	132	183
Mozzarella, whole milk	1 ounce	80	5.5	6.1	3.73	0.6	0.0	22	0.0	106	147
Muenster	1 ounce	104	6.6	8.5	5.42	0.3	0.0	27	0.1	178	203
Neufchâtel	1 ounce	74	2.8	6.6	4.20	0.8	0.0	22	0.1	113	21
Parmesan, grated	1 ounce	129	11.8	8.5	5.40	1.1	0.0	22	0.3	528	390
Parmesan Italian Topping, fat-free, grated	1 ounce	60	8.0	0.0	0.00	8.0	0.0	20	0.0	180	128
Provolone	1 ounce	100	7.2	7.5	4.84	0.6	0.0	20	0.1	248	214
Ricotta, lite	1 ounce	20	3.0	1.0	0.60	1.0	—	4	—	20	34
Ricotta, nonfat	1 ounce	20	4.0	0.0	—	2.0	—	3	—	15	48
Ricotta, part-skim	1 ounce	39	3.2	2.2	1.39	1.5	0.0	9	0.1	35	77
Romano, grated	1 ounce	110	9.0	7.6	4.85	1.0	0.0	29	—	340	302
Swiss	1 ounce	107	8.1	7.8	5.04	1.0	0.0	26	0.0	74	272
Swiss, processed, fat-free	¾ ounce	30	5.0	0.0	0.00	3.0	0.0	3	0.0	240	120
Swiss, reduced-fat	1 ounce	85	9.6	5.0	2.78	0.5	—	18	0.1	44	334
Cherries											
Dried	1 ounce	82	1.4	1.1	0.25	18.8	2.6	0	0.5	0	17
Fresh, sweet	½ cup	52	0.9	0.7	0.16	12.0	1.7	0	0.3	0	11
Sour, in light syrup	½ cup	94	0.9	0.1	0.03	24.3	0.1	0	1.7	9	13
Sour, unsweetened	½ cup	39	0.8	0.2	0.05	9.4	1.8	0	0.2	2	12

FOOD	APPROXIMATE MEASURE	FOOD ENERGY (CALORIES)	PROTEIN (GRAMS)	FAT (GRAMS)	SATURATED FAT (GRAMS)	CARBOHYDRATE (GRAMS)	FIBER (GRAMS)	CHOLESTEROL (MILLIGRAMS)	IRON (MILLIGRAMS)	SODIUM (MILLIGRAMS)	CALCIUM (MILLIGRAMS)
Chicken, skinned, boned, and roasted											
White meat	3 ounces	147	26.1	3.8	1.07	0.0	0.0	72	0.9	65	13
Dark meat	3 ounces	174	23.3	8.3	2.26	0.0	0.0	79	1.1	79	13
Liver	3 ounces	134	20.7	4.6	1.56	0.7	0.0	537	7.2	43	12
Chili sauce	1 tablespoon	18	0.4	0.1	0.03	4.2	0.1	0	0.1	228	3
Chives, raw, chopped	1 tablespoon	1	0.1	0.0	0.00	0.1	0.1	0	0.0	0	2
Chocolate											
Chips, semisweet	¼ cup	215	1.7	15.2	—	24.2	0.4	0	1.1	1	13
Sweet	1 ounce	150	1.2	9.9	—	16.4	0.1	0	0.4	9	27
Syrup, fudge	1 tablespoon	62	0.9	2.6	1.55	10.1	0.1	2	0.2	17	24
Unsweetened, baking	1 ounce	141	3.1	14.7	8.79	8.5	0.7	0	2.0	1	23
White, baking	1 ounce	169	1.5	11.9	7.18	14.6	0.0	4	0.0	35	49
Chutney, apple	1 tablespoon	41	0.2	0.0	—	10.5	—	—	0.2	34	5
Cilantro, fresh, minced	1 tablespoon	1	0.1	0.0	0.00	0.3	0.2	0	0.2	1	5
Clams											
Raw	½ cup	92	15.8	1.2	0.12	3.2	0.0	42	17.3	69	57
Canned, drained	½ cup	118	20.4	1.6	0.15	4.1	0.0	54	22.4	90	74
Cocoa powder, unsweetened	1 tablespoon	24	1.6	0.7	0.44	2.6	—	0	0.9	2	8
Coconut											
Fresh, grated	1 cup	460	4.3	43.5	38.61	19.8	11.7	0	3.2	26	18
Dried, sweetened, shredded	1 cup	463	2.7	32.8	29.08	44.0	4.9	0	1.8	242	14
Dried, unsweetened, shredded	1 cup	526	5.5	51.4	45.62	18.8	4.2	0	2.6	30	21
Cookies											
Brownie	2-ounce bar	243	2.7	10.1	3.13	39.0	—	10	1.3	153	25
Chocolate	1 each	72	1.0	3.4	0.90	9.4	0.0	13	0.4	61	18
Chocolate chip, homemade	1 each	69	0.9	4.6	—	6.8	0.2	7	0.3	30	7
Fig bar	1 each	60	0.5	1.0	0.26	11.0	—	—	0.5	60	10
Fig bar, fat-free	1 each	50	0.5	0.0	0.00	11.0	1.0	0	0.2	63	8
Fortune	1 each	23	0.3	0.2	—	5.0	0.1	—	0.1	—	1
Gingersnaps	1 each	36	0.5	1.3	0.33	5.4	0.0	3	0.4	11	14
Oatmeal, plain	1 each	57	0.9	2.7	0.68	7.2	0.4	9	0.3	46	13
Sugar wafers	1 each	47	0.6	2.4	0.48	5.9	0.0	7	0.1	61	4
Vanilla creme	1 each	83	0.8	3.6	—	12.1	—	—	0.4	61	3
Vanilla wafers	1 each	17	0.2	0.9	0.17	2.1	0.0	2	0.1	22	2
Corn											
Fresh, kernels, cooked	½ cup	89	2.6	1.0	0.16	20.6	3.0	0	0.5	14	2
Cream-style, regular pack	½ cup	92	2.2	0.5	0.08	23.2	1.5	0	0.5	365	4
Cornmeal											
Degermed, yellow	1 cup	505	11.7	2.3	0.31	107.2	7.2	0	5.7	4	7
Self-rising	1 cup	407	10.1	4.1	0.58	85.7	—	0	7.0	1521	440
Cornstarch	1 tablespoon	31	0.0	0.0	0.00	7.3	0.1	0	0.0	1	0
Couscous, cooked	½ cup	100	3.4	0.1	0.03	20.8	—	0	0.3	4	7
Crab											
Blue, cooked	3 ounces	87	17.2	1.5	0.19	0.0	0.0	85	0.8	237	88
Imitation	3 ounces	87	10.2	1.1	—	8.7	0.0	17	0.3	715	11
King, cooked	3 ounces	82	16.5	1.3	0.11	0.0	0.0	45	0.6	912	50
Crackers											
Butter	1 each	17	0.0	1.0	—	2.0	—	—	0.1	32	4
Graham, plain	1 square	30	0.5	0.5	—	5.5	—	—	0.2	48	1
Melba rounds, plain	1 each	11	0.4	0.2	—	2.0	—	—	0.1	34	0
Saltine	1 each	13	0.3	0.4	—	2.1	—	—	0.1	43	5
Saltine, fat-free	1 each	10	0.2	0.0	0.00	2.4	—	0	0.1	23	0
Whole wheat	1 each	33	0.7	1.3	0.33	4.7	0.3	0	0.0	60	0
Cranberries											
Dried, whole	1 ounce	85	0.0	0.4	0.14	20.3	1.6	0	0.0	1	3
Fresh, whole	½ cup	23	0.2	0.1	0.01	6.0	0.6	0	0.1	0	3

Dash (—) indicates insufficient data available

FOOD	APPROXIMATE MEASURE	FOOD ENERGY (CALORIES)	PROTEIN (GRAMS)	FAT (GRAMS)	SATURATED FAT (GRAMS)	CARBOHYDRATE (GRAMS)	FIBER (GRAMS)	CHOLESTEROL (MILLIGRAMS)	IRON (MILLIGRAMS)	SODIUM (MILLIGRAMS)	CALCIUM (MILLIGRAMS)
Cranberries *(continued)*											
Juice cocktail, reduced-calorie	½ cup	22	0.0	0.0	0.00	5.6	—	0	0.0	4	11
Juice cocktail, regular	½ cup	75	0.0	0.1	0.00	19.2	—	0	0.2	5	4
Sauce, sweetened	¼ cup	105	0.1	0.1	0.01	26.9	0.2	0	0.1	20	3
Cream											
Half-and-half	1 tablespoon	20	0.4	1.7	1.08	0.7	0.0	6	0.0	6	16
Sour	1 tablespoon	31	0.5	3.0	1.88	0.6	0.0	6	0.0	8	17
Sour, nonfat	1 tablespoon	10	1.0	0.0	—	1.0	—	0	—	10	—
Sour, reduced-calorie	1 tablespoon	20	0.4	1.8	1.12	0.6	0.0	6	0.0	6	16
Whipping, unwhipped	1 tablespoon	51	0.3	5.5	3.43	0.4	0.0	20	0.0	6	10
Creamer, nondairy, powder	1 teaspoon	11	0.1	0.7	0.64	1.1	0.0	0	0.0	4	16
Croutons, seasoned	1 ounce	139	3.0	5.0	—	18.9	—	—	0.3	—	20
Cucumbers, raw, whole	1 medium	32	1.3	0.3	0.08	7.1	2.4	0	0.7	5	34
Currants	1 tablespoon	25	0.4	0.0	0.00	6.7	0.1	0	0.3	1	8
Dandelion greens, raw	1 cup	25	1.5	0.4	—	5.1	0.9	0	1.7	42	103
Dates, pitted, unsweetened	5 each	114	0.8	0.2	0.08	30.5	3.6	0	0.5	1	13
Doughnut											
Cake-type	1 each	156	1.8	7.4	1.92	20.6	0.5	24	0.5	200	16
Plain, yeast	1 each	166	2.5	10.7	2.60	15.1	0.9	10	0.6	94	15
Egg											
White	1 each	16	3.4	0.0	0.00	0.3	0.0	0	0.0	52	2
Whole	1 each	77	6.5	5.2	1.61	0.6	0.0	213	0.7	66	25
Yolk	1 each	61	2.8	5.2	1.61	0.3	0.0	213	0.6	7	23
Substitute	¼ cup	30	6.0	0.0	0.00	1.0	—	0	1.1	90	20
Eggplant, cooked without salt	½ cup	13	0.4	0.1	0.02	3.2	0.5	0	0.2	1	3
Extract, vanilla	1 teaspoon	15	0.0	0.0	—	1.5	0.0	0	0.0	0	0
Fennel, leaves, raw	½ cup	13	1.2	0.2	—	2.3	0.2	0	1.2	4	45
Figs											
Fresh	1 medium	37	0.4	0.2	0.03	9.9	1.9	0	0.2	1	18
Dried	1 each	48	0.6	0.2	0.04	12.2	3.2	0	0.4	2	27
Fish, cooked											
Cod	3 ounces	89	19.4	0.7	0.14	0.0	0.0	47	0.4	66	12
Flounder	3 ounces	100	20.5	1.3	0.31	0.0	0.0	58	0.3	89	15
Grouper	3 ounces	100	21.1	1.1	0.25	0.0	0.0	40	1.0	45	18
Haddock	3 ounces	95	20.6	0.8	0.14	0.0	0.0	63	1.1	74	36
Halibut	3 ounces	119	22.7	2.5	0.35	0.0	0.0	35	0.9	59	51
Mackerel	3 ounces	134	20.1	5.4	1.53	0.0	0.0	62	0.6	56	11
Mahimahi	3 ounces	93	20.2	0.8	0.20	0.0	0.0	80	1.2	96	—
Perch	3 ounces	100	21.1	1.0	0.20	0.0	0.0	98	1.0	67	87
Pollock	3 ounces	96	20.0	1.0	0.20	0.0	0.0	82	0.2	99	5
Pompano	3 ounces	179	20.1	10.3	3.83	0.0	0.0	54	0.6	65	37
Salmon, sockeye	3 ounces	184	23.2	9.3	1.63	0.0	0.0	74	0.5	56	6
Scrod	3 ounces	89	19.4	0.7	0.14	0.0	0.0	47	0.4	66	12
Snapper	3 ounces	109	22.4	1.5	0.31	0.0	0.0	40	0.2	48	34
Sole	3 ounces	100	20.5	1.3	0.31	0.0	0.0	58	0.3	89	15
Swordfish	3 ounces	132	21.6	4.4	1.20	0.0	0.0	43	0.9	98	5
Tilapia	3 ounces	84	16.0	2.0	—	—	0.0	—	—	45	—
Trout	3 ounces	128	22.4	3.7	0.71	0.0	0.0	62	2.1	29	73
Tuna, canned in oil, drained	3 ounces	168	24.8	7.0	1.30	0.0	0.0	15	1.2	301	11
Tuna, canned in water, drained	3 ounces	111	25.2	0.4	0.14	0.0	0.0	—	2.7	303	10
Flour											
All-purpose, unsifted	1 cup	455	12.9	1.2	0.19	95.4	3.4	0	5.8	2	19
Bread, sifted	1 cup	495	16.4	2.3	0.33	99.4	—	0	6.0	3	21
Cake, sifted	1 cup	395	8.9	0.9	0.14	85.1	—	0	8.0	2	15
Rye, light, sifted	1 cup	374	8.6	1.4	0.15	81.8	14.9	0	1.8	2	21
Whole wheat, unsifted	1 cup	407	16.4	2.2	0.39	87.1	15.1	0	4.7	6	41

FOOD	APPROXIMATE MEASURE	FOOD ENERGY (CALORIES)	PROTEIN (GRAMS)	FAT (GRAMS)	SATURATED FAT (GRAMS)	CARBOHYDRATE (GRAMS)	FIBER (GRAMS)	CHOLESTEROL (MILLIGRAMS)	IRON (MILLIGRAMS)	SODIUM (MILLIGRAMS)	CALCIUM (MILLIGRAMS)
Frankfurter											
All-meat	1 each	138	4.9	12.6	4.63	1.1	0.0	22	0.5	482	5
Chicken	1 each	113	5.7	8.6	—	3.0	—	44	0.9	603	42
Turkey	1 each	103	5.6	8.5	2.65	1.1	—	42	0.8	488	60
Fruit bits, dried	1 ounce	93	1.3	0.0	—	20.0	—	0	0.5	24	—
Fruit cocktail, canned, packed in juice	½ cup	57	0.6	0.0	0.00	14.6	0.8	0	0.2	5	10
Garlic, raw	1 clove	4	0.2	0.0	0.00	1.0	0.0	0	0.1	1	5
Gelatin											
Flavored, prepared with water	½ cup	81	1.5	0.0	—	18.6	0.0	0	0.0	54	0
Unflavored	1 teaspoon	10	2.6	0.0	—	0.0	—	—	—	3	—
Ginger											
Fresh, grated	1 teaspoon	1	0.0	0.0	0.00	0.3	0.0	0	0.0	0	0
Crystallized	1 ounce	96	0.1	0.1	—	24.7	0.2	0	6.0	17	65
Grapefruit											
Fresh	1 medium	77	1.5	0.2	0.03	19.3	1.5	0	0.2	0	29
Juice, unsweetened	½ cup	47	0.6	0.1	0.02	11.1	0.0	0	2.5	1	9
Grape juice, Concord	½ cup	60	0.0	0.0	—	14.9	—	—	0.0	11	4
Grapes, green, seedless	1 cup	114	1.1	0.9	0.30	28.4	2.6	0	0.4	3	18
Grits, cooked	½ cup	73	1.7	0.2	0.04	15.7	—	0	0.8	0	0
Ham											
Cured, roasted, extra-lean	3 ounces	123	17.8	4.7	1.54	1.3	0.0	45	1.3	1023	7
Reduced-fat, low-salt	3 ounces	104	15.3	4.2	—	1.8	—	42	—	658	—
Hominy, white or yellow	½ cup	58	1.2	0.7	0.10	11.4	2.0	0	0.5	168	8
Honey	1 tablespoon	64	0.1	0.0	0.00	17.5	0.0	0	0.1	1	1
Honeydew, raw, diced	1 cup	59	0.8	0.2	0.08	15.6	1.5	0	0.1	17	10
Horseradish, prepared	1 tablespoon	6	0.2	0.0	0.01	1.4	0.1	0	0.1	14	9
Hot sauce, bottled	¼ teaspoon	0	0.0	0.0	—	0.0	—	0	0.0	9	0
Ice cream											
Chocolate, regular	½ cup	147	2.6	7.5	4.62	19.2	0.0	—	0.6	52	74
Chocolate, fat-free	½ cup	100	3.0	0.0	0.00	22.0	0.0	0	0.0	60	80
Vanilla, regular	½ cup	134	2.3	7.2	4.39	15.9	0.0	30	0.0	58	88
Vanilla, fat-free	½ cup	100	2.0	0.0	0.00	22.0	0.0	0	0.0	40	64
Vanilla, gourmet	½ cup	175	2.0	11.8	7.37	16.0	0.0	44	0.1	54	75
Ice milk, vanilla	½ cup	92	2.6	2.8	1.76	14.5	0.0	9	0.1	52	88
Jams and Jellies											
Regular	1 tablespoon	54	0.1	0.0	0.01	14.0	0.2	0	0.2	2	4
Reduced-calorie	1 tablespoon	29	0.1	0.0	—	7.4	—	0	0.0	16	1
No-sugar-added	1 tablespoon	40	0.0	0.0	0.00	10.0	—	0	—	0	—
Jicama	1 cup	49	1.6	0.2	0.07	10.5	0.7	0	0.7	7	18
Kiwifruit	1 each	44	1.0	0.5	0.08	8.9	2.6	0	0.4	0	20
Kumquat	1 each	12	0.2	0.0	0.00	3.1	0.7	0	0.1	1	8
Lamb											
Ground, cooked	3 ounces	241	21.0	16.7	6.91	0.0	—	82	1.5	69	19
Leg, roasted	3 ounces	162	24.1	6.6	2.35	0.0	—	76	1.8	58	7
Loin or chop, broiled	3 ounces	184	25.5	8.3	2.96	0.0	—	81	1.7	71	16
Rib, broiled	3 ounces	200	23.6	11.0	3.95	0.0	—	77	1.9	72	14
Lard	1 tablespoon	116	0.0	12.8	5.03	0.0	0.0	12	0.0	0	0
Leeks, bulb, raw	½ cup	32	0.8	0.2	0.03	7.3	0.6	0	1.0	10	31
Lemon											
Fresh	1 each	22	1.3	0.3	0.04	11.4	0.4	0	0.6	3	66
Juice	1 tablespoon	3	0.1	0.0	0.01	1.0	—	0	0.0	3	2

Dash (—) indicates insufficient data available

FOOD	APPROXIMATE MEASURE	FOOD ENERGY (CALORIES)	PROTEIN (GRAMS)	FAT (GRAMS)	SATURATED FAT (GRAMS)	CARBOHYDRATE (GRAMS)	FIBER (GRAMS)	CHOLESTEROL (MILLIGRAMS)	IRON (MILLIGRAMS)	SODIUM (MILLIGRAMS)	CALCIUM (MILLIGRAMS)
Lemonade, sweetened	1 cup	99	0.2	0.0	0.01	26.0	0.2	0	0.4	7	7
Lentils, cooked	½ cup	115	8.9	0.4	0.05	19.9	4.0	0	3.3	2	19
Lettuce											
Belgian endive	1 cup	14	0.9	0.1	0.02	2.9	—	0	0.5	6	—
Boston or Bibb, shredded	1 cup	7	0.7	0.1	0.02	1.3	0.4	0	0.2	3	—
Curly endive or escarole	1 cup	8	0.6	0.1	0.02	1.7	0.4	0	0.4	11	26
Iceberg, chopped	1 cup	7	0.5	0.1	0.01	1.1	0.5	0	0.3	5	10
Radicchio, raw	1 cup	10	0.6	0.1	—	1.8	—	0	—	8	8
Romaine, chopped	1 cup	9	0.9	0.1	0.01	1.3	1.0	0	0.6	4	20
Lime											
Fresh	1 each	20	0.4	0.1	0.01	6.8	0.3	0	0.4	1	21
Juice	1 tablespoon	4	0.1	0.0	0.00	1.4	—	0	0.0	0	1
Lobster, cooked, meat only	3 ounces	83	17.4	0.5	0.09	1.1	0.0	61	0.3	323	52
Luncheon meats											
Bologna, all-meat	1 slice	90	3.3	8.0	3.01	0.8	0.0	16	0.4	289	3
Deviled ham	1 ounce	78	4.3	6.7	—	0.0	0.0	—	0.3	—	1
Salami	1 ounce	71	3.9	5.7	2.29	0.6	0.0	18	0.8	302	4
Turkey ham	1 ounce	34	5.5	1.2	0.45	0.3	—	19	0.4	286	2
Turkey pastrami	1 ounce	33	5.4	1.2	0.43	0.1	—	18	0.4	283	2
Lychees, raw	1 each	6	0.1	0.0	—	1.6	0.0	0	0.0	0	0
Mango, raw	½ cup	54	0.4	0.2	0.05	14.0	1.2	0	0.1	2	8
Margarine											
Regular	1 tablespoon	101	0.1	11.4	2.23	0.1	0.0	0	0.0	133	4
Reduced-calorie, stick	1 tablespoon	50	0.1	5.6	0.93	0.1	0.0	0	0.0	139	3
Fat-free	1 tablespoon	5	0.0	0.0	0.00	0.0	0.0	0	0.0	90	0
Marshmallows, miniature	½ cup	73	0.5	0.0	0.00	18.5	0.0	0	0.4	9	4
Mayonnaise											
Regular	1 tablespoon	99	0.2	10.9	1.62	0.4	0.0	8	0.1	78	2
Nonfat	1 tablespoon	12	0.0	0.0	—	3.0	—	0	0.0	190	—
Reduced-calorie	1 tablespoon	44	0.1	4.6	0.70	0.7	0.0	6	0.0	88	1
Milk											
Buttermilk	1 cup	98	7.8	2.1	1.35	11.7	0.0	10	0.1	257	284
Buttermilk, nonfat	1 cup	88	8.8	0.8	0.64	12.0	—	8	—	256	288
Chocolate, low-fat, 1%	1 cup	158	8.1	2.5	1.55	26.1	0.1	8	0.6	153	288
Chocolate, low-fat, 2%	1 cup	180	8.0	5.0	3.10	25.8	0.1	18	0.6	150	285
Condensed, sweetened	1 cup	982	24.2	26.3	16.77	166.5	0.0	104	0.5	389	869
Evaporated, skim, canned	1 cup	200	19.3	0.5	0.31	29.1	0.0	10	0.7	294	742
Low-fat, 1%	1 cup	102	8.0	2.5	1.61	11.6	0.0	10	0.1	122	300
Low-fat, 2%	1 cup	122	8.1	4.7	2.93	11.7	0.0	20	0.1	122	298
Nonfat dry	⅓ cup	145	14.5	0.3	0.20	20.8	0.0	8	0.1	214	503
Powder, malted, chocolate	1 tablespoon	84	1.1	0.7	—	18.4	—	—	0.3	47	13
Skim	1 cup	86	8.3	0.4	0.28	11.9	0.0	5	0.1	127	301
Whole	1 cup	149	8.0	8.1	5.05	11.3	0.0	34	0.1	120	290
Mint, fresh, raw	¼ cup	1	0.1	0.0	—	0.1	—	0	0.1	0	4
Molasses, cane, light	1 tablespoon	52	0.0	0.0	—	13.3	0.0	0	0.9	3	34
Mushrooms											
Fresh	½ cup	9	0.7	0.1	0.02	1.6	0.5	0	0.4	1	2
Canned	½ cup	19	1.5	0.2	0.02	3.9	—	0	0.6	—	—
Shiitake, dried	1 each	14	0.3	0.0	0.01	2.6	0.4	0	0.1	0	0
Mussels, blue, cooked	3 ounces	146	20.2	3.8	0.02	6.3	0.0	48	5.7	314	28
Mustard											
Dijon	1 tablespoon	18	0.0	1.0	—	1.0	0.0	0	—	446	—
Prepared, yellow	1 tablespoon	12	0.7	0.7	0.03	1.0	0.2	0	0.3	196	13
Nectarine, fresh	1 each	67	1.3	0.6	0.07	16.1	2.2	0	0.2	0	7
Nuts											
Almonds, chopped	1 tablespoon	48	1.6	4.2	0.40	1.7	0.9	0	0.3	1	22
Cashews, dry-roasted, unsalted	1 tablespoon	49	1.3	4.0	0.78	2.8	0.5	0	0.5	1	4

FOOD	APPROXIMATE MEASURE	FOOD ENERGY (CALORIES)	PROTEIN (GRAMS)	FAT (GRAMS)	SATURATED FAT (GRAMS)	CARBOHYDRATE (GRAMS)	FIBER (GRAMS)	CHOLESTEROL (MILLIGRAMS)	IRON (MILLIGRAMS)	SODIUM (MILLIGRAMS)	CALCIUM (MILLIGRAMS)
Nuts *(continued)*											
Hazelnuts, chopped	1 tablespoon	45	0.9	4.5	0.32	1.1	0.3	0	0.2	0	14
Macadamia, roasted, unsalted	1 tablespoon	60	0.6	6.4	0.96	1.1	0.1	0	0.1	1	4
Peanuts, roasted, unsalted	1 tablespoon	53	2.4	4.5	0.62	1.7	0.8	0	0.2	1	8
Pecans, chopped	1 tablespoon	50	0.6	5.0	0.40	1.4	0.5	0	0.2	0	3
Pine nuts	1 tablespoon	52	2.4	5.1	0.78	1.4	0.1	0	0.9	0	3
Pistachio nuts	1 tablespoon	46	1.6	3.9	0.49	2.0	0.9	0	0.5	0	11
Walnuts, black	1 tablespoon	47	1.9	4.4	0.28	0.9	0.5	0	0.2	0	5
Oats											
Cooked	1 cup	145	6.1	2.3	0.42	25.3	2.1	0	1.6	374	19
Rolled, dry	½ cup	156	6.5	2.6	0.45	27.1	4.2	0	1.7	2	21
Oil											
Canola	1 tablespoon	117	0.0	13.6	0.97	0.0	0.0	0	0.0	0	0
Corn	1 tablespoon	121	0.0	13.6	1.73	0.0	0.0	0	0.0	0	0
Olive	1 tablespoon	119	0.0	13.5	1.82	0.0	0.0	0	0.1	0	0
Peanut	1 tablespoon	119	0.0	13.5	2.28	0.0	0.0	0	0.0	0	0
Safflower	1 tablespoon	121	0.0	13.6	1.24	0.0	0.0	0	0.0	0	0
Sesame	1 tablespoon	121	0.0	13.6	1.92	0.0	0.0	0	0.0	0	0
Okra, cooked	½ cup	26	1.5	0.1	0.04	5.8	0.6	0	0.3	4	50
Olives											
Green, stuffed	1 medium	4	0.0	0.4	—	0.1	—	—	—	290	—
Ripe	1 medium	5	0.0	0.4	0.08	0.3	0.1	0	0.1	35	4
Onions											
Green	1 tablespoon	2	0.1	0.0	0.00	0.5	0.2	0	0.1	1	5
Raw, chopped	½ cup	32	1.0	0.1	0.02	7.3	1.6	0	0.2	3	17
Cooked, yellow or white	½ cup	23	0.7	0.1	0.02	5.3	—	0	0.1	2	12
Orange											
Fresh	1 medium	62	1.2	0.2	0.02	15.4	5.8	0	0.1	0	52
Juice	½ cup	56	0.8	0.1	0.01	13.4	0.2	0	0.1	1	11
Mandarin, canned, packed in juice	½ cup	46	0.7	0.0	0.00	12.0	0.1	0	0.4	6	14
Mandarin, canned, packed in light syrup	½ cup	77	0.6	0.1	0.02	20.4	0.1	0	0.5	8	9
Mandarin, canned, packed in water	½ cup	37	0.0	0.0	—	8.4	—	—	0.4	11	—
Oysters, raw	3 ounces	59	6.0	2.1	0.54	3.3	0.0	47	5.7	95	38
Papaya											
Fresh, cubed	½ cup	27	0.4	0.1	0.03	6.9	1.2	0	0.1	2	17
Nectar, canned	½ cup	71	0.3	0.3	0.06	18.1	—	0	0.4	6	13
Parsley, raw	1 tablespoon	1	0.1	0.0	0.00	0.3	0.2	0	0.2	1	5
Parsnips, cooked, diced	½ cup	63	1.0	0.2	0.04	15.1	2.1	0	0.4	8	29
Passion fruit	1 medium	17	0.4	0.1	—	4.2	2.0	0	0.3	5	2
Pasta, cooked											
Macaroni or lasagna noodles	½ cup	99	3.3	0.5	0.07	19.8	1.1	0	1.0	1	5
Medium egg noodles	½ cup	106	3.8	1.2	0.25	19.9	1.8	26	1.3	6	10
Rice noodles	½ cup	138	3.1	1.3	—	28.6	—	0	2.2	—	40
Spaghetti or fettuccine	½ cup	99	3.3	0.5	0.07	19.8	1.1	0	1.0	1	5
Spinach noodles	½ cup	100	3.8	1.0	0.15	18.9	1.4	0	1.8	22	46
Tortellini, fresh, cheese-filled	½ cup	180	8.7	5.3	1.33	24.6	—	27	1.5	147	53
Whole wheat	½ cup	100	3.7	1.4	0.18	19.8	2.5	0	1.0	1	12
Peaches											
Fresh	1 medium	37	0.6	0.1	0.01	9.7	1.4	0	0.1	0	4
Canned, packed in juice	½ cup	55	0.8	0.0	0.00	14.3	0.6	0	0.3	5	7
Canned, packed in light syrup	½ cup	69	0.6	0.0	0.00	18.6	0.4	0	0.5	6	4
Canned, packed in water	½ cup	29	0.5	0.1	0.01	7.5	0.4	0	0.4	4	2
Juice	½ cup	57	0.0	0.0	—	13.6	—	—	—	5	—

Dash (—) indicates insufficient data available

FOOD	APPROXIMATE MEASURE	FOOD ENERGY (CALORIES)	PROTEIN (GRAMS)	FAT (GRAMS)	SATURATED FAT (GRAMS)	CARBOHYDRATE (GRAMS)	FIBER (GRAMS)	CHOLESTEROL (MILLIGRAMS)	IRON (MILLIGRAMS)	SODIUM (MILLIGRAMS)	CALCIUM (MILLIGRAMS)
Peanut butter											
Regular	1 tablespoon	95	4.6	8.3	1.38	2.6	1.0	0	0.3	79	5
Reduced-fat	1 tablespoon	90	4.0	6.0	1.00	7.5	0.5	0	0.4	70	—
No-salt-added	1 tablespoon	95	4.6	8.3	1.38	2.6	1.0	0	0.3	3	5
Pear											
Fresh	1 medium	97	0.6	0.7	0.03	24.9	4.3	0	0.4	0	18
Canned, packed in juice	½ cup	62	0.4	0.1	0.00	16.0	1.1	0	0.3	5	11
Canned, packed in light syrup	½ cup	71	0.2	0.0	—	19.6	3.1	0	0.3	6	6
Nectar, canned	½ cup	64	0.4	0.2	—	16.1	0.4	—	0.1	1	4
Peas											
Black-eyed, cooked	½ cup	90	6.7	0.7	0.17	15.0	1.5	0	1.2	3	23
English, cooked	½ cup	62	4.1	0.2	0.04	11.4	3.5	0	1.2	70	19
Snow pea pods, cooked or raw	½ cup	34	2.6	0.2	0.03	5.6	2.2	0	1.6	3	34
Split, cooked	½ cup	116	8.2	0.4	0.05	20.7	2.3	0	1.3	2	14
Sugar Snap	½ cup	42	2.7	0.2	0.04	7.5	2.6	0	2.1	4	43
Peppers											
Chile, hot, green, chopped	1 tablespoon	4	0.2	0.0	0.00	0.9	0.2	0	0.1	1	2
Jalapeño, green	1 medium	4	0.2	0.0	0.00	0.9	0.2	0	0.1	1	2
Sweet, raw, green, red, or yellow	1 medium	19	0.6	0.4	0.05	3.9	1.2	0	0.9	2	4
Phyllo pastry, raw	1 sheet	57	1.3	1.1	0.17	10.0	—	0	0.6	92	2
Pickle											
Dill, sliced	¼ cup	4	0.2	0.1	0.02	0.9	0.5	0	0.4	553	10
Relish, chopped, sour	1 tablespoon	3	0.1	0.1	—	0.4	0.2	0	0.2	207	4
Sweet, sliced	¼ cup	57	0.2	0.2	0.04	14.1	0.4	0	0.5	276	5
Pie, baked, 9-inch diameter, cut into 8 slices											
Apple, fresh	1 slice	409	3.3	15.3	5.22	67.7	3.5	12	0.8	229	37
Chocolate meringue	1 slice	354	6.8	13.4	5.38	53.8	0.5	109	1.2	307	130
Egg custard	1 slice	248	7.3	11.6	4.07	28.6	0.3	149	0.9	229	129
Peach	1 slice	327	3.2	11.0	2.74	55.1	0.8	0	1.0	339	35
Pecan	1 slice	478	5.8	20.3	4.31	71.1	0.5	141	2.4	324	51
Pumpkin	1 slice	181	4.0	6.8	2.24	27.0	0.8	61	1.1	210	78
Pimiento, diced	1 tablespoon	4	0.2	0.1	0.01	1.0	—	0	0.3	3	1
Pineapple											
Fresh, diced	½ cup	38	0.3	0.3	0.02	9.6	1.2	0	0.3	1	5
Canned, packed in juice	½ cup	75	0.5	0.1	0.01	19.6	0.9	0	0.3	1	17
Canned, packed in light syrup	½ cup	66	0.5	0.2	0.01	16.9	0.6	0	0.5	1	18
Juice, unsweetened	½ cup	70	0.4	0.1	0.01	17.2	0.1	0	0.3	1	21
Plum, fresh	1 medium	35	0.5	0.4	0.03	8.3	1.3	0	0.1	0	3
Popcorn, hot-air popped	1 cup	23	0.8	0.3	0.04	4.6	0.9	0	0.2	0	1
Poppy seeds	1 tablespoon	47	1.6	3.9	0.43	2.1	0.5	0	0.8	2	127
Pork, cooked											
Chop, center-loin	3 ounces	204	24.2	11.1	—	0.0	0.0	77	0.9	59	5
Roast	3 ounces	204	22.7	11.7	4.07	0.0	0.0	77	1.0	59	8
Sausage link or patty	1 ounce	105	5.6	8.8	3.06	0.3	0.0	24	0.3	367	9
Spareribs	3 ounces	338	24.7	25.7	10.00	0.0	0.0	103	1.5	79	40
Tenderloin	3 ounces	141	24.5	4.1	1.41	0.0	0.0	79	1.3	57	8
Potatoes											
Baked, with skin	1 each	218	4.4	0.2	0.05	50.4	3.6	0	2.7	16	20
Boiled, diced	½ cup	67	1.3	0.1	0.02	15.6	1.2	0	0.2	4	6
Potato chips											
Regular	10 each	105	1.3	7.1	1.81	10.4	1.0	0	0.2	94	5
No-salt-added	10 each	105	1.3	7.1	1.81	10.4	1.0	0	0.2	1	5
Fat-free, made with real potatoes	10 each	37	1.0	0.0	0.00	7.7	0.7	0	0.3	60	0
Pretzel sticks, thin	10 each	25	0.5	0.5	—	4.4	0.0	—	0.3	83	4
Prunes											
Dried, pitted	1 each	20	0.2	0.0	0.00	5.3	0.6	0	0.2	0	4
Juice	½ cup	91	0.8	0.0	0.00	22.3	1.3	0	1.5	5	15

FOOD	APPROXIMATE MEASURE	FOOD ENERGY (CALORIES)	PROTEIN (GRAMS)	FAT (GRAMS)	SATURATED FAT (GRAMS)	CARBOHYDRATE (GRAMS)	FIBER (GRAMS)	CHOLESTEROL (MILLIGRAMS)	IRON (MILLIGRAMS)	SODIUM (MILLIGRAMS)	CALCIUM (MILLIGRAMS)
Pumpkin											
Canned	½ cup	42	1.3	0.3	0.18	9.9	2.0	0	1.7	6	32
Seeds, dry	1 ounce	153	7.0	13.0	2.46	5.0	0.6	0	4.2	5	12
Radish, fresh, sliced	½ cup	10	0.3	0.3	0.01	2.1	0.3	0	0.2	14	12
Raisins	1 tablespoon	27	0.3	0.0	0.01	7.2	0.5	0	0.2	1	4
Raisins, golden	1 tablespoon	31	0.4	0.1	0.02	8.2	0.5	0	0.2	1	5
Raspberries											
Black, fresh	½ cup	33	0.6	0.4	0.01	7.7	5.0	0	0.4	0	15
Red, fresh	½ cup	30	0.6	0.3	0.01	7.1	4.6	0	0.3	0	14
Rhubarb											
Raw, diced	½ cup	13	0.5	0.1	0.02	2.8	0.4	0	0.1	2	52
Cooked, with sugar	½ cup	157	0.5	0.1	0.01	42.1	—	0	0.3	1	196
Rice, cooked without salt or fat											
Brown	½ cup	110	2.5	0.9	—	23.2	0.3	1	0.5	1	8
White, long-grain	½ cup	108	2.0	0.1	—	24.0	0.5	0	0.9	0	10
Wild	½ cup	83	3.3	0.3	0.04	17.5	—	0	0.5	2	2
Rice cake, plain	1 each	36	0.7	0.2	0.00	7.7	0.1	0	0.2	1	1
Roll											
Croissant	1 each	272	4.6	17.3	10.67	24.6	0.8	47	1.1	384	32
Hard	1 each	156	4.9	1.6	0.35	29.8	0.1	2	1.1	312	24
Kaiser, small	1 each	92	3.0	1.8	—	16.0	0.1	—	1.3	192	7
Plain, brown-and-serve	1 each	82	2.2	2.0	0.34	13.7	0.1	2	0.5	141	13
Whole wheat	1 each	72	2.3	1.8	0.51	12.0	0.8	9	0.5	149	16
Rutabaga, cooked, cubed	½ cup	29	0.9	0.2	0.02	6.6	0.9	0	0.4	15	36
Salad dressing											
Blue cheese	1 tablespoon	84	0.4	9.2	—	0.3	0.0	0	0.0	216	3
Blue cheese, fat-free	1 tablespoon	16	0.0	0.0	0.00	4.0	0.0	0	0.0	120	0
Blue cheese, low-calorie	1 tablespoon	59	0.9	5.8	1.40	0.8	—	11	0.1	171	24
Cucumber, fat-free, reduced-calorie, creamy	1 tablespoon	8	0.0	0.0	0.00	2.0	0.0	0	0.0	100	0
French	1 tablespoon	96	0.3	9.4	—	2.9	0.0	8	0.1	205	6
French, low-calorie	1 tablespoon	20	0.0	0.0	0.00	4.0	—	0	—	120	—
Italian	1 tablespoon	84	0.1	9.1	—	0.6	0.0	0	0.0	172	1
Italian, no-oil, low-calorie	1 tablespoon	8	0.1	0.0	—	1.8	0.0	0	0.0	161	1
Ranch-style, fat-free	1 tablespoon	16	0.0	0.0	0.00	3.0	0.0	0	0.0	150	0
Thousand Island	1 tablespoon	59	0.1	5.6	0.94	2.4	0.3	—	0.1	109	2
Thousand Island, low-calorie	1 tablespoon	24	0.1	1.6	0.25	2.5	0.2	2	0.1	153	2
Salsa, commercial	1 tablespoon	3	0.1	0.0	—	0.5	—	—	0.0	42	1
Salt, iodized	1 teaspoon	0	0.0	0.0	0.00	0.0	0.0	0	0.0	2343	15
Sauces											
Barbecue	2 tablespoons	23	0.5	0.5	—	4.0	0.2	0	0.3	255	6
Caramel	2 tablespoons	110	0.0	0.0	0.00	27.0	1.0	0	0.0	70	0
Hot fudge, light	2 tablespoons	90	2.0	0.0	0.00	23.0	2.0	0	0.8	90	32
Tartar, regular	2 tablespoons	143	0.3	15.2	2.35	1.4	0.1	14	0.2	426	6
Sauerkraut, canned	½ cup	22	1.1	0.2	0.04	5.0	1.3	0	1.7	780	35
Scallops, raw, large	3 ounces	75	14.3	0.6	0.07	2.0	0.0	28	0.2	137	20
Sesame seeds, dry, whole	1 teaspoon	17	0.5	1.5	0.21	0.7	0.1	0	0.4	0	29
Sherbet											
Lime or raspberry	½ cup	104	0.9	0.9	—	23.8	0.0	0	0.0	67	39
Orange	½ cup	135	1.1	1.9	1.19	29.3	0.0	7	0.1	44	52
Shortening	1 tablespoon	113	0.0	12.6	2.36	0.0	0.0	0	0.0	0	0
Shrimp											
Fresh, cooked, peeled, and deveined	3 ounces	84	17.8	0.9	0.25	0.0	0.0	166	2.6	191	33
Canned, drained	3 ounces	102	19.6	1.7	0.32	0.9	0.0	147	2.3	144	50

Dash (—) indicates insufficient data available

FOOD	APPROXIMATE MEASURE	FOOD ENERGY (CALORIES)	PROTEIN (GRAMS)	FAT (GRAMS)	SATURATED FAT (GRAMS)	CARBOHYDRATE (GRAMS)	FIBER (GRAMS)	CHOLESTEROL (MILLIGRAMS)	IRON (MILLIGRAMS)	SODIUM (MILLIGRAMS)	CALCIUM (MILLIGRAMS)
Soup, condensed, made with water											
Chicken noodle	1 cup	75	4.0	2.4	0.65	9.3	0.2	7	0.7	1106	17
Chili, beef	1 cup	170	6.7	6.6	—	21.4	1.4	13	2.1	1035	43
Cream of chicken	1 cup	117	2.9	7.3	2.07	9.0	0.1	10	0.6	986	34
Cream of chicken, low-salt, reduced-fat	1 cup	80	2.0	2.5	1.00	11.0	—	10	0.3	480	0
Cream of mushroom	1 cup	129	2.3	9.0	2.44	9.0	0.4	2	0.5	1032	46
Cream of mushroom, low-salt, reduced-fat	1 cup	70	2.0	3.0	1.00	9.0	—	10	0.0	480	16
Cream of potato	1 cup	73	1.7	2.3	1.22	11.0	—	5	0.5	1000	20
Onion	1 cup	58	3.7	1.7	—	8.2	—	0	0.7	1053	27
Tomato	1 cup	85	2.0	1.9	0.37	16.6	0.5	0	1.7	871	12
Vegetable, beef	1 cup	78	5.4	2.0	0.83	9.8	0.2	5	1.2	956	17
Soy sauce											
Regular	1 tablespoon	8	0.8	0.0	0.00	1.2	0.0	0	0.3	829	2
Low-sodium	1 tablespoon	6	0.0	0.0	0.00	0.0	—	0	0.0	390	—
Reduced-sodium	1 tablespoon	8	0.8	0.0	0.00	1.2	0.0	0	0.3	484	2
Spinach											
Fresh	1 cup	12	1.6	0.2	0.03	2.0	2.2	0	1.5	44	55
Canned, regular pack	½ cup	22	2.3	0.4	0.00	3.4	1.1	0	1.8	373	97
Cooked	½ cup	21	2.7	0.2	0.04	3.4	2.4	0	3.2	63	122
Squash, cooked											
Acorn	½ cup	57	1.1	0.1	0.03	14.9	1.2	0	1.0	4	45
Butternut	½ cup	41	0.8	0.1	0.02	10.7	1.2	0	0.6	4	42
Spaghetti	½ cup	22	0.5	0.2	0.05	5.0	1.0	0	0.3	14	16
Summer	½ cup	18	0.8	0.3	0.06	3.9	1.4	0	0.3	1	24
Squid, raw	4 ounces	104	17.7	1.6	0.41	3.5	0.0	264	0.8	50	36
Strawberries, fresh	1 cup	45	0.9	0.6	0.03	10.5	3.9	0	0.6	1	21
Sugar											
Granulated	1 tablespoon	48	0.0	0.0	0.00	12.4	0.0	0	0.0	0	0
Brown, packed	1 tablespoon	51	0.0	0.0	—	13.3	0.0	0	0.5	4	12
Powdered	1 tablespoon	29	0.0	0.0	0.00	7.5	0.0	0	0.0	0	0
Sunflower kernels	¼ cup	205	8.2	17.8	1.87	6.8	2.4	0	2.4	1	42
Sweet potatoes											
Whole, baked	½ cup	103	1.7	0.1	0.02	24.3	3.0	0	0.4	10	28
Mashed	½ cup	172	2.7	0.5	0.10	39.8	4.9	0	0.9	21	34
Syrup											
Chocolate-flavored	1 tablespoon	49	0.6	0.2	0.00	11.0	—	0	0.3	12	3
Corn, dark or light	1 tablespoon	60	0.0	0.0	0.00	15.4	0.0	0	0.8	14	9
Maple, reduced-calorie	1 tablespoon	30	0.0	0.2	0.00	7.8	0.0	0	0.0	41	0
Pancake	1 tablespoon	50	0.0	0.0	0.00	12.8	0.0	0	0.2	2	20
Taco shell	1 each	52	0.7	2.8	—	5.9	—	—	—	62	—
Tangerine											
Fresh	1 medium	38	0.5	0.1	0.02	9.6	1.6	0	0.1	1	12
Juice, unsweetened	½ cup	53	0.6	0.2	0.02	12.5	0.1	0	0.2	1	22
Tapioca, dry	1 tablespoon	32	0.0	0.0	—	8.4	0.1	0	0.2	0	2
Tofu											
Firm	4 ounces	164	17.9	9.9	1.43	4.9	1.4	0	11.9	16	232
Soft	4 ounces	60	7.0	3.0	—	2.0	—	0	1.4	5	100
Tomato											
Fresh	1 medium	26	1.0	0.4	0.06	5.7	1.6	0	0.6	11	6
Cooked	½ cup	30	1.3	0.3	0.04	6.8	0.9	0	0.7	13	10
Dried	1 ounce	73	4.0	0.8	0.12	15.8	—	0	—	594	31
Dried, packed in oil	1 ounce	60	1.4	4.0	0.54	6.6	—	0	—	75	0
Juice, regular	1 cup	41	1.8	0.1	0.02	10.3	0.9	0	1.4	881	22
Juice, no-salt-added	1 cup	41	1.8	0.1	0.02	10.3	0.9	—	1.4	24	22
Paste, regular	1 tablespoon	14	0.6	0.1	0.02	3.1	0.7	0	0.5	129	6
Paste, no-salt-added	1 tablespoon	11	0.5	0.0	—	2.6	—	—	0.2	6	4
Sauce, regular	½ cup	37	1.6	0.2	0.03	8.8	1.8	0	0.9	741	17

FOOD	APPROXIMATE MEASURE	FOOD ENERGY (CALORIES)	PROTEIN (GRAMS)	FAT (GRAMS)	SATURATED FAT (GRAMS)	CARBOHYDRATE (GRAMS)	FIBER (GRAMS)	CHOLESTEROL (MILLIGRAMS)	IRON (MILLIGRAMS)	SODIUM (MILLIGRAMS)	CALCIUM (MILLIGRAMS)
Tomato *(continued)*											
Sauce, no-salt-added	½ cup	40	1.2	0.0	—	9.2	1.6	—	—	24	—
Stewed, canned	½ cup	30	0.9	1.1	0.20	5.2	0.2	0	0.4	187	10
Whole, canned, peeled	½ cup	22	0.9	0.0	—	5.2	0.8	—	0.5	424	38
Whole, canned, no-salt-added	½ cup	22	0.9	0.0	—	5.2	0.8	—	0.5	15	38
Tortilla											
Chips, plain	10 each	135	2.1	7.3	1.05	16.0	0.2	0	0.7	24	3
Corn, 6″ diameter	1 each	67	2.1	1.1	0.12	12.8	1.6	0	1.4	53	42
Flour, 6″ diameter	1 each	111	2.4	2.3	0.56	22.2	0.9	0	0.8	0	27
Turkey, skinned, boned, and roasted											
White meat	3 ounces	134	25.3	2.7	0.87	0.0	0.0	59	1.1	54	16
Dark meat	3 ounces	159	24.3	6.1	2.06	0.0	0.0	72	2.0	67	27
Sausage link or patty	1 ounce	55	6.1	3.2	1.00	0.5	—	20	—	296	—
Smoked	3 ounces	126	20.4	4.9	1.45	0.0	0.0	48	2.3	586	9
Turnip greens, cooked	½ cup	14	0.8	0.2	0.04	3.1	2.2	0	0.6	21	99
Turnips, cooked, cubed	½ cup	14	0.6	0.1	0.01	3.8	1.6	0	0.2	39	17
Veal, cooked											
Ground	3 ounces	146	20.7	6.4	2.59	0.0	—	88	0.8	71	14
Leg	3 ounces	128	23.9	2.9	1.04	0.0	—	88	0.8	58	5
Loin	3 ounces	149	22.4	5.9	2.19	0.0	—	90	0.7	82	18
Vegetable juice cocktail											
Regular	1 cup	46	1.5	0.2	0.03	11.0	0.5	0	1.0	883	27
Low-sodium	1 cup	48	2.4	0.2	—	9.7	—	—	1.7	48	34
Venison, roasted	3 ounces	134	25.7	2.7	1.06	0.0	—	95	3.8	46	6
Vinegar, distilled	1 tablespoon	2	0.0	0.0	0.00	0.8	0.0	0	0.0	0	0
Water chestnuts, canned, sliced	½ cup	35	0.6	0.0	0.01	8.7	0.4	0	0.6	6	3
Watercress, fresh	½ cup	2	0.4	0.0	0.00	0.2	0.4	0	0.0	7	20
Watermelon, raw, diced	1 cup	51	1.0	0.7	0.35	11.5	0.9	0	0.3	3	13
Wheat germ	1 tablespoon	26	1.7	0.7	0.12	3.7	1.1	0	0.5	1	3
Whipped cream	1 tablespoon	26	0.2	2.8	1.71	0.2	0.0	10	0.0	3	5
Whipped topping, nondairy, frozen	1 tablespoon	15	0.1	1.2	1.02	1.1	0.0	0	0.0	1	0
Wonton wrappers	1 each	6	0.2	0.1	0.03	0.9	0.0	5	0.1	12	1
Worcestershire sauce											
Regular	1 tablespoon	12	0.3	0.0	0.00	2.7	0.0	0	0.0	147	15
Low-sodium	1 tablespoon	12	0.0	0.0	0.00	3.0	—	0	—	57	—
Yeast, active, dry	1 package	20	2.6	0.1	0.01	2.7	2.2	0	1.1	4	3
Yogurt											
Coffee and vanilla, low-fat	1 cup	193	11.2	2.8	1.84	31.3	0.0	11	0.2	150	388
Frozen, low-fat	½ cup	99	3.0	2.0	1.41	18.0	—	10	—	35	100
Frozen, nonfat	½ cup	82	3.4	0.0	0.00	18.1	—	0	—	60	129
Fruit varieties, low-fat	1 cup	225	9.0	2.6	1.68	42.3	0.2	9	0.1	120	313
Plain, low-fat	1 cup	143	11.9	3.5	2.27	16.0	0.0	14	0.2	159	415
Plain, nonfat	1 cup	127	13.0	0.4	0.26	17.4	0.0	5	0.2	173	452
Zucchini											
Raw	½ cup	9	0.7	0.1	0.02	1.9	0.3	0	0.3	2	10
Cooked, diced	½ cup	17	0.7	0.1	0.01	4.1	0.5	0	0.4	3	14

Dash (—) indicates insufficient data available

Source of Data: Computrition, Inc., Chatsworth, California. Primarily comprised of *Composition of Foods: Raw, Processed, Prepared.* Agriculture Handbook No. 8 Series. United States Department of Agriculture, Human Nutrition Information Service, 1976–1993.

Recipe Index

Subject Index

Acknowledgments and Credits

Oxmoor House wishes to thank the following individuals and merchants:

Annieglass, Santa Cruz, CA
Mrs. Gene Ball, Birmingham, AL
Barbara Eigen Arts, Jersey City, NJ
Birmingham Botanical Gardens, Birmingham, AL
Bridges Antiques, Birmingham, AL
Bromberg's, Birmingham, AL
Cassis & Co., New York, NY
Christine's, Birmingham, AL
Colonial Silver Shoppe, Montgomery, AL
Mr. and Mrs. Tom Curtin, Birmingham, AL
Fioriware, Zanesville, OH
Frankie Engel Antiques, Birmingham, AL
Goldsmith/Corot, Inc., New York, NY
Gorham, Providence, RI
The Holly Tree, Birmingham, AL
Homewood Sporting Goods, Birmingham, AL
Iden Pottery, c/o Edward Russell, Valhalla, NY
Izabel Lam, Long Island City, NY
Pan Lambert Pottery, Corrales, NM
Lamb's Ears Ltd., Birmingham, AL
Los Angeles Pottery, Los Angeles, CA
M's Fabric Gallery, Birmingham, AL
Maralyn Wilson Gallery, Birmingham, AL
Mariposa, Gloucester, MA
Mesa International, Elkins, NH
Old World Pewter, Gainesville, GA
Pillivuyt, Salinas, CA
Primitive Artisan, Pittsfield, MA
Rina Peleg Ceramics, Brooklyn, NY
Table Matters, Birmingham, AL
Vietri, Hillsborough, NC

You can order the heart-shaped pasta used in Heartfelt Pasta Salad (page 67) from Buckeye Beans & Herbs, Inc., P.O. Box 28201, Spokane, WA 99228.

Photography and photo styling by Oxmoor House Staff:

Photographers: Ralph Anderson and Jim Bathie
Photo Stylists: Kay E. Clarke and Virginia R. Cravens

Additional photography:
Gary Clark: pages 15, 25, 26, 31
Colleen Duffley: page 15
Tina Evans: pages 12, 19, 35, 210
Bruce Roberts: page 15
Charles Walton IV: page 15

Additional photo styling:
Bob Gager: pages 184, 192
Ashley Johnson: page 158